JUDICIAL INDEPENDENCE
IN THE AGE OF DEMOCRACY
Critical Perspectives from around the World

CONSTITUTIONALISM AND DEMOCRACY

KERMIT HALL AND DAVID M. O'BRIEN, EDITORS

JUDICIAL INDEPENDENCE IN THE AGE OF DEMOCRACY

Critical Perspectives from around the World

EDITED BY

PETER H. RUSSELL AND DAVID M. O'BRIEN

UNIVERSITY PRESS OF VIRGINIA

Charlottesville and London

The University Press of Virginia
© 2001 by the Rector and Visitors of the University of Virginia
All rights reserved
Printed in the United States of America
First published 2001

⊗The paper used in this publication meets the minimum requirements of the American National Standard for Information Sciences—Permanence of Paper for Printed Library Materials, ANSI Z39.48-1984.

Library of Congress Cataloging-in-Publication Data
Judicial independence in the age of democracy : critical perspectives from around the world / edited by Peter H. Russell and David M. O'Brien.
    p.   cm. — (Constitutionalism and democracy)
    Includes bibliographical references and index.
    ISBN 0-8139-2015-9 (cloth : alk. paper) — ISBN 0-8139-2016-7 (pbk. : alk. paper)
    1. Judicial power. 2. Judicial process. 3. Political questions and judicial power. I. Russell, Peter H. II. O'Brien, David M. III. Series.

K3367 .J828 2001
347'.012—dc21

                                                    00-043886

CONTENTS

TABLES

ACKNOWLEDGMENTS

This collection of studies originated with the work of the International Political Science Association's Research Committee on Comparative Judicial Politics. Several of the chapters were initially delivered as papers at the committee's 1996 meeting at Hebrew University in Jerusalem, Israel. Additional contributions were recruited and were delivered and discussed at the committee's 1998 meeting at Northeastern University in Boston, Massachusetts. The editors are grateful to all who contributed and discussed the papers at various stages, as well as to the anonymous reviewers of the collection. We are also indebted to Richard Holway, Ellen Satrom, Gary Kessler, and the staff of the University Press of Virginia for their patience and time and trouble in producing this collection.

Chapter 8, "Judicial Independence in England: A Loss of Innocence" by Robert Stevens, appeared in a different version in the *Oxford Journal of Legal Studies* 19 (1999): 365–402. It is printed here with the permission of Oxford University Press.

Peter H. Russell
David M. O'Brien

JUDICIAL INDEPENDENCE
IN THE AGE OF DEMOCRACY
Critical Perspectives from around the World

1

Toward a General Theory of Judicial Independence

PETER H. RUSSELL

I believe we need a theory of judicial independence. The "we" here refers to the world of liberal democracy and the discipline of political science. In today's world, there is a general trend toward liberal democracy. Judicial independence is generally viewed as an essential feature of liberal democracy.[1] And yet there is little agreement on just what this condition of judicial independence is, or on what kind or how much judicial independence is required for a liberal democratic regime, or on the societal conditions on which judicial independence depends.

For countries that are in a process of transformation from "peoples' democracies" or other kinds of authoritarianism to liberal democracy, the most pressing questions about judicial independence are apt to be about how to secure its minimal requirements. As the chapters in this volume on Eastern Europe, Russia, and Central America demonstrate, countries going through this transformative process are struggling with restrictions on judicial independence of the most fundamental kind—political direction of judicial decision making, bribery, corruption, and a nearly total absence of economic security for their judges. In the chapter on Hong Kong, we have the case of a political community, just as it is emerging from colonial rule, subjected to the sovereignty of a Communist regime that could hardly be said to be in transition to liberal democracy. In this context, judicial autonomy becomes a crucial condition of political autonomy. Conversely, chapters of this book on Australia, Israel, Japan, South Africa, Western Europe, the United Kingdom, and the United States deal with judicial independence in societies that consider themselves to be liberal democracies. In such settings, there is as much concern about the danger of taking judicial independence too far as there is with not taking it far enough.

If the movement of authoritarian regimes toward liberal democracy raises the question of the minimum conditions of judicial independence required for a regime to be truly liberal, the growth of judicial power within long-established liberal democracies and the assignment of major responsibilities to the judiciary in new or emerging liberal democracies raise the very opposite question of how independent a powerful judiciary can be without undermining democracy.[2] Here the liberal principle of judicial independence runs up against the democratic principle of accountability.[3]

The perspectives of political science are well suited for the analysis of a concept such as judicial independence. It is the province of political science to study the connections between different elements of the political system. Judicial independence is first and foremost a concept about connections—or, more precisely, the absence of certain connections—between the judiciary and other components of the political system. The traditional legal scholarship that has dominated the literature on judicial independence tends to be doctrinal and parochial, deriving its ideas from the precedents and practices of particular legal traditions.[4]

By way of contrast, political science (which, by the way, as this volume demonstrates, may be practiced as much by legal academics as by persons who call themselves political scientists) brings to the study of judicial independence a healthy skepticism about judicial independence and its sister concept, judicial impartiality. From the perspective of political science, everything in the political system is connected to everything else and nothing in the political system is without bias. Thus, for the political scientist studying the real world of politics, judicial independence and impartiality of necessity cannot be absolutes. The analytical challenge is to ascertain what kinds of independence (and impartiality) are possible and desirable.

Some might regard the attempt to develop a single, universal theory of judicial independence as a mistake. Undoubtedly, liberal democracies differ in their treatment of judicial independence. Judicial independence is a much more important principle of government for some than it is for others. Some countries have gone much further than others to constitutionalize judicial independence and to give the judiciary a major role in articulating and enforcing it. And there are remarkable differences in the components or elements of judicial independence that liberal democracies find most important and in the arrangements they put in place for securing its various components. While acknowledging this diversity of approaches to judicial independence, we still must ask whether there is a common "it" in all of this. Can we talk about "judicial independence" in terms that are sufficiently universal to enable us to compare how different polities treat "it"? Or is the concept so fundamentally variable that there is really no basis for comparative analysis in this field?

As an active member of an international political science research committee devoted to the comparative study of judiciaries, naturally I am compelled to believe it must be possible to arrive at an understanding that makes comparative study of judicial independence possible. Indeed, the primary purpose of the present project is to test that belief.

What Should We Expect of a General Theory?

The first requirement of a general theory of judicial independence is analytical clarity about the kind of phenomenon being referred to when we talk about judicial independence. Is judicial independence essentially about the relationships judicial institutions and individual judges should or should not have with other institutions, groups, or individuals? Or is it a concept that refers primarily to a certain kind of behavior or way of thinking or set of attitudes expected of judges? Or is it all of these things? And if it does encompass all of these things, how do these different ways of thinking about judicial independence relate to one another? Consensus on this matter is surely necessary if we are to have some assurance that when we discuss and debate issues of judicial independence across national and cultural borders, we are talking about the same kind of thing or things.

A second requirement of a general theory is to have some coherent idea of the purpose or rationale of judicial independence. Judicial independence is not an end in itself. Those who believe that some measure of judicial independence is desirable must hold this belief, because judicial independence is thought to serve some important objective, to contribute to some desirable state of affairs. If judicial independence is a means to some end, a theory of judicial independence must be based on some idea of what that end is. It must deal with the reason why judicial independence is considered to be a valuable feature of a political regime. Indeed, the end or objective of trying to ensure a modicum of judicial independence in a polity must be the key to assessing whether judicial independence is adequately established or maintained. Without some idea of the desirable state of affairs for which judicial independence is thought to be a necessary condition, it is difficult to see how arguments about judicial independence can be intelligibly arbitrated.

A third task for a general theory of judicial independence is to identify the major components or elements of judicial independence. If judicial independence is to be conceived at least in part, if not essentially, as a relational concept, that is to say a concept about the relationships judges and their institutions ought or ought not to have with others, then it is important to establish an inventory or menu of the relationships that are most essential to judicial independence. The study of judicial independence cannot possibly cover all of the connections between the judiciary and the world in which it is embedded. What are the relationships that are thought to have the greatest bearing on judicial independence in terms of enhancing or threatening judicial independence? The relative importance of various relationships or connections is bound to vary among regimes. Nonetheless, political science inquiry in this area should be built on a broad recognition of all relationships of potential importance to judicial independence. One of the most interesting findings in comparative research may well be variation in the relationships that are perceived to have the greatest bearing on judicial independence in different states.

While we can expect a general theory of judicial independence to provide reasonably complete and comprehensive positions on questions concerning the three aspects set out above—namely, the meaning of the concept, its rationale, and its principal elements—we cannot expect a general theory to produce definitive answers to the substantive normative and empirical questions that might be raised about judicial independence in various contexts. For example, a general theory of judicial independence cannot decisively settle whether or not pressures on judges generated from within the justice system, as disclosed by David O'Brien and Yasuo Ohkoshi in their chapter on Japan or by Todd Foglesong in his chapter on Russia, constitute a violation of judicial independence, any more than it can determine whether the media pressure, as described in Donald Kommers's chapter on Germany, which induced Judge Orlet to resign, is altogether incompatible with judicial independence.

At this stage in our study of judicial independence and liberal democracy, we should not expect political science to arrive at a theory of judicial independence that yields a touchstone of what judicial independence fundamentally requires. Judges interpreting constitutional guarantees of judicial independence in various regimes may be called upon to do that very thing. In doing so, they will draw on the precedents and experience of their societies. But a general political science theory of judicial independence should not be looked to for definitive answers to these questions. This is so for two reasons. First, the principle of judicial independence raises complex normative issues on which there neither is nor may ever be a consensus among political scientists. Most of the pressing issues of judicial independence—the issues that tend to get litigated in the courts or publicly ventilated—are questions about where the liberal requirement of judicial autonomy should give way to the democratic requirement of accountability. The position a political scientist takes on these issues will depend on the kind of balance one thinks appropriate between these competing principles. Second, even if there were a fair degree of consensus among political scientists on the normative issue, on the empirical side we lack hard knowledge of how a particular treatment of a judicial independence issue—for instance, removing partisan political control over judicial appointments or involving those who are not judges in the evaluation of judges—actually affects the fundamental purpose of judicial independence.

One other task a general theory of judicial independence cannot perform is to prescribe the social, economic, and political conditions required to produce and maintain the minimal requirements of judicial independence (assuming we could agree on what these are). It is a common observation among those who study the transition to liberal democracy, including contributors to this volume, to identify "the rule of law," or what Dick Howard in his chapter on post-Communist Central and Eastern Europe refers to as a "constitutional culture," as a condition of critical importance in moving toward an effective and credible judiciary. Michael Dodson and Donald Jackson's chapter on Central America sheds some new light on the internal and external conditions that may assist in this crucial dimension of liberalization. Still, how the rule of law is imbibed and fostered in a society remains one of the most challenging questions in contemporary political science.

Though a general political science theory of judicial independence cannot yield definitive answers to the substantive issues that arise in various jurisdictions, nonetheless it should serve as an organizing framework for research and debate about these issues. It should enable those who are dealing with specific issues of judicial independence in particular contexts to relate their concerns and findings to a reasonably clear and comprehensive understanding of the basic dimensions and elements of judicial independence and of its underlying rationale. So that is my principal expectation of a general theory of judicial independence: that it frame a discourse about judicial independence that identifies the key normative and empirical issues. Such a framework requires an unpacking of judicial independence into its main dimensions so that it is possible to identify the points on each dimension where judicial autonomy is most at issue and to assess the merits of different ways of dealing with each kind of threat. Comparative study based on such a framework should eventually yield a stronger basis than now exits for taking positions on substantive issues.

The Meanings of Judicial Independence

In political science literature, judicial independence has been used to refer to two concepts. One of these is the autonomy of judges—collectively and individually—from other individuals and institutions. Used in this sense, it is a relational term referring to crucial features of the relationship the members of the judiciary ought to have with each other and that the judiciary as a whole should have with other parts of the political system. Judicial independence is also used to refer to judicial behavior that is considered indicative of judges enjoying a high measure of autonomy. O'Brien and Ohkoshi, for instance, use the concept this way in their chapter when they talk about "assertions of judicial independence" by Japanese judges, and Foglesong also uses it when he asks how can it be that Russian judges, despite being increasingly vulnerable to political and other pressures, continue "to render decisions that appear independent."

These two senses of judicial independence are closely related. One is thought to be a means to the other. We want judges to enjoy a high degree of autonomy so that they can think and act independently rather than being controlled in their decision making by others. But closely linked though these two senses are, analysis will suffer if we run them together. A judge's capacity for independent thought and judgment—the second use of the concept—does not automatically result from enjoying what would be regarded as a high degree of autonomy—the first meaning of the concept.

We can all imagine judges, and perhaps some of us can even point to a few, who, despite lacking the main ingredients of judicial independence in the first sense, nevertheless were brave enough to defy those who could and would sanction them for their decision making and to assert judicial independence in the second sense. The odds, of course, are all against this happening very often—and that is precisely why we deem it so important to maintain a high measure of autonomy for judges. Nevertheless, judges who lack crucial aspects of that autonomy may defy the odds and act independently. Similarly, it is possible for judges who enjoy, by any standards, a great deal of autonomy in the first sense, to decide cases in a manner that is deferential to powerful "others." In other words, judicial independence in the first sense of autonomy does not guarantee that judges will think and act in an independent manner.

The chapters by O'Brien and Ohkoshi and by Foglesong present good examples of how political science analysis can benefit from separating the two senses of judicial independence. O'Brien and Ohkoshi show that Japanese judges, despite enjoying a high degree of formal autonomy from the other branches of government, behave in a very deferential manner and seldom "assert their independence" by challenging acts of government. The explanation they advance is not that this is an example of judges who enjoy a great deal of autonomy but who fail to assert it because they are, as it were, just naturally deferential. Instead, they view this deference as reflecting a situation in which formal institutional autonomy masks a lack of individual autonomy within the judicial hierarchy.

The O'Brien and Ohkoshi chapter, like other recent research, alerts us to the fact that judicial independence may be threatened not only in relatively well-known ways from the outside but also from inside the judiciary itself, by senior judges using administrative and personnel controls to direct the decision making of individual judges lower in the judicial hierarchy. In this context, the judicial elite would appear to serve as an instrument for maintaining the external political elite's control of the judiciary.

Conversely, Foglesong's paper indicates that in post-Communist Russia, a similar dependence of ordinary judges on their superiors and mentors in higher courts can result in decisions reflecting "an antistate, somewhat populist sentiment," stemming from judges' resentment of the government's reneging on promises to ensure judicial independence or to provide adequate funding for courts or pay regular salaries.

Though the infrequency of judicial decisions challenging the political arms of government may be a symptom of the absence of judicial autonomy, it is a mistake to equate judicial independence with a high frequency of judicial decisions reversing the other branches of government.[5] There are several reasons for not making this equation. The first is that judges who frequently render decisions that run counter to the government of the day may well enjoy a high degree of independence from that government but might be very susceptible to control by nongovernmental forces. Examples would be judges who rule against government prosecutors because they are in the pocket of organized crime, or who overturn government policy because the judges are closely aligned with an opposition interest group. Carlo Guarnieri's discussion of the Italian magistracy suggests that the price of hyperactivity by the judiciary in that country may be the increasing dependency of magistrates on political opposition forces and the media. Another factor is that the legal and constitutional systems of the state might provide relatively few legal grounds for over-turning legislation. Yet another is the possibility that actual violations of constitutional limits by the nonjudicial branches of government may be infrequent.

The point to be emphasized is that in trying to ascertain the degree or kind of judicial independence judges actually enjoy or ought to enjoy, the focus should be on the relational meaning of the concept rather than on its behavioral meaning. This is so for both practical and intellectual reasons. The focus of any practical endeavors to secure judicial independence must be on institutional arrangements designed to protect and foster independ-ence. Judicial independence of mind and behavior cannot be manufac-tured. But institutional arrangements considered to be conducive to an independent-minded judiciary can be established and maintained. As to what kind of arrangements are possible and desirable, again it is only through consideration of the full range of pressures and forces impinging on judges—the ambit of relationships they have with one another and with outsiders—that a comprehensive theory of judicial independence can be built.

In the phrase "judicial independence," there is another word that may need some clarification. That is the word "judicial." When we talk about the judiciary having or not having independence, is it always clear just which officials or institutions are being referred to? Does "judicial" or "ju-diciary" have a common enough meaning to enable us to construct a gen-eral theory of judicial independence? Shimon Shetreet in the concluding essay of a volume surveying judicial independence in twenty-nine coun-tries takes the position that for all of these states "The judiciary could be defined as the organ of government not forming part of the executive and legislature, which is not subject to personal, substantive and collective controls, and which performs the primary function of adjudication."[6]

While I can accept this position as far as it goes, I do not think applica-tion of the principle should be confined to functionaries called judges or institutions called courts (or their linguistic equivalents). Indeed, one way of undermining judicial independence is to transfer judicial functions from a judiciary enjoying a high degree of autonomy to officials and agencies that have very little independence.

Consequently, I prefer a functional rather than a formal or nominal no-tion of what constitutes the "judicial" realm. The "judiciary" for whom ju-dicial independence is a defining normative expectation are the officials and institutions that perform the central judicial function of adjudication. And what is adjudication? In the space of this chapter, I cannot do more than draw on the definition of adjudication advanced in my earlier writings, namely that adjudication is the provision of authoritative settlements of disputes about legal rights and duties.[7] Now, whether or not you accept this definition of adjudication, it is necessary to base a theory of judicial independence on some understanding of the essential function of the judiciary. For what other rationale could be advanced for judicial independence than that without it the judiciary would not be able to perform its essential function? This, then, brings us, logically, to the second part of a theory of judicial independence—namely its rationale.

Rationale of Judicial Independence

What do we expect of the judiciary in a liberal democracy? What essential public function do we want it to serve? The answer that is given to this question must be the key to considering—in any context—whether there is too much or too little or the right kind of judicial independence.

The judiciary's essential function derives from two closely related social needs. First, in a civil society we want some of our relations with each other and with our government to be regulated by reasonably well-defined laws setting out mutual rights and duties. Second, when disputes arise about these legal rights and duties, we want a mutually acceptable third-party adjudicator to settle the dispute.

For John Locke, meeting these needs was a fundamental reason for living under civil government rather than in a state of nature. "Wherever any two men are who have no standing rule and common judge to appeal to on earth for the determination of controversies of right betwixt them," he wrote in his *Second Treatise of Government*, "they are still in a state of nature."[8] Note that for Locke the crucial need is for a common adjudicator of disputes about rights. By that he means a judge who is genuinely a third party and not bound to or by either of the disputing parties. It stands to reason that if the person adjudicating a dispute is under the direct control or influence of one of the parties, that person will appear to be, of necessity, too partial to the controlling party to be accepted by the other party as a common judge.[9]

Settling disputes about legal rights and duties between private individuals or groups gives us only half of the rationale for judicial independence in a liberal democracy. Even in an illiberal, authoritarian regime, the government may support the functioning of a judiciary for settling civil disputes about the legal obligations of citizens to one another but be unwilling to submit disputes about its own legal obligations to a judiciary it does not control. Such a government is not subject to legal restraints.

Locke, of course, was alert to this possibility when he wrote as follows: "I desire to know what kind of government that is, and how much better it is than the state of nature, where one man commanding a multitude has the liberty to be judge in his own case, and may do to all his subjects whatever he pleases, without the least liberty to any one to question or control those who exercise his pleasure."[10] Replace "one man commanding a multitude" with "one government or party elected by a multitude" and you have the case for subjecting government itself—including popular, elected governments—to legal limits on its authority. This, of course, is a defining feature of a liberal, rule-of-law regime. For such a regime to be a reality, disputes about whether the nonjudicial branches of government have exercised their powers in a manner authorized by law must be decided by judges those branches do not control.

So here we find the fundamental purpose or rationale of the principle of judicial independence. We want judges to enjoy a high degree of autonomy so that, when disputes arise about our legal rights and duties to one another and in relation to public authorities and these disputes cannot be settled informally, we can submit them for resolution to judges whose autonomy or independence gives us reason to believe they will resolve the issues fairly, according to their understanding of the law, and not out of fear of recrimination or hope of reward.

This formulation of the rationale of judicial independence has many problematic features judicial realists will be quick to identify. The law judges are to apply does not have ready-made "neutral" or mechanical answers to many of the disputes about legal rights and duties that are submitted to them. The paradox of adjudication, as Martin Shapiro reminds us in the opening section of his chapter on the European Court of Justice, is that judges often make the law in the very process of settling disputes about the law. We also know that, because they are rendering authoritative judgments about the law that are expected to be backed up by the coercive arm of the state, judges themselves are state functionaries and, in that sense, part of the system of governance. Their institutions are established, maintained, and protected by other arms of the state. So their autonomy from other branches of public authority can only be partial. And that is not all. We realists know that judges come to their work with predispositions based on their pre-judicial experience and affiliations, and that these predispositions are not easily shed even if they are disciplined by new orientations after their appointment.

All of this is undoubtedly true. Like other political scientists who study the judiciary, I have "dined out" on exposing these "political" aspects of the judiciary. But none of this realism justifies abandoning the principle or ideal of judicial independence. A sound principle of government should not be discarded just because it cannot be fully realized. The job of the political scientist who believes in liberal democracy is to figure out what kinds of independence it is most essential to maintain. In this sense, judicial independence is one of those principles, like accountability or democratic representativeness, that is most easily dealt with at its negative margins—that is at the points where the absence of independence is most telling and destructive of the institution's claim to legitimacy.

So what I propose to do next is to sketch out the key elements of judicial independence—the directions in which we should look for the most telling threats to its existence and exercise. I will illustrate points with examples drawn from chapters in this book, augmented by developments in the Canadian judiciary—the judicial system with which I am personally most familiar.

Dimensions of Judicial Independence

Judicial independence as a relational term does not refer to a single kind of relationship—a single lack of dependency between two things. Judicial independence is best understood as a two-dimensional relationship. First, in terms of the sources of dependency, external controls and influences must be distinguished from internal controls and influences. Second, in terms of the targets of influence or control, the individual judge must be distinguished from the judiciary as a collective whole or institution.

The external category refers to all of those forces—governmental and nongovernmental, public and private—outside of the judiciary itself that can encroach on the autonomy of the judiciary collectively or of the individual judge. This is the most widely recognized dimension of judicial independence and embraces what is normally meant by the separation of powers principle. In England, as Robert Stevens's chapter shows, the participation of the Law Lords in the upper house of Parliament and the position of the lord chancellor as the senior judge, make having an institutional concept of judicial independence based on a rigid separation of powers impossible.

The internal dimension, however, refers to sources of influence and control within the judiciary itself. From the internal perspective, it is only the individual judge, not the judiciary in a collective or institutional sense, whose independence is at stake. Of course, not all influences of judges on one another are to be regarded as violating judicial independence. For example, the influence of the decisions of higher courts on lower court judges is surely not to be regarded as a violation of judicial independence.

A theory of judicial independence that is realistic and analytically useful cannot be concerned with every inside and outside influence on judges. Every moment of the day—and, perhaps in their sleep as well—judges are subject to many influences. In this respect, the definition of judicial independence adopted by the 1983 World Conference on the Independence of Justice is quite unreal when it states that "judges individually shall be free, and it shall be their duty, to decide matters before them impartially, in accordance with their assessment of the facts and their understanding of the law without any restrictions, influences, direct or indirect, from any quarter or for any reason."[11]

To formulate the principle of judicial independence in a way that requires judges to be totally uninfluenced by anybody whatsoever is totally unrealistic. Bora Laskin, a former chief justice of Canada, in a classic essay entitled "The Institutional Character of the Judge," identified a number of external influences on judges, such as critical writings of legal scholars and internal influences such as judges' exchanges with one another through memoranda and conferences—none of which he regarded as violating the principle of judicial independence.[12]

In identifying undue influences that endanger judicial independence, it is important to bear in mind, as I have argued above, the essential purpose of the judiciary and adjudication. Judicial independence is at risk when influences undermine a judge's capacity to adjudicate—that is to be accepted by the contesting parties as a common judge for the settlement of their legal dispute. Judges' capacity for adjudication is not undermined when they read widely about the law and discuss legal issues with their colleagues. It would be quite another matter, however, if the government or some outside organization controlled their library selections, or if senior judges used their positions to control what other judges read.

A general theory of judicial independence cannot deal comprehensively with all possible undue influences that may impinge on judicial autonomy. But what it might reasonably be expected to do is to identify the main points of interaction within the judiciary and between the judiciary and outside forces where undue influences may come into play and put judicial independence at risk. A complete theory would also deal with the institutional arrangements or protective devices that can be used at each of these points to safeguard judicial independence without going so far as to destroy the accountability that democrats wish to maintain for the judicial branch of government. Here I can only provide a sketchy catalogue of the key points of interaction at which undue influence may occur. The larger task of assessing the merits of the various rules and institutional arrangements for securing judicial independence must remain an ongoing project for the international community of political scientists interested in this subject.

Critical Points of Control and Undue Influence

The principal ways in which judicial independence, both collectively and individually, may be encroached upon can be grouped into four categories: structural, personnel, administrative, and direct. Below, I will outline the kinds of undue influence or control, external as well as internal, that may be encountered in each area.

Structural: By structural I refer to the power of governmental bodies outside the judiciary to create and modify judicial institutions. The judiciaries in all of the liberal democracies are vulnerable, in varying degrees, to the power of legislatures to create, modify, and destroy judicial structures as well as to establish and alter the system of appointing, removing, and remunerating judges. In some countries, this vulnerability is moderated by constitutional "guarantees" that restrict legislative control over the judiciary. Shimon Shetreet's chapter makes a strong case for such guarantees in Israel, where the judiciary has become involved in many controversial political issues. However, even in these countries, constitutional guarantees of judicial power will still provide a good deal of legislative leeway, and constitutional clauses themselves are subject to modification by nonjudicial political forces.

It would surely be wrong to regard every incidence of legislatures or leaders of the executive branch initiating changes in judicial structure as threats to judicial independence. Judicial structures must have some flexibility. They will need to be altered to fit the changing needs of the societies they serve. These major changes of judicial structure in a democracy should be made by accountable politicians. Martin Shapiro's chapter on the European Court of Justice contains a fascinating account of how national governments that have felt that court's constraining force on their policies have cautiously restricted its power in expanding the scope of European integration. So here the principle of democratic accountability must often take precedence over judicial independence. Judicial independence is at risk, however, when the "political branches" use or threaten to use their control over structure to shape adjudicative outcomes. It is at this point that external structural control may become undue and threaten judicial independence in the collective sense.

Franklin Roosevelt's "court packing plan," discussed in Henry Abraham's chapter on the politics of judicial independence in the United States, is a case in point. Here the American president's threat to add six justices to the Supreme Court was designed to change the way the Court decided constitutional cases. In Abraham's view, the struggle over Roosevelt's aborted bill indicated that "the country would not stand for any crass tampering with judicial independence." Roosevelt withdrew his bill, but there was a change in the position of the Court's majority—the "switch in time that saved nine." Whether Roosevelt's threat was justified depends on one's overall evaluation of the situation of the United States at that time and the long-term consequences of Roosevelt's actions for constitutional democracy. Here it is essential to bear in mind that however important a principle judicial independence is in a liberal democracy, it should never be elevated to such an exalted status that other principles of good government must give way.

Court packing is by no means the only way in which political authorities may abuse the power they possess over judicial structure. Governments may strip courts of their jurisdiction to adjudicate matters in which the government of the day has a vital interest, or they may transfer jurisdiction over such matters from the regular courts to tribunals whose decision makers lack the security of tenure enjoyed by the judiciary. We find an interesting variant of this structural threat to judicial independence in John Williams's chapter on Australia. Although the judiciary has read a very strict guarantee of the separation of powers into the Australian constitution, this has not prevented governments from getting rid of judges they find troublesome by dismantling or reorganizing the court on which they serve.

Personnel: Under this heading, I group together the policies and procedures that apply to all aspects of judicial personnel. These include the methods of appointing, remunerating, and removing judges—the traditional focal points of concern about judicial independence—as well as promotions and transfers, modes of discipline short of removal, professional evaluation, training, and continuing education—matters that are receiving more attention in contemporary discussions. In all of these areas, the independence of judges may be threatened by both external and internal forces.

Security of tenure traditionally has been regarded, and rightly so, as the sine qua non of judicial independence. It stands to reason that, if an officeholder can be removed for decisions someone else dislikes, that someone else is really in control of the decision maker. The security of tenure required for judicial independence is consistent with mandatory retirement and limited-term appointments. Indeed, for judges of constitutional courts exercising the extraordinary power of judicial review, appointments for a limited term rather than for life may well strike a better balance between democratic accountability and judicial independence. That is precisely the conclusion, as this volume shows, of Europe's newest constitutional democracies.

What is really essential for judicial independence is that removal should be very difficult and should be based on a demonstration, judiciously arrived at, that the judge is incapable of discharging the responsibilities of judicial office. A demonstrated pattern of rudeness or of racism or sexism in a judge's treatment of persons coming before the court might be reasonable grounds for removing a judge. It was for reasons of this kind that a recent Canadian inquiry recommended the removal of a Quebec superior court judge.[13] However, it is important to distinguish this kind of misbehavior, which may occur in the course of judicial proceedings, from the decisions rendered by judges. Judicial independence is seriously at risk when judges can be removed because their decisions have offended someone—be that someone a party to the proceedings, a senior judge, the government, the media, an interest group, or the general public. Judges who must placate some powerful individual or group in order to keep their job will not feel free to adjudicate in a fair and professional manner.

Several chapters in this book show that even where the formal mechanisms for removing judges meet a high standard of judicial independence, as is the case in the civil law countries of Western Europe and the common law countries of the English-speaking world, judges who make unpopular decisions or whose political orientation offends powerful politicians may be pressured into resigning. I have already referred to Donald Kommers's report of how a barrage of media ridicule of an opinion of the German judge, Rainer Orlet, led to the judge's early "retirement." In his chapter on judicial independence in England, Robert Stevens informs us of the more subtle ways in which British politicians arrange for the departure of judges who have become an inconvenience. More sinister is John Williams's account of how Lionel Murphy, as radical a jurist as ever sat on Australia's high court, was subjected to a parliamentary enquiry that ended only when it was disclosed he was dying of cancer.

At the other end of the political spectrum are countries that are just now—possibly—in transition to liberal democracy. In these countries, instead of encountering a few troubling lapses from well-established systems of secure judicial tenure, we find in their recent past a total absence of secure tenure and judiciaries totally lacking in public credibility. J. Michael Dodson and Donald W. Jackson's chapter on the status of the judiciary in Central America reports on the very low level of public trust in the El Salvador and Guatemala judiciaries even a few years after the introduction of judicial reforms. In these transition societies, including former Communist countries, the concern of judicial reformers to get rid of judges corrupted by the old system raises the question of "judicial cleansing." To the liberal democrat, such a concept is apt be anathema. Still, the question must be asked whether judges who served essentially as political lackeys of authoritarian governments that had no respect for the rule of law or an independent judiciary should be afforded the level of protection appropriate for judges in a well-established liberal democracy.

Judicial independence is less at risk at the front end of the personnel process—the appointing end—if there is a strong system of judicial tenure at the back end—the removal end. What Owen Fiss refers to as the "political insularity"[14] of the judge is compromised regardless of which of the three major systems of judiciary staffing is in place—election by the people, appointment by elected politicians, or appointment into a professional career judiciary. All three systems are open to the possibility of political forces outside or within the judiciary trying to influence the course of adjudication by putting persons on the bench who will take the appointers' position in applying and interpreting the law.

O'Brien and Ohkoshi's chapter shows how in the Japanese case a judicial elite with its own political agenda can use the staffing process to shape the basic orientation of a professional career judiciary. The absence of political insularity from the other two systems is obvious. However, if following their appointment, judges can decide cases in a manner that disappoints those who put them on the bench and get away with it, then we are not so concerned about political control at the entry point. It is precisely for this reason that popular election of judges poses a much greater threat to judicial independence. The elected judge who faces the prospect of standing for reelection may be unduly influenced by that prospect. Judges often have to decide cases involving the rights of unpopular individuals or groups. A system that requires judges to win popularity contests to retain office takes democratic accountability to the point of destroying judicial independence.

Where judges are appointed by politicians or recruited into a career judiciary—the systems that are most prominent in the common law and civil law worlds—the danger point for judicial independence may be more in the process of promotion and career advancement than initial appointment. Judicial tenure may be well protected. Yet, if those who control career advancement within the judiciary are perceived to reward or punish a particular ideological orientation in judicial decision making, judicial independence can be seriously compromised. O'Brien and Ohkoshi indicate that there is a strong possibility of this being a reality in the Japanese career judiciary.

In his chapter on judicial independence in the Latin countries of Western Europe, Carlo Guarnieri shows that apprehension of this kind of bias is so severe in Italy that advancement through the judicial ranks has come to depend entirely on seniority and not at all on merit. In the common law world, the implications of a system of judicial promotions receive too little attention. In countries like Canada and the United Kingdom, the very existence of promotions is denied: judges are not promoted; they are "elevated"—lifted mystically by some inhuman agency to a higher position.

The greatest danger to judicial independence from political manipulation of the staffing or promotion process is ideological conformity. In the American federal judicial system, especially in Supreme Court appointments, where the application of ideological litmus tests by the president is so blatant,[15] what happens if the pendulum of partisan politics stops swinging for a long time and the country's highest judiciary is staffed with nothing but judges who are ideologically in line with the governing party? How easy would it then be for all Americans to accept such a judiciary as "common judges" in John Locke's sense? The same danger exists in other common law countries like Australia and the United Kingdom, where the appointment process' lack of transparency makes it even easier for politicians to pack the judiciary with their political and social friends.

To guard against a politically unbalanced judiciary, liberal democracies are well advised to build social and political pluralism into their judicial appointing arrangements. Hugh Corder's chapter on South Africa shows how a carefully structured judicial service commission can give the judicial appointing process the pluralism—and transparency—essential for combining judicial independence with democratic responsiveness in this new multiracial constitutional democracy. Germany, as we can see through Donald Kommers's chapter, has been the most thorough of the European democracies in ensuring that the staffing of its federal judiciary is subject to a balance of political influences. Guarnieri's chapter shows how the Latin countries of Western Europe achieve a fair measure of political pluralism in the composition of the supreme judicial councils that govern their judiciaries. Of course, if there is no pluralism in a country's political system, there will be no pluralism in its judicial appointing system. It remains to be seen whether the very nonpluralist regime of the

People's Republic of China can tolerate the decisions of a Hong Kong judiciary selected by a reconstituted but independent judicial service commission. The chapter on Hong Kong by Jill Cottrell and Yash Ghai provides a gripping account of the tensions emanating from this situation.

Judicial remuneration is the other point where traditionally there has been concern about judicial independence. The old adage of "he who pays the piper calls the tune" is incompatible with judicial independence. Judges are bound to be dependent on others for meeting their personal material needs. The independence of individual judges can be put seriously in jeopardy if the support they receive is so inadequate that they are readily open to bribery or compromising business ventures. I found this danger to be very real when I studied the lower courts of Uganda shortly after independence.[16] Todd Foglesong's chapter reveals how in post-Communist Russia the very meager income and housing available for judges seriously undermines their independence.

The danger in more affluent countries is a system of remuneration (including pensions and other benefits) that subjects either the individual judge or the judiciary collectively to the unfettered discretion of political or judicial authorities. The possibility of undue influence opens up when judicial salaries and benefits are not set in a regularized manner according to established criteria but seem to depend on the whims of the paymaster. In one of the Canadian provinces, Alberta, the method of paying judges deteriorated to that point. In 1997 the Supreme Court of Canada reviewed the Alberta situation along with challenges to the remuneration systems in two other provinces and ruled that it is unconstitutional for the government to make any changes in judicial remuneration that have not been considered by an "independent, effective and objective" judicial compensation commission.[17]

Judicial independence should not mean that the level of judicial remuneration is never to be reduced. Governments elected on platforms calling for fiscal restraint do not jeopardize judicial independence when they apply a program of public sector pay reductions to judges. But what if a government applies a heavier form of restraint to the judiciary than to the rest of the public service? In Canada it was a situation of this kind that prompted an Alberta judge to find the government's rejection of an independent judicial compensation's recommended salary increase unconstitutional,[18] and similarly, an Ontario court to find a freeze of salaries of justices of the peace unconstitutional.[19] In terms of securing fair remuneration, Canadian judges appear to be at the cutting edge—and some might suggest that they are "pushing the envelope."

The growth of judicial power in liberal democracies has been accompanied by demands for new forms of judicial accountability. Public complaint procedures have been instituted in many jurisdictions to provide consumers of court services some redress when judges fail to treat them in a polite, fair, and efficient manner. Typically, these complaints raise matters that are not serious enough to be grounds for removal but that are serious enough to warrant some intermediate sanction such as a reprimand or temporary suspension. A number of U.S. states have introduced systems of performance evaluation for judges to foster high standards of professional conduct on the part of their judiciaries. Programs of initial and continuing education for judges are being augmented in a number of jurisdictions by "sensitivity training" designed primarily to make white, male judges more aware of the perspectives and problems of women and racial and ethnic minorities.

All of these initiatives have been questioned—particularly by judges themselves—for their compatibility with the principle of judicial independence. Programs in any of the areas mentioned above can certainly be mounted in a way that undermines judicial independence, but the point is that they need not be. Appropriate precautions can be taken in all of these areas to protect judicial independence. Complaint procedures can be conducted judiciously (which does not necessarily mean solely by judges), so that judges, while being induced to treat those who appear in their courts with due respect, are not constrained to alter their decision making. Performance evaluations can be conducted discreetly without degenerating into popularity contests and can be fruitful instruments of professional development.[20] Similarly, "sensitivity training," if organized in a noncoercive way by the judiciary itself and protected from capture by interest groups, can contribute to the cultivation of what Benjamin Cardozo referred to as a "judicial temperament," which, as he put it, "will help in some degree to emancipate (the judge) from the suggestive power of individual dislike and prepossession . . . to broaden the group to which his subconscious loyalties are due."[21] One context in which there is a clear need for judicial education of this kind is contemporary South Africa, where the black majority of a newly established liberal democracy is served by a predominantly white (and male) judiciary.[22]

Court Administration: The management of courts and judges' work is clearly an area in which the principles of democratic accountability and judicial independence need to be carefully balanced. Judges and courts provide a public service. In a democracy, there should be some public accountability for how well that service is provided and how public funds devoted to it are spent. Legislatures and executives led by elected politicians must assume some responsibility for the administration of courts. Conversely, if that responsibility is taken to the point where political authorities (who are a party to cases coming before the courts) also control vital aspects of adjudication, judicial independence can be seriously undermined.

In Canada, in the landmark case of *Valente*,[23] the first Canadian Supreme Court judgment on the guarantee of judicial independence in Canada's new constitutional Charter of Rights and Freedoms, Justice Gerald LeDain identified three aspects of judicial administration that he held must be under the judiciary's control. These are the assignment of judges to cases and courtrooms, the sittings of the courts, and court lists. These do clearly seem to be matters that no party to judicial proceedings, including the government, should control. If the executive could pick the judges who heard the cases it was involved in and determine their scheduling priority, it would appear to be controlling matters that are too integral to the adjudicative function itself. There are many other facets of court administration that might be under judicial control, including court budgeting, but it is not nearly so apparent that the principle of judicial independence requires this.

LeDain dealt only with the threat to the collective independence of the judiciary from external, governmental involvement in court administration. He did not address threats to the independence of the individual judge that may come from within the judiciary itself. O'Brien and Ohkoshi show how senior judges in the Japanese system can reward or punish judges by assigning them to different locations. David Marshall, an experienced Canadian judge and former director of Canada's National Judicial Institute, has courageously pointed out how chief justices can unduly influence judges on their court through administrative control over their assignments.[24]

Requiring that judicial administrators be accountable to their colleagues and building a culture of collegiality in the management of courts are important protections against this internal danger to judicial autonomy.[25] Foglesong's account of the Russian judiciary indicates that post-Communist reforms have done little to advance this component of individual judicial autonomy in that country.

Direct Approaches: In the first three categories of structural, personnel, and administrative threats to judicial independence, undue influence arises through connections that must exist among judges and between the judiciary and outside authorities. In none of the areas discussed could the judiciary be an island onto itself. The connections in these areas must continue. The challenge is to institute proper protections against influences flowing through these connecting links that may interfere with the judge's independence in performing adjudicative functions.

But, altogether outside these necessary connecting links there may be efforts to use the direct approach and try to influence judges directly to favor or disfavor a particular party or interest. Attempts at bribery or threats to the personal safety of the judge or the judge's family are obvious examples. The chapter by Dodson and Jackson reports how direct interference of this kind has been endemic in El Salvador and Guatemala.

Beyond such criminal activities, there are many other ways in which interested parties may try to bring pressure to bear on judges that may not be criminal but, if condoned, could certainly undermine independence. And, as Shetreet's chapter on Israel reports, these can most certainly occur in well-established liberal democracies. The options range all the way from telephone calls and private visits through huddled conversations at social events to high-pressure media campaigns.

One general defense against undue influences of the direct kind is requiring persons appointed to the bench to sever their association with political organizations, business corporations, and most social and professional bodies. Jurisprudence has developed in the liberal democracies under which judges can be disqualified if they have close ties to parties appearing before them and have not recused themselves. It appears from the chapters in this volume on Western Europe that Germany and Italy may be the most relaxed of the liberal democracies when it comes to judges retaining links with political parties. The most insidious direct approaches are those that take place covertly when an interested party, often an emissary of the government of the day, has a quiet chat with a judge about a case in which the government is interested. This continues to go on in the liberal democracies. As Robert Stevens's chapter shows, England is a case in point. Recently, the Supreme Court of Canada reviewed a situation in which a senior justice official had a private meeting with the chief justice of the federal court in order to influence the way a case involving accused war criminals was being handled.[26] The court reprimanded the participants in this affair for their breach of judicial independence but did not think the matter so serious as to make it impossible to proceed with the case. It may be that this sort of thing goes on frequently in other countries but is rarely exposed.

Open attempts through the media by politicians, pressure groups, or concerned citizens either to influence judges in the course of their decision making, or to criticize them afterward, are more tolerable. Most liberal democracies have strict laws or conventions restricting public comments on matters that are *sub judice*. But as the O. J. Simpson trial so vividly demonstrated, these rules can do little to shut up a noisy democracy whose attention is riveted on a judicial proceeding. These direct and open attempts to influence the judiciary are tolerable when the worst injury they can inflict is to make the judge feel unpopular.

Judges serving a vibrant liberal democracy must be prepared to take the slings and arrows of those who claim to speak for the multitude. In a democracy, it is not a bad thing for judges to be made aware of how their decisions are being received by the community they serve. The danger arises when the slings and arrows are directed to procedures that can sanction judges more concretely—above all to the removal process. When that occurs, judicial independence could be very much at risk.

Constitutional Guarantees

One of the institutional arrangements often looked to as the most fundamental way of protecting judicial independence is some "guarantee" of judicial independence in the country's written constitution. Constitutional recognition of the judicial power as a separate branch of government has featured prominently in the U.S. tradition. Many modern democracies, inspired by the American example, have included some such guarantee in their formal constitutions. Australia is a leading example.

Though constitutional entrenchment may be a useful device for safeguarding judicial independence, the comparative record of liberal democracies does not obviously support the generalization that it is a necessary condition. Look around the world of the liberal democracies and at their actual experience and ask yourself whether it is really clear that the judiciary in countries like Israel, New Zealand, the United Kingdom, or Sweden—all countries that have not constitutionally entrenched judicial independence—have enjoyed less independence than their counterparts in countries with constitutional guarantees—for example, the United States and Australia.

In emergent liberal democracies, where there has not been a strong tradition of judicial independence, it may be wise to ensure that judicial independence is included in the new constitution's catalogue of fundamental principles. As Dick Howard's and Hugh Corder's chapters show, this is very much the case in the constitutions of post-Communist Europe and in South Africa's new constitution. But valuable as such constitutional language may be in these contexts, particularly from a symbolic and educational perspective, it would be foolish to rely on constitutional protections—and their interpretation by the judiciary—for the implementation of judicial independence.

The problematic aspect of constitutional guarantees is indeed their interpretation and enforcement by the judiciary. In deciding cases in which the principle of judicial independence is alleged to have been violated, judges, in a sense, are acting as judges in their own case. Of course, the principle they are interpreting is important to the whole community, but still their own personal interests—sometimes in a very material sense—may be at issue. This has been very apparent in the recent spate of Canadian cases challenging salary freezes. When English judges threatened a court challenge to salary cuts during the 1930s depression, it was suggested that the case would have to be heard by a panel of retired judges.[27] This option was not available in Canada, where the explicit mention of judicial independence in its 1982 Charter of Rights made questions of judicial remuneration matters of judicial review for serving judges.

Precisely because judicial independence is such a complex, multifaceted principle whose proper ambit must always be weighed against other fundamental principles of liberal democracy, judges should not be given the last word in working out the concept's practical meaning.

Notes

1. On the difference between liberal democracy and other forms of democracy, see Giovanni Sartori, *Democratic Theory* (Detroit: Wayne State Univ. Press, 1962).

2. A 1995 volume of essays produced under the auspices of the International Political Science Association's Research Committee on Comparative Judicial Studies was devoted to this phenomenon. See C. Neal Tate and Torbjorn Vallinder, eds., *The Global Expansion of Judicial Power* (New York: New York Univ. Press, 1995).

3. This is the basic theme running through the most comprehensive survey of judicial independence, Shimon Shetreet and Jules Deschenes, eds., *Judicial Independence: The Contemporary Debate* (Dordrecht, Netherlands: Martin Nijhoff, 1985).

4. For two classic examples, see Irving R. Kaufman, "The Essence of Judicial Independence," *Columbia Law Review* 80, no. 2 (1980): 671–701; and William R. Lederman, "The Independence of the Judiciary," *Canadian Bar Review* 34, no. 7 (1956): 769–809.

5. For a leading example, see Theodore L. Becker, *Comparative Judicial Politics* (Chicago: Rand McNally, 1969).

6. Shetreet and Deschenes, *Judicial Independence*, 597–98.

7. See Peter Russell, *The Judiciary in Canada: The Third Branch of Government* (Toronto: McGraw-Hill/Ryerson, 1985), chap. 1.

8. John Locke, *The Second Treatise of Government* (New York: Library of Liberal Arts, 1952), 51.

9. For a classic analysis of the triadic nature of adjudication, see Martin Shapiro, *Courts: A Comparative and Political Analysis* (Chicago: Univ. of Chicago Press, 1981), chap. 1.

10. Locke, *The Second Treatise*, 9–10.

11. This document is included as chapter 39 in Shetreet and Deschenes, *Judicial Independence*.

12. Bora Laskin, "The Institutional Character of the Judge," *Israeli Law Review* 7, no. 3 (1972): 329–49.

13. "Report to the Canadian Judicial Council by the Inquiry Committee," *National Journal of Constitutional Law* 9 (1998): 357.

14. Owen M. Fiss, "The Right Degree of Independence," in *Transition to Democracy in Latin America: The Role of the Judiciary*, ed. Irwin P. Stokely (Boulder, Colo.: Westview Press, 1993), 55.

15. For a judicial defense of this practice, see William H. Rehnquist, *The Supreme Court: How It Was, How It Is* (New York: William Morrow, 1987), 236.

16. Peter Russell, *The Administration of Justice in Uganda: Some Problems and Proposals* (Entebbe: Government of Uganda Printer, 1971).

17. See Jacob S. Ziegel, "The Supreme Court Radicalizes Judicial Compensation," *Constitutional Forum* 9, no. 2 (1998): 31–41.

18. *Alberta Provincial Judges' Association v. The Queen*, Alberta Court of Queen's Bench (26 January 1999), not yet reported.

19. *Ontario Federation of Justices of the Peace Associations et al. v. The Queen*, Ontario Court of Justice (General Division) Divisional Court (16 March 1999), not yet reported.

20. For an analysis of evaluation systems, see Manitoba Law Reform Commission, *Independence of Provincial Judges* (Winnipeg, Canada: Queen's Printer of Maitoba, 1989), chap. 6.

21. Benjamin N. Cardozo, *The Nature of the Judicial Process* (New Haven, Conn.: Yale Univ. Press, 1921), 176.

22. Peter H. Russell, *Towards an Accountable and Responsive South African Judicial System* (Cape Town: Community Peace Foundation, 1996).

23. *The Queen v. Valente*, 2 S.C.R. 673 (1985).

24. David Marshall, *Judicial Conduct and Accountability* (Toronto: Carswell, 1995).

25. For suggestions on how these protections can be strengthened, see Martin Friedland, *A Place Apart: Judicial Independence and Accountability in Canada* (Ottawa: Canadian Judicial Council, 1995), chap. 9.

26. *Canada v. Tobiass*, 3 S.C.R. 673 (1997).

27. Robert Stevens, *The Independence of the Judiciary: The View from the Lord Chancellor's Office* (Oxford: Oxford Univ. Press, 1993), 59–60.

2

The Pillars and Politics of Judicial Independence in the United States

HENRY J. ABRAHAM

It is neither unusual nor surprising that the universe of judicial independence is a constant presence in the governmental process of a democracy. Although formal preoccupation by professional and lay observers with that process may wax and wane, it is always subject to critical analysis. Indeed, this has become increasingly so since the end of World War II. Whereas not so long ago judicial independence was treated only sporadically by scholars, columnists, and students laboring in the discipline, recent decades have evinced a burgeoning interest and concern and have done so not only with regard to the United States, which possesses one of the most powerful and most visible judicial branches in the world.

Because the role of the judiciary in the United States has served as a model for many other countries and regions, it is appropriate for this collection to address the centrality of judicial independence in the former in the hope that it may clarify the concept in a free and democratic universe.

Judicial Independence and the Impeachment Process

There is no doubt that the founding fathers considered an independent judiciary to be the cornerstone of a free society and the rule of law. Hence, they created Article 3 of the Constitution as a pillar of the separation of powers designed to provide genuine judicial independence. Although the judicial article implies necessary aspects of dependence on the legislative and executive branches—for example, the number of judges and justices, appropriations for operations, the level of salaries, jurisdiction over federal courts by Congress within the linguistic framework of Article 3, and execution of judicial mandates as well as selection of judges by the president—the article leaves no doubt of the framers' resolve to create a genuinely independent judicial branch: "The judicial power of the United States," states Section 1 of Article 3, "shall be vested in one Supreme Court, and in such inferior courts that the Congress may from time to time ordain and establish. *The Judges, both of the supreme and inferior courts* [the federal article of the Constitution does not deal with the organization and structure of the judiciaries of the several states] *shall hold their Offices during good Behavior,* and shall at stated Times, *receive for their Services, a Compensation, which shall not be diminished during their Continuance in Office.*"

The supplied italicization of the appropriate segments of Section 1 point to cardinal pillars of judicial independence. The first phrase guarantees that the judge cannot be removed so long as "good Behavior" is present, which, to all intents and purposes means life tenure, absent impeachable and convictable offenses (as outlined below). The second and concluding phrase ascertains that salaries may not be reduced while jurists hold their office. (Salaries may, of course, be increased, at Congress' pleasure.) These two guarantees constitute cardinal centricities of judicial independence that represent the envy of a good many judges laboring in systems abroad (and even by judges in some of the fifty states who do not enjoy life tenure but who have restricted, although usually, but not always, renewable terms, either by appointment or election).

That federal judges are removable, however, is demonstrated by the impeachment of thirteen, and conviction of seven, U.S. district-court-level judges between 1803 and 1989; nine others have resigned before formal charges were lodged against them.[1] The seven were convicted and removed in line with the authority provided by Article 1, Section 2, Clause 5; Section 3, Clauses 6 and 7; and Article 2, Section 4, with the latter providing also for removability from office of "civil officers of the United States [which includes judges] . . . on Impeachment for, and conviction of, Treason, Bribery, or other High crimes and Misdemeanors." Impeachment is voted by the House of Representatives by simple majority of the members present and voting (there being a quorum on the floor), but removal by the Senate can only come by an absolute two-thirds majority of the membership.

The seven judges impeached by the House and convicted and removed by the Senate were:

1. U.S. District Court judge John Pickering of New Hampshire, who was impeached in December 1803 on seven counts of "irregular judicial

proceedings, loose morals, and drunkenness" by a vote of 45-8. In March 1804 he was removed from office by the Senate by identical 19-7 votes on each of the articles.

2. U.S. District Court judge West H. Humphreys of Tennessee, who was impeached by voice vote in March 1862 on seven counts of "support of secession and holding Confederate office." The upper house convicted Humphreys on all but one of the charges, removing him from office by a 38-0 vote, and disqualifying him from holding any further public office by a 36-0 vote.

3. U.S. Commerce Court judge Robert Archbald of Pennsylvania, who was impeached in July 1912 by a vote of 223-1 on thirteen serious charges of misconduct in office, involving corrupt alliances with coal mine workers and railroad officials. Convicted by the Senate by voice vote on five of the articles in January 1913, he was disqualified from holding any further public office by a 39-35 vote.

4. U.S. District Court judge Halstead Ritter of Florida, who was impeached by the House (181-46) in March 1936 on seven counts of "bringing his court into scandal and disrepute," for actions including receipt of corrupt payments, practicing law while on the bench, and falsifying income tax returns. Acquitted on six of the seven counts, he was found guilty on the seventh, by a 56-28 vote. A motion to disqualify him from holding further public office lost by a vote of 76-0, however.

5. U.S. District Court judge Harry E. Claiborne of Nevada, who had been convicted and imprisoned on two felony counts of tax evasion in 1984. Judge Claiborne was impeached (413-0) on four counts of that offense in 1986. The Senate removed him late that year (87-10) for failure to report income, (90-7) for concealing income, and (89-8) for betraying his trust and "bringing disrepute" on federal courts. No vote was taken on disqualifying him from further public office.

6. U.S. District Court judge Alcee L. Hastings of Florida, who was impeached by a vote of 413-3 in August 1988 on seventeen counts of conspiracy to receive a bribe in a criminal case, making false statements during his 1983 trial on conspiracy and obstruction of justice charges, and disclosing confidential information from an FBI wiretap. The Senate found him guilty (69-26) in October 1989 of eight of the counts, of engaging in a "corrupt conspiracy" to extort a one-hundred-and-fifty-thousand-dollar bribe, of repeatedly lying under oath, and of forging letters to win acquittal. No vote to disqualify him from office was taken—and in November 1992 he was elected to the U.S. House of Representatives from a newly created, overwhelmingly black Florida district. The African American ex-judge

was sworn into legislative office without challenge and was reelected in 1994, 1996, and 1998.

7. U.S. District Court judge Walter L. Nixon of Mississippi, who was impeached by the House unanimously (417-0) in May 1989 for multiple perjury to investigators and a special federal grand jury. Sentenced to jail for five years, he was convicted and removed by the Senate later that year on two counts of perjury, by votes of 89-8 and 79-18. No public office disqualification was taken. Implicitly joined by Hastings, Nixon mounted an unsuccessful constitutional challenge against the Senate's procedures in federal court, which was turned aside (9-0) by the U.S. Supreme Court in 1993 as a nonjusticiable political question.[2]

Of the seven impeachment trials resulting in conviction described above, the first was probably unconstitutional as well as unjust—Pickering had been hopelessly insane and an alcoholic for three years preceding his impeachment, but he had committed no "high crimes and misdemeanors." The second, involving Humphreys, was at least questionable because of his Confederate involvement. But the other five were eminently justified and assuredly could not be regarded as a threat to judicial independence.

Yet, what of the impeachment but nonconviction of the six other judges? Two, U.S. District Court judges H. Delahay and George W. English, resigned before Senate action, believing the Senate would surely convict them. Four did go to trial in that body, all of which ended in acquittals of charges ranging from misconduct on the bench (Supreme Court justice Samuel Chase, 1804–05), to misconduct in office (U.S. District judge James H. Peck of Mississippi, 1830–31); "padding expense accounts, using railroad property in receivership of personal benefit, and misusing contempt of power" (U.S. District Court judge Charles Swayne of Florida, 1904–05); and "appointing incompetent receivers and allowing them excessive fees" (U.S. District judge Harold Louderback of California, 1933). With the possible exception of the sensational proceedings involving the sole U.S. Supreme Court justice to be impeached to date, Samuel Chase, none of the thirteen impeachments of federal judges can be justly charged to congressional assaults on judicial independence. Notwithstanding the voiced reservations in the Pickering and Humphreys cases, ample evidence of judicial impropriety existed to justify constitutionally authorized legislative action. Indeed, the latter branch normally invokes its impeachment authority with pronounced distaste and acute hesitancy. "When in doubt, don't," has been its motto in the universe of impeachment proceedings.

The exception, and arguably the only one on record, is the Samuel Chase impeachment. That controversial Supreme Court associate justice, who was George Washington's last appointment to the Court, joined that body in 1796. He was impeached by the House of Representatives in March 1804 by a vote of 72-32. Chase had made himself thoroughly obnoxious to the Jeffersonians and others by a long series of injudicious, often outrageously partisan, attacks against them, both on and off the bench; by his obvious favoritism toward fellow Federalists; and by his cavalier approach to the concept of impartial juries. His judicial posture was assuredly not an appropriate one; but he had probably not committed any impeachable offense per se under the "high crimes and misdemeanors" sanctions provision. Nonetheless, the now Jeffersonian Senate was obligated to try him, following the House's action, and it did so with considerable alacrity and amidst great ceremony. Vice President Aaron Burr presided, and Chief Justice John Marshall was an important defense witness.

Almost one year to the date after his impeachment, Chase was justly acquitted in March 1805, the Senate failing to attain the required two-thirds majority for conviction on any of the charges against him. With twenty-three votes needed for any removal at the time, the largest total attained against him on any of the counts was a vote of 19-15. The result was a signal victory not only for the narrow interpretation of the impeachment and conviction process but also for the principle of an independent judiciary. Chase, somewhat contrite, remained on the bench until his death at seventy in 1811, having served fifteen years.

Judicial Remuneration

The nondiminishing of compensation provisional safeguard is so clearly worded, and its intent so obvious, that it has not been a genuine factor in any question of judicial independence. That does not mean that the federal judiciary has always been happy with its compensation—but that is a judgmental matter. While the monetary rewards may not equal those of numerous lawyers in the private sector, the on-bench psychic income is surely a positive consideration, and the judiciary has not been ignored in periodic public service salary increases.

In 1976 a group of 140 federal judges entered litigation, alleging that, as a result of inflation, their constitutional guarantee against reduction in salary during their term in office had been violated. The U.S. Court of Claims, where the suit commenced, disagreed (4-2) in *Atkins v. United States*,[3] and the Supreme Court denied review a few months later.[4] But in 1980, following renewed litigation, the latter ruled (8-0) that two statutes of 1977 and 1980, which had revoked salary increases of 4.8 and 12.9

percent, respectively, in judges' compensation after those laws had taken effect, did constitute a violation of the compensation clause of Article 3 of the Constitution. Conversely, the Court held that that clause did not apply to the merely promised but not enacted 1978 and 1979 increases, which Congress had canceled before they went into effect.[5] The safeguards of the compensation clause are securely in place, and this clause is an important pillar supporting judicial independence in the United States.

Judicial Power and Political Reprisals

Realistically, as demonstrated above, the tenure and emolument guarantees of Section 1 of Article 3 have thus not been meaningful threats to judicial independence. Buttressing the latter significantly and centrally is the article's Section 2, which spells out the power of the federal judiciary in specific and generous detail, including the assignment of original jurisdiction to the Supreme Court in a wide range of particular subject matters, as well as appellate jurisdiction in all others covered by the section, while reserving to Congress the authority to alter appellate jurisdiction by law.

The Supreme Court's original jurisdiction, therefore, can only be altered by constitutional amendment, as Chief Justice John Marshall held so decisively in the seminal case of *Marbury v. Madison*,[6] wherein he pronounced the judiciary's most essential, and most awesome power—*judicial review* of the actions of the other two branches in the federal government (and, by subsequent extension, of those of the several states).

But Article 3, Section 2, does retain for Congress the authority to enact "Exceptions and . . . Regulations as . . . Congress shall make" to the Supreme Court's appellate jurisdiction, and it has done that, or tried to do that, on a number of occasions. Congress, for example, did so successfully when it repealed a law that had given the Court fast-track appellate jurisdiction in a famed post–Civil War Reconstruction case, *Ex parte McCardle*,[7] thus depriving the high tribunal of hearing the case, which had already been granted review.

Congress subsequently attempted to limit the Court's jurisdiction. But it succeeded only marginally, in a host of slaps at the liberal Warren Court during the mid and late 1950s, the high-water mark of the cold war and the reign of the McCarthy scares, in a far-reaching piece of legislation—the so-called Jenner-Butler bill. If it had been successful, this bill would have dramatically altered the judiciary's power to strike at allegedly illegal or unconstitutional legislation, largely in the national security realm. The bill narrowly failed to pass in what was a demonstrable attempt to lash out at judicial independence in statutory construction and constitutional interpretation. In the 1990s, Congress attempted to direct the Court's standard of review in cases involving the religion clauses of the First Amendment by spelling out legislatively in its Religious Freedom Restoration Act of 1993 that the standard should meet the so-called "compelling state interest" criterion in adjudicating apposite cases. When the issue reached the Supreme Court in the 1997 case of *City of Boerne v. Flores*,[8] the high tribunal struck down the law by a 6-3 vote, ruling that Congress had usurped the Court's power to define constitutional protections for religion (and, moreover, had intruded on the business of the states, as well as having misconstrued its authority under Section 5 of the Fourteenth Amendment).

Indubitably, the Court's power of judicial review—and that of the lower federal courts—is a constant source of both approbation and criticism-*cum*-assault by public as well as private institutions and observers. But the judicial branch cannot engage in a popularity contest; it must be free to call its interpretative shots as it sees them. It can be hoped that it will do so both wisely and appropriately—and, in general, it has opted for a role that is deferential to the two elected branches of government, unless it perceives clear violations of their authority. To address one aspect of the latter, statistics demonstrate beyond doubt that the Supreme Court, for one, does not lightly vote to strike down federal legislation. Thus, as of May 2000, out of approximately one hundred thousand laws enacted by Congress during its more than two hundred years of existence, the Court has declared unconstitutional only 157 or 158 (depending on one's count) provisions of federal law in whole or part[9] (while some twelve hundred state laws and provisions of state constitutions have run partly or wholly afoul of that judicial checkmate since 1789).

It is understandable that the seminal power of judicial review has often been under assault, especially since it is exercised by judges who serve for life—if their behavior is "good" and they choose to stay on—and who, while eminently subject to criticism, are not really effectively "touchable." The attacks on the judiciary center on its role of interpretation. Ideally, that role should normally be one of *pro*scription, or affirmation, that is, of saying "yes" and "no" rather than one of *pre*scription, that is, of engaging in what is regarded as judicial "legislating" rather than performing judicial judging, of substituting judicial value judgments and policy preferences for appropriate construction, and of "making" rather than "finding" law.

In theory, the members of the Supreme Court, at the apex of the judicial branch, are expected to approach their task of interpreting the law and the Constitution strictly and narrowly—they should resolutely shun judicial lawmaking. The line between proscription and prescription, however, is, of course, as narrow and elusive as it is controversial and complex.[10] It is, thus, hardly surprising that it has been the controversy of that line that has triggered some of the most serious attacks on the judicial role and judicial independence.

Examples abound. To cite merely some of the most well-known in what is in effect a lengthy history of what some would regard as "court bashing" and others as appropriate concern, one could begin by pointing to the aforementioned 1805 unsuccessful attempt to impeach the outspoken, partisan Federalist Supreme Court justice Samuel Chase. Another nineteenth-century illustration is the antijudicial campaign by the Radical Republican-controlled Congress in the aftermath of the Civil War, which enacted the controversial Reconstruction Acts. These acts included attacks on the Supreme Court through Congress' power to change the number of justices on the bench, either by increasing the latter—an option always available constitutionally—or by eradicating a vacant position. The Court's famous or infamous holding in *Dred Scott v. Sandford*,[11] the pre– Civil War 1857 decision upholding the tenets of slavery, and the 1869 *Ex parte McCardle* litigation, discussed earlier, are illustrative of the type of decision stimulating congressional anti-Court actions. The Fuller, White, and Taft Courts of the Progressive era also witnessed sundry attempts, though broadly unsuccessful, to intimidate the Court.

The high-water mark of assaults on the Court came during President Franklin D. Roosevelt's first and second terms in office (1933–39), reaching its crescendo with FDR's 1937 "Court packing plan."[12] The enormously popular president, flush with his ambitious New Deal legislative plan, so eagerly and overwhelmingly supported by Congress, saw his goals savaged by the "Nine Old Men" of the Supreme Court, five or six of whom combined to strike down no less than sixteen New Deal laws within a thirteen-month period.

Frustrated and angry because no vacancy had occurred on the Court in his first term, and seeing his program in shambles, Roosevelt devised a plan to pack the Court with presumably reliable supporters. The bill he sent to the Senate on February 5, 1937, largely drafted by Attorney General Homer Cummings, would have added one justice for every member of the Court who served ten years and who did not retire after his seventieth birthday, the additions to be limited to a total of six, thus potentially creating a Court of fifteen. (Similar provisions were included for the lower federal courts, up to a total of fifty.) A firestorm of opposition ensued within the halls of Congress, the press, and the public, the proposed legislation being perceived for what, in fact, it was: an assault on judicial independence.

While the Senate was biding its time, two decisive events occurred: (1) Led by Chief Justice Charles Evans Hughes, who managed to persuade Justice Owen Roberts to join him in most instances, the Court dramatically reversed itself between March and June on a number of major constitutional issues, with the four "Old Horsemen" now in dissent. The most important and first among these decisions was its 5-4 upholding of a Washington State minimum wage law for women and children on March 29, 1937.[13] (2) Taking advantage of an ultimately enacted judicial reform provision in the "Court packing plan," Justice Willis Van Devanter, one of the "Four Horsemen," retired on May 18, 1937, thus opening the way for FDR's first Court appointment—the loyal New Deal senator Hugo L. Black of Alabama. The Court was now safely transformed into a liberal majority, and the Senate recommitted the "Court packing plan" to its Judiciary Committee, where it died a deserved death.

Roosevelt had lost the battle but won the war; his program was safe. Still, the struggle over the aborted bill indicated with crystal clarity that the country would not stand for any crass tampering with judicial independence and that, when the proverbial chips are down, it prefers the judiciary over the other two branches.

That does not mean, however, that criticism of the judiciary has not continued. Criticism does continue, and not infrequently in lively mode, with particular emphasis on the issue of the parameters of judicial power and both the judiciary's and the public's perception thereof. It is centered in the application of the judicial role in drawing that controversial, elusive, yet so fundamental line between "judicial activism" and "judicial restraint," between what is acknowledged as the judiciary's appropriate role in interpretation, in judging, and its inappropriate one of "legislating"—a function presumably reserved to the legislative branch of government.

The indictment of the judiciary for the alleged transgression of its ordained role is that while, of course, courts must have the power to interpret legislation and, if absolutely necessary, hold unconstitutional a law or executive action that is clearly contrary to the Constitution, a line must be drawn between the exercise of judicial judgment and the imposition of judicial will—the latter by no means being confined merely to appellate courts. Indeed, the federal trial courts, that is, the U.S. district courts, are positioned to exercise "will" more than the other levels of the judiciary, if not finitely. Judicial "will" is accordingly equated with legislating, which is presumably reserved to Congress and the legislatures of the fifty states. How that line is to be drawn, by whom, where, and under what circumstances, represents the sine qua non of the troubling issue, which lies at the core of the issue of judicial independence. Like all fine lines, the one between "interpreting" or "judging" and "legislating" is thus highly tenuous.

Clearly, there is no simple or single response to the basic query, one so crucial to line drawing in general and the line at issue in particular. Justice Robert H. Jackson's memorable exhortation *cum caveat*, one year before his death in 1954, that "We [judges] are not final because we are infallible, but we are infallible only because we are final,"[14] is indeed apposite.

In theory, of course, the judiciary is not final, for it can be overturned by Congress, either statutorily or by constitutional amendment, and both tools have been used: The former—which, however, is again theoretically, if not perhaps politically, reversible in turn by the judiciary—had taken place in some hundred and thirty instances by 2000, in response to one or more Supreme Court decisions. During one five-year period, from 1985 to 1990, for example, the number of bills introduced in Congress to modify or overturn Supreme Court decisions totaled eighty-two, although, predictably, very few succeeded.[15]

Constitutional amendments—the ultimate and "safest" mode to "get at the Court"—have been used between six and nine times between 1789 and mid-2000 (depending on one's count and viewpoint) to reverse Supreme Court decisions, including aspects of the Thirteenth, Fourteenth, and Fifteenth Amendments (the Civil War amendments), the jurisdictional Eleventh Amendment, the Sixteenth (Income Tax) Amendment, and the Twenty-Sixth Amendment, which, overturning a 1970 decision to the contrary, granted suffrage to eighteen-year-olds at the state and local level. Some would include the Seventeenth Amendment (providing for the direct election of U.S. senators), the Nineteenth Amendment (granting women suffrage), and the Twenty-fourth Amendment (abolishing the poll tax in federal elections).

The Supreme Court, at the apex of the judiciary, sniffing the political wind, or patently perceiving prior decisional error, does, of course, at times overrule its precedents either confessionally or *sub silentio*. In other words, it can simply effect a change of its mind by virtue of distinguishing or overruling its own earlier holdings. Thus, although most of the Supreme Court's decisions stand as *res judicata*, quite a few are ultimately modified or neutralized by the Court itself or by valid action by the other branches of government, led by Congress. America's remarkable, potent, awe-inspiring system of judicial review indeed produces frustrations, but it has the saving grace of resiliency.

In any case, the Court has rarely remained indefinitely out of line with the policy views of the lawmaking—arguably, the people's—majority, with the probable exception of a host of libertarian decisions involving the interpretation of the Bill of Rights. On major public policy issues, both the president and the Congress may be expected to succeed, speaking generally and in the long run, though in the short run they may have to bow to the Court's educational role. If the Court is to thrive, as Professor Wallace Mendelson has said so well, it "must respect the social forces that determine elections and other major political settlements. No court can long withstand the morals of its era."[16]

The Court, to be sure, cannot be a mere register of public opinion; it has an obligation to become the latter's molder and leader in applicable interpretive opinion stances. Time and again, the Court has come through nobly when the constitutional chips have been on the line—as it did memorably in July 1974, when it was confronted with the expansive claims of executive privilege advanced by President Richard M. Nixon during the Watergate controversy. Its 8-0 holding, including three Nixon appointees to the Court (the fourth, then Associate Justice William H. Rehnquist, recused himself because he had been a member of the Nixon administration), against those claims[17] constituted a—probably the—major catalyst in Nixon's subsequent resignation from office on August 9, 1974.

The judicial branch of the United States thus functions in an institutional setting that forces responsibility on it. The justices, at the apex, may at times consult their own policy preferences in their approach to constitutional interpretation and statutory construction—not an astonishing fact in the face of such constitutional linguistic catch-all guarantees as "due process of law" and "equal protection of the law," for instance—but the public will continue to insist on its favorite branch's independence. Notwithstanding recurring, albeit consistently unsuccessful, legislative demands for reforms, such as a requirement for a two-thirds vote, or even a unanimous one, in declarations of unconstitutionality; a ten-, fifteen-, or twenty-year term limit; or reconfirmation of jurists every decade, there is broad agreement with the gravamen of orator Senator Daniel Webster's intonation in support of a judicial bill, that "the maintenance of the judicial power is essential and indispensable to the very being of the government. The Constitution without it would be no constitution; the government no government."[18]

More than a century and a half later, the vitality of federal judicial independence was ably echoed and reconfirmed in an exchange of views between federal appellate judges: "The independence of the federal judiciary is intact today. Federal judges regularly decide cases without being subjected to external pressures from other branches of government or to effective coercion by societal elements in general. Furthermore, orders of the Court are regularly respected and enforced, probably in large part because of the independence and impartiality of the judiciary."[19]

It is possible to identify some exceptions to the authors' conclusion that external pressures are absent, and there undoubtedly will be others; but the essence of the two wise statements just quoted remains both accurate and realistic. Judicial independence in the U.S. federal system is secure. It will, because it must, live in our evolving history—and emerging nations may well view it as a possible model.

Notes

1. For a detailed account of all impeachments and convictions, see Henry J. Abraham, *The Judicial Process: An Introductory Analysis of the Courts of the United States, England, and France.* 7th ed. (New York: Oxford Univ. Press, 1998), 44–51.

2. *Nixon v. United States,* 506 U.S. 224 (1993). For a detailed account of the Claiborne, Hastings, and Nixon cases, see Mary L. Volcansek, *Judicial Impeachment: None Called for Justice* (Champagne, Ill.: Univ. of Illinois Press, 1995). For one embracing all trials, see Eleanor Bushnell, *Crimes, Follies, and Misfortunes: The Federal Impeachment Trials* (Champagne, Ill.: Univ. of Illinois Press, 1992).

3. *Atkins v. United States,* 556 F.2d 1028 (1977).

4. *Atkins v. United States,* 429 U.S. 939 (1977).

5. *United States v. Will,* 499 U.S. 200 (1980).

6. *Marbury v. Madison,* 5 U.S. 137 (1803).

7. *Ex parte McCardle,* 74 U.S. 506 (1869).

8. *City of Boerne v. Flores,* 117 S.C. 2157 (1997).

9. For a complete table of the Court's rulings, see Abraham, *The Judicial Process,* 302–20.

10. Ibid., chaps. 7 and 8.

11. *Dred Scott v. Sandford,* 19 Howard 393 (1857).

12. See William E. Leuchtenburg, *The Supreme Court Reborn: The Constitutional Revolution in the Age of Roosevelt* (New York: Oxford Univ. Press, 1995).

13. *West Coast Hotel v. Parrish,* 300 U.S. 379 (1937).

14. *Brown v. Allen,* 344 U.S. 443, 540 (1953)(con. op.).

15. See, Abraham, *The Judicial Process,* 364–67.

16. Wallace Mendelson, *Justices Black and Frankfurter: Conflict and the Court,* 2d ed. (Chicago: Univ. of Chicago Press, 1966), 127.

17. *United States v. Nixon,* 417 U.S. 683 (1974).

18. As quoted by Chief Justice Earl Warren, "Webster and the Court," *Dartmouth College Alumni Magazine* 34 (19 May 1969).

19. Letter of 23 May 1994, from Judges James A. Redden and Randall R. Rader, quoted by L. Ralph Mecham, director, Administrative Office of the United States Courts, in his "Introduction to Mercer Law Review Symposium on Federal Judicial Independence," *Mercer Law Review* 46 (1995): 637, 644.

3

Stifling Judicial
Independence from Within

The Japanese Judiciary

DAVID M. O'BRIEN AND YASUO OHKOSHI

Japan and Competing Theories of Judicial Independence

Judicial independence in Japan has become a matter of considerable controversy. J. Mark Ramseyer has argued that judicial independence has been curbed by the Liberal Democratic Party (LDP).[1] Governing
from 1955 to 1993, the LDP controlled judicial appointments and, according to Ramseyer, manipulated judicial behavior in other ways. Following
William M. Landes and Richard A. Posner,[2] Ramseyer further argued that
from an econometric perspective, it is rational for single-party dominated
political systems to accord courts less independence because of the governing party's expectation it will continue to win elections, whereas competitive party systems favor greater judicial independence in order to
preserve a party's legislative gains while in office once it is out of power.
"Restated," Ramseyer claimed that, "American politicians [because of the
competitive two-party system] politicize appointments but depoliticize
control. Japanese politicians politicize control and therefore need not (because of the self-selection among judicial candidates) politicize appointments as strongly."[3]

Further developing and applying a rational choice model, Ramseyer
joined with political scientist Francis Rosenbluth, in their book *Japan's Political Marketplace,* to argue, more generally, that "Japanese judges are
agents of LDP principals; in practice, LDP principals treat Japanese agents
much as principal-agent theory suggests."[4] And Ramseyer, along with
Eric B. Rasmusen, subsequently developed further support for the theory,
by analyzing the personnel data (backgrounds, decisions, and judicial

assignments) of 274 lower court judges, that the LDP manipulated the careers of lower court judges by rewarding or providing incentives to those judges adhering to its party line.[5]

Notably, Ramseyer, Rosenbluth, and Rasmusen were not the first to argue that Japanese judges have been manipulated.[6] But, they were the first to do so on the basis of a "principal-agent theory," rather than with an analysis of the institutional dynamics of the Japanese judiciary and other anecdotal evidence. In doing so, they swept broadly and challenged more conventional studies and theories of the institutional dynamics of the Japanese judiciary. Japan scholar John O. Haley has countered the analysis of Ramseyer and his colleagues on, principally, two scores. First, for the postwar Occupation Forces, in drafting Japan's 1947 constitution, "judicial independence did not mean judicial autonomy." In short, Ramseyer and his colleagues overstate their argument. In Haley's words, "direct political control over the appointment of Supreme Court justices and lower career judges was intentionally provided. To argue that there has not been any political influence is to question this original design."[7]

Second, turning to the institutional history of the judiciary in Japan, Haley argues rather convincingly that "Japan's judiciary has almost from its inception been organized as a remarkably autonomous elite bureaucracy within the civil law tradition."[8] The postwar judicial reforms and management of the judiciary have served to further insulate the courts and reinforced the judiciary's institutional independence. Haley thus concludes with no uncertainty that, "Those [i.e., Ramseyer, Rosenbluth, and Rasmusen] who argue to the contrary that politicians in Japan direct the courts and its decisions distort the facts and profoundly mislead."[9]

"Judicial independence" is, of course, somewhat ambiguous, complex, and may connote the absence of any number of constraints—constraints ranging from the financial, ideological, and psychological to various mechanisms of political control. Fortunately, although disagreeing about the status of judicial independence in Japan, Ramseyer and his colleagues and Haley focus on one aspect of "judicial independence," namely, the *institutional independence* of the judiciary, which revolves around whether and to what extent courts are subject to external political controls. There is another, no less important factor, namely, the degree of independence enjoyed by individual judges on the bench, or *judicial independence on the bench.*

In terms of the debate over the institutional independence of the Japanese judiciary, our analysis of the operation of the judiciary largely supports Haley's rejection of the "principal-agent theory," as advanced by Ramseyer and others. Fundamentally, Ramseyer, Rosenbluth, and Rasmusen gloss over the pivotal role of the chief justice and the General Secretariat in recommending the appointment, reappointment, and assignments of lower court judges. Moreover, they present no evidence that the LDP (in contrast to higher court judges and the Supreme Court) actively intervened so as to control judicial decisions. In other words, lower court judges are manipulated, but they are manipulated by the chief justice and the General Secretariat. Through that judicial manipulation, the institutional independence of the judiciary has been preserved and reinforced.

The data and analysis presented here, however, leads us to reject Haley's assessment of the related issue of judicial independence on the bench. Remarkably, Ramseyer and his colleagues focus only on the lower courts and, rather oddly, pay no attention to the operation of the Supreme Court. By contrast, Haley understands that judicial independence cannot be adequately studied without examining the institutional linkages between the lower courts and the Supreme Court, especially in a judicial system operating with career judges and a tightly controlled judicial bureaucracy. Haley, nonetheless, underestimates the influence and control of the chief justice and the General Secretariat over the composition of the high court, no less than over the lower courts. More is at work than merely the fact that career judges make up over a third of those sitting on the Court at any given time. Appointments to the Court are manipulated by the chief justice in other ways as well. And they are manipulated by the chief justice and the General Secretariat so as to curb judicial independence on the bench.

Furthermore, whereas studies by some scholars of the voting behavior and opinion writing of justices during the first two decades of the postwar Supreme Court suggested a basis for optimism about the emergence of judicial independence on the Supreme Court, we present new data showing that expressions of individual judicial independence have in fact declined during the 1980s and 1990s. In short, as Haley correctly argues, contrary to Ramseyer and colleagues, the chief justice and the General Secretariat manipulates judicial appointments and assignments in order to maintain the judiciary's institutional independence. In addition, as documented here in the section entitled "Thwarting Judicial Independence in the Supreme Court," appointments to the Supreme Court are no less manipulated to curb and confine expressions of *judicial independence on the bench*, both in terms of the decisions rendered and opinion writing as measured by concurring and dissenting opinions.

Structure and Organization of the Japanese Judiciary

Almost a half century ago, the creation of Japan's postwar judicial system aimed to forge revolutionary change in the role of courts. Under the prewar Meiji Constitution, the courts and the Diet exercised their powers in the name of the emperor. That constitution specifically stipulated that the "Judicature shall be exercised by the Courts of Law according to Law, in the name of the Emperor." Although judicial independence was proclaimed and judges had lifetime appointments, subject to good behavior and disciplinary action, they functioned like bureaucrats under the supervision of the Ministry of Justice. Courts had no power of judicial review over either legislation or administrative actions. They could not even adjudicate disputes between citizens and the government; there were separate tribunals for such disputes.[10]

Against the background of the prewar constitution and judiciary, the reorganization of the courts in 1947 was revolutionary, or potentially revolutionary, in four respects. First, the constitution, promulgated on November 3, 1946, and put into effect on May 3, 1947, rejected the emperor's sovereignty. Popular sovereignty was proclaimed and a constitutional democracy was created in place of the previous constitutional monarchy. Second, a parliamentary system was erected, but unlike the system of parliamentary sovereignty in Great Britain, the courts were separated from the rest of the government for the first time in Japan's long history. Third, American-style judicial review was provided for, and courts were given the power to strike down laws that violate the constitution. Fourth, and finally, the basis for judicial independence was laid, at least on paper.

The reorganization of the Japanese judicial system, nevertheless, resulted in far less revolutionary change in practice. Article 76 vested the "whole judicial power" in the courts, and Article 77 shifted responsibility for judicial administration from the prewar Ministry of Justice to the Supreme Court. The latter acquired extensive ruling-making powers as well as authority over the training, nomination, assignment, and oversight of lower court judges. The courts were also empowered for the first time to exercise review over the constitutionality of legislation and administrative actions. Still, in spite of these parchment guarantees, the courts infrequently assert their power and have rarely challenged the government's interpretation of the constitution.

The Supreme Court and lower courts, more generally, tend to defer to the government.[11] The Japanese Supreme Court generally abides by a "rule of strict necessity" and "constitutional decision making is limited to the unavoidable."[12] In spite of its authority to enforce the constitution, the

Supreme Court has ruled that many constitutional questions are either "matters of legislative discretion" or "political questions" reserved for the Diet and other governmental agencies, not for the courts, to decide. Only six times in the entire postwar period has a regulation or law been declared unconstitutional by the Supreme Court.[13] Moreover, none of those rulings, arguably, brought about major social change. The Diet refused, for instance, to correct the malapportionment in the election of representatives, which the Court deemed to be constitutionally impermissible in 1976 and, again, in 1985.[14] In addition, lower court decisions that go against the government are almost invariably reversed by higher courts or the Supreme Court.

Whereas there has been a "judicialization" of politics in the United States, Western Europe, and elsewhere,[15] the exercise of judicial review in Japan remains extremely self-restrained. That results in large measure from the failure of judicial independence to develop within the ranks of the judiciary. Although the institutional independence and autonomy of the judiciary was secured, judicial independence on the bench remains sharply curbed. The judicial system operates in ways that discourage, and even punish, nonconformity in the lower courts and the Supreme Court.

The Japanese judicial system is unitary, unlike the system of judicial federalism in the United States. At its apex is the Supreme Court of Japan, which is composed of fifteen justices, who generally decide cases as petty benches composed of five justices. Each of the three petty benches has its own courtroom and sits twice a week. The first petty bench sits on Mondays and Thursdays, the second on Mondays and Fridays, and the third on Tuesdays and Fridays. Major cases and administrative matters are referred to the entire Court, which sits *en banc* as the grand bench to hear cases and, as a judicial conference, to dispose of administrative matters. These meetings of the entire Court are held on Wednesdays throughout the year, except during holidays and during vacation time in August.

The Supreme Court's docket of cases is crowded, as are those of the lower courts. The size of the docket runs contrary to the self-perpetuated myth of harmony in a country of "reluctant litigants."[16] More than seven thousand cases are annually filed or pending on the Japanese Supreme Court's docket in the 1990s, with the Court disposing of approximately five thousand each year. From a comparative perspective, the docket is as large as that of the U.S. Supreme Court, yet in a country with less than half of the population of the United States.[17]

Unlike the U.S. Supreme Court, the Japanese Supreme Court has no discretionary jurisdiction. Technically, it must decide all appeals. Appeals are basically of two sorts: *koso* appeals to high courts and *jokoku* appeals to the Supreme Court are limited to review for errors in legal interpretation, alleged conflicts with precedents, and misapplications of the Code of Criminal Procedure. But, they also allow for *de novo* review and a determination of whether there are other grounds for appeal. By contrast, a *kokoku* appeal must raise an alleged constitutional violation or conflict with precedent. In practice, both kinds of appeals are treated basically alike. Well over 95 percent are summarily dismissed, leaving the lower court rulings intact.

Of the five thousand-odd cases disposed of each year, fewer than one hundred cases a year arc granted oral arguments and decided by full written opinion. Each justice ostensibly reads all filings, but they are first screened by the Court's law clerks or research officials and then divided among the justices on the three petty benches. Unlike law clerks at the U.S. Supreme Court, who are recent law school graduates, who serve only a year, and who work for an individual justice, the law clerks in Japan are experienced judges assigned to the Court for three to five years. Notably, they work for the Court as a whole, not for individual justices. They screen and research cases, as well as draft most of the opinions of the petty and grand benches. There are currently twenty-nine law clerks. Among them, a chief supervises the work of seventeen assigned to a division handling civil and administrative cases, while the remaining eleven are assigned to the criminal law division.

On the three petty benches, each case is in turn assigned to an individual justice, who further studies it and recommends whether it should be granted oral arguments at the twice-weekly conference of each petty bench. Each justice reports on about one hundred to one hundred and fifty cases a month, or about eight hundred cases per petty bench each month. Yet, according to Justice Itsuo Sonobe, only a dozen or so cases "are seriously deliberated."[18]

The most important cases—those that raise unresolved constitutional issues or in which precedents will be established or changed—are transferred by petty benches to the grand bench. These select few cases are further researched by the law clerks, and some are eventually granted oral arguments. Oral argumentation carries little weight, however. As Justice Sonobe candidly concedes, "Oral argument is admitted in cases in which the lower court decision is [to be] reversed, and such oral argument is pretty formal and not substantial." Justices rarely ask questions from the bench.

In addition (and again unlike the U.S. Supreme Court, which publishes all of its opinions and decisions), the Japanese Supreme Court publishes only a few of its most important rulings each year. Two justices from each of the petty benches, along with two law clerks, form a committee that decides which ones should be published in the reporter of narrowly selected Supreme Court decisions, the *Saiko Saibansho Hanreishu*. The cases and opinions in that reporter are thus deemed important enough to have precedential value and to prove useful for practitioners. A more complete collection, containing many more but not all opinions, is available in a so-called unabridged reporter, the *Saiko Saibansho Saibanshu*, for criminal (*keiji*) and civil (*minji*) cases. This reporter of decisions neither includes all opinions nor is widely available, even in libraries.

Below the Supreme Court are eight high courts, located in the major cities of Tokyo, Osaka, Nagoya, Hiroshima, Fukuoka, Sendai, Sapporo, and Takamatsu, as well as six branches in other cities. These courts have territorial jurisdiction over their designated regions. They also have both appellate and original jurisdiction over civil and criminal cases. Each is supervised by a chief judge (or president) and typically functions in three-judge panels, with a senior judge presiding, although cases involving insurrection are heard by five-judge courts. There are approximately 285 high court judges. Appointed by the cabinet on the recommendation of the Supreme Court, they remain subject to periodic reappointments and to mandatory retirement at age sixty-five.

The number of judges sitting on a high court depends on its caseload and regional population. Assignments are made basically on the basis of seniority, along with the ranking of individual judges and courts. In 1991, 30,690 appeals were filed and another 15,824 cases were pending, for a total of 46,514 cases. Of those, decisions were rendered in 30,706 cases. Notably, there were roughly the same number of cases (a total of 44,465) in U.S. federal appellate courts.[19]

Appeals to high courts come from district courts and family courts, along with some cases directly from summary courts. District courts are the principal trial courts of the system. There are 50 of them, located in all major cities, and another 201 branches are located in other towns. District courts generally function as single-judge courts without juries. Three-judge district courts, however, decide appeals from summary courts as well as cases deemed especially important because of the constitutional issues raised. There are 910 district court judges and 460 assistant judges. They face heavy caseloads as well. In 1991, for instance, the district courts had 822,590 filings, had another 405,458 cases pending, and reached decisions in 813,634 cases. By contrast, U.S. district courts in 1991 faced filings of only 217,656 civil cases and 45,215 criminal cases, though state courts confronted far larger numbers.

The 50 family courts and their 201 branches are located alongside the district courts. Unlike district courts, they have specialized jurisdiction over family affairs and domestic matters, such as divorce and estates as well as juvenile delinquency. These courts use conciliation procedures to discourage adjudication of disputes. They are staffed by approximately two hundred judges and one hundred and fifty assistant judges, along with fifteen hundred probation officers. Below the family courts are 452 summary courts, with about 810 judges. These single-judge courts have original jurisdiction over civil cases involving claims of less than 900,000 yen ($9,000) and minor criminal cases for which fines may not exceed 200,000 yen ($2,000). The filings and pending cases in 1991 totaled 2,741,230, with decisions handed down in 2,637,938 cases.[20]

Crushing Judicial Independence in the Lower Courts

Judicial independence was ostensibly guaranteed in Japan by the reorganization of the courts and by provisions providing for the removal of judges from the bench through primarily impeachment proceedings. Yet judicial independence amounted to little more than the institutional separation of the courts from the rest of the government. Judicial independence on the bench has failed to take root for a number of reasons. The legacies of the prewar judicial tradition, the infrastructure, and legal culture bode ill for assertion of independence by judges. In addition, although the forces of the Occupation in the 1940s "purged" many high government officials, prewar judges were not among them, being deemed not important enough to purge. Prewar judges thus continued to exercise influence and arguably wielded greater power as a result of the reorganization of the courts. They were positioned to conserve as much as possible of the past and to rebuff efforts to enforce new constitutional guarantees for civil rights and liberties.

Moreover, as Ramseyer and others emphasize, the conservative Liberal Democratic Party (LDP) remained in power from 1955 to 1993—for almost four decades. The LDP therefore retained formal control over judicial appointments. But, no less important is how lower court judges are recruited and supervised. The Supreme Court—and in particular the chief justice and General Secretariat—oversees the training, nomination, reappointment, assignments, and salaries of lower court judges. The General Secretariat consists of one secretary general, seven bureau chiefs, and about eight hundred judges and other officials. As a result, Japanese judges and courts are tightly controlled, in contrast to the decentralized and far more independent federal courts in the United States.

In other words, the configuration of judicial politics changed in the postwar era, but it changed in ways that perpetuated bureaucratic methods for punishing assertions of judicial independence. No longer part of the prewar Ministry of Justice, the judiciary became a large bureaucracy in its own right. The judicial system now employs over twenty-one thousand judges, clerks, secretaries, marshals, and other personnel. There are bureaus for general, personnel, financial, civil, criminal, administrative, and family affairs. The Legal Training and Research Institute turns out virtually all of the country's attorneys, prosecutors, and judges. A research and training institute also exists for court clerks and another for probation officers. The entire system is supervised by the Supreme Court, with primary direction responsibility held by the chief justice and the General Secretariat.

Central to the operation of contemporary Japanese judiciary is the system of producing and promoting an elite cadre of professional judges. With the exception of the Supreme Court, the lower courts are staffed entirely by career judges, who must survive a series of professional and personal hurdles, beginning with their admission to a university. Unlike legal education in the United States, but like that in Great Britain, Germany, and France, students study law as undergraduates. After graduation, most students take bar exam cram courses in preparation for the National Law Examination. The test, which may be taken numerous times, is rigorous. Out of the more than twenty thousand students a year who take the test, only about seven hundred pass. (Before 1993, when the government increased the number, only about five hundred a year were successful.) Graduates of the leading law schools at the universities of Tokyo, Waseda, Chuo, Kyoto, and Keio tend to do well.

Only after passing a multiple-choice examination given in May, submitting a thesis in July or August, and passing an interview in October is a student admitted into the Legal Training and Research Institute. There, at government expense, he or she pursues a two-year course of study. During their time at the institute, students have four four-month internships — in an attorney's office, a prosecutor's office, a criminal court, and a civil court. Before graduating, students may apply to become assistant judges, although there are only as many positions as there are vacancies, which number about one hundred a year. Students seek mentors and advisers in choosing their legal careers and in deciding whether to apply for a judgeship. Those who are discouraged by faculty at the institute from applying for judgeships are, if they persist in applying, most likely to be denied judicial appointments.

Judicial careers begin with a ten-year appointment as an assistant judge, an apprenticeship. In actuality, assistant judges function like full judges after five years. They may become an associate judge on a three-judge court or preside over a single-judge court. After a decade, they become full judges, subject to reappointment every ten years. During the course of their careers, they will be reassigned many times and to several courts, or to other positions within the judiciary.

A judge may move from a district court to being an acting high court judge, sitting as a so-called left-hand associate. After five more years, the judge may then become a regular high court judge, sitting on the right side of a more senior presiding judge. Eventually, a judge may be elevated to the position of presiding judge on a three-judge court. A very few will then be given an opportunity to become chief judges (presidents) on the country's most prestigious high courts, those located in Tokyo, Osaka, and Nagoya. Later, from that select group, a few who have reached their mid-sixties are rewarded with an appointment to the Supreme Court, or to the most coveted position of chief justice. The chief justice ranks in status with the prime minister, the only other government official ceremoniously appointed by the emperor, as well as with the speakers of the houses.

What is pivotal to the operation of the Japanese judiciary, and what Ramseyer and his colleagues fail to fully appreciate in arguing that the LDP (principal) manipulates the judiciary (agent) is that the chief justice recommends to the judicial conference and to the cabinet all lower court appointees and their reassignments, no less than appointments to the Supreme Court. For example, as Haley notes, two months before the February 1990 appointment of Chief Justice Ryohachi Kusaba, the retiring chief justice, Koichi Yaguchi, paid a visit to the prime minister in order to inform him of the Court's choice for his successor. There was no objection to the recommendation, for as an official quoted in the *Mainichi Shimbun* put it: "We wouldn't have the vaguest idea who anyone they might suggest was, and we wouldn't have any way of finding out whether they would be suitable. The Supreme Court people have researched this. We trust their judgment."[21] In sum, the chief justice and the General Secretariat (not the prime minister, the LDP, or other governing parties) are the principals bearing responsibility for overseeing the careers of lower court judges as well as appointments to the Court.

Already selective, the judicial system becomes increasingly competitive the higher up a judge moves within the hierarchy of courts. Over the years and along the way, many are encouraged to abandon their careers and to go into private legal practice. Reassignment to less desirable courts, salary rankings, and the remote but real possibility of being denied reappointment are powerful incentives for achieving conformity. In addition, some are put on fast tracks, while many others reach dead ends sooner or later. Those serving on the Tokyo district and high courts fall into the former category. Within legal circles, the elite among the judicial elite are referred to as "triple crown winners." They have worked on the staff of the General Secretariat, served as law clerks at the Supreme Court, and later become teachers at the Legal Training and Research Institute. In contrast, those known as "triple handicaps" are kept in the lowest (fourth) pay grade, assigned to local branch courts, and never become presiding judges.[22]

The career of Supreme Court Justice Itsuo Sonobe, appointed to the Court in 1989 at age sixty, illustrates the fast track of a select few. After teaching administrative law for more than a decade at Kyoto University, he began a fifteen-year judicial career destined to culminate in a Supreme Court appointment. After two years as a district court judge, he moved to a high court for three years, and then became a chief judge on a district court for three years. Afterward, he served for five years as the head law clerk in charge of civil and administrative cases at the Supreme Court, followed by two more years as the chief judge of the Tokyo District Court. Sonobe then returned to academia, teaching in Tokyo for two years at Tsukuba University and another two at Seikei University, whereupon he was appointed to the Court as a professor, despite his extensive experience within the judiciary. His career was distinguished and exceptional. Rarely are legal scholars elevated to the highest bench. "In Japan," as Justice Sonobe explains, "the academic world is completely separated from the practicing world. Scholars are like octopus (*tako*) living in a small trap (*tsubo*). They don't know the outside world. So the academic world is called octopus-trap (*tako-tsubo*) society."

The experience of the overwhelming majority of career judges is vastly different and the pressures for conformity enormous. Some lower court judges have asserted their independence and ruled liberally on claims to civil rights and liberties. Yet their rulings tend to be reversed on appeal by higher courts. Moreover, a range of personal and professional sanctions may be brought to bear on them. Even former Chief Justice Takaaki Hattori acknowledged that "There is a potential conflict here between the judges' independence to decide cases and the Supreme Court's power of administrative supervision" over lower court judges.[23] Many lawyers and former judges contend that the conflict is blatant, with assignments and salary adjustments manipulated so as to reprimand certain judges.

Judges who are too independent or too liberal may be offered reassignments to less prestigious courts or to courts in less desirable locations, necessitating their moving their families. In this way, they are encouraged to leave the judiciary instead. Ramseyer and colleagues, as well as Haley and others, have demonstrated the impact of the manipulation of judicial assignments on the careers of lower court judges. But, they have not addressed how the General Secretariat also regularly discriminates in salary rankings against those who, after ten or twenty years, have proven too independent or less than absolutely loyal. After twenty years, career judges who are favored are promoted to the third grade of the salary scale, receiving 18.4 million yen (about $184,000). If they serve on a prestigious court in a major city, like Tokyo or Osaka, they receive an additional 2.2 million yen ($22,000), for a total of 20.6 million yen ($206,000).

By contrast, some of their peers, those who began their careers at the same time but who have fallen out of favor, remain stuck in the fourth salary grade. Because these judges are typically assigned to branch courts located in small towns, they receive no salary supplement and earn 15.42 million yen ($154,200). The prospect is not bright for these judges. The favored judges will continue to be promoted, while they will be kept in the lowest salary grade.

The disparity in salaries continues to grow throughout their careers. Even judges in the same rank do not receive the same salary, because special benefits, such as family allowances, may also be assigned. In any event, favored judges will reach the first grade, earning 24.81 million yen ($248,100), while the disfavored who remain on the bench earn 9,390,000 yen ($93,900) a year less. The burden on these judges grows greater as their children reach college age and they face the expenses of sending them to live in Tokyo, Kyoto, or Osaka, where the major universities are located. Yet such discrimination is defended as necessary to maintaining a judicial meritocracy, promoting the best and the brightest.

More direct assaults have been made on judicial independence in the lower courts, as Ramseyer, among others, have recounted. The most well-known instance occurred when the *Naganuma* case was pending before the Sapporo District Court.[24] That case involved a major controversy over the construction of a missile base. The plaintiffs also challenged the constitutionality of the Self Defense Forces under Article 9's stipulation that "land, sea, and air forces, as well as other war potential, will never be maintained" in postwar Japan. Chief Judge Kenta Hiraga sent a letter, which became known as the "Hiraga Memorandum," to two of the three judges deciding the case. In the letter, he offered presiding Judge Shigeo Fukushima and Assistant Judge Hiroshi Hirata some "friendly advice from a senior colleague."[25] And he proceeded to counsel them to be circumspect in their ruling.

After handing down the court's decision, Judge Fukushima brought Hiraga's letter to the attention of the Sapporo District Court's judicial conference, which leaked the matter to the press. Chief Judge Hiraga defended his action on the ground that Judge Fukushima was a member of the Young Jurists' Association, an association of lawyers, judges, and professors founded in 1954 to counter the influence and fierce anticommunist stance of Chief Justice Kohtaro Tanaka, who headed the judiciary from 1950 to 1960. Amid protests on all sides, Chief Judge Hiraga was subsequently "reprimanded" by being transferred to the more prestigious Tokyo High Court. The Supreme Court also admonished Judge Fukushima that "judges should not fall into the error of self-importance but should always be humble enough to try to build up character and competence by exchanging experience and knowledge among themselves."[26]

Judges belonging to the Young Jurists' Association were specifically singled out for recrimination, as Ramseyer and Rasmusen demonstrate in their study of the backgrounds and careers of lower court judges. The association was far too liberal in the view of the Supreme Court and the General Secretariat. Attorneys in the association were in the vanguard of defending victims of environmental pollution, and some of the judges finding in their favor and against the government were also members. As a result, they faced retaliation from the Supreme Court under both Chief Justice Tanaka and his successors in the 1970s. In particular, ultraconservative Chief Justice Kazuto Ishida (1963–73) sought to purge the bench of members of the association. In addition, the National Conference of High, District, and Family Courts passed a resolution calling for judges to resign from the Young Jurists' Association. A number of those working in the General Secretariat resigned. Others belonging to the association were denied assistant judgeships. And some of the association's judges were given undesirable transfer assignments.

In these ways, judicial independence on the bench in the lower courts was directly assaulted and undermined. On the basis of that record, Ramseyer and Rosenbluth assert that, "LDP leaders use their direct control over judicial appointments and indirect control over the Secretariat to shape judicial decisions."[27] Yet in drawing that conclusion, Ramseyer and

Rosenbluth gloss over the pivotal role of the chief justice and the General Secretariat in recommending to the prime minister and the cabinet the appointment, reappointment, and assignments of lower court judges. Furthermore, they present no evidence that the LDP actively intervened to control those and other judicial decisions.

Lower court judges are manipulated, but they are manipulated by the chief justice and the General Secretariat. Contrary to Ramseyer and Rosenbluth, Haley correctly concludes that the manipulation of lower court judges is part of "the judiciary's self-policing mechanisms to prevent ideological shifts leftward."[28] In sum, judicial independence on the bench is curbed and punished by the Supreme Court in order to preserve the judiciary's institutional independence and freedom from the kind of political controls that Ramseyer and Rosenbluth mistakenly and misleadingly argue the LDP exercised over the judiciary.

Thwarting Judicial Independence in the Supreme Court

Unlike lower court judges, not all members of the Supreme Court are career judges. Still, judicial independence is discouraged in a variety of ways, ranging from the selection process to the operation of the Court itself. The appointment process and tenure is different for Supreme Court justices than for lower court judges. The drafters of Japan's postwar constitution and the hastily written Court Organization Law of 1947 modeled the appointment process for justices along the lines of the so-called Missouri Plan. The Missouri Plan was first adopted by that U.S. state in 1940; subsequently almost one-half of the states have enacted some version of the plan. The plan embodies a merit selection system that the American Bar Association and the American Judicature Society championed as an alternative to partisan judicial elections and also as a means to improve the quality of judges sitting on state benches in the United States. The three basic elements are as follows: (1) a nonpartisan commission nominates three candidates for every vacancy, (2) from those the governor appoints one, and (3) the judge must be approved by the voters at the time of the next general election; if approved, he or she receives a twelve-year appointment.

Although modeled after the Missouri Plan, the constitutional and statutory provisions for the selection, appointment, and tenure of Japanese Supreme Court justices have been modified or circumvented in practice. The use of a nominating commission was short lived, for instance. In April 1947, an eleven-member Advisory Committee for Appointing Justices was appointed and nominated thirty candidates for justiceships and three for the chief justiceship. Later that year, however, the Japan Socialist Party (JSP) won the general election and temporarily controlled the government for one year.

Again, the selection process changed. A new fifteen-member nominating committee was created. This committee recommended thirty candidates, from which the JSP cabinet named the first fifteen justices to the postwar Court. A year later, in 1948, the JSP was driven from office. Nominating committees for selecting justices were never used again. Instead, when a vacancy occurs, cabinet officials consult with the chief justice and the General Secretariat, who exercise extraordinary influence over the appointments, especially if a career judge is elevated.

As with the selection and promotion of lower court judges, the chief justice determines the appointment of members of the Supreme Court, including his own successor. There is no "advise and consent" process, as with the U.S. Senate's confirmation of the president's judicial nominees. As a result, little media attention is paid to judicial appointments, and the appointment of Supreme Court justices frequently becomes known only after the fact. Moreover, only four chief justices in the entire postwar era have not served most of their previous careers in high positions within the judicial bureaucracy. In the 1980s and 1990s, all chief justices—specifically, Chief Justices Jiro Terada (1980–85), Koichi Yaguchi (1985–90), Ryohachi Kusaba (1991–95), and Toru Miyoshi (1995–)—have risen through the ranks of the General Secretariat. Each had previously served as chief of one or more of its bureaus before being elevated to the Court.

Chief Justice Koichi Yaguchi, who headed the Supreme Court and the judicial bureaucracy from 1985 to 1990, for instance, was known within Tokyo legal circles as "Mr. Judicial Administration" and said to even know "the number of mice that live within the Supreme Court building." He had been in the first graduating class of the Legal Research Institute in 1948 and had spent most of his career rising through the ranks of the judicial bureaucracy to its highest position as chief of the General Secretariat at the time of his appointment to the Court. Indeed, Yaguchi had served only twelve years (or one-third) of his career on the bench deciding cases. He also had been in charge of the General Secretariat's personnel bureau in the late 1960s and 1970s, when Chief Justice Ishida purged the judiciary of liberals associated with the Young Jurists Association.

The selection of justices is also conditioned by stipulations in Article 31(1) of the Court Organization Law that justices "shall be among persons of broad vision and extensive knowledge of law, who are not less than 40 years of age." That article also specifies that

> At least 10 of them shall be persons who have held one of the positions mentioned in item (1) or (2) for not less than 10 years, or one or more of the positions mentioned in the following items for the total period of 20 years or more: (1) President of the High Court; (2) Judges; (3) Judges of the Summary Court; (4) Public Prosecutors; (5) Lawyers; (6) Professors or assistant professors in legal science in universities which shall be determined elsewhere by law.

In practice, only those who have reached the pinnacle of their respective careers are considered. And an appointment to the Court is considered a crowning glory for those favored few.

A convention was established, in the words of former Chief Justice Takaaki Hattori, that "Supreme Court justices are appointed in roughly equal numbers from among three broad groups: (1) inferior court judges; (2) practicing lawyers; and (3) public prosecutors, law professors, or other persons of broad knowledge and experience."[29] However, that ratio in representation has changed over the years. The rule instead became six career judges; five or four practitioners; two former bureaucrats, including one diplomat; one or two prosecutors; and one law professor.

The six career judges on the Court in 1995–96, moreover, had spent most of their early careers in administrative, not judicial, positions. Chief Justice Toru Miyoshi spent twenty-two years of his early career in administration. Likewise, the other five career judges on the Court had spent most of their early careers in administrative posts. Although the chief justice held the record for administrative service, he was followed by Justices Katsuya Ohnishi, with twenty-one and a half years; Hideo Chigusa, with nineteen years; Masao Fujii, with eighteen years; Tsuneo Kabe, with seventeen years; and Motoo Ono, with fourteen years in administration rather than serving in the lower courts.

The prior positions of the 121 justices who have served on the Court between 1947 and 1995 are presented in table 3.1. Notably, as the ratio of career judges, lawyers, bureaucrats, and law professors changed, the balance tipped further toward reinforcing the influence of the chief justice and the General Secretariat over the composition and, arguably, the direction of the Court. With one exception, all appointees have been male. In 1994 Prime Minister Morihiro Hosokawa named the first female, a sixty-six-year-old former Labor Ministry official, Hisako Takahashi.

Somewhat like the Missouri Plan, the Constitution of Japan provides for a system of popular review. After their appointment, according to Article

TABLE 3.1

Prior Occupations of Justices on the Japanese Supreme Court, 1947–1995

Immediate Prior Position	Number	Percentage
Judge	46	38.0
Attorney	39	32.2
Prosecutor	13	10.7
Professor	10	8.2
Administrator	7	5.7
Diplomat	6	4.9
Total	121	99.7

Source: David M. O'Brien and Yasuo Ohkoshi, *To Dream of Dreams: Religious Freedom and Constitutional Politics in Postwar Japan* (Honolulu: Univ. of Hawaii Press, 1996).

79(2), justices "shall be reviewed by the people at the first general election of the members of the House of Representatives following their appointment." Thereafter, justices face election after each ten years of service. This provision is ostensibly a reflection of the postwar constitution's rejection of the emperor's sovereignty and recognition of popular sovereignty. Under the system, voters place an X in a box next to the name of a justice they think should be dismissed. Otherwise, their ballot is counted as a vote for retaining the justice.

Popular review nevertheless has been rendered virtually meaningless. Criticism of popular review has been leveled on several scores: Voters are more concerned with the election of their representatives. They pay little attention to justices on the ballot. They generally know little about the justices' qualifications or voting records. A ten-year interval is too long.[30] In addition, as Justice Sonobe points out, the "mass media doesn't take it seriously." Votes are cast "against some of the justices half in fun," because they were once bureaucrats. Votes for dismissal usually amount to only "10 percent or 15 percent at most." Justice Sonobe, among others, thus doubts whether "this system is effective and that the cost of carrying it out in every election of the House of Representatives has enough benefit."

Whatever the merits or limitations of popular review, an end run around the system was made by the practice of appointing older and older justices. Justices are simply not on the bench long enough to stand for election after ten years. Article 50 of the Court Organization Law mandates retirement at age seventy, and because justices are appointed in their sixties, few face elections. Furthermore, the average age of appointees has incrementally inched up. In the 1950s, the average age of justices at the time of their appointment was 61.2 years. In the 1960s, the average rose to 62.9 years, then reached 63.7 years in the 1970s, and 64 years for appointees in the 1980s. The average age of the twenty-one justices appointed between 1990 and 1995 was 64.2. As indicated in table 3.2, the average length of service is a little over six years. And as the age of appointees has risen, the corresponding average tenure has declined. The average length of service for those justices appointed in the 1940s and 1950s was over eight years, compared with five-and-a-half years for those named in the 1990s.

TABLE 3.2

Average Length of Service of Japanese Supreme Court Justices, 1947–1995

Prime Minister	Date of Appointments	Number of Appointees	Average Number of Years of Service
Katayama	1947	15	8.93
Yoshida	1948–54	7	8.28
Hatoyama	1955–56	4	8.75
Ishibashi	1956	1	4.00
Kishi	1957–60	2	6.00
Ikeda	1960–64	13	6.61
Sato	1964–72	14	7.00
Tanaka	1972–74	6	7.00
Miki	1974–76	4	5.75
Fukuda	1976–78	5	5.20
Ohhira	1978–80	7	6.57
Suzuki	1980–82	5	5.60
Nakasone	1982–87	13	5.30
Takeshita	1987–89	2	6.00
Kaifu	1989–91	9	5.55
Miyazawa	1992–93	4	5.25
Hosokowa	1993–94	4	5.30
Murayama	1994–95	6	6.50
Total		121	6.31

Source: O'Brien and Ohkoshi, *To Dream of Dreams.*

Age discrimination appears in the recruitment of justices from different career paths as well. The largest number of justices are either elevated from within the lower courts or named from private legal practice. The latter are deemed or are potentially more independent because they have not toiled within the judicial bureaucracy. Considering all justices recruited from 1947 through 1995, forty-six were former judges and thirty-nine were practicing attorneys. The average length of service for the former was 6.19 years, while the latter averaged 5.7 years. The average service for others was as follows: former (ten) law professors with 9.2 years, followed by (thirteen) prosecutors with 7.6 years, (seven) administrators averaged 7.2 years, and (six) diplomats with an average of 7.0 years. Thus, while the latter have longer tenures than former lower court judges or lawyers, their numbers are severely limited.

Justices appointed from outside of the ranks of career judges may have some experience in the courts or the government, as the earlier discussion of Justice Sonobe's career illustrates. Still, law professors, lawyers, and others appointed from outside of the judiciary are considered by the General Secretariat to be potentially more independent on the bench. By design, their numbers and service are thus limited. Most notably, only one of the fifteen seats on the high bench is designated for a legal scholar, a professional category that, as discussed below, exhibits the greatest independence in opinion writing. Hence, although justices who were previously law school professors have the longest tenures, their numbers are sharply limited and only one sits on the bench at a time.

Appointing older justices to the Court results in higher levels of turnover. The General Secretariat and the government therefore have more opportunities to reward a greater number of those who have reached the peak of their careers. Limited tenures, however, may also work to discourage judicial independence on the bench. To be sure, there was no tradition of individual concurring or dissenting opinions before establishment of the postwar Court. The Great Court of Cassation, under the Meiji Constitution, announced decisions in *per curiam* (unsigned) opinions. All decisions were unanimous. No dissenting or concurring opinions were filed, as remains the contemporary practice in Japanese lower courts.

Still, Article 11 of the Court Organization Law of 1947 mandates that "the opinion of every judge shall be expressed in written decisions." A basis was thus laid for introducing the practice of dissenting and concurring opinions, as is well established in the U.S. Supreme Court. The practice of the postwar Japanese Supreme Court has largely proven otherwise, however. All the justices sign opinions for the Court, and occasionally some attach supplemental opinions that are neither concurring nor dissenting per se and that may only invite confusion over the Court's ruling. Nevertheless, it seems fair to say that judicial independence, as registered in concurring or dissenting opinions and split decisions, remains far from the norm.

Because not all opinions are published, serious issues of the justices' accountability are apparent, and major methodological problems arise in measuring judicial independence in opinion writing.[31] Most studies of the Supreme Court's decision making are based on decisions reported in *Saiko Saibansho Hanreishu.* Yet as noted earlier, many more (but still not all) opinions are published in the less-accessible reporter *Saibansho Saibanshu.* An examination of all published and unpublished decisions and opinions, kept for civil and administrative cases in the clerk's office of the Supreme Court, underscores how few individual opinions are actually produced.[32] In 1989 the three petty benches and the grand bench rendered decisions in 2,243 cases, issued 474 orders, and ruled on another 464 miscellaneous matters. The Court took a total of 3,181 actions on pending civil and administrative filings. In addition, the Court disposed of 1,509 filings in criminal cases, with 76 written decisions, 1,101 orders, and 332 miscellaneous actions.

Of the civil and administrative cases, only thirty decided by the three petty benches were not unanimous decisions. The justices filed only sixteen dissenting opinions, seven concurring opinions, and five separate opinions. The grand bench handed down only one ruling that was not unanimous, and that one had only a single separate opinion. By that measure, the norm remains collective, not individualized, decision making. Moreover, the *Saiko Saibansho Saibanshu* published only the 1 grand bench decision and 16 petty bench rulings that were not unanimous, plus 65 unanimous rulings in civil cases, along with the decisions in 70 criminal cases, for a total of 152 reported decisions.

Even fewer were published in the *Saiko Saibansho Hanreishu.* It reported just the grand bench's 1 decision, 8 other decisions in civil cases, and 3 criminal cases that were not unanimous, with another 44 unanimous decisions (in 26 civil and 18 criminal cases), for a total of 56 reported decisions out of the 4,690 decisions and orders handed down in the Court's 1989 term.

A major study of the postwar Court's decision making, based on published opinions in *Saiko Saibansho Saibanshu,* suggested a basis for optimism about the development of judicial independence on the bench. Of the cases decided from 1947 to 1962, political scientist Takeyoshi Kawashima found 589 criminal cases and 161 civil cases in which split decisions were rendered.[33] A total of 750 split votes out of the 5,716 votes were taken in 4,729 criminal cases and 987 civil cases. Further analyzing those data, Kawashima found that the number of concurring and dissenting opinions gradually increased, and did so in relation to justices' length of service. Those who were elevated to the Court from outside the ranks of lower court career judges filed almost three times the number of concurring and dissenting opinions in the initial period from 1947 to 1950. But Kawashima concluded that by the late 1950s and early 1960s, each group tended to concur and to dissent about as often as the other.

Whatever movement there initially appeared toward individualism in decision making on the postwar Court soon abated, however. Indeed, judicial independence, as recorded in split decisions, concurrences, and dissents, has declined significantly over the last decade. A review of the published opinions in *Saiko Saibansho Saibanshu* from 1981 to 1993 reveals only 331 dissenting, concurring, and separate opinions. Notably, the number of individual opinions dropped to fewer than half of the number filed during the Court's first fifteen years: 331 separate opinions were filed between 1981 and 1993, as compared with the 750 between 1947 and 1962. As table 3.1 shows, justices sitting during the Court's first decades had longer tenures (an average of seven years) than those serving in the 1980s and early 1990s (who averaged a little over five years). Moreover, Kawashima found that the initial conventional ratio of five former judges, five lawyers,

TABLE 3.3

Individual Opinion Writing on the Japanese Supreme Court, 1981–1993

Justice	Prior Position	Years on Court	Concurring	Dissenting	Other	Total
Itoh	Professor	8.0	34	12	2	48
Taniguchi	Judge	6.0	16	13	15	44
Dando	Professor	3.0	9	11	4	24
Shimatani	Lawyer	6.0	4	13	2	19
Fujisaki	Diplomat	4.0		14	3	17
Yokoi	Prosecutor	3.5	2	11	6	19
Total			65	74	32	171

Source: O'Brien and Ohkoshi, *To Dream of Dreams.*

and five administrators or professors held true: among those serving in the period of 1947–62, former judges constituted 34 percent, lawyers 34 percent, and administrators or professors 31 percent.[34] By contrast, of the justices serving between 1981 and 1993, 40 percent were former lower court judges, 32 percent had been attorneys, and 10 percent had been prosecutors, while the percentage of former administrators, diplomats, and professors dropped to 18 percent.

What remains no less striking about individual opinion writing in the contemporary Japanese Supreme Court is how a very small number of justices authored a majority of all separate opinions. In other words, many justices authored few or no separate opinions. Between 1981 and 1993, 30 percent of the serving justices never filed a single individual opinion, whether a separate, concurring, or dissenting opinion. Moreover, little more than a handful of the justices wrote more than 50 percent of all separate opinions, or 171 out of the 331 individual opinions issued between 1981 and 1993. The six justices listed in table 3.3 were the only ones to file more than fifteen separate opinions during their tenures.

The sole former career judge to file a large number of individual opinions was Justice Masataka Taniguchi. Among the career judges appointed to the Court, he was truly exceptional in this regard. His productivity, however, was exceeded by the former University of Tokyo Law School professor Masami Itoh. The remaining "frequent filers" of dissenting, concurring, and separate opinions also had professional careers in areas other than the judiciary. If Justice Taniguchi's opinions are excluded, then three law professors accounted for 27.2 percent of all individual opinions; and ten attorneys contributed 23.4 percent; and nine former administrators, prosecutors, and diplomats wrote 23.2 percent. The number of individual opinions filed by twelve former lower court judges amounted to 20.7 percent (if Taniguchi's opinion writing is included, this rises to 31.7 percent). Notably, law professors are the most prolific independent opinion writers, yet their representation on the Court is the most severely limited as well. By contrast, former lower court judges are generally the least independent opinion writers but comprise the largest percentage of the occupational groups represented on the Court.

One more factor may contribute to the decline in the number of dissenting and concurring opinions by justices. Besides the shift toward naming older appointees and more career judges to the Supreme Court, the justices' opinion-writing process itself discourages individualism. As Justice Sonobe emphasizes, opinions for the Court are drafted by law clerks, not by the justices themselves. A justice filing a dissent or concurrance thus must draft the opinion alone. This not only entails a lot of work but pits the justice against colleagues, the law clerks, the Court's norms, and the legal culture.

Conclusion

Judicial independence in the lower courts and the Supreme Court of Japan has been curbed and punished by various means. To be sure, the prewar tradition weighs against individual expression, and the filing of separate opinions remains prohibited in the lower courts. The conservative LDP's long reign also ensured its monopoly over judicial appointments throughout most of the postwar era. Yet, judicial appointments are made largely on the recommendation of the chief justice and the General Secretariat. Lower court judges are more the agents of the chief justice and the General Secretariat than they are of the LDP or other political parties. In addition, the judicial bureaucracy promotes judges in ways calculated to reward conformity, and the Supreme Court's composition and operation discourages individualism on the bench. That is also to say that the politics of the judicial bureaucracy, electoral outcomes, and the governmental infrastructure matter a great deal more for establishing judicial independence—both institutional independence and judicial independence on the bench—and for the exercise of constitutional review than the parchment guarantees of Japan's 1947 Constitution. In sum, while the postwar Japanese judiciary has preserved its institutional independence, it has also sharply limited judicial independence on the bench both in the lower courts and in the Supreme Court.

Notes

1. J. Mark Ramseyer, "The Puzzling (In)Dependence of Courts: A Comparative Approach," *Journal of Legal Studies* 23 (1994): 721.

2. William M. Landes and Richard A. Posner, "The Independent Judiciary in an Interest Group Perspective," *Journal of Law and Economics* 18 (1975): 875.

3. Ramseyer, "The Puzzling (In)Dependence of Courts," 742 n. 93.

4. J. Mark Ramseyer and Frances McCall Rosenbluth, *Japan's Political Marketplace* (Cambridge: Harvard Univ. Press, 1993), 178.

5. J. Mark Ramseyer and Eric B. Rasmusen, "Judicial Independence in a Civil Law Regime: The Evidence from Japan," *Journal of Law, Economics, and Organizations* 13 (1997): 259.

6. See Percey R. Luney Jr., "The Judiciary: Its Organization and Status in the Parliamentary System," in Percey R. Luney and Kazuyuki Takahashi, eds., *Japanese*

Constitutional Law (Tokyo: Tokyo Univ. Press, 1993); see also J. Mark Ramseyer and Eric B. Rasmusen, "Skewed Incentives: Paying for Politics as a Japanese Judge," *Judicature* 83 (January–February 2000): 190–95.

7. John O. Haley, "Judicial Independence in Japan Revisited," *Law in Japan* 25 (1995): 1.

8. Ibid., 3.

9. Ibid., 10.

10. Meiji Constitution, Articles 57 and 61. On the history of the Meiji Constitution, see, generally, Hideo Tanaka, *The Japanese Legal System* (Tokyo: Tokyo Univ. Press, 1977).

11. See Frank Upham, *Law and Social Change in Postwar Japan* (Cambridge: Harvard Univ. Press, 1987). For criticisms of his thesis, see Yoshiharu Matsuura, "Review Essay: Law and Bureaucracy in Modern Japan," *Stanford Law Review* 41 (1989): 1627.

12. *Tomabechi v. Japan*, 7 Minishu 350 (S.Ct., April 15, 1953), quoted and discussed by Nobuyoshi Ashibe, "Human Rights and Judicial Power," in Lawrence Beer, ed., *Constitutional Systems in Late Twentieth Century Asia* (Seattle: Univ. of Washington Press, 1992), 243.

13. See *Kunihiro v. Japan*, 16 Keishu (S.Ct., G.B., Nov. 28, 1962); *Aizawa v. Japan*, 27 Keishu 265 (S.Ct., G.B., April 4, 1973); *Umehara v. Japan*, 29 Minshu 572 (S.Ct., G.B., April 30, 1975); *Kano v. Hiroshima Election Management Commission*, 39 Minshu 1100 (S.Ct., G.B., July 17, 1985; *Kurokawa v. Chiba Prefecture Election Commission*, 30 Minshu 223 (S.Ct., G.B., April 14, 1976); and *Hiraguchi v. Hiraguchi*, 41 Minshu 572 (S.Ct., G.B., April 30, 1975).

14. See Hiroyuki Hata, "Malapportionment of Representatives in the National Diet," *Law & Contemporary Problems* 1990 (1990): 35.

15. See, e.g., C. Neil Tate and J. Vallender, eds., *The Global Expansion of Judicial Power* (New York: New York Univ. Press, 1995).

16. See, e.g., J. Mark Ramseyer, "Reluctant Litigant Revisited: Rationality and Disputes in Japan," *Journal of Japanese Studies* 14 (1988): 111; John O. Haley, "The Myth of the Reluctant Litigant," *Journal of Japanese Studies* 4 (1978): 359; and V. Lee Hamilton and Joseph Sanders, *Everyday Justice: Responsibility and the Individual in Japan and the United States* (New Haven, Conn.: Yale Univ. Press, 1992).

17. For a discussion of the U.S. Supreme Court's caseload, see David M. O'Brien, *Storm Center: The Supreme Court in American Politics,* 5th ed. (New York: Norton, 2000), chap. 3.

18. Interview with Justice Itsuo Sonobe (Tokyo, 19 July 1993).

19. Administrative Office of U.S. Courts, *Federal Judicial Caseload: A Five Year Review, 1989–1993* (Washington, D.C.: 1994), 12.

20. General Secretariat, *Justice in Japan* (Tokyo, 1990).

21. Quoted in Haley, "Judicial Independence in Japan Revisited," 10.

22. See interview with former Judge Teruo Ikuta in *Shukan Kin'Yobi (Weekly Friday)* 59 (27 January 1995): 50–53.

23. Takaahi Hattori, "The Role of the Supreme Court of Japan in the Field of Judicial Administration," *Washington Law Review* 60 (1984): 69, 82.

24. The Naganuma Case, *Ito et al. v. Sakurauchi, Minister of Agriculture, Forestry, and Fishery*, 712 Hanrei Jiho 20 (Sapporo Dis. Ct., 7 September 1973).

25. Quoted in Hiroshi Itoh, *The Japanese Supreme Court* (New York: Markus Wiener, 1989), 266–67.

26. Quoted by Frank G. Miller, "The Naganuma Case: Judge Fukushima and the *Seihokyo*," paper presented at the 1974 Association for Asia Studies meeting (New York), as quoted in Itoh, *The Japanese Supreme Court*, 268.

27. Ramseyer and Rasmusen, "Judicial Independence in a Civil Law Regime," 20.

28. Haley, "Judicial Independence in Japan Revisited," 12.

29. Hattori, "The Role of the Supreme Court of Japan," 72.

30. Hideo Tanaka, "The Appointment of Supreme Court Justices and the Popular Review of Appointments," *Law in Japan* 11 (1978): 25.

31. Besides the problem of selective publication of opinions, other methodological difficulties arise from the high turnover of the justices and the time lag between the actual decision making and the announcement of decisions. See Miroshi Itoh, "Judicial Decision-Making in the Japanese Supreme Court," *Law in Japan* 3 (1969): 128; and David Danelski, "The Supreme Court of Japan: An Exploratory Study," in *Comparative Judicial Behavior*, eds. Glendon Schubert and David Danelski (New York: Oxford Univ. Press, 1969), 121, 137–38.

32. The Supreme Court of Japan granted permission to examine all records and opinions, for which we are grateful. The Court, however, does not maintain the records for criminal cases, and thus analysis of those cases was impossible. This data is further analyzed in David M. O'Brien and Yasuo Ohkoshi, *To Dream of Dreams: Religious Freedom and Constitutional Politics in Postwar Japan* (Hawaii: Univ. of Hawaii Press, 1996), 65–84.

33. Takeyoshi Kawashima, "Individualism in Decision-Making in the Supreme Court of Japan," in Schubert and Danelski, *Comparative Judicial Behavior*, 104.

34. Ibid., 105.

4

The Dynamics of Judicial (In)dependence in Russia

TODD FOGLESONG

At the end of August 1992, one month after the adoption of the Law on the Status of Judges of the Russian Federation, which introduced for the first time life-term appointments for judges, as well as other major improvements in their work conditions and salaries, V. M. Lebedev, the chairman of the Supreme Court of Russia, was ecstatic about judicial independence. His satisfaction was so great that, in jest, he announced: "Now I can retire."[1]

Lebedev's sense of accomplishment was understandable, for much hard political lobbying had been required to get the law adopted, and the law indeed dramatically raised the status of judges in Russia. But his confidence in the security of judicial independence in Russia now seems naive. Crucial provisions of the Law on the Status of Judges are routinely flouted by officials in the executive, and legislators have extensively amended laws designed to insulate judges from political pressures, despite the re-constitutionalization of judicial independence in Russia in 1993.[2] In addition, the deep socioeconomic crisis of the last seven years, combined with the unruliness of the Russian state and its chronic inability to govern, have had catastrophic consequences for the courts. Courthouses have been deprived of electricity and mail services, judges have been evicted from their buildings for not paying rent, and, in some cases, they have been beaten up or murdered by thugs, disgruntled litigants, and hired hands of criminal groups. Neither the state nor the constitution have protected judges. Judicial independence in Russia appears quite tenuous.

It is thus odd that in the past six years, Russian judges have displayed a remarkable amount of "independence." In a wide array of cases, courts have ruled against powerful and influential political figures, state agencies, and economic organizations. Four-fifths of all requests for restitution and remedial action in suits against acts and decisions of government officials and agencies are granted by courts.[3] One-fifth of all habeas corpus-like petitions are granted, with detainees freed from police custody.[4] Some 99 percent of wage-arrears suits, and 65 percent of wrongful dismissal claims—many lodged against company town–like employers—are found in favor of the plaintiff. Lower-level courts rule illegal or *ultra vires* local and regional government ordinances and laws regulating commerce or modifying electoral procedures.[5] And there have been several instances of courts ignoring government decrees and presidential edicts they think contravene the constitution. All of this activity seems unthinkable in a dependent judiciary.

The incongruity of these two developments—the increased vulnerability of Russian judges to political and other pressures, on the one hand, and the growing assertiveness of judicial authority on the other—is puzzling. What has enabled or induced Russian judges to render decisions that appear independent? Are they uninfluenced by or immune to the pressures to which they are daily subjected? How can we account for assertions of authority in a judiciary that lacks the kind of guarantees of security typically thought to be a condition of such behavior?

These specific questions prompt more general ones about the relationship between the two distinct dimensions of judicial independence, which might be labeled "structural" and "behavioral."[6] Do the various formal (constitutional and legal) protections afforded judges actually promote or foster independent judicial decision making? If so, how, and to what degree? Which of the arrangements established by states to insulate judges from pressures to administer the law in a particular or prejudiced manner matter most to decision making—the appointments process, judicial training and education, systems of remuneration, court organization, judicial administration, procedure? Do judges in civil and common law countries require the same kind, or amount, of independence? And finally, if judges can act independently without the guarantees we think both constitute and cause judicial independence, what is its purpose, rationale, and justification?

Answering these questions raised by the Russian judiciary illuminates problems in the current conceptualization of judicial independence in both political science[7] and legal scholarship.[8] Obviously, it makes little sense to describe the Russian judiciary as both "dependent" and "independent." But that is the conclusion these findings dictate. Such a conclusion, however, does not aid our understanding of the relationship between the constituent elements of judicial independence or help us discover its "optimal forms," as Peter Russell encourages. More troublesome is that the paradox in the developments just described presents problems for an appraisal of judicial independence in Russia. In what terms should the status and performance of Russian courts be assessed?

Lacking a new or better vocabulary for the analysis, I use the term "independence" in both its prefixed and unprefixed forms below. Perhaps the awkward terminology will draw attention to the cumbersome character of the concept. After outlining court organization and structure in Russia, the judicial selection and appointments processes are described, and then judicial independence in Russia is evaluated, along with a tentative explanation for the unexpected assertiveness of Russian judges.

Court Organization and Structure

Russia has three separate and unequal judiciaries: the Constitutional Court, the arbitration courts, and the courts of general jurisdiction.[9] The Constitutional Court has exclusive jurisdiction over complaints and inquiries into the constitutionality of legislation, and now over all normative acts of the state.[10] The Constitutional Court is so large, powerful, and productive that it could be treated as a separate judiciary.[11] Arbitration courts handle all disputes arising between legal entities, such as state enterprises, private companies, and governmental bodies or administrative agencies.[12] The courts of general jurisdiction handle all civil suits, criminal trials, and misdemeanor hearings, as well as all nonconstitutional administrative disputes between citizens and the state. They are the most numerous—with 2,500 courts and 15,500 judges in the 89 Subjects of the Russian Federation—and are what most Russians think of when they hear the word "court."

The focus here is exclusively on the courts of general jurisdiction, for that is where most of the formal administration of justice in Russia takes place. In 1998–99 there were approximately twenty-four hundred and fifty district (*raionnye*) courts, with approximately twelve thousand judges. Formerly called "people's courts," district courts are the lowest-level courts in Russia and are exclusively trial courts. Few of these district courts are formally divided into civil and criminal panels; most lower court judges consider themselves generalists, trying all manner of cases. The volume of litigation is astonishing. In 1997 district courts disposed of nearly four million civil suits, one and a half million criminal cases, and almost two million "administrative materials"—that is, misdemeanor charges.[13] The caseload per judge was approximately nine criminal, twenty-three civil, and twelve administrative trials each month, nearly twice the allowable norm established by a 1996 joint decree of the ministries of justice and labor.[14] Delays are, consequently, common, and reformers of all stripes have advocated introducing justices of the peace [JPs] for several years. However, JPs are not likely to be introduced in large numbers before 2001, and thus district courts will remain the primary court of general jurisdiction for some time into the current century.

The second level of courts of general jurisdiction is the regional (*oblastnoi*), territorial (*kraevoi*), or republican court. Each of the eighty-nine Subjects of the Russian Federation has such a court, and whether that court is "regional," "territorial," or "republican" depends on the constitutional status of the individual subject of the federation. All regional courts are both appellate and trial courts and employ approximately twenty-five hundred judges. As trial courts, regional courts have a limited caseload, operating as a court of first instance only for especially grave crimes (capital murder and rape, bribery, and other "crimes of state officials" in particular) and for civil suits deemed of "special social significance." Regional courts are thus consumed primarily with appellate work, which, in Russia, has two very different and complex dimensions—"cassation" and "supervision."[15] First, each regional court has two "cassation colleges"—one each for appeals of civil and criminal trials conducted in district courts. Second, each regional court has a presidium, which reviews "in supervision" (*v nadzore*) appeals or protests of decisions in district courts that were not the subject of cassation proceedings or that have entered into legal force. The presidium comprises the five or seven most important judges of the court. The unusually broad scope of appellate review in Russia, combined with the regional court's invisible hand in judicial administration, creates special problems for the independence of lower court judges.

The highest court and ultimate arbiter of nonconstitutional law in Russia is the Supreme Court. It has 115 judges, divided into four separate chambers or divisions (*kollegii*): criminal, civil, military, and the "cassation panel" (*kassatsionnaia palata*), a special board that handles only appeals of jury trial verdicts. Though the court occasionally conducts trials, especially in cases deemed "of special social significance," most of its work is appellate, generated either by cassation appeals or supervisory reviews. The majority of its judges work in three-judge panels that review cases from a particular geographical zone. The court also has a presidium, comprising the chairman, the first deputy chairman, six other deputy chairman, and five other judges. The presidium is unique and powerful, itself a court of last resort. It hears appeals from contested rulings of Supreme Court cassation panels, and it can review in supervision (*nadzor*) any ruling, decision, or verdict made by any court in Russia. Moreover, the seven ex officio members of the presidium are authorized to summon on their own initiative the files from any case in any court in Russia if the integrity or legality of the case's disposition is in doubt.

Upon review of the case, a protest can be submitted to and reviewed by the presidium itself. The fact that, with enough patience or clout, any dissatisfied litigant can obtain an audience with one of these seven judges gives the members of the presidium enormous opportunities for shaping the administration of justice in Russia.

Perhaps the most important and powerful feature of the Supreme Court is the plenum. The plenum, which is a meeting of all the judges on the court, convenes between four and six times a year to discuss problem areas in judicial practice and to issue "explanations" (*raz"iasneniia*) of the law in order to ensure uniformity in the administration of justice. Typically, the plenum meets only after a study (*oboshenie*) of mistakes in judicial practice has been distributed to all eighty-nine regional courts and ample time has been given for discussion and commentary of a draft of the court's "explanation." While these explanations are not in theory "binding" on lower courts, Supreme Court and regional court judges routinely reverse lower court rulings that run afoul of the explanations, and they often cite specific points in the court's explanation.[16] The plenum is thus the institutional incarnation of a case-based law of precedent in Russia. The Supreme Court's discretion in selecting the "precedents" has important implications for the behavioral independence of trial judges.

Staffing the Courts

There is no centralized or organized system of judicial selection in Russia. Lacking a national institute for preparing judges, Russia relies on local government agencies and the courts themselves to find recruits.[17] The requirements of candidates for judicial posts are neither numerous nor onerous. For example, candidates for a district court-level position must be twenty-five years old, not have committed any "compromising acts" (*po-*

rachashchie postupki), possess a higher legal education, and have five years of work experience "in the juridical profession." The first real hurdle faced by candidates for judicial posts is an examination, administered by judges elected to the Judicial Qualification Commission (JQC) of the region. The examination is supposed to test only a candidate's legal knowledge and professional preparation, although it is impossible to know what questions are posed and what form the exam takes. Candidates who pass this exam must then obtain a "recommendation" from that JQC before having their name forwarded for consideration to the chairman of the Supreme Court of Russia. Before the chairman can present that candidate to the president of Russia for formal appointment, he must first obtain the "agreement" of the legislature of the region in which the appointee is to serve.

The guarantees of judicial immunity are formidable. Judges cannot be detained, arrested, investigated, or charged with criminal offenses unless the procurator general himself first convinces and obtains the consent of the relevant JQC. Judges cannot be transferred to another post without their written consent, nor can they be suspended or removed from the bench without the permission of the JQC. The grounds for suspension are: disappearance, participation or success in an electoral campaign, or being charged with a criminal offense. The grounds for removal are also tightly constrained, with two exceptions: "engaging in activity incompatible with the position of a judge," and "committing an act that disgraces the honor and dignity of a judge (*pozoriashchii chest' i dostoinstvo sud'i*) or denigrates the authority of the judiciary" [*umaliaiushchii avtoritet sudebnoi vlasti*].[18] These two grounds furnish the JQCs with considerable discretion, which is discussed further below.

The Russian Constitution requires that courts be financed directly from the federal budget and at a level that "ensures the possibility of the complete and independent administration of justice."[19] More recent laws add that the lines in the budget for funding the courts must be "protected" and that no reduction in the amount of financing provided to the judiciary take place without the consent of the Congress of Judges. Judges' salaries cannot be reduced and are fixed by rank in relation to the chairman of the Supreme Court. That is, the chairman of a regional court, for example, will receive 80 percent of what the chairman of the Supreme Court receives; the chairman of a district court will receive 72 percent, and a rank-and-file judge on a district will receive 67 percent. Judges do not pay income tax. They receive raises for seniority and rank, earn annual and quarterly bonuses, and are entitled to a large array of perks, benefits, and salary supplements, including free public transportation, a 50 percent reduction on rent and housing payments, food support stipends, and a generous retirement package.[20] Most important, judges are to be given appropriate housing within six months of their appointment.

Appraising Judicial Independence

As this short description of the status of Russian courts and judges shows, the Russian judiciary enjoys an expansive, even enviable, list of formal guarantees of independence. The principle of life-term appointments for all judges at all level of courts is particularly impressive, unequaled in either Europe or the Americas. But against what standard and by what yardstick should judicial independence in Russia be measured? The "level" of independence obtained in the civil-law countries of Western Europe? The recent Soviet past? Moreover, can judicial independence be measured as a whole, or should it be measured by estimated degrees of (in)dependence by level of court and perhaps even by kind (civil, criminal, administrative) of proceeding? Finally, how can something be measured in a nonnarrative fashion that Peter Russell rightly calls "relational"?

It has been suggested that there are four extant "methods" of measuring judicial independence.[21] One—let us call it "legalist"—assays the degree of insulation from partisan political pressures afforded the judiciary by the (typically constitutional) provisions for appointment, security of tenure, and remuneration.[22] A second—"behavioralist"—analyzes judicial decision making, and in particular, whether courts administer the law in ways hostile to or in disregard of (i.e., "without fear or favor") the wishes of those with political power and influence (of which the executive and legislature are the main sources).[23] Both qualitative and quantitative devices are used to gauge the independence of decisions; textual analyses and codings of rulings, rates of acquittal and conviction, and the number or frequency of dissenting opinions are common indicators of independence. A third method—"culturalist," perhaps—analyzes the estimations of independence given by judges themselves, or legal officials, or other participants in the administration of justice, using the utterances of the subjects of scrutiny for insights into the character or extent of judicial independence.[24] A final method—"careerist"—focuses on the determinants of appointment and promotion in judicial careers, using biographical attributes of judges as signs of both the effort used to influence judicial performance and the loyalties of decision makers.[25]

Many scholars use more than one "method," of course (the David O'Brien and Yasuo Ohkoshi chapter in this volume is a good example), and for a comprehensive, and convincing, study of judicial independence in any one country, all four methods probably should be employed (which the earnest methodologist might call "quadrangulation"). Ideally, close attention would be paid also to differences in the results yielded by each particular method of measurement; variation could tell us about the relationships between the various dimensions of independence.

Unfortunately, it is very difficult to access the kind of data and information in Russia necessary for a sophisticated and multidimensional study of judicial behavior. The approach here is one-sided in that it addresses only the "structural" dimension of independence and focuses primarily on the formal arrangements under which judges are hired, paid, and fired and courts are funded and administered. I begin by considering the "institutional independence" of the courts and move then to the individual independence of judges. The guiding questions are: upon whom are judges and courts most dependent? To which agents and agencies do power and influence accrue in the process of financing, administering, and staffing the courts? By what course are pressures on judges propagated?

Autonomy: Court Financing and Judicial Administration

In 1997 the Russian judiciary acquired a "protected" place in the Russian federal budget, a privilege shared only by the military. But this was not so much a sign of the respect accorded courts in Russia as a recognition of the extent of the crisis from which the judiciary needs protection. The combination of a massive drop in Russia's recorded gross domestic product, the failure of the government to collect taxes, and international pressure for fiscal restraint left the judiciary woefully underfunded in the late 1990s. In both 1995 and 1996, the budget for the courts was one-third of the amount deemed by the Supreme Court chairman as "essential" to basic operations. Furthermore, in both years, the government reneged on its budgetary commitments, which had been arrived at only after protracted political negotiations and agreements and which had failed to deliver a substantial portion of the funding allocated to the courts. Consequently, in 1996 and 1997 the money allocated to the courts barely covered judges' wages; virtually nothing was left to pay for operating costs (paper, stamps, telephone service, heating, and electricity), not to speak of repairs and improvements.[26] The debts—to electricity companies in particular—amassed by the judiciary were enormous. By April 1998 the chairman of the Tambov Regional Court reported an overall debt of one and a half billion rubles. It is remarkable that the courts themselves were not sued by their creditors.

Although the Constitutional Court promptly ruled in favor of the Supreme Court, and the legislature soon thereafter passed a new law to govern the financing of the judiciary, the problems of ensuring courts with appropriate funding have endured. District- and regional-level courts today remain substantially dependent on local government authorities for subventions, credits, and in-kind assistance—despite an apparent desire by the federal government to insulate courts from local pressures.[27] In short, interagency conflict within the executive as well as courts between national and subnational governing bodies repeatedly have subverted efforts to make Russian courts financially autonomous.

Complaints of judicial officials and the ostensibly self-governing associations of judges, in particular the Congress of Judges and its executive body, the Council of Judges—prompted an official inquiry into the misallocation of funding in 1997 and a promise from the president to "protect" from sequestration all funds designated to the courts in the budget. Nevertheless, in mid-April of 1998, the new Russian government—which was directly accountable to the president—decided to reduce the budgetary allocation to the courts of general jurisdiction in the second quarter of the year by 26.5 percent.[28] On 1 June, again after lobbying from leading judicial officials and representatives from the upper house of the Federal Assembly, Boris Yeltsin ordered his new prime minister to work out a "special system of measures" to ensure that violations of the Federal Law on the Judiciary did not occur again in the future. The prime minister had one of his deputies assure the president in a letter of 16 June that the required funding had been dispersed, but court officials reported that the government had not yet complied with the president's demand.[29] In anticipation of such noncompliance, the Supreme Court in May 1998 petitioned the Constitutional Court to investigate the constitutionality of Article 102 of the 1998 Law on the Federal Budget of the Russian Federation.[30]

The character of the courts' reaction to the financial crisis of the 1990s illustrates well the Russian judiciary's lack of autonomy. Rank and file judges did not issue protests or sue the state, but rather petitioned the president, sometimes directly and sometimes via the Council of Judges. Many of these oddly titled "solicitations" (*obrashcheniia*) contain unctuous requests for the president's "intercession" and that he correct the situation. Though clearly rooted in traditional patterns of administrative exchange, the solicitousness of the courts in these matters undermines respect for their autonomy.

The consequences for Russian courts of the crisis in judicial funding have been predictable: there are grave concerns about impartiality in the administration of justice. In many cases, judges have received, and in some cases actively solicited, support from local governments and economic organizations whose acts and actions they are increasingly asked to adjudicate. According to a survey of more than three hundred district court judges, in 1996–97, 58 percent of courts received some "help" from local governments, and one out of every seven judges reported receiving aid from private sources.[31] Although in most regions, the amount of "help" has not been large and has consisted of emergency contributions or in-kind assistance—envelopes, cars, photocopiers—some courts have accrued sizable new "debts." This has created expectations of some form of repayment, if not direct pressures for reimbursement, and, among judges, a sense of obligation: some 7 percent of the judges surveyed, for example, reported that specific demands accompanied the assistance they received, and of those receiving support from private firms, 22 percent admitted that the support had some influence on their handling of cases.

Perhaps more worrisome than the opportunities for peddling influence in the courts is that judges have been turned into petitioners. Court leaders are now clearly accustomed to acts of supplication, imploring, requesting, and beseeching local officials for money. The tenor of their entreaties, moreover, is likely timorous, since those they approach have no constitutional or legal obligation to respond favorably. It is not inconceivable that some form of haggling accompanies these "exchanges" between local officials and judges. It is also possible that the perceptions of fealty aroused in the public by reports of judges approaching the executive "with extended hands" infect judges' own attitudes about the role of courts in society.[32] At the very least, judges seem resigned to the torpor of financial dependency. Such is the despondence of leading officials about the state of judicial finance and government's respect for courts' independence that V. A. Tumanov, former chairman of the Constitutional Court and now head of the President's Council on Questions for Improving Justice, suggested at a May 13, 1998, meeting that further appeals for proper funding would amount to "howls in the desert" (*vopli v pustyne*).[33]

The Ministry of Justice played the most important role in judicial administration in the late Soviet period of Russian history, during which it held exclusive control over most facets of maintaining and operating the courts. The ministry's monopoly on selection and training, its pivotal role in promotion and disciplinary proceedings, and its stranglehold over judicial financing, gave it and its detachments in the regions even greater influence over judges and courts than the Communist Party once had had. However, since the adoption of the law on the status of judges in 1992, which took away most of the ministry's functions, and especially after the recent allegations of misallocation of court funding and embezzlement, judges have displayed enthusiastic support for institutions of judicial self-government. These include the Congress of Judges—the general assembly of judges that elects the Council of Judges—the Judicial Qualification Commissions, and, most recently, the Judicial Department.

The Congress of Judges, representing the whole judicial community, is elected by regional conferences of judges. It has played an important role in forging a distinct corporate identity for judges, calling public attention to judicial affairs, and securing governmental action to benefit the courts.[34] The Congress elects a Council of Judges (of 114 members, presently), which meets two to three times a year and which drafts and discusses legislation and resolutions on matters of importance to judicial reform and court operations—including the Code of Judicial Ethics, the Law on the Judicial Community, and most recently, a law on financing the courts. The presidium of the Council of Judges has lobbied the president, represented the judiciary in parliament, and even issued quasi-legal "instructions" and "recommendations" on how courts should interpret various provisions of the Law on the Status of Judges. Both among judges and in the public at large, the Council of Judges is seen as the protector of the judiciary's interests.

The judicial qualification commissions, which are elected by regional councils of judges from lists of judges nominated at meetings of regional conferences of judges, are the most important organs of self-government. The JQCs have a monopoly on the administration of entrance exams, issue all decisions to nominate candidates for all judicial posts and to remove judges from the bench, and authorize criminal investigations of the judiciary.

The Judicial Department, which received legislative approval in 1988, is supposed to acquire responsibility for all other functions of judicial administration—including matters pertaining to cadres (determining caseload norms, need for new positions, recruitment, training, scheduling vacations), organization (court records, archives, statistics), and resource questions (building rentals, equipment, technical support, and so forth). The department is subordinate to both the Council of Judges and the chairman of the Supreme Court, but there are concerns that it will become the handmaiden of the latter, or worse—ineffectual. The department has yet to reach agreement with the government on the size of its staff and units in the regions, and thus has an operating budget only for its central apparat. In the meantime, on the basis of an "understanding" between the chairman of the Supreme Court and the minister of justice, the ministry continues to perform most functions related to judicial administration.[35]

None of the organs of judicial self-government are financially independent and thus cannot be considered autonomous. Both the Council of Judges and the Supreme Judicial Qualification Commission (SJQC) occupy space ceded temporarily by the Supreme Court. In order to convene meetings, conduct business, and publish rulings or the results of their deliberations, the council and SJQC rely on favors from "sponsors," private donations, and government subventions, all obtained through negotiations and by the initiative of the heads of these organs.[35] Most of the members of these bodies must travel considerable distances to attend meetings and participate in judicial administration, incurring expenses that are rarely reimbursed. As if to underscore the hobbylike nature of such participation, judges involved in judicial administration call themselves (with a mixture of pride and self-deprecation) "enthusiasts." Good-natured irony about the crisis in judicial finance is likely to be short-lived, however, for their continued financial dependence creates a danger that they will become supplicants of the Supreme Court.

Indeed, the crisis in judicial funding and the survival strategies of judges have aggravated an important dynamic of judicial dependence in Russia. The chairmen of courts have always been unusually powerful figures within the judiciary, and their pivotal new role in finding funding for operations increases their influence over rank-and-file judges. The case of Bondarev, chairman of the Railroad District Court in Ryazan, illustrates the power some chairmen have over judges and shows the potential for patronage politics to swamp the courts if the federal government continues to underfund the judiciary.

Resentful of the underfunding of the courts, and frustrated by the unresponsiveness of local government to his requests for aid, Bondarev obtained the consent of the "judicial enforcers" on his court to use as he saw fit a large sum of money that should have been given to enforcers as a reward for their successful implementation of an arbitration court decision against a local refinery.[37] As a result of his administrative acumen, and a certain amount of entrepreneurialism, three judges (including Bondarev) received new apartments, and the entire court obtained new typewriters, pencils, and paper as well as other essential materials, and even a car (in this case, a jeep). None of the judges, secretarial staff, or bailiffs-enforcers objected to Bondarev's scheming, even though the legality of his undertaking was quite questionable. Moreover, and not surprisingly in light of the benefits received, all avowed deep gratitude and "profound respect" to Bondarev in written affidavits when the chairman's actions became the subject of a misconduct proceeding in 1997.[38] Bondarev was later removed from the bench by the local judicial qualification commission.

Although Bondarev's case is extreme, the role of chairmen in securing the welfare of their judges in Russia is great in all courts. The chairman of a court in Russia exercises control over many administrative functions that affect the work lives and economic well-being of judges. For example, most benefits accorded judges—especially housing—cannot be obtained without the energetic lobbying of the chairman, and all judges, veteran and new, depend on the chairman for the scheduling of vacations, help in obtaining holiday packages, arranging of health and child-care services, and gaining of access to scarce consumer goods. In addition to possessing economic clout, the chairman also controls caseloads and distribution and writes performance evaluations. The combination of a monopoly over quasi-procedural functions and great authority in matters affecting careers gives chairmen power over judges. The crisis in judicial finance has no doubt broadened the role of the chairmen as benefactors and deepened concerns about their influence in the administration of justice.[39]

In short, Russian courts clearly lack autonomy in the etymological sense of the word. Their inability to control levels of funding and the pattern of expenditures has left judges exposed and susceptible to many forces and interests, especially to those executive agencies and private organizations with discretionary income. It must be emphasized, though, that the course of any ensuing influence on judges is channeled through the chairmen of individual courts, whose own power is enhanced by their informal and growing role in judicial administration. The absence of autonomy thus reinforces and makes more cogent the vertical, or "internal," dimension of judicial dependence, which is likely to grow even stronger in the near future with the transfer of authority for judicial administration from the Ministry of Justice to the courts themselves.

Changes in Appointment and Promotion Procedures

Two major modifications to the Law on the Status of Judges have compromised the tenure security of Russian judges, and thus personal independence. First, in April 1993 an amendment to the status law introduced a five-year fixed term for judges elected for the first time. In July 1995 a further amendment reduced this initial term to three years. Only after completion of this probationary period can a judge stand for lifetime appoint-ment.[40] Second, the 1996 Law on the Court System introduced a new stage into the appointments process: before forwarding names to the president for final appointment, the chairman of the Supreme Court must first obtain formal approval by the legislative assembly of the region in which the judge is to serve.

These changes generate great incentives for the judiciary to cooperate with and avoid offending local political officials, especially since the consent of regional legislatures is required for both the initial appointment and any change in the position occupied by the judge. Ambitious judges thus will come under the scrutiny of the legislature many times during their careers—at the time of the initial probationary appointment, the appointment for life, appointment as a chairman of a court, and all subsequent promotions short of elevation to the Supreme Court. Consequently, the careers of Russian judges today are not very secure. Possibly, they are less independent than they were ten years ago.

This conclusion does not apply to all judges equally. As tables 4.1 through 4.3 on security of tenure of the judiciary show, higher-level judges enjoy much greater levels of formal independence. Perhaps three-fourths of the 111 Supreme Court judges, and four of its six deputy chairmen, already enjoy life-term appointments. And nearly three-fourths of all judges

Table 4.1
Tenure Security of Russian Judiciary as of 1 January 1998

	All Courts	
Total No. Occupied Judicial Posts	14,457	
Appointed to Life Terms	3,426	(23.6%)
Elected for 10-year terms	6,219	(43.0%)
Appointed to 5-year terms	2,350	(16.2%)
Appointed to 3-year terms	2,385	(16.4%)

Source: A. A. Pakholkov, deputy director, Department of Cadres, Russian Supreme Court. Unpublished figures given to the author in March 1998; numbers as provided.

on regional courts have been appointed "without limitation of terms." (See table 4.2.)

Clearly, superior court judges can administer the law without worrying about being removed from office. The situation of lower court judges, however, is not nearly so comfortable. As the data in table 4.3 show, only 15 percent of district court chairmen and fewer than 12 percent of all judges in district courts enjoy life-term appointments. In other words, more than 85 percent of all judges working in district courts will face reappointment of some kind in the next few politically tumultuous years.

The differences in the level of professional security enjoyed by the judges of the three levels of courts in Russia make it difficult to assess the personal independence of judges as a whole. Indeed, the great gap between the tenure security enjoyed by regional- and district-level judges of the Russian judiciary is divided in two separate estates, or castes—one virtually untouchable, the other within arm's reach of local political figures. When better access to data on decision making in these courts becomes

TABLE 4.2

Tenure Security of Russian Regional and Republican-Level Courts as of 1 January 1998

	All Judges	Chairmen	Deputy Chairmen	Judges
Total No. Occupied Judicial Posts	2,629	83	204	2,342
Appointed to Life Terms	1,963 (74.7%)	56 (67.5%)	155 (75.9%)	1,752 (74.8%)
Elected for 10-year terms	571 (21.7%)	26 (31.3%)	47 (23.0%)	498 (21.3%)
Appointed to 5-year terms	11 (0.4%)	0	0	11 (0.4%)
Appointed to 3-year terms	31 (1.2%)	1	0	30 (1.3%)

Source: A. A. Pakholkov, deputy director, Department of Cadres, Russian Supreme Court. Unpublished figures given to the author in March 1998; numbers as provided.

available, we may explore the hypothesis that differences in degrees of structural independence have consequences for judicial behavior.

How have the legislatures and the president used their discretion in the process of appointing judges? Have there emerged any detectable patterns or principles of selection? Unfortunately, we know next to nothing about how regional legislatures have used their power to veto candidates for judicial posts. There are, of course, anecdotes and stories of arbitrary and predetermined rejections of candidates, some of whom lack the requisite political profiles or ethnic credentials, especially in national republics such as Tatarstan, Bashkortostan, and Tyva. Such pressures are expected, because between 1989 and 1992, when judges were elected to ten-year terms by regional legislatures, deputies enthusiastically embraced ideas of democratic accountability and used their authority to browbeat, insult, and badger judges standing for election. But presently no data are available on the number of judges and candidates for judicial posts rejected by legislatures in the subjects of the federation.

TABLE 4.3

Tenure Security of Russian District Courts as of 1 January 1998

	All Judges	Chairmen	Deputy Chairmen	Judges
Total No. Occupied Judicial Posts	11,828	2,327	606	8,895
Appointed to Life Terms	1,463 (12.3%)	347 (14.9%)	101 (16.6%)	1,015 (11.4%)
Elected to 10-year terms	5,648 (47.8%)	1,716 (73.7%)	432 (71.2%)	3,500 (39.3%)
Appointed to 5-year terms	2,339 (19.7%)	164 (8.6%)	52 (8.6%)	2,123 (23.9%)
Appointed to 3-year terms	2,354 (19.9%)	93 (4.0%)	18 (3.0%)	2,243 (25.2%)

Source: A. A. Pakholkov, deputy director, Department of Cadres, Russian Supreme Court. Unpublished figures given to the author in March 1998; numbers as provided.

We know a little more about the work of the presidency in staffing the courts, but not much more. There appear to be two bodies with responsibility for reviewing the candidates forwarded to the president for appointment: one is the Commission of the Council on Cadres Politics of the President of the Russian Federation, and the other is the Department of Cadres Policy (*upravlenie kadrovoi politiki*) of the Presidential Administration. Whereas the commission is intergovernmental, with more or less ex officio representation and is chaired by the minister of justice, the Department of Cadres Policy is the president's personal creation, directly subordinate and presumably loyal only to him. According to Yeltsin's former legal adviser, the Department of Cadres Policy meets after the commission, and thus affords the president with one more opportunity to use the privilege of the chief executive in appointing judges.[41]

Data from the Department of Cadres in the Supreme Court show that each year a number of candidates for judgeships forwarded to the president by the chairman of the Supreme Court are not appointed. For example, in 1994 and 1995 combined, 2,706 candidates for district court posts were presented to Yeltsin, but only 2,105 were actually appointed. Unfortunately, because of inconsistencies in the way the data are recorded by the Supreme Court, we cannot be confident of the precise number of rejections, or by which body they were made, or on what grounds.

Consider the report for 1997. In that year, 1,108 candidates for district court posts were "presented" (*predstavleno*) to Yeltsin for appointment. In the same year, 752 (including 48 candidates "presented" in the last three months of 1996) were actually appointed. But we cannot conclude that 404 (36.5 percent) of the 1,108 candidates presented in 1997 were rejected by the commission, department, or president, and thus that selecting judges is a highly contentious affair. First, some—perhaps most—of these 404 candidates were probably approved later, in 1998. Second, the report specifically indicates that twenty-four candidates were "rejected" (*otkloneno*) by the president, one was rejected "on the basis of the conclusion of the Commission" (*po zakliucheniiu kommissii*) and another five were "recalled" (*otozvany*) by the chairmen of the courts to which they would have been appointed. If this information is complete and accurate, it means that the process of appointing judges is merely very time consuming, and that, eventually, more than 98 percent of candidates for judicial posts are approved. In short, it may well be that staffing the lower courts in Russia is a heavily bureaucratized, but not politicized process.

This conclusion is warranted for several reasons. First, President Yeltsin did not exert much control over, or express much interest in the selection of cadres, even to positions of authority and power far greater than that of a judge. M. A. Krasnov, Yeltsin's legal adviser until April 1998, claimed that he had to fight hard to get the president to pay attention to constitutional issues, let alone judicial affairs. He suggested that Yeltsin was not particularly concerned about staffing the courts and that the primary concern of the commission and department was whether or not the candidate or judge awaiting appointment might be corrupt.

But there are more important reasons to suspect that the role of the president in staffing the courts (and influence in choosing judges) is relatively minor. First, there is both a dearth of persons willing to become judges and considerable pressure on the president to fill the posts. Caseloads, and hence delays, have grown exponentially in the last few years, just as conditions in the courts have worsened and salaries for lawyers in private practice have skyrocketed. With an acknowledged crisis in the courts, there is an urgency to staffing matters. Accordingly, the president has much to lose by blocking the appointment of someone who is willing, eligible, and even marginally qualified to become a judge. Second, the president has few incentives to reject candidates and little to gain by doing so. Since judges have no party affiliation and, since most candidates to district court positions have not yet administered the law in any meaningful way, there is little basis to predict which way judges will administer justice. Third, so much prior agreeing and politicking takes place before a candidate is forwarded to the president for appointment that he has few reasons or grounds to reject candidates already vetted and endorsed. Arbitrary appointments are risky, and likely are rare.

Consequently, the greatest role in staffing the courts is played by judges—specifically the chairman of the Supreme Court and members of the judicial qualification commissions—and it is the endorsement or approval of higher courts and judges that is most important for candidates to obtain.

As the only nominating authority, the chairman of the Supreme Court plays a decisive role in determining who sits on the bench. All judges interested in promotion need to appear obedient and display loyalty to the chairman, and all jurists wishing to serve in the courts must not alienate him. But the impact of this discretion to nominate, or "present," candidates is probably greater on already-employed judges than ones being recruited to the bench. There are two main reasons: First, the shortage of jurists willing to work in the courts limits the chairman's choices. Lebedev would look foolish, and risk deceiving the president, if he rejected reasonable candidates for judicial posts at the same time as decrying the impossibly high workloads of judges. The fact that the "hunger for cadres" is well known to prospective judges diminishes the debt they acquire through his sponsorship of their candidacy. Second, only working judges have a reliable means of displaying loyalty to the chairman—namely, issuing verdicts and rulings in accord with the adjudicative preferences or policy "line" he embraces and supports. Furthermore, the predilections or predisposition of prospective judges cannot be easily ascertained, because the court's Department of Cadres is too small to have an investigatory capacity and the chairman has little time available to research these propensities. Prospective judges thus enjoy, in effect, a kind of presumption of loyalty. At least in relation to new recruits, therefore, these factors substantially constrain the chairman's discretion in judicial selection and reduce the amount of fealty owed him for a nomination.

The most important body and group with whom both present and future judges must curry favor is thus the Judicial Qualification Commission. The JQCs in each region comprise between nine and seventeen judges, who are usually elected proportionally from district and regional courts. For example, the Moscow Region JQC consists of sixteen judges, eight from the regional court and eight from district courts (six chairmen and deputy chairmen, and two rank-and-file judges). No one can be appointed to a judicial post without a recommendation from a JQC. Consequently, the JQCs are the main filters of the judiciary, the first and perhaps only sieve in judicial selection. However, even the JQCs seem to have little choice in judicial selection.

In 1997 the JQCs did not recommend 13.2 percent of jurists aspiring to become judges.[42] While the rate of rejection in the preceding year was lower (7.9 percent) and there are some indications that the JQCs are becoming more demanding, it appears that most jurists who meet the statutory requirements of judges are approved.[43] Indeed, many jurists who should not have been approved are ultimately appointed to the bench. In several cases, jurists with criminal records and mercenary motives for becoming judges have been admitted to the bench.[44] The embarrassments caused by the need to remove such judges later vex the chairman of the Supreme JQC, who recently blasted lower-level commissions for a "purely formal" approach to selection. According to Zherebtsov, "the majority of JQCs in the regions see their contribution to staffing the courts not in selection, but in filling vacancies."[45] The deputy chairman of the Yaroslav Regional Court, also a member of the SJQC, was more blunt: "the existing difficulties with cadres," she reported, "make judicial qualification commissions hostages of the current situation."[46]

This and other evidence suggest that the shortage of jurists willing to become judges severely limits the discretion of the JQCs—and possibly their influence on judges—by imposing on them a highly pragmatic calculus in judicial selection. For example, it appears that both the sex of the applicants and their housing status play decisive roles in choosing judges. In an unusual case from the Ryazan region in 1997, where there were two applications for one spot—one from a man, the other from a woman—the JQC gave preference to the male applicant because he was likely to miss fewer work days on account of child-care problems and, unlike his competitor, he had his own apartment. Other stories told by senior judges suggest that the housing status of a prospective judge indeed plays a large role in selection.[47] Clearly, more research is required to investigate this apartment or "cadre shortage" hypothesis.[48] But a pragmatic approach to hiring judges makes much sense, especially since forwarding for nomination the name of a judge who does not require an apartment (or other favors) from local government and, more important, the expenditure of scarce political capital by the chairman of his court in securing it, greatly reduce the amount of work, and potential headaches, in "filling vacancies." The underfunded and fatigued enthusiasts on JQCs could be forgiven such utilitarianism.

By law, the level of remuneration for Russian judges is irreducible, but it is not indexed to inflation, and sometimes salaries are not received. Judges therefore remain vulnerable to the vicissitudes of the Russian economy and the government's attempt to reform it. A greater determinant of the wealth and livelihood of judges, however, is their access to scarce public goods, such as good housing, telephone lines, quality health and day care, and education for their families. Again, by law, judges are to be given priority access to housing and telephones, but local officials frequently fail to deliver these entitlements to judges. In 1996 thirty-six hundred judges (more than one quarter) lived in dormitories, communal (i.e., shared) apartments, or with friends, and one half lacked telephones at home.[49] In the still highly bureaucratic Russian economy, access to such goods is indirect and must be mediated by a public figure, such as the chairman of a court. Furthermore, the continued practice of giving judges monetary bonuses and benefits for good work accords the chairman even greater potential influence, because the disbursement of bonuses hinges on the performance reports the chairman writes. A judge's total income and career success are thus heavily dependent on the chairman.

The JQCs handle all complaints against judges as well as allegations of criminal or professional misconduct. The standards on which decisions are made in such proceedings, unfortunately, are not particularly clear or well established and thus afford the JQCs with some arbitrary discretion and power. For example, the JQCs have approved requests to charge and try judges for criminal offenses in some cases merely on the basis of the "large amount of investigatory work completed," and "on account of the need to remove the suspicions aroused" by a preliminary investigation.[50] The JQCs have also frequently removed judges for excessive delays and "red tape." Judges have good reason to be wary of the JQCs, for these organs of judicial self-government appear to amplify the power of higher courts and senior judges over lower-level ones.

In most cases, the JQCs have jealously guarded the immunity of their fellow judges. Although half of all requests to initiate criminal proceedings against judges are approved, the JQCs are not really so evenhanded. Some well-warranted requests are not granted. Such caution and apparent corporatism has led to public charges that the JQCs are "protectionist" organizations. But the JQCs have also vigorously cleansed the corps of drunks, slackers, and mavericks: seventy-five judges were removed in disgrace in 1997, and almost a hundred in both 1996 and 1998. It is likely also that a considerable number of judges voluntarily exiting the corps were, in fact, ushered out for other reasons. In addition, in some misconduct proceedings, judges have been removed for "insignificant oversights," and "without regard for the judge's claims." In a few cases, judges were ousted simply because they had a verdict overturned.[51] Such decisions fuel concerns that the JQCs are tools in the hands of higher court judges and can be used to square accounts.

This evidence makes the JQCs seem volatile, almost unpredictable. The fact that there is substantial regional variation in the practices of the JQCs contributes to the impression that the behavior of these organizations is highly idiosyncratic and that their conduct is shaped by the particular "correlation of forces" in each region. On the whole, however, it appears the JQCs have been mild, if not indulgent, in meeting out justice within the corps—much to the dismay of Zherebtsov, the chairman of the Supreme JQC. Zherebtsov, who attributes the bureaucratization of justice and much of the crisis of confidence in the courts, to the "arrogance and brutishness" (*chvantsvo, grubost'*) of certain judges who, "intoxicated with independence," have become "completely irresponsible and uncontrolled (*bezotvetstvennye i beskontrol'nye*)," has pushed hard to establish rigid rules for judging judicial conduct and ethics.[52] Nevertheless, many misconduct hearings conclude with "warnings" given to judges, even though the JQCs presently lack statutory authority to deliver such admonitions. Also, many judges on the JQCs report that they stop short of removal if "harmful consequences" do not ensue from the objectionable conduct and if the judge in question has an otherwise honorable service record. Indeed, the obsession with "mitigating factors" at JQC hearings indicates that the strict liability approach to judicial discipline advocated by Zherebtsov is alien to Russian judges' sense of justice. It also suggests that concerns about caseload (and especially the sudden increase in backlog that ensues from any removal), the shortage of experienced judges, and even friendship exert a strong influence on the behavior of the JQCs, moderating the management of misconduct.

Conclusion

This discussion of "independence" suggests that although both the executive and legislature in regions and at the national level play a role in staffing the courts, their discretion and potential influence on judges—especially at the district court level—is mitigated substantially by the shortage of qualified jurists and the pressing need to fill vacancies. Consequently, the primary patrons, main benefactors, and biggest potential threats to the independence of judges in Russia come from other judges. Actual control over decisions that matter most to a judge, privately and professionally, rests with other judges. In other words, the most salient dimension of (in)dependence in Russia is vertical, or "internal." But even, or perhaps especially, within the judiciary, it appears that the dearth of promising prospects for judgeships, the indulgence of judicial qualification commissions, and utilitarian approach to judicial selection all conspire to give judges some insulation from the influence of their colleagues and superiors. In this sense, perhaps the judiciary really is the least dangerous branch.

The Russian judiciary is neither autonomous nor independent. Both institutionally and individually, judges are exposed and vulnerable to pressures to administer the law in ways desired by those with whom decisions on appointment, promotion, remuneration, and removal rest. However, the fact that the judiciary itself is master of most of these decisions and that its discretion is curbed by an internal politics of shortage, compromise, and realism means that judges enjoy some insulation from both external and internal influences, and it may be possible for them administer the law in ways that accord with their own understanding of it.

This conclusion helps account for the recent assertiveness of Russian courts. If judges in Russia are most dependent on other judges, and their primary loyalty is to their vertical superiors and mentors in higher courts, then the pattern of judicial behavior I outlined in the introduction becomes less puzzling. Court decisions that appear "independent" of political power may actually reflect an antistate, somewhat populist sentiment born of judges' resentment of the government for consistently reneging on its promises to ensure judicial independence, or even maintain consistent court funding and regularly pay salaries. It is also possible that rulings against local authorities and potentates, especially in matters of administrative law, are so common precisely, if perversely, because they are irregularly and incompletely implemented. The more often their own claims about law and legal rights are ignored and flouted, the greater symbolic solidarity with litigants judges display and their rulings acquire. It can also be surmised that, as the amount of perceived disorder in the state and scale of corruption and arbitrary behavior among public officials grows, judges have become more adamant about upholding legal norms. This would not be the first time in Russian history that a dearth of order was combated with a surge of formal legal accountability.

Of course, this is a highly speculative explanation of Russian judicial behavior. Clearly, understanding how the formal, or structural, dimensions of (in)dependence affect judicial behavior requires an appreciation of judges' mind-sets, psychology, and even the law—factors more proximate to, and thus potentially more influential on, the process of adjudication than the politics of appointment, removal, and remuneration. Without a detailed analysis of the socialization of judges—the process by which they are educated, trained, and absorbed into the judiciary—and the politics of the judicial process itself—the character of trials and correlation of forces in the courtroom—accounts of patterns of judicial decision making based on assessments of (in)dependence will be superficial. Such an analysis is beyond the scope of this chapter, but in light of the arguments I have advanced here, it merits mentioning that these dimensions of judicial politics in Russia, too, afford higher court judges with power and influence over their subordinates. Senior judges train new recruits, and the appellate process operates like a machine for preventing, or at least diminishing, dissent.[53] Not only do Russian judges not come to the bench "independent," there is little to foster or encourage "independence" once the judges are inside the corps. There is thus something of an ontological problem of judicial independence in Russia. One cannot simply limit incursions into or remove restrictions on judges' liberties and expect to discover judicial independence. Where, then, does it come from?

Notes

1. Author's interview, 24 August 1992.

2. See especially Articles 120 and 121 of the 1993 Constitution.

3. See "Rabota sudov RF po rassmotreniiu grazhdanskikh del (pervoe polugodie 1997 goda)," *Rossiiskaia iustitsiia* 1 (1998): 51.

4. See Todd Foglesong, *"Habeas Corpus* or Who Has the Body? Judicial Review of Arrest and Detention in Russia," *Wisconsin International Law Journal* 14 (1996): 541.

5. For more on the use of such powers in Russian courts, see Peter H. Solomon Jr. and Todd S. Foglesong, *Courts and Transition: The Challenge of Judicial Reform in Russia* (Boulder, Colo.: Westview Press, forthcoming).

6. See Todd Foglesong, "The Politics of Judicial Independence and Administration of Criminal Justice in Russia, 1982–1992" (Ph.D. diss., University of Toronto, 1995).

7. For a recent overview of studies of judicial independence in political science, see Christopher Larkins, "Judicial Independence and Democratization: A Theoretical and Conceptual Analysis," *American Journal of Comparative Law* 44 (1996): 605.

8. For a discussion of the meaning of "judicial independence" by an American judge, see the remarks of Judith Kaye in the "Symposium on Judicial Independence," *Hofstra Law Review* 25 (1997): 709.

9. The military courts are part of the courts of general jurisdiction. But in practice they work fairly independently from other courts, and, in effect, they form a separate judicial hierarchy.

10. See Peter Krug, "Departure from the Centralized Model: The Russian Supreme Court and the Constitutional Control of Legislation," *Virginia Journal of International Law* 37 (1997): 725. The most recent and controversial ruling of the Constitutional Court was published in *Rossiiskaia gazeta* on 30 June 1998, p. 6.

11. See Robert Sharlet, "Transitional Constitutionalism: Politics and Law in the 2nd Russian Republic," *Wisconsin International Law Journal* 14 (1996): 495.

12. For two excellent studies on the evolution and current operation of the arbitration courts, see Kathryn Hendley, "Remaking an Institution: From State Arbitrazh to Arbitration Courts," *American Journal of Comparative Law* 46 (1998): 1; and "An Analysis of the Activities of the Russian Arbitrazh Courts: 1992–1996," A report submitted to the National Council on Soviet and East European Research (1997).

13. See the "Spravka o rabote sudov za 1997 god" (Report on court work for 1997), prepared by the deputy director of the Ministry of Justice's Department of Statistics.

14. See "Normy nagruzki sudei," *Rossiiskaia iustitsiia* 2 (1997): 54–56.

15. Cassation proceedings in theory check only for legal error but in practice extend to questions of fact. A review in supervision reexamines the entire case file and history, but typically without the participation of the parties. Christopher Osakwe, "Modern Soviet Criminal Procedure," *Tulane Law Review* 57 (1985): 484, suggests that scope of cassation in the USSR was "narrower than review *de novo* but wider than review for error."

16. The court distributes to all judges the explanations and recommends they be used as "guidance" (*rukovodstvo*) in the application of law. For the court's most recent defense of its prerogative to issue such explanations and understanding of their significance as a source of law, see "O roli i znachenii postanovlenii plenuma Verkhovnogo Suda RF," *Biulleten' Verkhovnogo Suda RF* 3 (1998).

17. In May 1998 President Yeltsin signed a decree establishing an Academy of Justice, which is, reportedly, modeled on the Ecole Nationale de la Magistrature in France. See A. Kamakin, "V Rossii sozidaetsiaa akademiia pravosudiia," *Nezavisimaia gazeta*, 13 May 1998, p. 2, and D. Sokolov, "Novoe pokolenie rossian budut sudit' professionally. Ikh obuchat v Akademii pravosidiia," *Obshchaia gazeta*, 16–22 April 1998, p. 2.

18. Article 14, paragraphs 7 and 9, of the Law on the Status of Judges in the Russian Federation.

19. Article 124 of the constitution.

20. Law on Supplemental Guarantees for the Social Protection of Judges and Court Workers of the Russian Federation, 10 January 1996.

21. See Gretchen Helmke, "Methods for Measuring Judicial Independence: Preliminary Findings for the Case of Argentina (1975–1995)" (unpublished paper, 1998).

22. See, for example, the essays in Irwin Stotzky, ed., *Transition to Democracy in Latin America: The Role of the Judiciary* (Boulder, Colo.: Westview, 1993).

23. See, for example, Gerald Rosenberg, "Judicial Independence and the Reality of Political Power," *Review of Politics* 54 (1992): 3; and C. Neal Tate and Stacia Hynie, "Authoritarianism and the Function of Courts: A Time Series Analysis of the Philippine Supreme Court, 1961–1987," *Law and Society Review* 27 (1993): 707.

24. See, for example, Jose Toharia, "Judicial Independence in an Authoritarian Regime: The Case of Contemporary Spain," *Law and Society Review* 9 (1975): 475.

25. See, for example, Mark Ramseyer, "The Puzzling (In)dependence of Courts: A Comparative Approach," *The Journal of Legal Studies* 23 (1994): 721.

26. Iurii Feofanov, "Nishchii sud k pravosudiiu ne goden, *Izvestiia*, 19 July 1996, and "Sudebnaia vlast v finansovom tupike," *Rossiiskaia gazeta*, 14 November 1996, p. 5.

27. See Vladimir Kovalev, "Kremlin Tightens Grip on Courts," St. Petersburg *Times*, 18 April 2000, p. 1.

28. Igor Iurev, "Tikhii sekvestr pravosudiia. Minfin sdaet slug zakona v polzovanie regionalnym elitam," *Obshchaia gazeta*, 7–13 May 1998, p. 3.

29. Letter from Vladimir Khristenko, "On the course of implementing the President's directive from June 1, 1998, No. Pr-762," dated 16 June 1998, No. 2966p-P4. See also the commentary in "Sudy podaiut v sud," *Rossiiskie vesti*, 8–14 July 1998, p. 11.

30. Decree no. 12 of the Plenum of the Supreme Court of the Russian Federation, 27 May 1998. The Constitutional Court quickly ruled in favor of the Supreme Court and indicated that the government "must" (*nadlezhit*) correct the situation. *Rossiiskaia gazeta*, 30 July 1998, p. 5.

31. For details about the survey, see Solomon and Foglesong, *Courts and Transition*.

32. Oleg Odnokolenno, "A sud'i—eto voobshche kto? Sudebnaia vlast na izhdi-venii mestnoi elity," *Kommersant-deili,* 29 April 1998, p. 3.

33. *Stenogramma zasedaniia Soveta pri Prezidente Rossiiskoi Federatsii po voprosam sovershenstvovaniia pravosudiia* (Moscow: Spark Publishers, 13 May 1998), 43.

34. Several laws, presidential decrees, and governmental resolutions benefiting judges or courts have followed or immediately preceded meetings of the congress. See *Sbornik normativnykh aktov o sude i statuse sudei Rossiiskoi Federatsii* (Moscow: Spark Publishers, 1996), 93–95.

35. See Lebedev's discussion of the funding crisis and the Judicial Department in "Nevozmozhno gosudarstvo bez pravosudiia," *Iuridicheskii vestnik* 13 (June 1998): 9.

36. Author's interviews with Iu. I. Sidorenko, chairman of the Council of Judges, March 1997, and A. V. Zherebtsov, chairman of the Supreme Judicial Qualification Commission, June 1997.

37. Since 1992, to stimulate initiative in the enforcement of court decisions, enforcers have been entitled to a reward of 5 percent of the value of property, assets, or penalties awarded by courts in criminal and civil proceedings. In 1996, after a few particularly fortunate enforcers retired soon after claiming their 5 percent rewards in great cases, a governmental decree limited the enforcers to more modest honoraria (a one-time payment of ten times the monthly minimum wage).

38. The inquiry was prompted by the discovery of the unseemly enrichment of the railroad court by that district's commissioner (*glava administratsii*), who requested that the Accounting Chamber of the Parliament investigate.

39. For reports of chairmen using their power to facilitate a kind of judge shopping, see Solomon and Foglesong, *Courts and Transition,* 68.

40. Article 11, paragraph 3, Law on the Status of Judges in the Russian Federation.

41. Interview with M. A. Krasnov, 2 July 1998. Krasnov, it should be pointed out, was not deeply involved in cadre questions for the courts and was not completely sure about the sequence in which the two bodies meet.

42. Data supplied by the Supreme Judicial Qualification Commission.

43. Many chairmen of regional JQCs reported at the November 1997 seminar on judicial discipline that the most common grounds for rejection were the absence of five years prior work experience and excessive age. It turns out that many retired jurists apply for judgeships to generate income and secure augmented pensions.

44. Several judges have been removed from the bench upon discovery that they joined the judiciary solely to obtain apartments and pensions. For more details, see Foglesong, "Judging Judges in Russia."

45. Author's interview with Zherebtsov, June 1997.

46. Stenographic record of the three-day seminar on judicial discipline, 24–27 November 1997, 4, 18.

47. Author's interviews with a member of the Judicial Qualification Commission of the Moscow Region and two senior consultants to the Supreme Judicial Qualification Commission, June 1997.

48. There appears to be considerable regional variation in the choosiness of the JQCs. In 1997 in Stavropol, sixteen of thirty-six (44.4 percent) applicants were rejected; in Astrakhan, twelve of thirty-two (37.5 percent) were refused; in Moscow, only twelve of eighty-five (14.1 percent) were not recommended. If data on vacancies were available by region, the shortage hypothesis could be explored by examining whether vacancies and indiscriminate hiring are correlated.

49. See "Koe-chto o 'beloi kosti'" *Trud,* 19 June 1997.

50. See "Spravka po rezul'tatam obobsheniia praktiki rassmotreniia v 1996 godu materialov kvalifikatsionnymi kollegiiami sudei," 5–7.

51. See "Spravka o rabote Vysshei kvalifikatssionoi kollegii sudei RF za 1997 god," 3–4.

52. Stenographic record of the 24–27 November 1997 Seminar on Judicial Discipline, 2–3. See also Zherebtsov, "Kodeksu etiki-pridat' normativnyi kharkter," *Rossiiskaia iustitsiia* 8 (1997).

53. For an elaboration of this argument, see Todd Foglesong, "The Evolution of Judicial Dependence and Reform of Criminal Justice in Late Soviet Russia," in *Reforming Justice in Russia, 1864–1994: Power, Culture, and the Limits to Legal Order,* ed. Peter H. Solomon Jr.(Armonk, N.Y.: Myron Sharpe, Inc., 1996).

5

Judicial Independence in Post-Communist Central and Eastern Europe

A. E. DICK HOWARD

The collapse of Communism in Central and Eastern Europe in 1989 brought in its wake efforts to create societies based on principles of constitutionalism and democracy.[1] Any attempt to achieve a transition from authoritarianism to constitutional democracy requires the nurturing of the rule of law. Essential to the rule of law is the creation and maintenance of an independent judiciary.[2]

An independent judiciary can serve several important functions. At the most basic level, an independent judiciary helps to ensure individual justice by providing a neutral third-party arbiter to resolve disputes between parties. More generally, if the judiciary is to act as an effective check on the other branches of government and monitor the constitutional separation of powers, it must be free from the undue influence of the legislature and the executive.[3] Moreover, independence from popular demands is necessary in order for the judiciary to protect minority rights against majoritarian tyranny. Finally, of particular importance in a post-Communist society, judicial independence promotes the rule of law by nurturing the development of a constitutional culture, heightening constitutional literacy, and stimulating constitutional dialogue between the branches of government and among the nation's people.

The struggle for judicial independence in Central and Eastern Europe is the focus of this chapter. In the years since the Velvet Revolution, how successful have the countries of the region been in developing an independent judiciary? What role has the judiciary played in their transition to democracy? What promise does judicial independence hold for the future? The first section provides the historical, cultural, and political background necessary to appreciate the region's current efforts to establish and protect an independent judicial branch. The second section offers a theoretical framework in which to define and discuss judicial independence. The third section examines the pressures that confront the judiciaries in constitutional democracies and the methods adopted to insulate them from such threats. Finally, the fourth and fifth sections explore some of the larger implications of judicial independence by focusing on the power of judicial review.

Post-Communist Central and Eastern Europe

In assessing judicial independence in Central and Eastern Europe, the unique historical, cultural, and political background of the region should be appreciated. After nearly a half century of Soviet domination, the legacy of Communism inevitably left its mark. Also, the continental civil law system has had an important influence on these nations. These legal traditions, as well as cultural factors such as religion and ethnicity, should inform any conversation concerning Central and Eastern Europe's democratic transition. It is within this context that the countries of the region have struggled to develop the legal culture necessary to nourish an independent judiciary.[4] Although many countries in the region have professed a commitment to this goal,[5] their histories are not steeped in the traditions normally associated with judicial independence. Not only must these countries devise organizational guarantees of judicial independence and provide the courts with functional power, but they also must confront a strong historical current running counter to the basic tenets of such independence.

The lingering effects of almost a half century of domination and control under the Communist legal order should not be underestimated as an impediment to the creation of an independent judiciary. Not only were many of today's judges trained under this legal system, but the assumptions on which it rested cannot be wiped out overnight. As a theoretical matter, the principal legacy of soviet constitutionalism is unity of state power.[6] Under this tradition, all government power, derived from the proletariat, is concentrated in one legislative body. An independent judicial branch was antithetical within the communist paradigm; no separation of power exists, because the proletariat cannot act against their own interests.[7] In Communist states, judges were seen as merely servants of the state, party loyalists who often did not need explicit directions from political leaders on how to rule.[8] As a practical matter, Communism translated into corruption and "telephone" justice.[9]

The legacy of Communism aside, few of the countries in the region had their own pre-Communist traditions for guidance in establishing an independent judiciary. Only Czechoslovakia created a relatively successful democracy during the interwar period. And even though Czechoslovakia established a Constitutional Court in 1920, that tribunal, in fact, never heard any cases.[10] Given the dearth of historical precedents within their own region, to whom should these countries look in establishing a system of government based on the separation of powers and rule of law with a structurally independent judiciary?

An American might suppose the United States to be the logical choice. After all, the United States has a democratic system of government with an independent judicial branch that has been functioning successfully under a written constitution for over two hundred years. The countries in Central and Eastern Europe, however, have looked to the example of their Western European neighbors. At first blush, this fact may seem surprising, as an independent judiciary is a relatively new idea in Western Europe, an area where civil law systems predominate. Influenced in part by the French judicial experience during the ancien régime, Western Europeans traditionally have tended to look to legislatures and not to the judiciary to give shape to the constitutional and legal order.

Thus the Continental legal systems envisioned a limited role for the judiciary: Judges were seen as civil servants, government bureaucrats who did not make law but rather determined the facts to which codified laws could be applied. Not having the principles of precedent and *stare decisis* and not being influenced by the legal realism movement, a very formalistic judicial style resulted in which the judiciary was perceived as "merely an administrative tool for the implementation of legislatively determined policies."[11]

The French tradition of legislative supremacy and legal positivism pervaded Europe until this century. It was not until after the horrors of World War II that these nations began to question the limited role played by the judiciary within their legal order. They reacted to the undermining of their faith in a strictly codified legal system by expanding judicial power and by establishing independent courts with the power, among other things, to protect individual rights. Germany, for example, rather than massively reforming its former judiciary, instead established an independent Constitutional Court separate from the regular judiciary and from the other branches of government to deal specifically with constitutional issues. Even the French, notoriously leery of judicial power, established the Conseil Constitutionnel to review the constitutionality of legislation.

Both the French and the German models of bifurcated justice have been very influential in the emerging democracies of Central and Eastern

Europe.[12] Such a structural system is more appealing to these countries than is the decentralized American model for several reasons. There is a political factor: Central and Eastern European countries hope to be admitted to European institutions such as the Council of Europe. Moreover, before the Communist era, with the exception of Hungary's common law experience, the countries' legal traditions paralleled that of Western Europe, operating under a civil law system. Trained under that system or the socialist legal order, the judges in these nations were not prepared to implement a decentralized judicial network with the responsibility of judicial review. Also, during the Communist regime, the role of the regular judiciary undermined its legitimacy in the public's eyes. Once Communism collapsed, there were advantages in advancing constitutional change by creating one new institution rather than enhancing the power and independence of organs that had been tarnished in the public's view. The new constitutional courts were to serve as symbols of the new governments' openness.

The Idea of Judicial Independence

Despite pervasive support for the normative value of an independent judiciary, scholars continue to struggle to articulate this concept. Part of the problem in defining an independent judiciary is that it cannot be observed in its pure "ideal" form. Rather, it is often best studied at its negative margins, where pressures threaten the institution or its members.

In chapter 1, Peter Russell offers an analytical framework for assessing judicial independence. First, he identifies judicial independence as relational, having two principal dimensions—sources of dependency (external or internal) and sources of influence and control (collective or individual). Viewing the impartial adjudication of disputes as the goal of judicial independence, Russell would focus on those threats that interfere with this capacity. In addition to direct threats, he categorizes other pressures as those related to personnel, administration, and structure. Undue influence concerning personnel involves such issues as the method of appointing, remunerating, and removing judges as well as how judges are promoted, transferred, disciplined, trained, and evaluated. Coercion through administration encompasses how the work of the court and of individual judges is managed. Structural threats are implicated when the political branches use their power to create and modify judicial institutions in an attempt to shape adjudicative outcomes.

Although Russell's framework contributed to the theoretical underpinnings of this chapter, the approach here toward judicial independence differs from his approach in several respects. Specifically, rather than adopt wholesale the categories he establishes, this chapter conceives of the multiple factors bearing upon judicial independence as falling along a spectrum. At one extreme are those threats against which most observers would agree the judiciary should be protected. At the other end of the spectrum are those influences that generate debate as to whether they undermine the judiciary's independence or whether they are, in fact, desirable checks on judicial power. Bribery of judges and threats to their physical safety are obvious examples of the former, while denying judicial review that enforces "fundamental" rights is more debatable.

Against this theoretical backdrop, this chapter examines judicial independence in the emerging democracies of Central and Eastern Europe. The chapter's third section offers an empirical account of the regular courts and constitutional courts in the decade following the fall of Communism. It focuses predominately on those factors most would agree impinge on judicial independence and on how various countries have responded to these pressures. In particular, it provides an overview of how judges are appointed, paid, and removed; how they are promoted, transferred, disciplined, trained, and evaluated; and how the work of the courts and of individual judges is managed.

The chapter's fourth section takes our enquiry closer to the heart of the debate over the place of the courts in a constitutional democracy. That part focuses on constitutional courts and judicial review, probably the most novel innovation on the constitutional scene in Central and Eastern Europe. A look at judicial review invites this question: Once the courts, specifically the constitutional courts, are formally independent, what power should they exercise? This section discusses structural threats such as those arising when the political branches use their power to create and modify judicial institutions in an attempt to shape adjudicative outcomes. The concluding section examines the close link between judicial review and a constitutional culture.

An Empirical Account of the Judiciary and of Judicial Independence in Central and Eastern Europe

Judicial independence does not occur in a vacuum. For judicial independence to thrive, a country must provide an appropriate juridical environment. In particular, it must be dedicated to a democratic system of government based on a separation of powers and the rule of law. In form, at least, the countries of Central and Eastern Europe declared these principles. For example, the Polish Constitution, adopted in May 1997, provides that "the system of government of the Republic of Poland shall be based on the separation of and balance between the legislative, executive, and judicial powers."[13]

Such language, however, does not guarantee judicial independence. The courts now functioning in Central and Eastern Europe are being subjected to great pressures as these countries struggle to develop constitutional democracies.

Constitutional Structure of the Courts

All the countries in the region, with the exception of Estonia, have adopted a bifurcated system of justice. In addition to the regular courts, their constitutions establish a constitutional court distinct from the ordinary judiciary and separate from the other branches of government. Underscoring the disjunction, the constitutions often deal with the two judicial systems in different sections. The respective bodies are considered separate judicial organs and are often treated differently in terms of structure, function, and tradition. Therefore, analysis of judicial independence in constitutional courts is distinguished from that of regular courts.

The regular judiciary often consists of one or two supreme courts,[14] courts of appeal, and regional and district courts. As the competence, organization, and procedures of the regular judiciary are usually to be determined by future legislation, the possibility for variation among countries is great. In contrast, the region's constitutional courts tend to follow a pattern. Most such courts consist of nine to fifteen justices,[15] serving seven- to ten-year nonrenewable terms.[16] In this respect, Bulgaria is typical. Its Constitutional Court is composed of twelve justices, each elected for one nine-year term.[17] One third of its members are selected by the National Assembly, one third by the president of the republic, and one third by the two supreme courts. Most countries divide the selection authority in some way between the legislative and executive branches.[18]

Many of the countries' constitutions contain explicit guarantees of judicial independence both as an institution and for individual judges. For example, Slovakia's Constitution provides that the Constitutional Court "is an independent judicial body charged with protecting constitutionality." Additionally, it states that judges "are independent in making decisions and bound solely by the law."[19]

However, much debate exists in the literature concerning the importance of a written constitution in securing democracy in general and its effect on creating an independent judiciary in particular.[20] A written constitution is, of course, no assurance of judicial independence. Great Britain reminds us that democracy and the rule of law are possible without a written constitution. As to those countries having a written constitution, it should be recalled that countries in the Soviet bloc often had eloquently written constitutions yet were not democratic nor did they have an independent judiciary. Even in Western Europe, a constitution's provisions may sometimes be seen as symbolic and aspirational rather than judicially enforceable. Nonetheless, given the civil law background of countries in Central and Eastern Europe, codifying an independent judiciary can be the first step to institutionalizing independent courts.

Implementing the Constitutional Judicial Plan

Written guarantees of judicial independence alone do not ensure the actual implementation and maintenance of an independent judiciary. The method of appointing, remunerating, and removing judges, as well as the procedure for promotions, transfers, evaluation, discipline, training, and continuing education all potentially affect the court's actual autonomy. How the courts' and judges' work is managed is also relevant to this enquiry.

Not surprisingly, the organizational framework of the regular judiciary differs significantly from that of the constitutional courts. Constitutional provisions for appointment of the regular judges vary. In Hungary and the Czech Republic, the president appoints judges, while in Bulgaria, a judicial committee serves this role. Lithuania, Poland, and Romania have adopted a combination of these procedures, with a judicial committee recommending judges for presidential appointment.[21] In contrast, the parliaments in these countries are much more active in the appointment process of justices to the constitutional courts, although most countries still divide the appointment power between the executive and legislative branches. By and large, little difference in status seems to result from the various election and appointment procedures.[22] Appointments may have political overtones,[23] but, provided other structural safeguards are in place, the selection process seems to have minimal impact on judicial independence in this region.

In the end, nothing seems more essential for the independence of both the regular judiciary and the constitutional court than security of tenure. For regular judges, this security is often provided by life tenure or by a term limited only by mandatory retirement.[24] Under these circumstances, promotions, transfers, and remuneration become more important. The relevance of these factors is further enhanced by the civil law training of the justices and by the tradition of a career judiciary. In this respect, the judicial councils established in Bulgaria and Poland seem to provide the greatest protection from attempts at external manipulation. Indeed, the explicit purpose of Poland's National Council of the Judiciary is to "safeguard the independence of the courts and judges."[25] To the extent they remain apolitical bodies, such organs reinforce the principle of judicial independence for the region's regular court systems.

Security of tenure takes a different form as regards the constitutional courts. Rather than enjoying life tenure, constitutional court justices usually serve between seven and ten years. The relatively short tenure arguably serves as a counterbalance to the countermajoritarian objection to the judicial review powers of these tribunals. According to this argument, judges serving for a limited time are more likely to be in touch with and reflect society's prevailing views than those who serve for life. At the same time, a limited term often is associated with less judicial independence.[26] Whatever their ideals, the justices must also be concerned about securing their future employment. This risk seems minimal, however, for two reasons. First, appointment to the constitutional court often occurs at the pinnacle of a career, coming later in life, when retirement is the most logical next step upon expiration of a justice's term. Second, justices often are also law professors, who are allowed to maintain their academic posts while serving on the court. In practice, it has been observed that, although they serve limited terms, these justices nonetheless displayed "little deference to [those who] appointed them."[27]

More important than the length of tenure is the job security that exists during a judge's time in office. In this respect, the various constitutions make it fairly difficult to remove judges in general and constitutional court justices in particular. They are not removable from office save for limited exceptions, such as conviction for a crime committed outside the scope of employment or incapacitation—both usually judicially determined. Moreover, they often enjoy the same immunity as legislators, who may be removed only with the court's approval.[28]

These formal protections have not prevented all threats of removal against individual judges. For example, the Bulgarian Parliament amended the Act on the Supreme Judicial Council to require fifteen years legal experience and five years experience as a judge in order to serve on the Supreme Court. This change was initiated to remove the chairman of the Supreme Court, Ivan Grigorov, who openly favored the opposition party. On a more general level, the amendment was seen as a potential tool for the socialists in power to attack judges suspected of sympathizing with their political opponents. Although the Constitutional Court ruled unconstitutional the use of the act to remove incumbent judges, the parliamentary majority elected eleven new members to the Supreme Judicial Council before the decision was published in the State Gazette. The court declared this attempt to subvert the court's pronouncement unconstitutional as well.[29]

Although the legislators eventually respected the court's decision, their attack on the regular judiciary seemed to shift to the Constitutional Court. As is often the case, rather than removal, the external pressure exerted on the Constitutional Court concerned its budget. The ruling majority in Bulgaria first attempted to amend the Act on the Constitutional Court to cut justices' salaries and abolish their right to retire with pensions. Later, in response to the court's refusal to dismiss a case against the Communist Party, the executive branch reduced the court's budget allocations by cutting benefits and compensating investigative magistrates from the budget of the Ministry of Justice rather than from that of the Ministry of the Interior. In addition, the prime minister attempted to evict the court from its office building.[30] Contrary to their intentions, these blatant attacks on the judiciary actually seemed to solidify the court's position in Bulgaria. In ruling these various attempts unconstitutional, the court's public stature was enhanced, as it was seen as the "last bulwark against an ominous, large-scale campaign of re-communization."[31]

Internal factors can compromise the constitutional court's and the regular judiciary's administrative independence. First, concentration of power within the judicial branch can threaten the independence on the constitutional court. In Albania, the chairman of the Constitutional Court determines who on the court considers the questions presented by the parties, and he sets the date for adjudication. If he chooses to ignore a petition, the court can be paralyzed.[32] Just as separation of power between the branches of government can protect the judiciary from external interference with its functioning, so too can division of authority within the branch promote judicial autonomy.

A more basic internal problem confronts the regular judiciary: a shortage of qualified judges. For example, in the Czech Republic in 1994, half of the 2002 judges in the country had less than two years' experience, and approximately three hundred positions remained vacant.[33] Many countries passed lustration laws to purge the government of former Communists likely to undermine the transition to democracy. As a result, some judges were dismissed or retired voluntarily. At the same time, the need for judges was increasing as new areas of private law burgeoned. Yet the working conditions for the regular judiciary have dissuaded people from pursuing such a career. Office facilities and space are often inadequate, and the pay as well as social status of judges is often below that of private attorneys. For example, in Lithuania in 1994 it would have taken half of the average monthly salary of a judge to buy a pair of shoes.[34] Add to the mix the increasing workload, and the result is a seriously understaffed, underpaid, and overworked judiciary.

The newly emerging democracies have attempted to insulate the judiciary from direct threats by requiring judges to sever their connections with political and business organizations. Nonetheless, widespread corruption in some countries makes bribery a concern.[35] and parliamentary actions against Albanian Justice Zef Brozi arguably employed physical intimidation.[36] These examples and the case of the Balkan judge who was ordered to report to combat duty the day after releasing a former military official suggest that direct approaches to influence the judiciary are not a chimerical threat.

Of particular consequence to the regular judiciary and the constitutional courts is the legacy left by decades of Communist rule. The lasting imprint of socialist control may dissuade ordinary judges from initiating judicial review and discourage constitutional court justices from provoking parliaments. The emerging democracies have attempted to deal with this issue in a number of ways. A complete overhaul of the judiciary, while advocated by some, would undermine the institutionalization process integral to developing judicial independence. Instead, screening the judges carried over from the Communist era with competency exams seems a more effective way to "purge" the branch of the unqualified. Bulgaria adopted the latter approach, removing twenty-three judges of the eighty-three legal professionals reviewed.[37] Most constitutions make "high professional quality" an eligibility requirement for judges, although they define differently what this qualification means. In addition, it is understood that the success of judicial independence is dependent on judicial competence, and many countries have established training and continuing education programs for their judges.

In sum, the countries in this region have placed great reliance on their written constitutions to secure judicial independence. They have created governments predicated on separation of powers and the rule of law. Furthermore, the provisions establish the method of appointing, remunerating, and removing judges as well as the procedure for promotions, transfers, evaluation, discipline, training, and continuing education, all of which are consistent with a respect for judicial independence. For the most part, this structure has enabled the courts in the region to withstand the most direct assaults on their autonomy.

Judicial Review in Central and Eastern Europe

Security of tenure may be the key to establishing a framework within which judges can effectively execute their adjudicative role, but, without power to resolve disputes, this framework serves no real purpose. This is especially true of constitutional courts, whose role is to help give reality to the goal of constitutional democracy. The constitutional courts are the ones empowered by the region's constitutions to engage in judicial review. Focusing on the constitutional courts is further justified because these courts have been the ones most emphasized in the literature and media. Just as most American commentary tends to concentrate on the U.S. Supreme Court, so too have constitutional courts captured the most attention when the subject is judicial activity in post-Communist Europe.[38]

There is yet another dividend to this approach. Because constitutional courts are new institutions, the confounding effect of past traditions should be lessened, thus enabling us better to isolate judicial independence. On the individual level, rather than being staffed by career judges, constitutional courts have legal scholars and other judges more inclined to assert their independence. Thus, by concentrating on these courts, we are more likely to observe acts of individual autonomy that, in turn, may provoke threatening responses directed against the court. Therefore, unless stated otherwise, further references to courts and justices in the following section refer to the constitutional courts in Central and Eastern Europe.

Two core functions of the constitutional courts are to maintain the constitutionally established separation of powers and to protect individual and minority rights. To accomplish these goals, the power of judicial review is crucial. Unlike the U.S. Constitution, the constitutions in this region place judicial review within the purview of the constitutional courts.[39]

Judicial review is better understood by asking three questions: What is the appropriate forum? When does review commence? Who are the interested parties? In answer to the first, judicial review can be diffuse or concentrated. In response to the second, it can be initiated *a priori* (before a law is enacted) or *a posterior* (after a law is passed). As to the third, review can be abstract (not connected with any specific case or controversy) or concrete (incidental).

The American diffuse system of subsequent concrete review has not been the model for the emerging democracies in Central and Eastern Europe. Instead, most countries follow the German pattern of *a posterior* abstract review, although Romania's system more closely resembles the French *a priori* abstract model and Hungary has adopted a mixture of the two.[40] Just as it helps explain their choice of a bifurcated system of courts, the civil law and socialist legal ties in these countries throw light on their opting for concentrated review. The distinguishing feature of these constitutional courts' jurisdiction is their capacity to engage in abstract constitutional review.

In contrast with the passive approach to judicial review in the United States—where various techniques are often used to avoid reaching constitutional questions—the constitutional courts are expressly empowered to grapple with such issues through abstract review. Their primary responsibility is to interpret the constitution, not to adjudicate cases. Thus, they are not restrained by the political question doctrine and, in fact, are encouraged to resolve political disputes. In other words, their constitutions mandate judicial activism.[41]

Nonetheless, this power of judicial review can be limited in various ways, among them, limiting the court's jurisdiction, undermining the finality and binding nature of a decision, and restricting access to the courts. First, although the scope of constitutional court authority in Central and Eastern Europe surpasses that of the U.S. Supreme Court, parliaments in Central and Eastern Europe, like the U.S. Congress, often have the power to restrict the court's jurisdiction by law.[42]

As to the effect of constitutional court decisions, in most countries in the region those decisions are considered final and binding. In this respect, until the adoption of the 1997 Constitution, Poland presented a somewhat anomalous constraint on judicial review. Decisions of the Constitutional Tribunal regarding statutes could be overturned by a two-thirds majority vote by the Sejm. The 1997 Constitution makes all Tribunal decisions final and binding, including those reviewing acts of Parliament.[43]

Every system of judicial review sets the stage for potential disputes between the judiciary and the other branches of government. It is no surprise that activist decisions of constitutional courts in Central and Eastern Europe have sometimes encountered resistance from other political institutions. For example, in Slovakia, angered by constitutional rulings, Prime Minister Vladimir Meciar proposed legislation that would require the vote of eight of the ten justices to invalidate any law. In practice, however, political bodies are more likely to undermine judicial review by ignoring a court decision rather than attempting legislation making it more difficult to overturn a statute. Such has been the case in Bulgaria, where Parliament has openly defied the court by readopting laws declared unconstitutional.[44] The Constitutional Court in Hungary confronted a similar test when Parliament failed to pass the legislation ordered by the court.[45] Given the inclusion in the region's constitutions of positive rights, which are inherently less amenable to judicial enforcement, this type of resistance seems the most probable obstacle to enforcement faced by the constitutional courts.

A constitutional court's ability to protect individual rights may be further restricted by limiting access to this forum. Hungary offers the most open access for the airing of constitutional grievances, but Poland's 1997 Constitution moves that country in the direction of easy access. Previously, Polish citizens had no right to petition the court directly for redress of constitutional violations but instead had to rely on an ombudsman. Similarly, Romania and Slovenia employ this method of securing the court's attention.[46] Most restrictive is Bulgaria, which not only prohibits individual access but also prevents lower courts and the Constitutional Court itself from initiating review.[47] Granting courts the right to initiate review is symbolic of the trust given to courts. When it is withheld, that trust is undermined. Bulgaria does allow abstract review by political actors. But all other countries in the region provide this access because it is a very effective way to exercise structural judicial review.[48] When it is limited to *only* these figures, however, the court's ability to protect minority and individual rights is seriously compromised. Thus, in order for the courts to perform effectively their role as protector of individual rights and governmental separation of powers, they must be accorded a large scope of authority, their decisions must be final and binding, and access to them should be open.

Judicial Review and Constitutionalism

For judicial review to be effective, there must be an environment that fosters an understanding of constitutional limits on government's power and in which decisions of a constitutional court are accepted. The "environment" contains both political institutions—the legislature and the executive—and the citizenry at large. For a constitutional culture to be considered fully developed, both political institutions and the public must respect the power of judicial review.

Fostering a constitutional culture is one of the greatest challenges facing countries making the transition to a constitutional democracy. Particularly in Central and Eastern Europe, where the judiciary was long seen as a tool of the state, creating and nurturing an understanding of and respect for judicial review is a serious hurdle. Further complicating the matter, presenting an uncontroversial theory of judicial review to the public is almost impossible. A look at international agreements and standards highlights this difficulty.

The Council of Europe's Committee of Ministers issued Recommendation No. r(94)12 on the independence, efficiency, and role of judges; nowhere does it mention judicial review.[49] Principle II, which concerns the authority of judges, states that "all persons connected with a case, including State bodies or their representatives, should be subject to the authority of the judge." If state actors are not "connected with a case" because of a lack of jurisdictional power, then this clause provides no basis for judicial review. Principle II grants that judges "should have sufficient powers and be able to exercise them in order to carry out their duties and maintain their authority and the dignity of the court." This in no way provides for judges to have the power of judicial review.

The United Nation's "Basic Principles on the Independence of the Judiciary" does little to protect or foster judicial review. The closest affirmation of judicial review comes in paragraph 4, which states: "There shall not be any inappropriate or unwarranted interference with the judicial process, nor shall judicial decisions by the courts be subject to revision. This principle is without prejudice to judicial review or to mitigation or commutation by competent authorities of sentences imposed by the judiciary, in accordance with the law." [50]

This serves to protect decisions made by a court but does not affirm the power of the judiciary to review the actions of other state actors. Unlike aspects of human rights, judicial review is not a principle readily agreed to by the international community; even long-standing democracies such as the United Kingdom and some of the Scandinavian countries do not have judicial review.

International support for judicial review is important, because judicial review can be especially difficult to accept for state actors and publics experiencing democracy for the first time. The U.N.'s Special Rapporteur captured this challenge:

> The Special Rapporteur has already observed a considerable misunderstanding on the part of governmental authorities and even parliamentarians. The misconception seems to be that judicial review is a matter of substituting the opinions of judges for the determinations or acts of the competent authorities within or under the executive or legislative branches of government. The often heard argument is: "How could judges, who are merely appointed, set aside the decisions of the elected representatives of the people and substitute their own decisions?"[51]

For a constitutional culture to exist, state actors and the public must overcome this theoretical challenge. As the special rapporteur notes, "The function of judicial review serves only to ensure that the executive and legislative branches carry out their responsibilities according to law, and that their determinations or acts do not exceed their accorded powers."

Bulgaria provides an example of a constitutional court, using the public's perception of events to foster respect for judicial review and further develop the constitutional culture. In an interview with two Bulgarian Constitutional Court justices, the interviewer noted the surprising development of Bulgarian constitutionalism, given the lack of "a long-standing tradition or institutional conventions," as well as "an environment where respect for legal norms and procedural intricacies is apparently not very great." In response, Justice Todorov observed that the early constitutional conflicts involved attempts by the Parliament (after the 1994 electoral victory of the Bulgarian Socialist Party) "to undermine judicial independence, to roll back the process of reintroducing private property, and to resubjugate the newly 'independent' media." These efforts "inevitably set the parliamentary majority against the Court," and in "this situation, the Court rather abruptly emerged as the true champion of the principles of constitutionalism."[52]

At least in retrospect, the justices were aware of public perception and the development of constitutional culture. According to Justice Todorov, "the incipient civil society, including all the non-communist political forces as well as the general public, came to perceive the Court as the last institutional barrier capable of stemming the tide of neo-communism." The attacks of the Bulgarian Socialist Party "actually raised the Court's stature in the public's eyes and elevated its institutional prestige," and the court "gradually acquired an aura of authority." Justice Hadjistoichev was even more explicit in his recognition of public opinion, claiming that the "Court's claim to authority rests on the public's recognition of the institution's salutary and indispensable role."

The prospects for a constitutional culture are enhanced when state actors come to see the legitimacy of judicial review and are willing to accept decisions they do not like. Justice Hadjistoichev believed that "both political and civil leaders grew aware of the fact that, without the Court's strategic interventions, maintaining the balance of power, necessary for Bulgaria's peaceful transition to democracy, would be difficult if not impossible." Those political actors who do not accept judicial review on this theoretical ground may feel obliged to accept it for political reasons; Justice Todorov asserted that "even politicians who are implacably hostile to the Court are aware that a policy of open defiance of the Court is incompatible with their claim to 'respect' the Constitution."[53]

This is probably the most optimistic view that could be taken of the events in Bulgaria. As political scientist Albert Melone observes, there "is a widespread perception that by rendering opinions that elected officials find unacceptable, judges may set back the cause of an independent judiciary and a law-governed state."[54] The Bulgarian court's handling of the Turkish party issue suggests the limits of a constitutional culture in

Bulgaria. The Bulgarian Constitution provides that no parties shall be based on racial, ethnic, or religious lines. The Bulgarian Socialist Party sought to have the Turkish ethnic movement, the Rights and Freedom Movement (RFM), declared illegal. Six justices voted to ban the RFM, five voted to find the party legal, and one justice was absent. A majority of the twelve-person court (seven justices) is required, so the petition was denied. The court's decision "defused a fractious constitutional controversy,"[55] but only a minority of the court supported that result.

Justices may have to make tough decisions regarding the impact a judgment will have on constitutionalism and a nation's constitutional culture. Often, judges in the region may have to choose between two evils: make the legally correct decision and face the prospect of no compliance, or make a decision that is not legally or constitutionally sound but saves institutional capital for another case. Judges in Central and Eastern Europe doubtless are aware of events in countries to their east, where political resistance to constitutional court decrees has often been a manifest problem. After having many presidential decrees annulled by the Constitutional Court of Belarus, the president announced he would not obey the rulings. Some situations have been even worse, resulting in a constitutional court being stripped of important powers. In Kazakhstan, the president was so angered by the Constitutional Court that, in his new constitution, he abolished the court and replaced it with a weak Constitutional Council that he chaired and controlled.[56]

Russia provides another example of an active court that was reined in by other political actors. In 1992 Herman Schwartz wrote that "the Russian Constitutional Court has established itself as an aggressive tribunal determined to safeguard the emerging Russian democracy" and went so far as to say that the politically active chairman of the Russian court, Valery Zorkin, "might well be Russia's John Marshall."[57] But the court was viewed as highly political, at least by other state actors, and in 1993 the court lost significant portions of its authority. It can no longer consider cases on its own initiative, and it cannot review the constitutionality of acts of top officials. The court now acts in a timid manner; when asked if difficult decisions are avoided out of a concern for survival, Justice Ebzeev stated that the concern is not with survival, but rather with "reviving our prestige and status."[58]

Because of its legal tradition, Hungary has a considerable advantage among the countries of Central and Eastern Europe. The Hungarian court is strikingly active and "has in fact been characterized as the most powerful constitutional court in the world."[59] Geza Herczegh, a former member of the Hungarian Constitutional Court, claims that "Hungarians are a nation of lawyers" and that jurists "have always played a great role in the Hungarian society." Hungary has legal traditions that were preserved during the Communist era, and on the Hungarian "heritage and with its elements we could build—rebuild—a rule of law system after fifty years of dictatorial regimes."[60] But the differences between Hungary and its neighbors are such that Hungary may prove atypical in the region.

The Bulgarian justices focused on building constitutional culture by taking advantage of the court's ability to appear above politics in cases involving separation of powers. Decisions involving the rights of unpopular groups—for example, ethnic or religious minorities—may hurt a court's standing in the public eye, if the public supports the legislative attack against the minority group. In a country with a firmly entrenched constitutional culture, an unpopular decision may not provoke a direct challenge to a court's authority. Unfortunately, the inchoate status of constitutional culture in some countries makes it more likely that a court will take public opinion and the likelihood of compliance into consideration. Bulgaria may have been fortunate to have cases come before the court that so clearly put the court in an advantageous position. The Russian court suffered institutional damage because the court expended institutional capital it simply did not have.

Balancing the short-term interest of protecting rights and defending separation of powers with the long-term concern of developing a constitutional culture remains a significant challenge to the region's constitutional courts. Justice Jan Drgonec of the Slovakian Constitutional Court underscored this concern when he succinctly stated that the courts of the region "can be effective only if there is political and legal culture that commands respect for their decisions."[61] Developing this constitutional culture continues to be one of the main challenges to Central and Eastern Europe as it attempts to create effective constitutional democracy.

Notes

1. This chapter focuses on Poland, Hungary, the Czech Republic, Slovakia, Bulgaria, and Romania. Reference at times is also made to the Baltic countries of Lithuania, Latvia, and Estonia; to Albania, Bosnia Herzegovina, Croatia, and Slovenia; and, in the fifth part ("Judicial Review and Constitutionalism"), to Russia, Belarus, and Kazakhstan.

2. See Christopher M. Larkins, "Judicial Independence and Democratization: A Theoretical and Conceptual Analysis," *American Journal of Comparative Law* 44 (1996): 605, 606.

3. Sandra D. O'Connor, "The Life of the Law: Principles of Logic and Experience from the United States," *Wisconsin Law Review* (1996): 1, 3–4.

4. Robert F Utter and David C. Lundsgaard, "Comparative Aspects of Judicial Review: Issues Facing the New European States," *Judicature* 77 (1994): 240–44.

5. Jane R Roth, "Judging in New Born Democracies," *Ohio State Law Journal* 54 (1993): 1109; Joan Davison, "America's Impact on Constitutional Change in Eastern Europe," *Albany Law Review* 55 (1992): 793.

6. Ruti Teitel, "Post-Communist Constitutionalism: A Transitiorial Perspective," *Columbia Human Rights Law Review* 26(1995): 167, 168–69.

7. See Utter and Lundsgaard, "Comparative Aspects of Judicial Review"; Rett R Ludwikowski, *Constitution-Making in the Region of Former Soviet Dominance* (Durham, N.C.: Duke Univ. Press, 1996), 39–43.

8. William W Schwarzer, "Democracy's Dawn: American Judges and the Rule of Law Abroad," *Judges' Journal* (Fall 1992): 31, 34.

9. Mark S Ellis, "Getting Judges to Hang Up on 'Telephone Justice,'" *Washington Post,* 22 June 1997, p. C3.

10. Lloyd N. Cutler and Herman Schwartz, "Approaching Democracy: A New Legal Order for Eastern Europe—Constitutional Reform in Czechoslovakia: E Duobus Unum?" *University of Chicago Law Review* 58 (1991): 511, 515.

11. Utter and Lundsgaard, "Comparative Aspects of Judicial Review," 241.

12. Austria, in 1920, was the first European country to establish a separate constitutional court. See Georg Brunner, "Development of Constitutional Judiciary in Eastern Europe," *Review of Central and Eastern European Law* 18 (1992): 535, 536.

13. Polish Constitution, Chapter 1, Article 10. To like effect, see Czech Constitution, Chapter 1, Article 2 ("The people shall be the source of all power in the state; they shall exercise it through the authorities of legislative, executive, and judicial power."); Bulgarian Constitution, Chapter 1, Article 8 ("The power of the state is divided between a legislative, an executive, and a judicial branch").

14. For example, the Czech Republic maintains a Supreme Court and a Supreme Administrative Court, and Bulgaria has a Supreme Court of Cassation and a Supreme Administrative Court. Czech Constitution, Chapter 4, Article 91; Bulgarian Constitution, Chapter 6, Article 119.

15. Lithuania, Romania, Bosnia, Macedonia, and Slovenia have nine justices. See constitutional provisions, Chapter 8, Article 103; Title V, Article 140; Article 6, Paragraph 1; Chapter 4, Article 109, Part 8; Article 163, respectively. Slovakia has ten members. See Slovak Constitution, Chapter 7, Article 134. Hungary and Croatia maintain eleven judges. See constitutional provisions Chapter 4 Article 32A, Chapter 5, Article 122, respectively. Bulgaria's court consists of twelve jurists. See Bulgarian Constitution, Chapter 8, Article 147. The Czech Republic and Poland have fifteen justices each. See constitutional provisions, Chapter 4, Article 84 and Chapter 8, Article 194, respectively.

16. Slovak justices enjoy a seven-year term (with an implicit right of reelection). Slovakia Constitution, Chapter 7, Article 134. The Czech Republic's constitution is similarly silent about the possibility of multiple ten-year terms. Czech Constitution, Chapter 4, Article 84. Bosnia has limited its first court to a five-year term; subsequent members enjoy tenure until the mandatory retirement age of seventy. Bosnian Con-

stitution, Article 6, Paragraph 1. With the exception of Hungary, which allows one re-election, the remaining countries in the region provide for one nine-year term for their Constitutional Court justices. Lithuanian Constitution, Chapter 8, Article 103; Ethan Klingsberg, "Judicial Review and Hungary's Transition from Communism to Democracy: The Constitutional Court, the Continuity of Law, and the Redefinition of Property Rights," *Brigham Young University Law Review* (1992): 41, 53–54; Polish Constitution, Chapter 8, Article 194; Romanian Constitution, Title V, Article 140; Macedonian Constitution, Chapter 4, Article 109; and Slovenian Constitution, Part 8, Article 165.

17. Bulgarian Constitution, Chapter 8, Article 147.

18. In Lithuania, the Parliament selects the justices upon proposal of the president, chairman of Parliament, and chairman of the Supreme Court. (See Lithuanian Constitution, Chapter 8, Article 103.); In the Czech Republic, the president appoints the justices with the consent of the Senate. (See Czech Constitution, Chapter 43, Article 84.); In Hungary, Parliament elects justices by a two-thirds majority upon nomination by the nominating committee, which is composed of one member of each political party represented in Parliament (Chapter 4, Article 32); In Poland, justices are chosen by the Sejm, while the president and vice president of the court are appointed by the president of the republic (Polish Constitution, Chapter 8, Article 194); In Slovakia, the president appoints justices from a list of twenty nominated by the National Council (Slovak Constitution, Chapter 7, Article 134); In Croatia, justices are elected by the House of Representatives at the proposal of the House of Counties (Croatian Constitution, Chapter 5, Article 122); In Slovenia, justices are elected by National Assembly upon nomination by the president (Slovenian Constitution, Part 8, Article 163).

19. Slovak Constitution, Chapter 7, Articles 124 and 144.

20. See James P McGregor, "Constitutional Factors in Politics in Post-Communist Central and Eastern Europe," *Communist and Post-Communist Studies* 29 (1996): 147; Mark Ramseyer, "The Puzzling (In)dependence of Courts: A Comparative Approach," *Journal of Legal Studies* 23 (1994): 721; Andrzej Rapaczynski, "Constitutional Politics in Poland: A Report on the Constitutional Committee of the Polish Parliament," *University of Chicago Law Review* 58 (1991): 595.

21. Hungarian Constitution, Chapter 10, Article 48; Czech Constitution, Chapter 4, Article 93; Slovak Constitution, Chapter 3, Article 86; Bulgarian Constitution, Chapter 6, Article 129; Lithuania Constitution, Chapter 9, Article 112; Polish Constitution, Chapter 8, Article 179; Romania Title III, Chapter 6, Articles 132, 133.

22. Alexander Fira, "A Constitutional-Theoretical Approach Viewed through the Yugoslav Constitutional System," *Beijing Conference on the Law of the World* 1(22–27 April 1990): 8.

23. See "Constitution Watch: Romania," *East European Constitutional Review* 4 (Winter 1995): 28.

24. See Czech Constitution, Chapter 4, Article 93; Polish Constitution, Chapter 8, Articles 179, 180 In the Slovak Republic, judges are initially elected for a four-year term. If they are reelected, they are granted life tenure (Slovak Constitution, Chapter 7, Article 145). After three years, justices in Bulgaria are irremovable (Bulgarian Con-

stitution, Chapter 6, Article 129); Cheryl W. Gray, Rebecca J. Hanson, and Michael Heller, "Hungarian Reform for the Private Sector," *George Washington Journal of International Law and Economics* 26 (1992): 293; Matthias Hartwig, "The Institutionalization of the Rule of Law: The Establishment of Constitutional Courts in the Eastern European Countries," *American University Journal of International Law and Policy* 7 (1992): 449.

25. Polish Constitution, Chapter 8, Article 186.

26. Especially if the limited term is coupled with a possibility of reelection or reappointment, as in Slovakia and Slovenia. The Hungarian and Croatian constitutions allow justices to serve two terms. See Herman Schwartz, "The New East European Constitutional Courts" in *Constitution Making in Eastern Europe,* ed. A. E. Dick Howard (Washington, D.C.: Woodrow Wilson Center, 1993), 163.

27. Schwartz, "The New East European Constitutional Courts," 176.

28. See Polish Constitution, Chapter 8, Articles 180, 181, 196, 200; Slovak Constitution, Chapter 7, Articles 136, 138; Bulgarian Constitution, Chapter 8, Articles 147, 148; Romanian Constitution, Title V, Article 140, Law on the Constitutional Court, Chapter 4, Article 42 and 43; Croatian Constitution, Chapter 4, Articles 119, 120; and Mark F Brzezinski, "The Emergence of Judicial Review in Eastern Europe: The Case of Poland," *American Journal of Comparative Law* 41 (1993): 153; but see also Herman Schwartz, "Taking the Heat," *ABA Journal* 82 (1996): 66. Article 315 of the Albanian Penal Code makes it a crime to impose an "unjust verdict." This article has been manipulated to threaten and prosecute judges.

29. "Constitution Watch: Bulgaria," *East European Constitutional Review* 3 (1994): 5; "Constitution Watch: Bulgaria," *East European Constitutional Review* 4 (1995): 7.

30. "Constitution Watch: Bulgaria," *East European Constitutional Review* (1995); Victor Gomez, "Constitutional Court v Government," *Transition* 1 (1995): 29.

31. "Bulgaria: Interview with Constitutional Court Justices Todor Todorov and Tsanko Hadjistoichev," *East European Constitutional Review* 6 (1997): 65.

32. In the winter of 1995, three justices resigned in protest over the chairman's lack of action on a petition. "Constitution Watch: Albania," *East European Constitutional Review* 4 (1995): 3.

33. "Constitution Watch: Czech Republic," *East European Constitutional Review* 3 (1994): 8.

34. William H. Walters, "Legal Reform in Lithuania," *Oregon State Bar Bulletin* 54 (1994): 21.

35. See Schwartz, "Taking the Heat"; "Constitution Watch: Romania," *East European Constitutional Review* 4 (1995): 27; "Constitution Watch: Albania," *East European Constitutional Review* 4 (1995): 3.

36. Initially, Parliament had sought to lift the immunity of the chairman of the Supreme Court of Cassation, Zef Brozi, because he reversed a lower court's decision freeing a Greek businessman. After further antagonizing opponents by reopening the case of opposition leader Fatos Natos, Brozi was finally dismissed from his post. "Constitution Watch: Albania," *East European Constitutional Review* 4 (1995): 1.

37. An additional 77 voluntarily retired, and 243 left their positions without explanation. In Poland, six justices on the Constitutional Tribunal were replaced in November 1989. With these changes, the court became more active. See Mark F. Brzezinski and Leszek Garlicki, "Judicial Review in Post-Communist Poland: The Emergence of a Rechtsstaat?" *Stanford Journal of International Law* 31 (1995): 13; Mark Brzezinski, *The Struggle for Constitutionalism in Poland* (New York: Columbia Univ. Press, 1998), 162–65.

38. Frederick P. Furth, *Courts of Ultimate Appeal: The Constitutional and Supreme Courts of the New Democracies of Central and Eastern Europe and the former Soviet Union* (San Francisco: Scott Foresman, 1993), 4.

39. Lithuanian Constitution, Chapter 8, Articles 102, 105; Czech Constitution, Chapter 4, Articles 83, 87; Hungarian Constitution, Chapter 4, Article 32A; Polish Constitution, Chapter 8, Articles 188, 189; Slovak Constitution, Chapter 7, Articles 124–29; Bulgarian Constitution, Chapter 8, Article 149; Romanian Constitution, Title V, Articles 144, 145; Bosnian Constitution, Article 6, Paragraph 3 and 4; Croatian Constitution, Chapter 5, Article 125 and 126; Macedonian Constitution, Chapter 4, Articles 110, 112; Slovenian Constitution, Part 8, Article 156, 157, Part 160, 161.

40. Sara Wright Sheive, "Central and Eastern European Constitutional Courts and the Antimajoritarian Objection to Judicial Review," *Law and Policy in International Business* 26 (1995): 1208. See also Jon Elster, "Constitutionalism in Eastern Europe: An Introduction," *University of Chicago Law Review* 58 (1991): 447.

41. The activism of these courts through abstract review poignantly raises the issue of the countermajoritarian objection to judicial review. Critics claim this type of review enables the courts to act as a second legislature by permitting courts to intervene in the legislative process and extend it when legislative minorities abuse it to achieve political ends. Supporters of abstract review usually respond with one of three arguments. Some accept the criticism as a necessary sacrifice to protect fundamental rights as well as monitor and control elected officials. Another approach emphasizes the representative nature of the courts—their election by representative bodies, their limited tenure, and the resulting reflection of the enduring wishes of the community against temporary tyrannical legislative minorities. A third position accepts the countermajoritarian nature of abstract review but asserts that many aspects of modern government are similarly nondemocratic. See Robert F. Utter and David C. Lundsgaard, "Judicial Review in the New Nations of Central and Eastern Europe: Some Thoughts from a Comparative Perspective," *Ohio State Law Journal* 54 (1993): 559.

42. This external control over jurisdiction is more threatening to judicial independence than self-imposing restrictions like those adopted by the Hungarian Constitutional Court to deal with their overwhelming caseload. One way to counter this threat is through a constitutional provision forbidding the parliament from limiting the constitutional court's jurisdiction beyond the constitutional restrictions. This approach was adopted by Bulgaria (Bulgarian Constitution, Chapter 8, Article 149); Albert P. Melone and Carol E. Hays, "The Judicial Role in Bulgaria's Struggle for Human Rights," *Judicature* 77 (1994): 248.

43. Polish Constitution, Chapter 8, Article 190, Chapter 13, Article 239.

44. "Constitution Watch: Bulgaria," *East European Constitutional Review* 5 (1996): 6.

45. "Constitution Watch: Hungary," *East European Constitutional Review* 3 (1994): 11.

46. Romanian Constitution, Title II, Chapter 4; Slovenian Constitution, Part 7, Article 159.

47. Rett R Ludwikowski, "Fundamental Constitutional Rights in the New Constitutions of Eastern and Central Europe," *Cardozo Journal of International and Comparative Law* 3 (1995): 73.

48. Lithuanian Constitution, Chapter 8, Article 106; Hungarian Constitution, Chapter 2, Article 26; Polish Constitution, Chapter 8, Articles 191–93; Slovak Constitution, Chapter 7, Article 130; Bulgarian Constitution, Chapter 8, Article 150; Romanian Constitution, Title V, Article 144; Bosnian Constitution, Article 6, Paragraph 3.

49. This material is cited in "Report of the Special Rapporteur on the independence of judges and lawyers", U.N. ESCOR, 52d Sess., Agenda Item 8, para. 18–24, U.N. Doc. E/CN.4/1996/37 (1994).

50. "Basic Principles on the Independence of the Judiciary," Seventh United Nations Congress on the Prevention of Crime and the Treatment of Offenders," U.N. Doc. A/CONF. 121/22, Chapter 1, Section D (1985), 59–60.

51. "Independence and Impartiality of the Judiciary, Jurors and assessors and the independence of lawyers," U.N. ESCOR, 51st Sess., Agenda Item 10, para. 56, U.N. Doc. E/CN.4/1995/39 (1995).

52. "Bulgaria: Interview," 66.

53. Ibid., 67.

54. Albert P. Melone, "Judicial Independence and Constitutional Politics in Bulgaria," *Judicature* 80 (1997): 280.

55. Melone and Hays, "The Judicial Role in Bulgaria," 253.

56. Schwartz, "Taking the Heat," 67–68.

57. Herman Schwartz, "The New East European Courts, *Michigan Journal of International Law* 13 (1992): 741, 777–78.

58. Leonid Nikitinsky, "Russia: Interview with Boris Ebzeev, Justice of the Constitutional Court of the Russian Federation," *East European Constitutional Review* 6 (1997): 83, 87.

59. Jon Elster, "On Majoritarianism and Rights," *East European Constitutional Review* 1 (1992): 19, 22.

60. Geza Herczegh, "The Evolution of Human Rights Law in Central and Eastern Europe: One Jurist's Response to the Distinguished Panelists," *Connecticut Journal of International Law* 8 (1993): 323, 325.

61. Andrej Skolkay, "Slovakia: Interview with Jan Drgonec, Justice of Constitutional Court of the Slovak Republic," *East European Constitutional Review* 6 (1997): 88, 91.

6

Judicial Independence in Latin Countries of Western Europe

CARLO GUARNIERI

The four countries of Latin Europe—France, Italy, Portugal, and Spain—are relatively homogeneous. All belong to the European Union; subscribe to the European Convention for the Protection of Human Rights and Fundamental Freedoms, with all its guarantees; and share the same democratic setting. Although there are some differences among them in institutional configuration, they share roughly the same levels of socioeconomic development. Their judiciaries enjoy a relatively high level of security: judges are ordinarily protected from outside threats.[1] Moreover, the judiciaries of Latin Europe share the same organizational heritage. All belong to the civil law, bureaucratic type of judicial system and, specifically, to the so-called "Napoleonic system," which is marked by a deep separation between the judiciary and other legal professions as well as by a somewhat stronger role of the political branches in judicial management.[2]

There are also some important differences, however. Most important is the variation in the power enjoyed by the political branches, because it affects more or less directly the degree of judicial independence. In this regard, France stands apart from the other three countries. Since the French Revolution, the judiciary has never played a significant role in the political process: "after the demise of the Ancien Régime, the depoliticization of the judicial function has been systematically pursued."[3] Guarantees of judicial independence have always been limited, while the executive has been entrusted with important prerogatives. To be sure, political power, especially in the executive, over the judiciary has enjoyed a stronger position in the French political system than in the other systems. Conversely, the troubled democratic development in the other three countries, which

111

have experienced long authoritarian periods, especially on the Iberian Peninsula, has brought about, at least in the postwar period, a general reinforcement of constitutional guarantees against the misuse or abuse of political power and, therefore, has strengthened the independence, scope, and depth of judicial decision making.[4]

Structure and Organization of the Judiciaries

The fragmentation of the jurisdiction of courts is a typical feature of the civil law tradition.[5] With the exception of Spain, the countries being considered share a basic judicial bifurcation, primarily as a consequence of the adoption of the Napoleonic model of judicial organization, between ordinary courts, which handle civil and criminal matters, and administrative courts, which have jurisdiction over complaints involving public agencies. Moreover, ordinary and administrative courts do not provide the only division in these countries; specialized courts also exist here.

In France, Italy, and Portugal, administrative judges form a separate body: their guarantees of independence, although growing, are less strong than those granted to the ordinary judiciary. Moreover, the councils of state—the highest administrative courts—perform advisory functions for the government, a role providing an additional connection between the administrative judiciary and the political system, even though the French Council of State has considerable autonomy. By contrast, Spain represents a special case. Disputes between private citizens and public agencies here are handled by specialized panels of ordinary courts.

As for the rest of Latin Europe, ordinary courts retain sole jurisdiction for trying civil and criminal matters. Apart from some minor exceptions, appeal is possible. Unlike the U.S. Supreme Court, which has almost complete discretionary jurisdiction, supreme courts in Latin Europe have to hear all cases filed. Moreover, while the supreme courts in this region formally have to deal exclusively with issues of legal interpretation, not purely factual disputes, in practice they function as appellate courts, reviewing issues of both fact and law. As a result, a sizeable part of the whole judicial workload may reach the top of the Latin European judicial systems.

A citizen's right to appeal to the supreme courts, and consequently the courts' crowded dockets, account for the excessive staffing of these courts.[6] Actually, they seem to perform their institutional function with increasing difficulty. Even though supreme court precedents are not formally binding—the doctrine of *stare decisis* has never been recognized in continental systems—their "persuasive" force has always been strong.[7]

Traditionally, this influence has been strictly connected to the bureaucratic arrangement of Continental judiciaries and especially to the role played in the process of career promotions by the judicial elite. Still, as discussed later, the position of the judicial elite appears to be growing weaker.[8]

After the ancien régime experience with the parliaments, that is, the appellate courts that claimed to be the guardians of the "Kingdom's fundamental rules,"[9] it was not until the twentieth century that judicial review of legislation was reestablished on the European continent. Moreover, not until after World War II did the exercise of judicial review begin its cross-national expansion. The Italian *Corte Costituzionale,* which was provided for in the 1948 Constitution, was, in fact, instituted in 1956. Two years later, the transition to the Fifth Republic in France brought about the establishment of the *Conseil Constitutionnel,* which, notwithstanding its peculiar features, plays an increasing role in the political system. The Iberian countries joined this European trend in 1978 and 1983, with the creation in Spain and Portugal respectively of separate constitutional courts.

The nine members of the French Constitutional Council[10] are appointed in the same proportions by the president of the republic and the presidents of the Senate and of the National Assembly respectively. Rather surprisingly, no specific qualification is required to be eligible for appointment, not even a law degree.[11] The twelve judges on the Spanish court are individually chosen by the following formula: the two chambers of parliament, on a three-fifths majority vote, each elect four members; the executive appoints two; the Higher Council of the Judiciary selects the remaining two. In Portugal, of the thirteen constitutional judges, ten are elected by the National Assembly by a two-thirds majority vote, and the remaining three are chosen by the court itself. Finally, in Italy, the fifteen judges of the court are appointed or elected in the same proportions by the president of the republic, both chambers of parliament sitting in common session by a three-fifths majority vote, and the highest courts, both ordinary and administrative.

The composition of constitutional courts is important, but their place within a country's judicial system must also be considered in assessing their roles in a political system. The first element to take into account is the institutional locus of constitutional adjudication. In this regard, the classic distinction contrasts "centralized" with "diffuse" judicial review. Under the former, judicial review is entrusted to a single court, whereas with the latter, every court has the power to declare a law inconsistent with constitutional obligations. Centralized review has marked the expansion of constitutional justice all over continental Europe. However, it should be noted that Portugal has also adopted a sort of diffuse review: the ordinary judiciary there can directly exercise judicial review of legislation, but if it does, the prosecutor must appeal to the constitutional court.

The second element concerns when constitutional adjudication may be activated. There are two alternatives available: constitutional adjudication may be invoked either before or after the enactment of the law. The so-called *a priori* review is typical of the French Constitutional Council, which may be asked to review legislation only in the short span of time between the passage of a law and its promulgation by the president of the republic. Once promulgated, the law cannot be challenged in the courts and can be amended only by the legislature itself, which retains its traditionally central position in the political process. By contrast, *a posteriori* review, found in all other Latin European countries, allows for constitutional challenges to legislation at any time.

Two further aspects deserve attention. First, in some countries, any citizen may bring a so-called "abstract review" lawsuit to invoke the protection of a fundamental right against any alleged encroachment by a public agency. This is the case for the *recurso de amparo,* recognized in the Spanish Constitution, which covers about the 90 percent of the workload of the constitutional court.[12] Second, in other countries, access is equally open to all citizens but only on the condition that they are involved in an actual dispute. Through the so-called "incidental" proceeding, litigants have the chance to challenge the law that should be applied in their case. If this occurs, the ordinary court has to assess whether the issue is groundless or not and, ultimately, refer the case to the constitutional court. In other words, ordinary courts are a filter between the litigants and constitutional adjudication.

The incidental proceeding produces the so-called "concrete" review of legislation, because it is triggered by the application of the law in individual disputes. This kind of review is found in Spain, Italy, and, to some extent, also in Portugal. The exception, again, is the French Constitutional Council, which reviews legislation not yet enforced and, thus, exercises only "abstract review." Under abstract judicial review, enacted legislation can be challenged only by public authorities, with the exception of the judiciary: the executive, the legislature, the local governments, and even (in Spain and Portugal) the Ombudsman. Even so, abstract judicial review has had considerable impact in France; indeed, it appears to have gone well beyond the intentions of its initial supporters.[13]

Beyond the specific features of the Latin European constitutional courts, it is clear that none have bound themselves to what Hans Kelsen termed "negatively legislating." Their task is not only to answer "yes" or "no" to a constitutional complaint. The decision-making techniques and opinion writing the courts have developed and elaborated more or less every-where allow them to participate in an active way in the policy process. To be sure, by comparison with judges in the United States, Latin European ordinary judges have a much reduced role in the constitutional review of legislation, because final review is always given to special constitutional courts. Still, together with the establishment and gradual expansion of supranational systems of justice, like those created by the European Community or the European Convention for Human Rights, ordinary courts have enlarged their discretionary powers and role and their scope of judicial review.

Judicial Recruitment

In general, civil law judiciaries do not basically differ from the bureaucratic machinery of the state.[14] They are grounded on the classic European conception of the judge as a mere executor of the law, based on technical legal knowledge. Therefore, the bureaucratic arrangement characterizing the European administration of justice expresses the old and sharp distinction between law and politics. In other words, judges, like other civil servants, merely apply preexisting legal rules without interfering in the prerogatives of the political branches. The basic analogy with civil service clearly emerges when the recruiting methods are examined.

Traditionally, entrance into the judiciary takes place on the basis of competitive examinations much like those that govern access to other bureaucratic corps. In all civil law countries, public competition is the main or the only way to become a career judge. Merit selection is considered to be the most effective instrument to ensure both professional qualifications and effective independence of the judiciary.

Leaving aside the peculiar traits of each system, the general features are as follows: Legal education is typically multipurpose, providing a general overview of all relevant areas of law, without any specialization. Competitions are open to young law graduates, usually with scarce or no previous professional experience. Consequently, the process of legal education and recruitment leaves little or no room for the "practical side" of the law that the recruits will eventually perform and is based solely on written and oral exams, which test their theoretical knowledge of the law. Judges are supposed to be able to perform the whole range of tasks they could be assigned—from adjudicating criminal and civil cases to serving as a public prosecutor. Legal training is basically carried out on the job, supervised by senior judges, and thus fosters the reproduction of a dominant professional ethos. To put it differently, judicial socialization takes place within, and is therefore essentially controlled by, the judicial organization. All these elements, and especially the reluctance to acquire professional experiences developed outside the judiciary, result in the strengthening of the *esprit de corps* and in the "balkanization" of the legal professions.[15]

However, in Latin European countries, recruitment by public competition has undergone some major developments, often aimed at solving problems typically associated with the bureaucratic model. Lateral entry into the judicial corps, accessible to lawyers or civil servants on a merit basis, has somewhat opened up the profession. Judicial schools have also been founded to provide training programs for new judges. In this respect, the French system has been in the forefront. Legal education and training of judges and public prosecutors is entrusted to the *Ecole Nationale de la Magistrature* (ENM), officially established in 1970 but actually at work since 1958. This institution has provided a model for other countries, such as Spain and Portugal. The so-called *concours etudiant,* namely the competition open to young law graduates, is by far the most important recruiting channel, but there also are other ways to enter the school. Leaving aside the specific qualifications required, all forms of competition share a common goal, namely, to open the judiciary to candidates from different professional environments.[16] Although they are deemed not sufficient to keep magistrates in touch with society,[17] these programs allow an "external ventilation" for judges that is still lacking in Italy.

The *concours étudiant* is open to candidates who are at least twenty-seven years old and, since 1992, who hold a law degree. The written and oral exams determining the admission to the school are highly selective. Successful candidates are integrated into the judiciary as *uditeurs de justice,* (judicial trainees) receive a salary, and enjoy certain guarantees of independence. The training period, currently fixed at thirty-one months, consists of two phases: the first is general training and is carried out both in the school and in the courts; the second, lasting six months, is devoted to more specialized training related to the *uditeurs* later assignment of the trainee within the judiciary. The apprenticeship involves working in law firms and other public organizations, so that trainees have "the opportunity to discover public or private institutions governed by different logic, and to get rid of the judicial monoculture."[18] During the training period, the young magistrates are subject to different evaluations, and their ranking entitles them to choose, from among the vacancies, the positions to which they will be assigned.

Judicial recruitment in Italy, however, still remains closer to the traditional continental model. Public competition on a national basis is the only way to enter the judiciary, both for judges and public prosecutors. A constitutional provision provides for the appointment of experienced lawyers and law professors to the Court of Cassation, the highest court of the country, but so far the rule has never been applied. Since people are recruited at a young age and usually serve until retirement, the Italian judiciary appears to be an "entrenched corps." After education at university law faculties, selection and subsequent training of judges and public prosecutors is controlled by the Higher Council of the Judiciary, an institution composed of a qualified majority of magistrates. The ministry of justice plays no part in the recruitment process nor in subsequent decisions concerning the status of judges and public prosecutors.

Unlike recent developments in the French system, time devoted to legal training in Italy has been shortened. Since 1988, legal apprenticeships are approximately fifteen months but may, in fact, vary according to the position to be filled. In the absence of any judicial school, apprenticeship takes place in courts and prosecutorial offices under the supervision of senior magistrates. Courses and seminars organized by the Higher Council last a few days and do not seem to follow a systematic plan. Most important, evaluations of personal performances by the Higher Council are almost invariably positive and, therefore, the initial national competition remains the critical point in the selection process.

As noted earlier, Spain and Portugal have followed the French model and established judicial schools. The main distinctive feature of the Portuguese *Centro de estudos judiciarios* is that after entering the school, trainees have to choose whether to become a judge or a public prosecutor. The distinction between judges and prosecutors is even more marked in Spain. The *Centro de studos judiciales,* dating to 1986 but having a precedent in the 1950 *Escuela judicial,* selects future judges by means of public competitions open to law graduates and is in charge of their education and training. However, in both countries lateral access to the corps has been established for jurists "of recognized competence," and there is a reserved quota of these positions at the different ranks.

In sum, in all Latin European countries, a judicial career begins at a relatively young age. The institutions in charge of training only partially compensate for their recruits' substantial lack of practical experience. Notably, the recruits' professional socialization is achieved almost exclusively within the judiciary, and merit standards largely govern the recruitment of judges. Still, with the remarkable exception of Italy, where the judicial recruitment process is under the complete control of the judiciary itself, judicial recruitment is monitored by the ministries of justice, which can exert, at least to some extent, an influence therein.

Institutional Independence

In all of the Latin European judicial systems, judicial independence is established in similar terms: in principle, judges are subordinate only to the law and their jurisdiction, especially in the criminal field, and are constitutionally insulated from outside infringements.[19] However, in practice, judicial independence is constrained by the organizational hierarchies of the judicial system. In addition, the well-known distinction between the external independence of the relations between the judiciary and the other branches of government and the independence of individual judges must be considered.[20]

The judiciaries in continental Europe have traditionally been characterized by a pyramid-like structure. As would be expected, salary, prestige, and personal influence depend on a judge's position on the hierarchical ladder and can be improved only through promotions. Positions are gained on a competitive basis and according to a combination of two criteria: seniority and merit. The latter is based on evaluations by higher-ranking judges. Even when the final decision on a judge's promotion is technically that of the minister of justice, or another institution, promotions rely heavily on an assessment of the judge's peers, that is, the formal, written evaluations of higher-ranking judges. Moreover, other actors outside the judicial system, especially in the executive branch and the ministry of justice, often influence the promotion process. Traditionally, such external intervention, although with different forms, represented the most important institutional link connecting the judiciary with the political system.

However, in Latin European countries, the prominent role traditionally played by the executive branch has been remarkably weakened, largely as a result of the creation of new institutions, like the higher councils of the judiciary, which were designed to strengthen the independence of the bench. All higher councils share a single feature: although in different proportions, members of the judiciary are always granted representation therein. (See table 6.1.) The higher councils of the judiciary are pivotal in the relationships between courts and other political institutions in these countries. Despite their common features, however, the composition and role of higher councils does vary in the different systems. And it is therefore necessary to compare their composition and functions and composition: above all, the ratio between judicial and lay members and the ways these groups are chosen. Of course, the level of judicial independence tends to be higher where judges are granted the majority of the seats on the councils and are directly elected by their colleagues.

TABLE 6.1

Composition of the Higher Councils of the Judiciary in France, Spain, Portugal, and Italy

	France Conseil superieur de la magistrature	Spain Consejo general del poder judicial	Portugal Conselho superior da magistradura	Italy Consiglio superiore della magistratura
Judicial members	**7:** 5 judges and 1 prosecutor indirectly elected by the corps; 1 councillor of state elected by his/her colleagues	**13:** 12 judges appointed by Parliament; the president of the Supreme Court is ex officio	**9:** 7 judges elected directly by the corps; 1 appointed by the president of republic; the president of the Supreme Court is ex officio	**22:** 20 magistrates elected directly by the corps; 1 each appointed by the president and the attorney general of the Court of Cassation
Lay members	**5:** 3 appointed respectively by the president of the republic, the president of the senate, and the president of the National Assembly; the minister of justice, the president of the republic	**8:** all lawyers appointed by Parliament	**8:** 7 lawyers appointed by Parliament, 1 by the president of the republic	**11:** 10 lawyers appointed by Parliament and 1 by the president of the republic

Source: C. Guarnieri and P. Pederzoli, La puissance de juger (Paris: Michalon, 1996), 74.

Established in the second half of the nineteenth century under the influence of the Napoleonic model, the Italian judiciary was much like that in France. Its hierarchical structure did not undergo dramatic changes even during the fascist regime, whose main strategy in the administration of justice was that of establishing regime-controlled special tribunals in charge of politically significant crimes. Because the bureaucratic structure of the judiciary was not questioned, even during the transition to democracy after World War II, a movement toward a substantial alteration of the traditional organization of the judiciary did not occur until the early 1960s. Among the many factors contributing to that judicial reform were (1) the institution of the Higher Council of the Judiciary, which although envisaged by the 1948 Constitution, did not actually begin operating until 1959; (2) the role played therein by the National Association of Magistrates, a union-like association internally divided into several organized factions that came to dominate the council's decisional process; and (3) above all, the dismantling of the traditional system of promotions by virtue of a large part of the judiciary coming to recognize the traditional career patterns and the underlying hierarchical relationships as inconsistent with the very notion of judicial independence.

The Italian Higher Council was entrusted with making all decisions related to the status of both judges and public prosecutors. More precisely, their recruitment, appointment, promotions, transfers, and disciplinary proceedings were removed from the minister of justice, who now has only the power to start disciplinary proceedings. Thus, the council became the main, if not the only, institutional bridge between the judiciary and the political system. At present, the council consists of (1) three ex officio members—the president of the republic, who presides; the president; and the prosecutor general at the Court of Cassation—and (2) twenty magistrates directly elected by the judiciary, as well as (3) ten lay members elected by Parliament among experienced lawyers and university law professors. In practice, the lay participants are chosen so as to reflect the strength of the different political parties in Parliament.

The reforms approved from 1963 to 1979 and, above all, the ways they were implemented incrementally but effectively dismantled the traditional hierarchy. As a result, today, promotions of Italian magistrates follow a quite unusual pattern. The traditional system of promotions, based on competitive examinations or on comparative assessments of the magistrates' work by higher-ranking judges, has been abolished. Technically, promotions are based on consideration of judges' seniority and merit, the latter determined by the Higher Council's evaluation. But, in practice, advancements depend almost exclusively on seniority. Professional evaluations have little practical significance, because they are almost invariably positive.

Promotions also no longer depend on the availability of vacant positions in higher courts. Thus, any magistrate can attain the highest ranks in twenty-eight years, or at least the corresponding salary.

Judicial promotions are, therefore, virtually automatic and deemed to encourage the proliferation of both part-time and full-time extrajudicial activities—a phenomenon that has developed in other countries as well, but in Italy it is more widespread. By allowing magistrates to establish relations, sometimes for a very long time, with other political and economic institutions,[21] the level of professionalism may be eroded, especially given the certainty of automatic career advancements and the lack of effective civil and disciplinary liability.[22] Hence, magistrates are encouraged to look for gratification outside the judiciary, in politics and even in the media.

The Italian experience has proven to be particularly attractive to the younger Iberian democracies, emerging from the fall of the authoritarian regimes. The Spanish judiciary, for instance, is quite similar to that in Italy in its bureaucratic organization. In its transition to democracy, marked by the 1978 Constitution, Spain reentered the mainstream of the Western constitutional tradition with a separation of powers and guarantees for judicial independence. Notably, the *Consejo general del poder judicial* was created to secure the independence of the third branch vis-à-vis the executive. Following the Italian model, the Spanish constitution provides that the majority of the Higher Council will be judges. This provision was enacted through the *Ley organica* of 1980, according to which the Higher Council is presided over by the chief of the Supreme Court and is composed of twenty members, twelve of whom are judges directly elected by their peers. The rest are appointed in the same proportions by both chambers of Parliament. As in Italy, the minister of justice only oversees the administration of justice. After the victory of the Socialist Party in 1982, however, the new government clashed with the conservative majority of the Higher Council.

That conflict led three years later to the reform of the *Ley organica* and resulted in judicial members of the Higher Council being elected by Parliament. That gave rise to both complaints from judges and controversies in Parliament. Although rejecting a legal challenge to that judicial reform, the constitutional court raised doubts about the introduction of an appointing mechanism that appeared to threaten the "partisan logic" of the Higher Council's decision making.[23] With respect to the developments observed in Italy, parliamentary election of judicial members, while fostering collaboration with the political forces, seems to have lessened the role of judicial associations. The Spanish council is in charge of appointments and promotions, according to procedures that vary with the judicial position to be filled. In principle, advancements depend on seniority and, to a lesser extent, on merit. But appointments to the highest positions also take into account the need to ensure the representation of linguistic minorities.

In Portugal, after the fall of the dictatorship of António de Oliveira Salazar and Marcello Caetano, major innovations took place. Among the measures immediately adopted, in 1974, was the direct election of the president of the Supreme Court and the presidents of courts of appeal by their peers. In so doing, the judicial hierarchy became elected by the judicial corps, with no intervention on the part of the executive and of the Higher Council. The principles regulating the Higher Council of the Judiciary were set forth in 1976 in the newly established constitution in rather laconic terms: Article 223 stipulates that the Higher Council "include members elected by and among judges." Conversely, the council was given responsibilities of remarkable latitude, ranging from making judicial appointments and transfers to promotions and disciplinary proceedings.

Following a 1982 constitutional amendment, the Higher Council now consists of seven judges, directly elected by their colleagues through a proportional system; seven members elected by Parliament; and two other members appointed by the president of the republic, one of them necessarily being a judge. Moreover, the Higher Council is chaired by the president of the Supreme Court, himself elected by his fellow judges. The judges, thus, were given the majority of the seats on the Higher Council, and that arguably strengthened the institutional independence of the Portuguese judiciary.

The French Higher Council is different in two important respects, namely the role preserved for the executive and the relatively narrow scope of its functions.[24] Although there have been different "versions" of the Higher Council in France from 1958 to 1993, the president of the republic and the minister of justice have always been included. At the same time, the council's tasks do not include judicial selection and training.

Created in 1946 to preserve the independence of judges, the French Higher Council was a true mutation under the Constitution of 1958. The role of the president of the republic inside the Higher Council came at the expense of the legislature. Nine counselors, sitting with the minister of justice and the president of the republic, were appointed by the latter. A 1993 constitutional amendment, however, brought about significant changes.

At present, the Higher Council, while still a single body, consists of two different panels for overseeing judges and public prosecutors, respectively. It is now composed of twelve members: the president of the republic; the minister of justice; a councillor of state elected by her peers; three lay members appointed respectively by the president of the republic, the president of the Senate, and the president of the National Assembly; and six magistrates representing the various hierarchical ranks, who are elected by their colleagues. It is precisely the composition of the latter segment of the Higher Council that changes, according to the type of panel: it consists of five judges and one public prosecutor when measures concerning judges are under consideration, whereas these proportions are reversed in the case of decisions affecting public prosecutors. The reform has also increased the functions of the Higher Council. The council now is in charge of the disciplining of judges and makes direct appointments to all important positions.

In conclusion, the French Higher Council has been entrusted with functions that are undoubtedly more important than those in the past but still not as broad as those vested in its Italian counterpart. The position of individual judges, the functions they perform, their prestige, and their salary are largely determined by career advancements. However, French judges nonetheless show higher levels of mobility than do judges in common law countries.[25]

Judicial Independence and Constitutional Courts

It is not easy to provide a grounded assessment of judicial behavior in the countries considered here, because there are no systematic data on the subject. In fact, in continental Europe, analysis of judicial behavior presents some special problems. For example, appellate civil law judges decide cases on panels and, as a rule, no dissenting or concurring opinions are allowed. In addition, academic research in Europe has, at least until recently, taken the traditional view that judges are only the "mouth of the law," and therefore scholars have concentrated on analyzing the law and the way legal texts are interpreted.[26]

Still, the significance of at least constitutional courts has notably expanded throughout Latin Europe, but especially in Southern Europe—that is, Italy, Portugal, and Spain. In those countries, constitutional courts were introduced with the aim of reinforcing citizens' guarantees against parliamentary legislation. However, "besides the general post-war cultural and political climate favourable . . . to the expansion of judicial review, one of the reasons that led to the creation of constitutional courts is intimately related to the process of institutionalization of judicial independence . . . career judiciaries were generally deemed unsuited by political elites to perform a function such as judicial review that required from them all that they appeared to lack: a high level of individual autonomy, prestige, and legal scholarship, as well as modern legal values and approaches to judicial decision making." Constitutional courts were, therefore, organized to be responsive to the new democratic political actors, a fact assured by the political nature of the process of appointment to such courts: "constitutional courts were the device through which that broad responsiveness was transmitted even to the staunchly insulated Southern European judiciaries."[27]

On the whole, the institution of judicial review has brought about deeper changes on judicial behavior by triggering an evolution in the prevailing conceptions of the judicial role, helping the diffusion of a more critical attitude toward legislation, and therefore contributing to the erosion of the traditional executory definition.

The case of the French Constitutional Council is only partly different. Created by Charles De Gaulle with the aim of having an instrument for checking parliamentary encroachments on executive prerogatives, the council's role changed after the reform of 1974 and the weakening of the Gaullist majority. The alternation of different political forces in the government—and the cohabitation of the 1980s and the 1990s—have furthered the council's independent role in the complex web of relationships between parliamentary forces, the government, and the president.[28]

Moreover, in recent years, even ordinary courts have experienced an extraordinary expansion of judicial power.[29] The growing intervention of courts in the political process has become a permanent trend. Italy is, without doubt, the most striking case. Since the 1970s, the judiciary has been increasingly involved in politics. Italian magistrates have played a crucial role in the fight against terrorism and organized crime. This development reached its apex, perhaps, in 1992, triggering a set of dramatic changes in Italian politics. Public prosecutors started a systematic campaign against political corruption, given the name "Clean Hands," aimed openly not only at prosecuting specific cases but at moralizing and mobilizing public opinion. As a consequence, Italy has experienced an unprecedented level of judicial activism, which played a significant part in the transition to the so-called Second Republic.[30] Moreover, judicial activism in Italy has not been restricted to the area of criminal law. Interest groups have discovered the effectiveness of courts in forging public policy. For example, in a recent case, courts have forced a reluctant government to organize the experimentation of an anticancer therapy, even though it would involve the diversion of resources already allotted to more orthodox treatments.[31] In short, the kinds of disputes adjudicated are no longer restricted to the private sphere and to the "classical" contentions between the citizens and the state, but now regularly involve disputes among and with other public institutions.[32]

Similar trends have also appeared in Portugal and Spain. Since the end of the 1980s, the Spanish Socialist government has been a target for judicial investigations concerning the alleged "dirty war" against the Basque terrorist organization ETA, a process that has made Baltasar Garzòn, the investigating judge, a kind of national hero.[33] The investigations discovered the involvement of police officers in the actions of the *Grupos Antiterrorista de Liberacion* (GAL), and the GAL case was only the beginning of Socialists' problems with the courts. Controversies over the illegal funding of the party's electoral campaign, charges of tax evasion, and outright corruption discredited the Socialist Party and contributed to its electoral defeat of 1996.

Nor has Portugal escaped this trend. The Social Democratic Party, in power from 1985 to 1995, was seriously affected by judicial investigations, along with media allegations, of corruption and tax evasion by party members. By the early 1990s, Prosecutor General Cunha Rodrigues had become one of the most visible and respected public figures in the country. The political scandals, carefully seized by the opposition parties, tarnished the image of the Social Democratic Party and were a factor in its defeats in the 1995 and 1996 elections.[34]

Neither has France been spared by the general trend toward increased judicialization of politics.[35] Since the end of the 1980s, a wave of judicial investigations has touched the political elite on the Left and the Right, reaching also top executives of big private corporations. The investigations have, likewise, concerned corruption, illegal use of private and public funds, and tax evasion. On the whole, the attitude of the French judiciary has been slowly evolving toward a more independent stance vis-à-vis the executive. Highly significant, for example, is the 1995 decision of the Court of Cassation that broadened the jurisdiction of ordinary courts on crimes committed by high public officials.

Still, admittedly, assessing the actual independence of the judiciary in Latin Europe is not easy. First of all, the fact remains that all maintain bureaucratic judiciaries, once under the control of the executive and of the judicial elite. Nonetheless, the growing institutional independence and the erosion of the judicial hierarchy has freed judges from some of the traditional forms of control. In addition, the institution of self-governing judicial bodies has enhanced the role of judicial associations, allowing the emergence of even strong differences inside the judiciary. In other words, the weakening of traditional dependencies, both external and internal, appears to have increased the relevance of the relationships between judges and the political and social environment. In all four countries, a new and strong relationship has developed between judges (as well as prosecutors) and the media: Baltasar Garzòn in Spain, Thierry Jean-Pierre in France, Antonio Di Pietro in Italy are only a few examples of magistrates whose initiatives have been strongly supported by public opinion and by the media. In fact, the media, whose interests often coincide with those of the judiciary, is especially able to support and draw attention to the actions of judges and public prosecutors.[36]

Conclusion

In democratic regimes, the relationships between the judiciary and other political institutions have traditionally been arranged in two ways: in civil law countries, the political branches exercise considerable influence over judicial bureaucracies, while in Anglo-Saxon countries, the influence of the executive and legislature primarily focuses on the judicial recruitment process. Nonetheless, these two legal families have approached the traditional tension between independent judges and democracy in not-so-different ways. Generally speaking, in the civil law systems of continental Europe, the role of the judge has been defined as that of a simple executor of the legislative will, therefore suppressing at its roots the aforementioned tension. In other words, there is no tension, because judges, although independent, just execute the will of the democratic majority. In the common law tradition, judicial creativity has always been recognized, and yet judicial law making has been controlled by some sort of self-restraint on the part of the judges and has been reflected in the mechanisms of judicial socialization at work in these countries.

Thus the institution of Higher Councils marks a radical change in the traditional way of arranging political-judicial relationships in civil law countries. This third channel of political influence can be interpreted mainly as a consequence of the slow but steady diminishing of public trust in executive power. As a consequence, the Higher Councils tend to erode the powers of the executive and of the old judicial hierarchies.

We are left, however, with a sort of paradox: more institutional independence does not appear to have resulted in more independence on the bench. Judicial independence from the executive has increased everywhere in Latin Europe. The importance of judicial associations has increased everywhere because of the role they play in the self-governing bodies. In some ways, they have replaced the old hierarchical structure: instead of a small group of higher-ranking judges, the judiciary is now run by the leaders of different judicial groups, whose influence depends to a large extent on their capabilities of attracting the support of their fellow magistrates.[37] On balance, in Latin European countries the slow but steady dismantling of the Napoleonic model of judicial organization has been associated with the judicialization of politics, marked by both growing judicial policy making and the development of a sort of criminalization of political responsibility.[38]

Notes

1. But not at every time and everywhere: terrorism in Italy in the 1970s and today in Spain as well as organized crime in certain areas of southern Italy have often hit judges and prosecutors. In Italy, between 1976 and 1980, ten magistrates were killed by terrorist groups, while between 1971 and 1992, twenty-four of them were victims of the mafia.

2. See John Henry Merryman, *The Civil Law Tradition* (Stanford, Calif.: Stanford Univ Press, 1985). The implicit comparison here is with Germany and the Scandinavian countries.

3. George Lavau, "Le juge et le pouvoir politique," in *La justice* (Paris: Presses Univ. de France, 1961), 59.

4. See C Neal Tate, "Courts and Crisis Regimes: A Theory Sketch with Asian Cases," *Political Research Quarterly* 46 (1993): 311.

5. This chapter borrows to a large extent from C. Guarnieri and P. Pederzoli, *La puissance de juger* (Paris: Michalon, 1996), to which I refer for a more detailed analysis.

6. See Martin Shapiro, "Appeals," *Law and Society Review* 14 (1980): 624; Mirjan Damaska, *The Faces of Justice and State Authority* (New Haven, Conn.: Yale Univ. Press, 1986); Mauro Cappelletti, *The Judicial Process in Comparative Perspective* (Oxford: Clarendon Press, 1989).

7. Marc Ancel, "Reflexions sur l'étude comparative des Cours supremes et le recours en cassation," in *Annales de l'Institut de droit comparé de l'Universitè de Paris* (Paris, 1934): 300.

8. It is not by chance that the decline of the Supreme Court's influence is particularly visible in Italy, where the traditional career has been dismantled, even though the decline of the Supreme Court's influence seems to be occurring also in France. See Giovanni Tarello, *Cultura giuridica e politica del diritto* (Bologna: Il Mulino, 1988); Michele Taruffo, *Il vertice ambiguo* (Bologna: Il Mulino, 1991); Sergio Chiarloni "La dottrina fonte del diritto?", *Rivista trimestrale di diritto e procedura civile* 47 (1993): 439; Antoine Garapon, *Le gardien des promesses* (Paris: Odile Jacob, 1996).

9. Cappelletti, *The Judicial Process in Comparative Perspective*, 124.

10. Former presidents of the republic may also sit as ex officio members. Whereas Vincent Auriol and René-Jules-Gustave Coty, who had held this position in the Fourth Republic, have exploited this chance, none of their successors in the Fifth Republic has done so.

11. In the course of its evolution, especially since the presidency of Valéry Giscard D'Estaing, the trend has nonetheless emerged toward appointing candidates with legal experience. Yet, François Mitterand revived the tradition based on standards of personal loyalty. See Alec Stone, *The Birth of Judicial Politics in France* (Oxford: Oxford Univ. Press, 1992), 51.

12. From the legal point of view, this procedure cannot be used for challenging a parliamentary law. In practice, however, it is likely that a decision against public administration will also affect the subtended legislation. Furthermore, the tribunal has shown a propensity to enlarge the scope of the *recurso* so to grant a more effective protection to individual rights.

13. The recent developments of the constitutional council illustrate the point. At the outset, the council could act only upon referral of four state authorities: the president of the republic, the prime minister, and the presidents of the Senate and of the Assembly. After the 1974 reform that granted this power also to sixty members of either chambers of the parliament—fixing therefore a threshold that oppositions could easily cross, referrals have known a dramatic growth. Abstract review has proved to be an attractive device to transfer political conflicts from the parliamentary into the judicial arena, which in this case tends to act more and more as a true "third chamber." See Martin Shapiro, "Judicial Politics in France," *Journal of Law and Politics* 6 (1990): 531.

14. See Merryman, *The Civil Law Tradition;* Giorgio Freddi, *Tensioni e conflitto nella magistratura* (Bari, Italy: Laterza, 1978), 62; Giuseppe Di Federico, "The Italian Judiciary and its Bureaucratic Setting," *The Juridical Review* 1 (1976): 40; Giorgio Rebuffa, *La funzione giudiziaria* (Torino, Italy: Giappichelli, 1993).

15. Merryman, *The Civil Law Tradition*, 102.

16. An accurate analysis of the different recruiting methods is provided by Anna Mestitz, *Selezione e formazione dei magistrati e degli avvocati in Francia* (Padova, Italy: Cedam, 1990).

17. See Daniel Soulez-Larivière, *Du cirque médiatico- judiciaire et des moyens d'en sortir* (Paris: Seuil, 1993).

18. Hubert Dalle, "Le recrutement et la formation des magistrats: une question de légitimité," *Revue française d'administration publique* 57 (1991): 53, 59.

19. See Christine Van Den Wyngaert, ed., *Criminal Procedural System in the European Community* (London: Butterworths, 1993).

20. See Shimon Shetreet, "Judicial Independence: New Conceptual Dimensions and Contemporary Challenges," in Shimon Shetreet and Jules Deschenes, eds., *Judicial Independence: The Contemporary Debate* (Dordrecht: Nijhoff, 1985), 637–38.

21. We can sketch out here only the most frequent and remarkable cases. The institutions with magistrates among their staff include Parliament, the central government (especially the ministry of justice, which is virtually colonized), the presidency of the republic, regional and provincial governments, as well as a range of administrative agencies. This phenomenon also includes the possibility of acting as arbitrators, which bring members of the judiciary in touch with decisions having considerable financial consequences. See Francesca Zannotti, *Le attività extragiudiziarie dei magistrati ordinari* (Padova, Italy: Cedam, 1981); and Giuseppe Di Federico, "The Crisis of the Justice System and the Referendum on the Judiciary," in Robert Leonardi and Piergiorgio Corbetta, eds., *Italian Politics: a Review* (London: Pinter, 1989), 25–49.

22. Disciplinary proceedings can be initiated by the minister of justice—actually in most cases by the prosecutor general at the Court of Cassation—and take place before the standing committee of the Higher Council, which does not seem to show any inclination toward severity. Legislation on civil liability, passed in 1987 following a popular referendum, supplies magistrates with so strong guarantees as to make its implementation very difficult. See Di Federico, "The Crisis of the Judicial System."

23. Perfecto Andrès Ibañez, "Espagne: justice et transition démocratique," in *La formation des magistrats en Europe et le role des syndicats et des associations professionnelles* (Padova, Italy: Cedam, 1992), 69.

24. A constitutional reform is presently under way in France, changing once again the composition and the powers of the Higher Council. According to the project, besides the president of the republic and the minister of justice, it will be composed of twenty-one members, ten elected by the judiciary and eleven appointed by different authorities (the Council of State will select a councillor and the president of the republic, the presidents of the Senate and of the National Assembly and the president of the Socioeconomic Council will appoint two members each); finally the vice president of the Council of State and the presidents of the Court of Cassation and of the Court of Accounts will jointly appoint other two members. The council will have jurisdiction over both judges and public prosecutors.

25. The procedure of advancements is, indeed, rather complicated. It will suffice here to emphasize once again the role of the judicial hierarchy. Evaluations on work performances are drafted by higher-ranking magistrates and recorded in personal reports, which are then made available to all actors taking part in the decision-making process. Hierarchical superiors represent, thus, a sort of interface between individual judges and appointing authorities. Besides the Higher Council and the minister of justice, the so-called commission for advancements also plays a role in career advancements, for it has the task of drafting the annual list of magistrates deemed qualified to be promoted. Since candidates to promotions must necessarily be drawn from this list, the commission represents a delicate element of the appointing machinery. While in the past it was staffed by magistrates appointed by the minister of justice, a reform in 1992 has made it possible for the commission to boast a more balanced

composition, including not only executive officials but also magistrates directly elected by their peers. See especially Roger Perrot, *Institutions judiciaires* (Paris: Montchrestien, 1993), 354–55; and Thierry Renoux and Andrè Roux, *L'administration de la justice en France* (Paris: PUF, 1994), 67–85.

26. See Merryman, *The Civil Law Tradition*.

27. Carlo Guarnieri and Pedro Magalhàes, "Democratic Consolidation, Judicial Reform and the Judicialization of Politics in Southern Europe," in *Democratic Consolidation in Southern Europe*, eds. Nikiforos Diamandouros, Richard Gunther, and Gianfrano Pasquinos (forthcoming).

28. See Stone, *The Birth of Judicial Politics in France;* and Doris Marie Provine, "Courts in the Political Process in France," in *Courts, Law and Politics in Comparative Perspective*, ed. Herbert Jacob (New Haven, Conn.: Yale Univ. Press, 1996), 177–247.

29. C. Neal Tate and Torbjorn Vallinder, *The Global Expansion of Judicial Power* (New York: New York Univ. Press), 519.

30. For what follows, see P. Pederzoli and C. Guarnieri, "The judicialisation of politics, Italian style," *Journal of Modern Italian Studies* 3 (1997): 321.

31. The Di Bella therapy (named after its inventor, a retired university professor) has been dealt with by all sorts of courts, including the constitutional court itself.

32. According to the well-known classification by Lawrence Friedman, "Trial Courts and Their Work in the Modern World," in *Zur Soziologie des Gerichtsverfahrens*, eds. L. Friedman and M. Rehbinder (Opladen, Germany: Westdeutscher Verlag, 1976), 25–38.

33. Garzòn is central instructing judge, with nationwide jurisdiction over major crimes, such as terrorism, drug trafficking, and organized crime.

34. In August 1998 the executive in charge of the Expo 1998 in Lisbon was arrested on charges of corruption.

35. A. Garapon and Denis Salas, *La Rèpublique penalisée* (Paris: Hachette, 1996); Denis Salas, *Le tiers pouvoir* (Paris: Hachette, 1997). For the SIDA case see Provine, "Courts in the Political Process of France," 228.

36. See Pier Paolo Giglioli, "Political Corruption and the Media: the Tangentopoli Affair," *International Social Science Journal* 149 (1996): 381.

37. The judicial associations have begun to play a role at the European level. We can mention here MEDEL (*Magistrats Européens pour Démocratie et la Liberté*), an international association of "progressive" magistrates, which advocates the creation of an "European judicial space" and the adoption of the "Italian model."

38. For this phenomenon, see Tate and Vallinder, *The Global Expansion of Judicial Power;* and Bonaventura Sousa Santos, *Os Tribunais nas sociedades contemporaneas* (Lisbon: Afrontamento, 1996), 20.

7

Autonomy versus Accountability

The German Judiciary

DONALD P. KOMMERS

Introduction

In an essay on courts and the rule of law in the Federal Republic of Germany (FRG), Edward Blankenburg recently wrote: "The [German] judiciary has become a separate institution emphasizing autonomy from politics at the same time that it has gained considerable political power."[1] He supports this assertion by referring to the "tight control" Land (state) ministries of justice wield over legal education, judicial recruitment, and the promotion of judges; the high number of professional judges relative to the population; a highly specialized court system; civil litigation rates that are among the highest in the world; and a mode of judicial review that "binds public decision makers to the letter of the law." What distinguishes this system at the end of the day, he concludes, is that "the legal profession in Germany emphasizes professional autonomy rather than democratic legitimation."[2] The author's message: judicial autonomy in Germany has been maintained at the cost of democracy.

This chapter examines judicial independence in Germany. In doing so, it tries to assess the integrity of Blankenburg's thesis. The relationship, however, between judicial autonomy, accountability, and independence is complex. Germany's legal system equates judicial independence with an institutionally autonomous judiciary. Institutional autonomy is a requirement of judicial independence. As some critics have alleged, however, this very autonomy threatens judicial independence in the face of a court system dominated by career judges drawn from a narrow slice of society and known more for their passivity than for their creativity. Accountability, however, also endangers independence, if, as in the former German

Democratic Republic (GDR), judges are beholden to their political superiors. But, again, as in the FRG, critics (such as Blankenburg) find that judges who function in an autonomous environment are often insufficiently accountable to the political democracy they are sworn to uphold and foster.

A dramatic illustration of the tension between independence and accountability occurred in the well-known Deckert trial of 1994. Günter Deckert, a militant anti-Semite, publicly vilified Germany's Jews for their claims about the Holocaust. A Mannheim criminal court found Deckert guilty of fomenting racial hatred under the applicable statute, but it let him off with a light sentence, because in the court's view, he was an "upright citizen" and "a good family man."[3] The author of the opinion — Judge Rainer Orlet — was impressed with Deckert's long years of dedicated political activity and the fact that he conscientiously (albeit mistakenly) believed in his anti-Jewish campaign, one prompted, the court seemed to suggest, by the defendant's understandable impatience with continued Jewish demands for compensation fifty years after World War II.

Were it not for these morally obtuse comments about Deckert's character and Jewish claims in an otherwise able opinion, it is unlikely the case would have exploded into a major public scandal. The hostility of the public reaction, and even opposition to Deckert within the judiciary itself, was meant to bring the judges to account for their alleged mistakes and indiscretions. The parliamentary reaction took the form of the "Auschwitz Lie" statute explicitly banning the denial of the Holocaust.[4] Most German commentators appeared to agree that the new statute was a justifiable rebuke to the judiciary for its lack of democratic accountability.

There was less agreement, however, on the issue of judicial independence. The external attack on Mannheim's court was fierce. The media subjected Judge Orlet to a constant drumbeat of vilification and ridicule. Representatives in Baden-Württemberg's parliament threatened to impeach him if he were not internally disciplined even though his behavior could not plausibly be regarded as an impeachable offense under the state constitution.[5] In the prevailing view of some observers, the principle of judicial independence would be flagrantly violated if an otherwise able judge could be sacked for injudicious remarks in the course of an otherwise competent judicial work product, especially in response to outside political pressure.

The heat was equally intense within the trial court itself. Over the objection of two of their colleagues, the full court issued an apologetic press release "disassociating itself from any far-right or anti-Jewish views that might have been conveyed by the judicial opinion." But in the same breath, the court "deplored all attacks on the principle of judicial independence."[6] The court then announced, amid rumors of internal dissent, that Judge Orlet was to be reassigned to another panel of the trial court. Meanwhile, he had taken a temporary sick leave from his official duties, yet the court insisted that his "illness" had nothing to do with the Deckert opinion.[7]

Judge Orlet returned to the court in the face of renewed threats of impeachment and the refusal of the court's lay judges to sit with him. The sorry scene ended shortly thereafter with Orlet's early retirement from the judiciary, one that appears to have been "forced" by internal as well as external pressure. Was the principle of judicial independence violated by these events and reactions? Many German lawyers and judges thought so. Indeed, by its relentless attacks on the judge's character, the press itself may have contributed to the erosion of the principle. Or did the press play a constructive role in making the judiciary accountable to Germany's political democracy? The question is worthy of serious reflection.

As the Deckert controversy demonstrates, judicial independence is taken seriously in Germany. It is a major linchpin of Germany's written constitution. It is equally entrenched in Germany's legal culture, so much so that any political attack on the judiciary is likely to be seen as an assault on the rule of law itself. Even a recent North-Rhine Westphalia proposal to combine the Justice and Interior ministries into a single administrative unit drew the fire of the state's leading judges. "The independence of judges must be defended" against any such interference with the Justice Ministry's governance over the judiciary, wrote Gero Debusmann, president of Hamm's State Court of Appeal in an open letter signed by twenty-three of his colleagues.[8] Political commentators and critical legal scholars, however, interpreted these reactions as defiant attempts to preserve the privileges of a judicial elite unresponsive to public needs and political democracy. Rolf Lamprecht, a columnist for *Der Spiegel*, Germany's leading news magazine, advanced this view in a popular book on the myth of judicial independence.[9] Again, we are faced with the question of what judicial independence means in Germany's legal culture.

In delving more deeply into this issue, we need to consider (1) the idea and nature of the German Rechtsstaat (constitutional state), (2) the structure and composition of the judiciary, and (3) the system of training and recruiting judges. The analysis here focuses heavily on the four "critical points of control" discussed by Peter Russell in the opening chapter. Each control point, as he rightly notes, affects the autonomy or independence of the judiciary. Germany's legal system pays meticulous attention to each control point in an effort to insulate judges against external and internal pressures that might compromise their independence.

Historical and Political Background:
The Judiciary and the Rechtsstaat

The judiciary is the backbone of the German Rechtsstaat, loosely translated as "a state based on the rule of law." The traditional Rechtsstaat, which has not always been associated with liberal democracy,[10] evolved into a form of juridical positivism based on the supremacy of statutory law (*Gesetz*). Its crowning achievement was the establishment of a unified court system staffed by highly trained, university-educated judges, selected on the basis of merit and vested with guarantees of life tenure and a fixed income. This system—the one still prevailing today—traces its birth to the Organization of Courts Act, enacted in 1877, six years after Germany's unification.[11] Besides creating a uniform court system, the act provided for uniform appellate procedures, uniform rules of judicial administration, and a uniform system for educating and training judges.

What stamped the judicial system with the indelible mark of a Rechtsstaat was its association with the principles of the rule of law *and* state sovereignty. In the prevailing jurisprudence of the German Empire (1871–1918), the state represented a supreme and indivisible unity—a *potestas suprema*-subject to no power other than law itself. The judiciary was an integral part of this system. Although judges were part of the civil service, legislation sought to secure their independence from monarchical control as well as from their administrative superiors. In short, the Rechtsstaat sought to protect judges against extraneous influences, both internal and external. Under the laws of Imperial Germany, for example, judges could not be removed from office, transferred, or retired for any reason having to do with their performance as judges.[12] The Rechtsstaat, in short, bound the state and its agents to law. By law, however, Germans meant those general laws laid down by the sovereign legislature, the state's ultimate authority and the highest expression of its will. Accordingly, the role of courts was one of applying these laws as written, a task that required, above all, an independent judiciary. Judicial independence in this sense implied the presence of a mind-set that virtually required judges to insulate themselves from forces, ideas, or even notions of justice located outside the formal structure of the legal system.

In emphasizing the supremacy of law and the importance of an independent judiciary, the Rechtsstaat embraced an important principle of constitutionalism, namely, equal justice *under law*. This tradition extended into the Weimar Republic, except that now the Rechtsstaat was associated with the principle of popular democracy. Law was regarded even then largely as a command issued by the sovereign power, the predominant organ of which was the popularly elected legislature (Reichstag). In the democratic Rechtsstaat, an independent judiciary was as essential as ever, not only to enforce the general norms of *private* law (civil and criminal) but also, and equally important, to ensure the proper and equal enforcement of *public* law. This sharp distinction between public and private law manifested itself, before and after the Weimar Republic, in the structure of the judiciary, a brief description of which will yield a fuller appreciation of judicial structure in the contemporary Germany.

The judicial system established in 1877 embraced ordinary courts of civil and criminal jurisdiction as well as a variety of specialized public law tribunals. This system was carried over and expanded in the Weimar Republic, which at the highest appellate levels witnessed the creation of several national courts. These included the Reichsgerichtshof (National Supreme Court), Reichsverwaltungsgericht (National Administrative Court), Reichsarbeitshof (National Labor Court), Reichsfinanzhof (National Finance Court), and the Staatsgerichtshof (Constitutional Court). Each of these courts, however, was quite limited in its jurisdiction. In any event, Germany would retain, develop, and streamline this system of public law courts in the years following World War II.[13]

Before proceeding to a discussion of judicial independence in the Federal Republic, a final remark on the traditional Rechtsstaat may be warranted. The pre-1933 Rechtsstaat was indifferent to the state's political organization or the particular government of the day. As the experience of the Weimar Republic showed, judges could harbor antidemocratic instincts while insisting on their independence and remaining faithful to the letter of the law.[14] Weimar's experience also showed that the formal Rechtsstaat was as important as any political constitution. Indeed, the legal positivism that prevailed in Germany at the time placed ordinary law on the same level as the constitution. All this changed with the adoption of the 1949 constitution, known as the Basic Law. The new constitutional order continued to herald the traditional Rechtsstaat but yoked it to a constitutional democracy bound, in the words of Article 20, by both "law and *justice*" (emphasis added).[15] In addition, the Basic Law subjected the judiciary as well as the legislature to the higher law of the constitution. The Basic Law defined itself as the supreme law of the land and created a special tribunal empowered to review the constitutionality of laws and other state actions.

Judicial Independence under the Basic Law

The principle of judicial independence is hammered into the Basic Law, reinforcing the equally entrenched doctrine of separation of powers. Article 20 (2) underscores the judiciary's organizational autonomy by requiring that "all public authority . . . shall be exercised by specific legislative, executive, and judicial organs." Accordingly, just as executive and legislative officials may not simultaneously serve as judges, the latter are barred from exercising nonjudicial functions.[16] In addition, Article 92 unambiguously declares that "judicial power shall be vested in the judges" and "shall be exercised by the Federal Constitutional Court, the federal courts provided for in this Basic Law, and the courts of the *Länder* [states]." This guarantee of institutional independence finds additional pillars of support in two clauses of Article 101. First, it bans special or extraordinary courts, a command that would exclude, for example, the creation of special courts to deal with sex offenders or drug dealers. The prohibition would also bar the establishment of what are called federal legislative courts in the United States. Second, it forbids the removal of any person from the jurisdiction of his or her lawful judge, effectively barring legislatures as well as judicial authorities from arbitrarily shifting cases, once allocated under a court's case distribution plan, from one judge to another. Article 97 (1), finally, pounds these principles home even further by commanding that "judges shall be independent and subject only to the law," a provision designed to secure the so-called substantive (*sachliche*) independence of judges. Paragraph 2 of the same article guarantees a judge's independence within the judiciary, a principle that may have been violated in the Deckert case.

These principles of judicial autonomy were embedded and amplified in the German Judges Act of 1961.[17] In addition to its provisions on judicial independence, the act includes 113 sections dealing with the qualifications, duties, tenure, and discipline of both federal and state judges. Its sections on judicial independence (sections 25–37), which implement the constitutional guarantees mentioned in the previous section, seek mainly to preserve a judge's personal autonomy within the judiciary. For example, judges may be transferred to other judicial offices without their consent only if their salaries remain undiminished and only pursuant to a judicial decision. These rules apply to discharges or transfers in disciplinary proceedings or in the interest of improved judicial administration. (As noted later, a different procedure applies to federal judges.) They do not apply if a judge is reassigned or removed pursuant to the reorganization of courts or judicial districts. Any such restructuring, however, must be authorized by statute and carried out by the cabinet official entrusted by law with its execution. Judges affected by such measures must be retained on full pay and reassigned, if at all possible, to a judicial office of the same rank, salary, and pension rights.

By granting judges an independent legal status outside of and apart from the civil service, the Judges Act constituted a defining moment in the history of the German judiciary. Judges were no longer classified as servants of the state, as are civil servants, and they would now enjoy more autonomy than under any previous national constitution. Judges would be subject to supervision, as are civil servants, but any internal judicial administrative decision or even a formal judicial proceeding that interferes with their personal independence is subject to further judicial scrutiny. Any disciplinary measure resulting from alleged incompetence, neglect of duty, or misbehavior on the bench is ultimately appealable to the Disciplinary Chamber (Dienstgercht des Bundes) of the Federal Supreme Court (Bundesgerichtshof).[18] Occasionally, these cases even reach the Federal Constitutional Court. One important decision involved an admittedly stubborn and uncooperative trial court judge who found his docket virtually empty under his court's case assignment plan. Over the objection that such a plan is an exclusively internal matter of judicial administration, the Constitutional Court ruled in a sharply worded decision that the court below had violated the judge's independence within the meaning of Article 97 (1) of the Basic Law.[19]

Despite these decisions upholding judicial independence, German law permits judges to join political parties and to speak out on political issues. Judges aspiring to higher judicial office may even find it to their advantage to join a political party, especially one of the two major parties, namely, the Social Democratic Party (SPD) or the Christian Democratic Union (CDU). Moreover, judges may hold office in a political party or other organization with political objectives. They may even serve on a city council. Heinrich Maul, a judge of the Federal Supreme Court, was recently identified as the Social Democratic chairperson of Karlsruhe's city council,[20] a fact reported without comment within a larger story on the city's municipal election. From an American perspective, the holding of a leadership position on a city council—a position of party leadership no less—by a judge would offend the principle of incompatibility. The rule, however, that judges may not simultaneously occupy legislative or executive positions does not apply to local councils that exercise quasi-legislative and quasi-executive powers.

Even as they are permitted to engage in political party activity, judges are required in their off-the-bench behavior to conduct themselves in a manner that will not compromise their independence on the bench. Since judges, like civil servants, represent "the whole people," they are required as a matter of legal formality to remain politically neutral. It is difficult, however, to reconcile such neutrality with active membership in a political party or with active support of partisan measures. According to the leading commentary on the Judges Act, a judge violates the principle of neutrality only when he divulges his political views in a highly partisan and provocative manner or advances his political aims by means other than substantive argumentation (*sachliche Darlegung*).[21] But is it possible to draw a bright line between "partisan" and "substantive" argumentation?

The Federal Administrative Court tried to do so in a decision involving the presiding judge of a Land court and thirty-four other judges (and prosecutors) who published a signed letter in a daily newspaper, the *Lübecker Nachrichten*), strongly opposing the stationing of American cruise missiles on German soil.[22] Their judicial superiors accused them of failing to exercise the restraint necessary to maintain public confidence in their independence. They were then warned to cease and desist from publishing any further letters or advertisements of this kind. The judges protested in a petition to the Federal Administrative Court, claiming that the warning not only conflicted with the terms of the Judges Act but also violated their constitutional right to freedom of speech. The Administrative Court rejected both arguments, claiming that in the circumstances of the present case, the judges offended the principle of judicial independence by appealing to the public *as judges*, thus failing to distinguish properly between their political and judicial roles.[23]

Political roles of any kind by judges would be regarded as highly improper in countries such as England, Canada, or the United States. Conversely, from a German perspective, disbarring judges from such activity would interfere with precious political rights enjoyed by other citizens and deprive them of full participation in the life of the very democracy they have sworn to uphold under the Basic Law. Another perspective might be suggested: Germany's guildlike system for training and recruiting judges produces a huge bureaucracy of nonpolitical judicial technocrats. Critics often allege that these judges are wedded to a legal formalism that makes them insensitive to social reality. Permitting them to join political parties and associated groups may help to expose career judges to the values, needs, and problems of the community as a whole, perhaps producing as a consequence a better balance between autonomy and accountability. As we shall see, party membership plays virtually no role in staffing the lower and intermediate levels of the judiciary. It takes on some importance, however, in staffing the highest positions in the state judiciary, particularly the presidents (i.e., chief judges) and vice presidents of the various courts as well as those presiding judges who chair collegial panels within the higher courts. Party membership is crucially important at the federal level where politically balanced staffing is the norm. This contrasts with the process of selection in the United States, where all appointees to the federal bench tend to be members of the president's party.

In some respects, however, the Basic Law does not go as far as the U.S. Constitution does in protecting the judiciary against the legislature. Judges, for example, could lose their positions as a consequence of court reorganization. Relatedly, the legislature regulates judicial tenure. Career judges are required by law to retire at the age of sixty-five. Finally, under the incompatibility provisions of the Judges Act, federal and state judges may not simultaneously serve in legislative or executive positions. But they are permitted to run for political office, in which case they may be granted an unpaid leave of absence for the purpose of campaigning during the last two months before an election, a practice that would not be tolerated in the United States. If elected to the national or a state parliament, however, or appointed to a post in the executive branch, the judge is required to give up his or her judicial post.

The most publicized event in recent years concerning a judge who stood for political office involved no less than Roman Herzog, president of the Federal Constitutional Court. In early 1994 he informed the Christian Democratic Party of his willingness to stand as its candidate for federal president, a decision on his part that invited a challenge to his participation in a pending constitutional case. Over the objection that he had compromised his independence, the Federal Constitutional Court ruled (in his absence) that merely agreeing to be a candidate for a political party was not in present circumstances a legitimate basis for believing that President Herzog could not exercise an impartial judgment.[24] After his nomination, as the law provides, he took a leave of absence from his judicial duties. He retained his post until his election as federal president in late 1994, at which time he was legally required to resign. Had he lost the election, he would have been able to resume his post as president of the Constitutional Court.

Exceptional instances of political involvement by federal judges such as Roman Herzog should not darken one's view of judicial independence in Germany. The ruling norm of judicial behavior prompts judges to refrain from such involvement. Most German judges would describe themselves as politically neutral and accountable only to the law, an orientation that conforms to a deeply entrenched conception of the judicial role as one where judges decide cases exclusively on the basis of preestablished rules. Judicial realists know, however, that every judge, German or American, harbors personal or political views likely to inform his or her judicial decisions. According to some estimates, about one-third of all lower-court judges in Germany are members of a political party. Yet judicial independence is in part a function of accountability; within the judiciary, judges can be called to account for their obvious biases either through disciplinary procedures or the process of appellate review.

Court Organization

Germany has a decentralized system of state and federal courts marked by their subject-matter specialization, collegial character, and unified appeals structure. In the FRG's federal system of government, all lower and intermediate courts of appeal are state (Land) courts, whereas all courts of final appeal are federal tribunals. Federal law specifies the basic organization and jurisdiction of state courts,[25] but their administration and staffing, including the training of judges, is under the control of the Länder. Within the framework of federal law, the Länder remain free to regulate the organization, number, and procedures of their courts.

Except for courts of minor jurisdiction, all trial courts are collegial tribunals. Most operate in three-judge panels. In addition to the regular courts, which handle ordinary civil and criminal cases, the system features four sets of autonomous courts hierarchically organized and entrusted with the exercise of specialized jurisdiction. Apart from constitutional courts, these include administrative, labor, social, and finance courts. The high federal courts cap these respective judicial hierarchies. Germany's integrated appeals system, in which cases begin in state courts and end in federal appellate courts, causes few problems, because almost all statutory law is federal law.

Table 7.1 includes a list of federal and state courts and the number of judges staffing them as of December 31, 1996.[26] The regular courts of ordinary jurisdiction exemplify the basic structure of the court system. Local courts (Amtsgerichte), ordinarily presided over by a single judge, line the bottom of the judicial pyramid. District courts, however, are collegial tribunals organized into civil, criminal, family, juvenile, and commercial panels. Bochum's district court is typical: headed by a president and vice president, the court consists of 103 judges, who sit in panels of three.

The state courts of appeal (Oberlandesgerichte) within the regular judiciary hear appeals on matters of law and fact—except in those instances where review is restricted to law—from lower courts. Most of the Länder have one such tribunal. In Sachsen-Anhalt, for example, the court consists of a president, vice president, and fifteen judges, five of whom preside over three-judge panels called senates. The Federal Supreme Court (Bundesgerichtshof), the court of last resort in civil and criminal matters, has 122 judges who sit in five-judge senates. The court as a whole consists of twelve civil senates, five criminal senates, and seven additional senates specializing in particular subject areas. The court's president is responsible for internal judicial administration. In nonjudicial matters, he is subject to the supervisory authority of the federal minister of justice.

The specialized courts of public law are similarly structured, except that most of them are organized at fewer levels than the regular courts. Reflecting their huge caseloads, only administrative courts are organized at three levels within the various Länder. Labor and social courts operate within a two-tiered structure (local and district courts), whereas the finance courts function only at the district court level. Although the rules may vary from state to state, nearly all of these courts sit in panels consisting of professional judges and lay judges, usually one of the former and two of the latter, each of whom enjoys an equal voice and vote in the disposition of cases. The highest court of appeal in each of these areas is, respectively, the Federal Administrative Court, Federal Labor Court, Federal Social Court, and Federal Finance Court. Like the Federal Supreme Court, these

TABLE 7.1

The German Judiciary

Land Courts	Judges	Federal Courts	Judges
Regular	16,338	Supreme Court	22
Administrative	2,506	Administrative Court	67
Social	1,141	Social Court	41
Labor	1,077	Labor Court	34
Finance	550	Finance Court	60
Constitutional	91	Constitutional Court	16
Total	21,703		340

Source: Statistisches Jahrbuch für die Bundesrepublik Deutschland 1997 (Wiesbaden: Statistischen Bundesamt, 1997), 364.

tribunals are headed by a president and are divided into senates of five judges each. The Federal Labor and Social Courts also include lay judges. The Federal Constitutional Court (Bundesverfassungsgericht) is the highest court of review for constitutional cases.

The Federal Constitutional Court occupies a special place in Germany's constitutional order. Unlike other federal courts, it is not a part of the regular judiciary. Statutorily defined as a "federal court of justice independent of all other constitutional organs," it enjoys equal rank with the Federal Parliament (Bundestag), Federal Council (Bundesrat), federal president, and the federal government (chancellor and cabinet). Other federal high courts are subject to the administrative and financial supervision of the Federal Justice Ministry. As the "supreme guardian of the Basic Law, the Constitutional Court is accountable to no other institution or branch of government. Constitutional and statutory provisions reinforce the court's autonomy and independence. For one thing, the court prepares its own budget, which requires the approval of the Bundesrat and not, as with other federal tribunals, the Ministry of Justice; for another, all of its powers and wide-ranging jurisdiction are laid down in the Basic Law itself.

Over the last fifty years, finally, the court has evolved into one of the most powerful and authoritative institutions in Germany's governmental system.[27] It has struck down untold numbers of laws, both federal and state. And while legislators have decried many of its decisions, they have seldom, if ever, failed to comply with its judgments. In fact, the parliament often legislates with one eye on the court's jurisprudential views, so much so that the "judicialization" of politics has become a common lament among the court's critics.[28]

The Constitutional Court's independence, however, like that of the U.S. Supreme Court, could be compromised by parliament's control over its organization and the allocation of its constitutionally prescribed jurisdiction. Parliament has chosen to divide the Constitutional Court into two senates—the first and the second—equal in power but exercising mutually exclusive jurisdiction. Each senate speaks in the name of the court as a whole, and the justices of one panel may not exchange places with those of the other except when, "in a particularly urgent case," a quorum is lacking in one senate, in which case a judge of the other senate may be chosen by lot to meet the quorum. (Any other arrangement would conceivably violate the constitutional provision barring the removal of persons from "the jurisdiction of their lawful judge.") The division of jurisdiction between the senates is specified by law, and if the political complexion of one senate is different from the other, parliament could shift authority over a given issue from one senate to another in the hope of influencing judicial outcomes.[29]

As for the scope of the judicial system as a whole, finally, we might note that Germany, with one-third the population of the United States, has nearly three times as many judges. Huge caseloads and a judge-dominated system of civil and criminal procedure helps to account for the FRG's large number of judges. Moreover, Germany is one of the world's most litigious societies. In 1995, 3.4 million cases were filed in trial courts of ordinary jurisdiction, not to mention 1.5 million cases carried over from the previous year. Over 1.2 million additional cases were docketed in the specialized public law courts. The right to sue is taken seriously in Germany, and suing is relatively inexpensive. Indeed, the tradition of the Rechtsstaat is reflected in the constitutional right of any person to resort to the courts when that person believes his or her rights have been violated by public authority. Individual Germans have been particularly willing to file complaints with the Federal Constitutional Court. By 1997 the court had received and acted on 107,890 complaints in defense of personal *constitutional* rights, arguably one sign of popular trust in the court's independence.

Training and Selection of Judges

Legal education in Germany is extensively regulated by national law, and it is designed to produce standardized jurists who meet the qualifications for judicial office. The system is divided into two phases: an intensive and largely prescribed course of university studies lasting three and a half years, followed by at least two years of preparatory training. A major state examination, consisting of written and oral parts, follows each of these stages. State justice ministries, assisted by university law faculties, prepare and administer the first examination. On passing it, students may proceed to the preparatory, or practical, stage of their training. During this phase, trainees serve for prescribed periods of time (usually three months or longer) as apprentices, respectively, in a civil court of ordinary jurisdiction, a criminal court or prosecutor's office, an administrative agency, and a private law office. In the year or more that remains of the *training* period, depending on supplementary state requirements, students may train in courts or agencies of their own choosing. The entire preparatory period is organized and managed by state justice ministries. Finally, any student wishing to advance into the judiciary must pass the second state examination with high honors. The examination is prepared, conducted, and graded by committees made up of judges, senior civil servants, and law professors.[30]

This system of legal education produces highly trained legal professionals, but it has been severely criticized for its length, its narrow focus on codes and statutes, and its tendency to produce jurists with civil service mentalities. The traditional university law curriculum and the preparatory period's emphasis on judicial training, these critics allege, ignore the social and economic complexities of modern society and disassociate law from the social sciences and other disciplines. In the 1970s, some Land governments tried to break down the two-stage system of legal education and to diversify the law school curriculum, but these efforts foundered on the opposition of law school faculties, ministries of justice, and the post-1982 conservative government in Bonn. At its sixty-second annual meeting in 1998, the Association of German Jurists also opposed any major overhaul in the system of legal education.[31]

Recruitment of State and Local Judges

As for recruiting new career judges at the state level, the process is as meritocratic as the system of legal training itself.[32] (Fewer than 50 percent of all law students complete the two-stage program of study.) Trainees become full jurists when they pass the second state examination. Now they are qualified to enter the judiciary or any other branch of the legal profession, including the civil service. In choosing the judiciary, candidates usually file an application with the appropriate ministry in a given state. Competition is open, but the standard of admission is extremely high. Unless candidates achieve a high score on their second state examination, they have little chance of success, regardless of their political orientation.

State ministries, and the Justice Ministry in particular, play a central role in selecting new judges, as they do in promoting tenured judges. In some states, they are assisted by judicial selection committees comprised of legislative and executive officials as well as tenured judges and private attorneys. When social and labor court judges are to be selected, these committees may include representatives of labor and management. Depending on the particular state, appointments to the judiciary may be subject to cabinet approval. Not all states use the committee system or require cabinet approval, however, in which instance the key figure in selecting new judges is ordinarily the minister in charge of the court being staffed. The vetting at this stage appears to involve little or no political screening. It is possible that a largely self-initiated candidacy produces judges with certain mind-sets or predispositions. One occasionally hears, for example, that labor and social court judges tend to be more liberal than their colleagues on other courts, but in the absence of empirical studies of judicial attitudes, such generalizations must be viewed with caution.

Successful applicants for the judiciary are initially appointed as probationary judges. To broaden their experience, they may be appointed initially to a prosecutor's office or to a position in the legal department of the Justice Ministry, a practice that would by barred by the American doctrine of separation of powers at least at the federal level. More often, they begin the probationary period with a judicial appointment, usually in a lower trial court, in which capacity they decide cases like any other judge and with the same guarantees of judicial independence. They also participate in seminars with senior judges. The probationary period lasts three years, during which trainees are subject to continuous evaluation. If they survive this period, and most do, they are rewarded with lifetime tenure with all the accompanying benefits and prestige that accompanies the status of a career judge. As already suggested, party or ideological considerations—apart from proven loyalty to the spirit and letter of the Basic Law—do not appear to play a significant role at this stage of the selection process.

Promotion to the high state appellate bench is also based on merit and is followed by intense screening within the judicial establishment and the Justice Ministry. In one five-state study, the investigator found that all of these judges had significant trial court experience, often at both the district and circuit levels, although in some states, these judges also had backgrounds in prosecutorial office or in the Justice Ministry or both.[33] Political considerations do play a role, however, in the promotion of tenured judges to leading positions in the state judiciary, whether at the trial or appellate level. Competence remains the standard in selecting presidents, vice presidents, and presiding judges of panels in the various courts, but nearly all commentators agree that judges promoted to these positions of leadership are likely to mirror, to some extent, the political orientation of the ministry or government choosing them.

What we do know from studies of the judiciary is that the overwhelming majority of career judges are disproportionately the sons and daughters of university graduates and civil servants.[34] Very few trace their origin to working-class families. Judges, like civil servants, also rank high in Germany's status structure. To this extent, the selection system produces a judiciary unrepresentative of the population. But whether these background and status factors make the judiciary any less accountable politically or less representative of community values than, say, the U.S. judiciary, is a difficult question. German judges enjoy a high measure of public trust, esteem that seems related to the general belief that judges are nonpolitical agents of the state, who apply existing rules of law impartially in the interest of the common good. That judges constitute a professional elite largely invisible to the public reinforces the notion of an Olympian judiciary bound to and by the law.

Legal critics have greeted this view of the judiciary—and its vaunted independence—with devastating scorn. They have faulted judges variously for their arrogance, their conservatism, their passivity, their insularity, and even their lack of social consciousness. They have sought to explode, as a leading columnist recently put it, the "myth of judicial independence."[35] There is little empirical data, however, to justify the views of the judiciary's most outspoken critics. Usually, they rely on impressions derived from such unpopular decisions as the Deckert case.

Indeed, the notion of judicial independence is often used as a political weapon. Judges, of course, behave like judges when they defend their independence in the face of hostile, and even legitimate, criticism. Reform-minded critics, however, find judges lacking in independence if they are too conservative, too unimaginative, too deferential to legislators, or too unwilling to make new law. But would judicial independence be better served in the presence of liberal, imaginative, and creative judges? Some critics seem to think so. Others, taking aim at Germany's twenty thousand-person-plus court system, portray the judiciary as a bureaucracy that inhibits independence as well as accountability. "The more judges we have," one commentator is quoted as saying, "the fewer will be the number of really independent judges,"[36] as if to suggest that judicial independence is a function of numbers. One of Germany's angriest judicial critics, finally, finds that judges who are entirely unengaged politically promote a mythical neutrality that actually undermines judicial independence. It suffices to remark that the inconsistency of these reproofs adds little clarity to our understanding of judicial independence.

The charge that the bulk of German judges are insular, noncreative, and bureaucratically oriented (and thus not as independent as they might be) confronts other realities. After all, Germany's contemporary judges are the products of their society and are immersed in its culture. Whatever may have been the character of the German judiciary in the early decades of the federal republic, most of today's judges are relatively young, sophisticated, and democratic. There is no reason to believe they are any more or less diverse politically, socially, or religiously than Germany's official elite. Moreover, judgeships are presently occupied by an increasing number of women. In 1963 the judiciary was a male bastion; women occupied only 4 percent of all judgeships. By 1996 the proportion of women was 27 per-cent, while no less than 47.7 percent of all probationary judges were women.[37] In this respect, at least, the judiciary is beginning to reflect the balance of the sexes in the larger society.

Recruitment of Federal Judges

A different system of recruitment prevails in the federal high courts, as would be expected in the light of their preeminent importance in the realm of public policy. Judges of these highest courts of appeal must have all the qualifications for judicial office and have reached the age of thirty-five. Conversely, the minimum age of Federal Constitutional Court judges is forty years; as for tenure, they are elected for a single nonrenewable term of twelve years but in any case must retire when they reach the age of sixty-eight. All other judges remain in office until sixty-five years of age. Finally, merit seems as important at the federal level as in the state judici-ary, but here politics plays a major role. However impressive the creden-tials of federal judicial candidates, they pass through a demanding filter designed to achieve some measure of political balance on the nation's highest courts, for which reason federal judges are more diversified in so-cial background than those of the regular state judiciary.[38]

The Basic Law itself specifies the mode of selection. For the highest courts other than the Federal Constitutional Court, judges are "selected jointly by the appropriate Federal Minister and a selection committee composed of the appropriate Land ministries and an equal number of members elected by the *Bundestag*." Thus, a vacant judgeship on the Fed-eral Supreme Court would be filled by a committee made up of the sixteen state justice ministers and an equal number of parliamentary representa-tives, whose partisan coloring would be proportionate to the numerical strength of each political party in the Bundestag. If the Federal Labor Court were involved, the committee's composition would vary accord-ingly. Still, its members would be almost exclusively legislators, because the ministry officials are also members of their respective parliaments, a mechanism that accords a measure of democratic legitimacy to the selec-tion of federal judges. The local and national political interests represented on the committee ensure that judgeships will be distributed proportion-ately on the basis of geographical origin and party affiliation. Yet, as Clark reports, professional qualifications and previous judicial experience remain important, because "a candidate's state examination grade and performance reports must be good."[39] Whatever the order of priority among these three factors—that is, geographical origin, party affiliation, and professional qualifications—federal judicial recruits are secure in the knowledge that their independence enjoys the support of both law and the constitution.

One of Germany's most respected public lawyers, however, recently deplored what he regards as the increasing influence of "party cartels" (Kartellparteien) over the process of judicial selection. Screening judges mainly for their political credentials, he charged, produces a federal bench staffed by party loyalists instead of neutral agents of the state, thus posing a serious threat to the judiciary's independence. The feature article in which these concerns were raised drew a sharp line, as does German constitutional theory, between political parties and the organs of the state.[40] This theory holds that political parties overstep their constitutional roles of influencing public opinion and organizing the government when they identify themselves with the apparatus of the state itself, particularly the judiciary and the civil service. Still, it would be difficult to show that American federal judges, nearly all of whom are members of or in sympathy with the party of the president who appoints them, are any more or less independent than Germany's federal judges.

Political parties play their most prominent role in selecting the justices of the Federal Constitutional Court.[41] The Basic Law places their selection in the hands of the Federal Parliament (Bundestag) and the Council of State Governments (Bundesrat), with each house electing one half the justices on each of the two senates. Party control of the recruitment process, however, seemed less threatening to judicial independence than parliament's control over the number and tenure of the court's members. Each of the court's two senates originally consisted of twelve justices, four of whom were elected from the federal judiciary and given lifetime tenure (i.e., until the compulsory retirement age of sixty-eight). The remaining eight justices of each senate were appointed for eight-year terms with the possibility of reelection.

Early on, the government tried to reduce the court's membership amid speculation that Chancellor Konrad Adenauer and his cabinet wanted to get rid of several justices up for reelection in 1956, all of whom were believed to have had doubts about the constitutionality of German rearmament.[42] The effort failed. By 1963 the court's total membership had been slashed from twenty-four to sixteen justices, but this result seemed dictated less by politics than by the need for administrative and adjudicative efficiency. At least no justice lost his seat in midterm as a result of the cutback. In 1970, finally, and largely to allay any suspicion that legislators would play politics with judicial tenure, parliament amended the Constitutional Court Act to limit all justices to a single nonrenewable term of twelve years. Moreover, the new rule had no adverse consequences for already-sitting justices. Federal judges elected for life were permitted to retain their seats until retirement, while those whose eight-year terms expired after 1970 were invariably reelected to a single twelve-year term.

The single twelve-year term of office was thought to be an effective way of balancing the principles of judicial independence and accountability. As noted, however, political parties would control the balance. Under the Federal Constitutional Court Act, the Bundestag elects its quota of justices indirectly through a twelve-person judicial selection committee. Party leaders choose the committee at the outset of each parliamentary term, and its party representation is proportionate to each party's strength in the full house. The Bundesrat, however, votes as a whole. A two-thirds vote in each house is required to elect a justice, so no candidate can be elected over the objection of the major opposition party.

As a consequence of the two-thirds rule, the recruitment process has turned into a highly collaborative exercise between the ruling coalition and main opposition parties in both houses. The settled practice of allowing each party to fill specified seats on the Constitutional Court actually began with the original appointment of twenty-four justices in 1951.[43] Since then, the court's two senates have been divided almost evenly between Christian and Social Democrats. Two justices in each senate are nominally neutral—that is, they are not members of a political party—but they too are nominated respectively by the SPD and the CDU/CSU. (The "neutrals" tend to be law professors.) When ruling in coalition with the small Free Democratic Party (FDP), a perennial partner in coalition governments, the main partner in the coalition may occasionally yield one of "its" seats to a member of that party. This bartering, in turn, overlaps with intraparty negotiations. Christian Democrats can no more ignore the legitimate claims of their Catholic and Protestant constituencies, or the federal interests of Bavaria's CSU, than Social Democrats can ignore the claims of their left and right wings. This mode of selection imitates the politics of consensus that governs so many other aspects of German public life. It results in a politically balanced tribunal and vests it with a large measure of democratic legitimacy.

Yet the politicization of the appointment process has invited strong criticism from commentators troubled by its implications for judicial independence.[44] It is doubtful, however, whether Germany's way of filling seats on its highest court threatens judicial independence any more or less than the constitutionally prescribed method of appointing the members of the U.S. Supreme Court. This also holds for confirmation hearings in the U.S. Senate. Any public fixation in Germany on how a judicial nominee might vote in a particular case or in a wide range of cases would be seen as a potential threat to the independence of that nominee. Similarly, the passionate partisanship displayed before the Judiciary Committee, often accompanied by threats of retaliation against senators who vote the wrong way, would be regarded as an interference with the independence of those entrusted with the duty of confirming or rejecting a judicial nominee. In addition, the public exposure of every facet of a judicial nominee's life and personality would be regarded as an egregious invasion of his or her privacy.

German law prohibits legislators from holding open hearings on judicial nominees.[45] Indeed, the ban has been imposed in the interest of independence and accountability. The American habit of allowing interest groups to testify openly for or against a presidential nominee, with all that this implies in terms of outside pressure on the Senate, is to obliterate the distinction between law and politics (in the German view) and to destroy the "myth" of the court's neutrality. The United States separates the appointing authority from the advise and consent power, whereas the Germans confer the whole appointing power on parliament. But parliamentary election by no means grants to any single group or political party decisive control over the selection process.

The special twelve-member electoral committee in the Bundestag consists of each party's most distinguished legal experts, while as noted earlier, party representation on the committee is proportionate to each political party's strength in the house as a whole. It is possible to argue that a similar result takes place in the U.S. Senate when its rejection of a judicial nominee forces the president to name another candidate more acceptable politically to a Senate majority. The point of these remarks, however, is not that one system is superior to the other, but that the German method is no more or less harmful to the principle of judicial independence than the method by which Americans choose their Supreme Court justices.

Conclusion

This essay began with references to Edward Blankenburg's recent study of the German judiciary. He observed that Germany's judiciary emphasizes professional autonomy over accountability. In the light of the present study, Blankenburg's conclusion needs to be qualified. Professional autonomy is clearly a central feature of Germany's judicial establishment. It is also one of its great merits, because judicial independence is rooted in the judiciary's autonomy. Judicial accountability in Germany has not been sacrificed to judicial autonomy. The former, however, may be said to be in tension with the latter, as it probably is and must be in most constitutional democracies. Judicial accountability in Germany can certainly be compared favorably to that of these other democracies. This is certainly true of Germany's highest and most respected tribunal, the Federal Constitutional Court, a tribunal whose democratic legitimacy is well founded in the parliamentary selection of its members and in their limited nonrenewable terms of office. The Federal Constitutional Court may, as Blankenburg suggests, follow a mode of judicial review that "binds public decision makers to the letter of the law," but a *constitutional* democracy could surely do much worse.

Notes

1. Erhard Blankenburg, "Changes in Political Regimes and Continuity of the Rule of Law in Germany," in Herbert Jacob et al., *Courts, Law, and Politics in Comparative Perspective* (New Haven, Conn.: Yale Univ. Press, 1996), 249.

2. Ibid.

3. Decision of 22 June 1994, Landgericht Mannheim (6. Grossen Strafkammer), *Neue Juristische Wochenschrift* 249 (1994).

4. *Strafgesetzbuch* (as amended, 28 October 1994), sec. 130 (3).

5. Rudolf Wasserman, "Richterklage im Fall Orlet?" *Neue Juristische Wochenshrift* 48 (1995): 303.

6. Statement of Landgericht Mannheim (typewritten and signed by Dr. Deichfuss, the court's press secretary), 15 August 1994.

7. *Der Spiegel* 42 (1994): 26.

8. *Süddeutsche Zeitung,* 27 and 28 June 1998, p. 5.

9. Rolf Lamprecht, *Vom Mythos der Unabhängigkeit* (Baden- Baden: Nomos Verlagsgesellschaft, 1996), 40.

10. The best short treatment of the history of the concept of the Rechtsstaat is Ernst-Wolfgang Böckenförde, "Entstehung und Wandel des Rechtsstaatsbegriffes," in *Festschrift für Adolf Arndt* (Frankfurt am Main: Europäische Verlagsanstaalt, 1969), 53–76.

11. Gerichtsverfassungsgesetz (hereinafter cited as GVG), 27 January 1877, *Reichsgesetzblatt,* 77.

12. See Georg Meyer and Gerhard Anschütz, *Lehrbuch des Deutschen Staatsrecht,* 17th ed. (Munich and Leipzig: Verlag von Duncker & Humblot, 1919), 723–36.

13. For a discussion of these national courts and their jurisdiction during the time of the Weimar Republic, see Johannes Mattern, *Principles of the Constitutional Jurisprudence of the German National Republic* (Baltimore: The Johns Hopkins Press, 1928), 562–613.

14. These antidemocratic instincts are often cited as a major reason for the judiciary's submission to the Nazi dictatorship. Commentators have also blamed the

judiciary's capitulation to Nazism to the triumph of legal positivism and the attendant failure of judges to coalesce around any notion of substantive justice outside
law. On this point see Eberhard Schmidt, *Gesetz und Richter: Wert und Unwert des Pos-
itivismus* (Karlsruhe: C. F. Müller Verlag, 1952) and Hubert Schorn *Der Richter im Dritten Reich* (Frankfurt am Main: Vittorio Klostermann, 1959), 26–32. For the most
comprehensive treatment of judicial administration during the Nazi period, see
Lothar Gruchmann, *Justiz im Dritten Reich 1933–1940* (Munich: R. Oldenbourg Verlag,
1988). See also Richard L. Miller, *Nazi Justiz* (Westport, Conn.: Praeger, 1995) and Ingo
Müller, *Hitler's Justice* (Cambridge: Harvard Univ. Press, 1990). On how lawyers and
the private bar succumbed to Nazism, see Kenneth F. Ledford, *From General Estate to
Special Interest 1878–1933* (Cambridge: Cambridge Univ. Press, 1996).

15. Grundgesetz [Basic Law] (hereafter cited as GG), art. 20 (3).

16. This is not an ironclad rule, however. The Federal Constitutional Court has permitted local government officials to serve as judges in private disputes in very limited circumstances. For a discussion of this and several other related constitutional
decisions, see David P. Currie, *The Constitution of the Federal Republic of Germany*
(Chicago: Univ. of Chicago Press, 1994), 153–62.

17. Deutsches Richtergesetz (German Judges Act), 8 September 1961, *Bundesgesetzblatt,* Part I, 1665. The following discussion relies on the 1993 version of this statute.
It also relies heavily on Günther Schmidt-Räntsch and Jürgen Schmidt-Räntsch,
Deutsches Richtergesetz Kommentar (Munich: C. H. Beck'sche Verlagsbuchhandlung,
1995).

18. The work of this chamber is substantial and important in the defense of judicial
independence. See Helmut Grimm, *Richterliche Unabhängigkeit und Die Diestaufsicht in
der Rechtsprechung der Bundesgerichtshof* (Cologne and Berlin: Carl Heymens Verlag,
1972).

19. See 17 *Entscheidungen des Bundesverwaltungsgerichts* (hereafter cited as BverfGe
252 (1964).

20. *Stuttgarter Zeitung,* 21 July 1998, p. 6.

21. Schmidt-Räntsch, *Richtergesetz,* 534–35, 540–41.

22. The letter claimed, among other things, that the presence of such missiles in
Germany would be unconstitutional in the absence of a law expressly authorizing
their installation. They also claimed that the missiles would endanger the lives of
German citizens and thus violate their constitutional right to life and bodily integrity
secured by Article 2 (2) of the Basic Law. The text of the letter is reproduced in the
court's decision. See 78 BverfGe 217 (1988).

23. Ibid., 222–23.

24. 89 BVerfGE 359 (1994). When a judge's impartiality is challenged in a pending
case, he is required to furnish his colleagues with a written statement of reasons in
defense of his participation. In the challenged judge's absence, they are then required
to rule on the motion to exclude in a published opinion. See Bundesverfassungs-
gerichtsgesetz (Federal Constitutional Court Act), 12 March 1951, as amended up to
11 August 1993 (*Bundesgesetzblatt* I, 1493), section 19.

25. Gerichtsverfassungsgesetz (Judiciary Act, hereafter cited as GVG), as enacted in the version of 9 May 1975, *Bundesgesetzblatt,* I, 1077.

26. A more recent statistical overview records only minor variations on these figures. See *Deutsche Richter Zeitung 76* (1998): 84. The table does not include the Federal Patent Court. This tribunal, which resides in Munich, consists of 146 judges who preside over twenty-eight panels. Appeals from their decisions may be taken to the Federal Supreme Court.

27. See Donald P. Kommers, "The Federal Constitutional Court in the German Political System," *Comparative Political Studies* 26 (1994): 470–91.

28. See Christine Landfried, "The Judicialization of Politics in Germany," *International Political Science Review* 15 (1994): 113.

29. The first senate's foot-dragging in the Communist Party Case triggered rumors that the Adenauer government would try to pass a law transferring its jurisdiction over petitions to declare political parties unconstitutional to the second senate, which was thought to be more favorable to the government. See Donald P. Kommers , *Judicial Politics in West Germany* (Beverly Hills, Calif.: Sage Publications, Inc., 1976), 190.

30. See Alfred Rinken, *Einführung in das juristische Studium,* 3d ed. (Munich: C. H. Beck'sche Verlagsbuchhandlung, 1996), 1–11. See also David S. Clark, "The Selection and Accountability of Judges in West Germany: Implementation of a Rechtsstaat," *Southern California Law Review* 61 (1988): 1802.

31. *Frankfurter Allgemeine Zeitung,* 26 September 1998, p. 4.

32. As David S. Clark has written, "The principal aim in Germany is to find and to promote the best legal talent available for the bench, which Germans believe can be accomplished by mediating the role of politics in the process." "Selection and Accountability," 1801.

33. Daniel J. Meador, "German Appellate Judges: Career Patterns and American-English Comparisons," *Judicature* 67 (1983): 23.

34. Dietrich Ruerschemeyer's finding that "40 to 45 percent of all German lawyers have grown up in families of *Beamten* [civil servants]" is a pattern that by recent estimates applies also to the judges. See *Lawyers and Their Society: A Comparative Study of the Legal Profession in Germany and the United States* (Cambridge: Harvard Univ. Press, 1973), 40.

35. See Lamprecht, *Vom Mythos,* 20–37.

36. Ibid., 30.

37. Rinken, *Einführung,* 51.

38. See Meador, "German Appellate Judges," 25. See also Glen N. Schram, "The Recruitment of Judges for the West German Federal Courts," *American Journal of Comparative Law* 21 (1973): 691; and Johann Feest, "Die Bundesrichter," in *Beiträge zur Analyse der deutschen Oberschicht* (Tübingen, Germany: Wolfgang Zopf, 1964), 134–49.

39. Clark, "Selection and Accountability," 1825.

40. Jochen A. Frowein, "Parteien und Verfassungsstaat," *Frankfurter Allgemeine Zeitung* (Feuilleton Section), 13 September 1996, p. 44.

41. See Donald P. Kommers, *The Federal Constitutional Court* (Washington, D.C.: American Institute for Contemporary German Studies, Johns Hopkins Univ., German Issues 14, 1994).

42. See Kommers, *Judicial Politics*, 135.

43. See Ibid., 120–28, for a discussion of the process surrounding the selection of the court's first twenty-four justices.

44. See generally Wilhelm Karl Geck, *Wahl und Amtsrecht des Bundesverfassungsgerichts* (Baden-Baden, Germany: Nomos Verlagsgesellschaft, 1987); Werner Billing, *Das Problem der Richterwahl zum Bundesverfassungsgericht* (Berlin: Duncker & Humblot, 1969); and Klaus Stern, "Gedanken zum Wahlverfahren für Bundesverfassungsrichter," in Wilfried Fiedler and Georg Ress, *Verfassungsrecht und Völkerrecht* (Berlin: Carl Heymanns Verlag KG, 1989), 885–96.

45. The Federal Constitutional Court Act provides that the special judicial selection committee of the Bundestag charged with electing one-half of the court's sixteen members shall conduct its proceedings behind closed doors. In addition, Article 6, paragraph 4, of the act requires committee members "to keep secret the personal circumstances of candidates made known to them as a result of their committee activities." The proceedings in the Bundesrat (the "upper" house in which the various German states are corporately represented), entrusted with electing the other eight justices, are also held behind closed doors.

8

Judicial Independence in England

A Loss of Innocence

ROBERT STEVENS

In England the concept of judicial independence, an integral part of the separation of powers, is an inchoate one, developed without much concern for the theoretical issues Peter Russell sets out at the beginning of this volume. One might have thought that, since many of the early ideas about the separation of powers developed in England, the concept of judicial independence might be articulately analyzed in the legal literature there. Far from it. In modern Britain, the concept of the separation of powers is cloudy and the notion of the independence of the judiciary remains primarily a term of constitutional rhetoric. Certainly its penumbra, and perhaps even its core, are vague. No general theory exists, although in practice, the English have developed surprisingly effective informal systems for the separation of powers. The political culture provides protections for the independence of the judiciary, which are missing in the law.

It was these very issues—judicial independence, the significance of judicial views, the role of judges in cases with a significant political element—that appeared to reach their climax in Britain as the country reached the millennium. It is true that, for the previous forty years, the courts had been directed or the judges had drifted back into those policy areas they had largely left or had been excluded from by the time of World War I. In the 1950s, it was competition law, the 1960s saw a formalized change to *stare decisis,* the 1970s saw the renewed incursion into labor law, the renewal of judicial review of administrative acts, and the arrival of the European Union (EU). The 1980s confirmed an increasingly creative approach to the common law, while the early 1990s provided a much wider approach to statutory interpretation.[1]

England Reexamines the Role of the Judiciary

The arrival of the New Labour government in May 1997 set off a series of events that would bring the legal culture to a point where a serious re-analysis of the role of the judiciary in public law was inevitable. The background ranged from plans for reform of the House of Lords and proportional representation for the House of Commons to the incorporation of the European Convention on Human Rights and devolution for Scotland and Wales. As the Human Rights Act became law, the chorus grew louder, suggesting that having unelected judges interpreting a far-reaching statute would pose a serious question of democratic legitimacy. The implications were widespread. Could judges still be chosen in the secretive way that had produced generations of judges whose elegant work in private law was much admired and had helped make London the major center for international commercial work? Would the new political burdens put on the judiciary in public law cases make it possible to continue to ignore the personal views of the judges, something that, at least since World War I, the English had opted to do?

The government itself, in early 1999, raised some of the issues that verged on structural changes in the separation of powers. In establishing a Royal Commission on the House of Lords, the terms of reference called for the Commission (under Lord Wakeham) to decide whether the House of Lords should remain the final court of appeal, with judges performing both judicial and legislative roles. The commission was forbidden from considering the possibility of a separate constitutional court, as had been suggested by Lords Goodhart and Lester during the debates on devolution for Scotland, where the legislation called for cases arising out of devolution to be heard by the amorphous Judicial Committee of the Privy Council.[2]

These same debates had already allowed the Scottish judges to articulate the need for entrenching judicial independence in Scotland. Lord Mc-Clusky, one of the Scottish judges, made the point most powerfully, responding to the lord advocate's assertion that it was "beyond belief" that the new Scottish first minister would recommend to the assembly the dismissal of High Court judges without cause, arguing that it was a real possibility. It was such arguments that gave Lord Lester the opportunity to press for a constitutional judicial commission to select judges to sit in constitutional cases, in lieu of the casual membership of the Judicial Committee of the Privy Council. Such a commission would also be responsible for disciplining and dismissing judges.

Nothing, however, so galvanized the issues relating to the independence of the judiciary and the separation of powers as the Pinochet case. In October 1998, General Augusto Pinochet, the former dictator of Chile, was in the U.K. receiving medical attention, when a Spanish judge issued an international warrant for his arrest to face charges in Spain relating to crimes against humanity (torture, hostage taking, and murder). The case came before the House of Lords on appeal from a divisional court ruling that the general was protected from extradition by sovereign immunity. To the considerable surprise of the profession, the House of Lords, in a five-judge panel (Nicholls, Steyn, and Hoffmann forming the majority) were not prepared to allow immunity. The underlying assumption of the majority was that the international law of crimes against humanity took precedence over English law.[3]

As the press went to work, together with the politicians, led by Lady Thatcher, an admirer of General Pinochet, it emerged that Lord Hoffmann had failed to disclose in public that he was the chair of the charitable wing of Amnesty International and that his wife was employed full time by that same human rights organization. In an action unprecedented in modern times, although normal in the United States, there was a petition for re-hearing. Perhaps surprisingly, after two days of hearings, Lord Browne-Wilkinson, the presiding law lord, announced that the case would have to be reheard, with the trenchant observation that "Lord Hoffmann who did not disclose his links with Amnesty International was disqualified from sitting."[4] The law lords made it clear that Lord Hoffmann's interest was not a marginal one, and Lord Chancellor Irvine called for a register of judges' interests. The law lords were careful, however, to say there was no evidence of bias on the part of Lord Hoffman. But appearances were as bad as reality. A third Pinochet case in the Lords was inevitable.

By mid-January 1999 the case was before the House of Lords, this time being heard by seven law lords. The result was to uphold some but not other parts of the first House of Lords case. Some things were already clear. The bungling had caused acute embarrassment to a judiciary that likes to pride itself on the respect in which it is held in other countries. Moreover, however the new hearing comes out, it was a no-win situation for the formalistic traditions of English law. No events could have more obviously underlined the element of judicial creativity and the importance of personal views in the final appeal court.[5] No case had so sorely tested the concept of judicial independence.

The advertising of the creative role of the judiciary and the inevitable importance of personal views in such creativity was highly significant. Yet in a constitutional sense, the focus was turned sharply on judicial independence—even if commentators often missed that point—and on the role of a final appeal court. Those who might not be ready to endorse creation of a constitutional court could not fail to be embarrassed by the lottery that surrounded the panel system in the House of Lords. The link between the legislature and the final court of appeal came under fire. Even in England the separation of powers has some meaning, even if it is more political than legal.

The English Tradition

Such excitement, at least by the standards of English constitutional law, must raise the question of where these problems have been for the last seventy years. What do the English mean by the independence of the judiciary, and how does that fit into the English view of the separation of powers? The most obvious observation that emerges as these questions are asked is that the English analysis in political terms has its own character.

When it comes to talking about judicial independence as part of the separation of powers in England, it is clear the concept has been more obviously important as a piece of political rhetoric than as a series of legal concepts. It is rarely, if ever, defined.[6] It is generally asserted. Lord chancellors, who embody the judicial, executive, and legislative, will claim Britain does or does not have separation of powers, depending on the context. They never deny that judges are independent.

It is, however, assumed that such independence was settled by Locke, Hale, Montesquieu, and Blackstone.[7] In fact, Locke and Hale offer only rudimentary notions of judicial independence, and Montesquieu, writing of England, seemed to confuse judges with the jury. It was Blackstone who gave a modern focus to the separation of powers,[8] although his legal impact was appropriately greater in North America than in Britain. In England until the nineteenth century, the chief justice sometimes sat in the cabinet; the lord chancellor still does.

The protections of judicial independence in England, as Blackstone realized, are primarily political rather than legal. This is perhaps inevitable in a system of responsible government that merges the executive and the legislature. It is indeed a monument to the generous liberal temper of British politics that judicial independence has been so well respected in England. Such political protection has been all the more important and significant in the light of the overwhelming belief in and power of the sovereignty of Parliament. For much of modern British history, parliamentary sovereignty has allowed little breathing space to the substance rather than the form of judicial independence, yet the concept has survived relatively unscathed.

Independence of Individual Judges

It is acceptable, if not entirely accurate, to say that the judiciary in England is independent in the sense of independence of an individual judge. To take what are conventionally seen as the hallmarks of such independence—security of tenure, fiscal independence, impartiality, and freedom from executive pressure—at the core, there is little doubt that England qualifies under any reasonable standard of judicial independence with respect to individual judges. Even more than other countries, however, the English scene has to be examined historically, and, at least to some extent, sociologically.

Traditionally—and rightly—we look to the Act of Settlement of 1701 as the basis of judicial independence—for by that act judges were not to be dismissed without addresses by both houses of Parliament. That protection should be seen in the context of eighteenth century society—a period of rationality and right order. Judges were still best understood as part of the medieval King's Council. Many of the officers of state had lifetime appointments—the bishops, what we would now call civil servants, and holders of lesser offices. Like the parson and the squire, the judge was thought to hold the freehold of his office. The problem was that James II had attempted to replace judges and to intimidate bishops. Good governance—in the sense the Whig ascendancy understood it—would not tolerate such behavior. A modified form of impeachment was therefore introduced to protect the judiciary. At the same time, however, the Glorious Revolution and the Hanoverian Succession ensured that, with the executive and legislature effectively merged, the judges would be lions under the mace rather than lions under the throne. The contrast with the remarkable separation of powers at the Constitutional Convention in Philadelphia seventy-five years later could not have been greater.

The tenure of English judges since 1714 has been relatively peaceful. The closest that a judge has come to being dismissed after addresses by both houses was Mr. Justice Barrington—an Irish judge—for alleged bribery. The fact that there were so few ripples to disturb the peace of judicial independence over three hundred years is mainly a tribute to the staid quality of the English judiciary and the political process that has protected it. The advent of parliamentary supremacy, however, confirmed under George I and II and only marginally challenged under George III, meant a diminishing—and less controversial—role for the judges. Moreover, with the arrival of a reformed and more democratic House of Commons beginning in 1832, in which virtually all legitimate power resided, the creative role of the courts was limited by the political culture as well as the reforms engendered by utilitarianism.

Even so, a few caveats in the litany of praise for judicial protection and integrity should be inserted, even as the English courts became less politically important. Politics did enter in. Until 1905, a political background helped in appointment to the bench, and thereafter politics were not unimportant. Lord Trevethin, appointed lord chief justice in 1921 to keep the seat warm for Sir Gordon Hewart, was required to sign an undated letter of resignation by that devious prime minister, Lloyd George, when he was appointed. When the coalition government broke up in 1922, Trevethin read of his resignation in the *Times*.[9] Justice was, however, done. Hewart was not an admired chief justice, and ultimately he too was dismissed by a telephone call from 10 Downing Street—in 1940, when Winston Churchill, in the darkest days of the World War II, needed to find a berth for Viscount Caldecote, his less than effective dominions secretary.

In 1928 the first Lord Hailsham asked for Lord Atkinson's resignation as a law lord because the Canadian press said there were too may "old fogies" in the Privy Council and, as Atkinson reported, "I was the oldest of the old fogies."[10] Certainly, the introduction of a mandatory retirement age in 1959 helped, but the second Lord Hailsham, lord chancellor for Edward Heath and Margaret Thatcher, had to urge Lord Chief Justice Widgery and Lord Denning on their way. Judges also police their own. Early in 1998, Mr. Justice Harman of the Chancery Division, much criticized by the legal press for arrogance, felt obliged to resign after particularly damning condemnation of his casualness and tardiness by the Court of Appeal.

Protection from politicians and political winds is, however, significantly by tradition. One must also remember that the vast bulk of the full-time judiciary in England (now some seven hundred and fifty, including the backbone of the professional judiciary, some five hundred and fifty circuit judges) have no protection under the Act of Settlement, although they have limited protected status under other statutes, and the Lord Chancellor's Department handles dismissals with considerable natural justice. When thinking about security of tenure, we must also remember that the English increasingly use a probationary period before substantive appointment. The recorder and assistant recorder—both part-time appointments—are used as training grades, although they at least have term

appointments. Appreciably more obvious is the old system of commissioners and the more recent system of deputy high court judges. That is
patently a probation system—preparatory to appointment to the High
Court, with appointments on an ad hoc basis. For the man in the street,
such arrangements are an understandable and probably desirable
arrangement to protect the quality of a judiciary, which provides, through
the courts, an important social service. The constitutional purist, however,
would argue such probationary arrangements are inconsistent with the
Montreal Declaration on the Independence of the Judiciary.[11]

Judicial independence is, in traditional studies, also closely associated
with fiscal independence for the judges. There is, no doubt, an important
element of public interest in this. An inadequately paid judiciary will be
prone to temptation, and the convention that the government of the day
accepts the advice of the Senior Salaries Review Body seems to have ensured an adequate, if not opulent, salary. If we look back to the seventeenth and eighteenth centuries, however, the great offices of state,
including the judiciary, were an opportunity to accumulate wealth.
Judges, often from modest circumstances, not infrequently ended as significant landowners and members of the aristocracy. While judicial
salaries were low, judges received a multitude of fees from all stages of
litigation. They were free to sell the right to become "court officials"; for
instance, until well into the nineteenth century, the masterships (interlocu-
tory judges), themselves lucrative, fetched very significant sums.

The system was put on a more rational basis under the influence of the
utilitarians. High Court judges' salaries were set at £5,500 in 1825—an immense sum for those days—reduced to £5,000 in 1832, the year of the
Great Reform Act. Such salaries still enabled judges to compete in wealth
with the great landowners. Indeed, economic historians tell us that during
the nineteenth century, Britain's economic fortunes meant that £5,000 became worth more, not less. Yet when, in the 1870s, William Gladstone
talked of cutting salaries, he was greeted with cries of horror by the
judges, who refused to discuss his reforming Judicature Bill while the
threat existed. In the twentieth century, the judges may well have had
more cause for complaint about salaries—but that complaint is probably
best looked at under the collective aspect of judicial independence.

As already suggested, the English judges rank high on any international
table of impartiality, particularly with respect to individual litigants. In the
twentieth century, London strengthened its reputation as the center of
commercial litigation primarily because of the judicial reputation for integrity and technical competence. Impartiality can, however, be an
ephemeral concept, and we are all conscious that despite the efforts of

philosophers and psychologists, we still have only an amateur notion of what we mean by the concept. Winston Churchill, as a minister in a Liberal government at the turn of the nineteenth century, warned against allowing judges to decide cases where "different classes" were concerned,[12] while in the 1940s Aneurin Bevan refused to allow appeals to judges in National Health Service matters for fear of "judicial sabotage."[13]

As we seek to reconcile these concerns with the reputation for impartiality in the broader sense of values, we need to remember that other constraints are at work that help to justify the judicial reputation for impartiality. English judges operate in a highly formalized doctrinal system, with a strong belief in law as a series of objective rules, which can be enforced impartially. Artificial as these claims may be, intellectually, judges are traditionally thought to be both pushed toward objectivity and kept up to the mark by a functionally separate bar, which itself has a reputation for independence and impartiality. This is, at least, the accepted position, and it contains an important element of truth. The formality of English law, a relatively small bar, a divided profession and the orality of English courtroom procedure are normally said to keep a judge's prejudices and predispositions to a minimum, because they emphasize the apparently objective element in the formal legal system. (The sceptic might, however, say they underline the prejudices held by both bench and bar).[14] Where the judge has discretion, however, whether it be over sentencing, the interpretation of statutes, or restating the common law principles—the inevitably creative elements in the judicial process—the judges have more opportunity to express their views.

In the actual operation of the separation of powers in Britain, there is a working relationship between the branches of government that surprises Americans. The different branches of government interact constantly. The executive frequently calls on judges to conduct inquiries into highly charged political issues. Senior judges and ministers meet to discuss possible sources of conflict, and there are instances of powerful exchanges of view. During the Labour government of 1945–51, Lord Chancellor Jowitt wrote to Lord Goddard, the lord chief justice, whom he had appointed, to the effect that he sincerely hoped "that the judges will not be lenient to these bandits (who) carry arms (to) shoot at the police." Conversely, the attorney general (Shawcross) wrote to the chief justice complaining that the Court of Criminal Appeal had gone too far in restricting questions about how confessions had been obtained. The chief justice agreed and said he would raise the complaint with his fellow judges. Americans might well believe these to be examples of the executive inappropriately interfering with the judiciary, as President Franklin D. Roosevelt's relationship with

Mr. Justice Felix Frankfurter and President Lyndon Johnson's with Mr. Justice Abe Fortas have been regarded as suspect. In England, such relationships are seen as ensuring the smooth running of the system.

Such relationships exist within the acceptable levels of tolerance of the English concepts of separation of powers. They arguably reflect a more flexible—and not irrational—sense of balance of powers and functions. A more egregious example of executive interference is, however, one of the most recent. In the early 1970s, while the Industrial Relations Court under Sir John Donaldson felt free to resort to imprisonment to break the strike mentality in England, the Court of Appeal, under Lord Denning, as master of the rolls, thought that imprisonment was not an appropriate way to settle industrial disputes. Lord Chancellor Hailsham, direct as ever, was furious. He sent for Denning while he was presiding in the Court of Appeal. Denning refused to adjourn court to wait upon the head of the judiciary (and cabinet member). When they did meet, Hailsham accused Denning of deliberately directing certain cases to his court. (He after all assigned cases in the Court of Appeal.) Denning insisted he merely applied law to the facts.[15] There was, however, something rather unsatisfactory about the encounter, at least as far as the absence of executive influence over the judiciary is concerned. Lord Donaldson and Lord Hailsham continued to have encounters that questioned a formal separation of powers. It emerged in 1983 that Lord Donaldson, by then master of the rolls, had been consulted by civil servants on "how the judiciary could play a more constructive role in industrial relations." Lord Hailsham defended such meetings as normal.[16]

As Russell points out in his introductory essay, judicial independence on occasion has to defer to judicial accountability—although this is a balance that has never been definitively analyzed. To take the most extreme example, Lord Eldon's delays in the Chancery Court would not be acceptable in terms of judicial accountability today. No matter how strong judicial independence is, the situation is obviously a delicate one. When Lord Mackay, lord chancellor from 1987 to 1997, was faced with a situation, as he saw it, of inefficiency and considerable waste of public money in the Employment Appeals Tribunal, he required the High Court judge then serving as president to follow certain administrative procedures to clear the backlog of cases. The judge resigned from the bench rather than accept the directive. A debate in the House of Lords alleged a serious breach of judicial independence. (Mackay had apparently invited Wood to "consider his position.") The matter, however, petered out without any discussion of where independence ended and judicial accountability began.[17]

The conflict between independence and accountability will no doubt produce more disputes as the courts are increasingly expected to offer an improved social service to their clients or customers. Indeed, the so-called Woolf reforms, which are currently being implemented, will call on judges not only to control and monitor their cases more closely, but also to be business managers of litigation. With these changes, there will then have to be more effective administrative controls to ensure judicial accountability. There is always a chance that a cry of judicial independence might be used to attempt to undermine judicial accountability.

Although the line between individual and collective independence of the judiciary is artificial, it does help focus arguments. With respect to individual independence, while there not surprisingly are issues at the penumbra, England can claim an eminently respectable basis for the independence of individual judges. What then of the collective situation?

Judges as a Separate Branch of Government

In England, the judges are not a separate or coequal branch of government. While the assertion is sometimes made that judicial independence in the corporate sense exists, it exists primarily in the minds of judges and a few liberal politicians to be produced at convenient moments in political and constitutional debate. The concept of parliamentary sovereignty ensures that separate branches of government do not exist.

In England, the lord chancellor is the senior judge, a cabinet member, and frequently an active politician, as well as head of a significant executive department. The current lord chancellor, Lord Irvine, is appreciably more active in politics than were his recent predecessors. He chairs many constitutional committees emerging from the cabinet, ranging from political programs to constitutional issues, such as devolution and the Bill of Rights. His is an important voice in developing the political program of the party. He joins actively in political debates.

The Office of Lord Chancellor was pilloried by Gilbert and Sullivan as "the embodiment" of "all that is good and excellent." Conversely, the system was justified in 1943 by that powerful mandarin—and permanent secretary to the lord chancellor—Lord Schuster, who wrote of the "advantages which accrue to the Cabinet from the presence of a colleague who is not only of a high judicial reputation, but who can represent to them the view of the judiciary; to the legislature from the presence in it of one who is both a judge and a minister; and to the judiciary from the fact that its President is in close touch with current political affairs."[18] The Schuster statement is remarkably revealing both about the concept of the judicial role and the perception of judicial independence in England. It is the rationale for a system that reflects the immense power of parliamentary sovereignty in Britain. It justifies a system that has worked relatively smoothly in practice.

Enthusiasm for the status quo, inevitable as it may be while parliamentary sovereignty looms so large, has not been shared by reformers. In the 1870s, as part of the great utilitarian reform of the courts, the judges opposed the idea of a ministry of justice to handle the administrative powers being taken from the old court structure and insisted that power be exercised by the lord chancellor. Hence the establishment of the Lord Chancellor's Office (now Department) in 1880. The hope that the reformers had held in the 1870s for a ministry of justice did not, however, die. Lord Haldane, in the report of his Committee on the Machinery of Government in 1918 called for a ministry of justice—although he still saw the need for a more restricted office of lord chancellor. The chief justice of the 1920s and 1930s—Lord Hewart—was paranoid that a plan to establish such a ministry was under way.

There was talk of splitting the post of lord chancellor in the Labour government of 1964–70, but Harold Wilson's lord chancellor, Lord Gardiner, was a conservative in professional matters, and nothing happened. In the early 1990s, there was much talk by Liberal and Labour reformers that the office should be split, but there has been little evidence that this has had any support from Lord Irvine since his appointment in 1997. That has not prevented a segment of Labour backbenchers suggesting that greater separation of powers at the top is necessary.

The position of the lords of appeal in ordinary—the judges of the House of Lords who serve as the final court of appeal, also undermines any basic concept of separation of powers. In the 1870s, the intention of the reformers—Lords Cairns and Selborne—had been to end both the House of Lords and the Judicial Committee of the Privy Council as judicial bodies.[19] In place of these two would be an aggrandized Court of Appeal sitting in the new Law Courts to be built in the Strand. A group of Tory right-wingers, led by Sir William Charley, although aided more thoughtfully by Lord Salisbury, harassed Benjamin Disraeli's administration after 1873 to restore the appeal to the lords to "protect the dignity" of the House of Lords.

In theory, the law lords are supposed to speak only on legal matters. That has not always deterred some of them from participating in policy debates. Perhaps the most dramatic recent example came in the late 1980s, when Lord Mackay introduced Green Papers designed to make the courts and the profession more efficient and responsive to the needs of the public, primarily by introducing market reforms. The retired law lords behaved in a remarkable manner during the legislative debates. No less than three—Lords Elwyn-Jones, Donaldson, and Lane (then retiring as lord chief justice)—implied that the Conservative lord chancellor (Mackay) was guilty of Nazi tendencies and, of course, of violating the independence of the judiciary.

The debate scarcely enhanced the reputation of the law lords. It also failed to clarify the issue of whether the law lords really belonged in the upper house. Some critics thought their presence an anachronism. There clearly were some advantages to the existing arrangement, and it certainly attracted the support of some commentators. In 2000, the Royal Commission in the House of Lords blessed this arrangement, but many believe the *McGonnell* case in the European Court of Human Rights may herald the beginning of the end of the system.

Related to the issue of judicial independence is the method of choosing the judges. They are chosen, as they are in most other common law countries, by a politician—basically the lord chancellor. While the English like to say judicial appointments in their country are nonpolitical, or even that they are apolitical, (and there are, in fact, no former MPs currently serving as judges), Europeans find it difficult to comprehend how a system that leaves the final say for choosing most judges with an active politician—the lord chancellor, with appointments to the House of Lords and Court of Appeal made by the prime minister—can be an apolitical system. (Even the House of Commons Select Committee on Home Affairs has described the prime minister's involvement in senior judicial appointments as "nothing short of naked political control.")[20] While civil servants in the Lord Chancellor's Department are influential and the lord chancellor consults the judicial heads of divisions, each lord chancellor boasts that the decisions are his and has rejected the idea of a judicial appointments commission. The lord chancellor, Lord Irvine, at first embraced the idea and then "put it on a back burner" and abandoned it. Yet in a very real sense, the claims of the apolitical nature of the process are true. While the judiciary is chosen primarily from the English bar, it is possible to argue that success and reputation at the bar far outweigh other attributes.

Parliamentary sovereignty and the wide jurisdiction of the lord chancellor, together with the political appointment of judges by a politician and the dual roles of the law lords, make it difficult to have an institutional concept of judicial independence based on a notion of separate branches of government. That, however, has rarely discouraged the English judges from believing that there is such a concept as the independence of the judiciary in some kind of ethereal collective sense. As academics are inclined to see violations of academic freedom whenever they are faced with decisions they do not like, English judges tend to announce violations of judicial independence when events occur that they think undermine their dignity—and until recently, English judges were big on dignity.

In terms of judicial self-perception, the most significant claims of violations of judicial independence have been those relating to the fiscal independence of judges. The most spectacular example of this was during the economic crisis in the 1930s. In 1931 the National Recovery Act cut the salaries of public servants, and the Order in Council implementing it cut judicial salaries, even though they were paid out of the Consolidated Fund. The judges were outraged. While in Northern Ireland the judges were said to have stood and sung "God Save the King" when they heard about the cuts, as Lord Schuster noted, the "English judges are in a mood where they are far more likely to sing 'The Red Flag' than 'God Save the King'." The insurrection was undignified and, in the traditional English way, ended in a compromise. A bill was introduced saying that judges' salaries could not be cut (subject to appeal, as is all British legislation).

For all the rhetoric, judicial independence—at least for the judges as a class—is not a legal concept in England. At the same time, its rhetoric is politically important in a body politic without a written constitution, which relies on a congeries of statutes, delegated legislation, custom, and convention for making the system work. Politically, the rhetoric normally does maintain a semblance of the separation of powers.

The Future

The question is, should there be a "real" separation of powers and a more meaningful concept of judicial independence in England? It may be a good moment to be asking this question, since the Tony Blair administration is clearly committed to reform of the constitution. The reform of the House of Lords, devolution, and the Human Rights' Act provide the framework for rethinking the separation of powers. Adherence to the EU has accelerated the process of undermining parliamentary sovereignty. Nevertheless, to transform the constitution so that there is a more realistic separation of powers will require a significant rethinking of political philosophy and the abandonment of various fundamental conventions and myths that, in many ways, operate satisfactorily in practice.

There is little doubt that the role, power, and self-perception of the judiciary has changed over the last thirty years. Perhaps nothing changed the judges more than the long period of Conservative rule between 1979 and 1997. For the first decade, there was effectively no political opposition, for Labour was split and then drifted leftward and into the political wilderness. The decline in the concept of an opposition coincided with the realization of the declining importance of the House of Commons. Lord Hailsham caught the atmosphere with his phrase "elected dictatorship" to describe the relationship of legislature and executive. The government made laws; backbench MPs were cannon fodder. The declining independence of MPs, even the decreasing importance of question time, inevitably appeared to leave a vacuum, particularly with respect to controlling the executive. It was into that vacuum that the judges increasingly stepped, as they hinted they would help "remedy the democratic deficit.[21]

Skirmishing over powers tends to lead to conflict. The conflict between the judges and the Conservative government became most public in the battles between Lord Taylor, the late lord chief justice, and Michael Howard, the last Conservative home secretary, over penal policy.[22] The interesting question now is what will the impact of all this be following the 1997 Labour landslide. With a massive, and, at this stage, docile majority of Labour members in the House of Commons, and apparently a chronically weak opposition, will the judges once again feel they are faced with the task of keeping some sense of balance in the constitution? Or, the sceptic might even ask, do they feel more comfortable with New Labour than they felt with Old Conservative?

It would be wrong, however, to think of these developments as some sudden kind of judicial putsch. For thirty-five years, the atmosphere has made it inevitable that judges would have more influence in the day-to-day running of the constitution. In the 1950s, 1960s, and 1970s, Parliament, by legislation, in effect instructed the judges to return to matters relating to competition and labor relations. By the 1960s, the judges had moved to renew judicial review of administrative decisions. From the mid-1960s onward, the appeal judges have been more willing to reclaim their traditional role of pushing the boundaries of the common law forward. In a wide range of cases, they have opened up new areas of negligence,[23] instilled notions of *bona fides* and instrumentalism in contracts, and rationalized criminal law. They have been much more activist in their interpretation of statutes. In 1993 in *Pepper v. Hart*,[24] in a 4-1 decision (the dissenter being Lord Chancellor Mackay), the House of Lords allowed leg-islative debates, under certain circumstances, to be introduced in inter-preting statutes. The opportunities for judicial creativity in this area are only now being fully realized.

Britain's changing relationship with the remainder of Europe also had its impact on the English judges. When Edward Heath eventually negoti-ated Britain's entry into the EU, the judges found they were, de facto, making decisions about the constitutionality of British statutes. While Lord Mackay explained this away by saying that what the judges were doing was merely interpreting one British statute in the light of another (the implementing legislation of 1972), it did not seem an adequate expla-nation for those watching events unfold. When, in 1994, the House of Lords held that British legislation relating to part-time employees violated European directives and was therefore unenforceable—or more accurately, the directive was automatically enforceable[25]—the *Times* concluded that "Britain may now have, for the first time in its history, a constitutional court.[26] The courts had already suspended a British statute while the Euro-pean courts tested its validity.[27] It was certainly not business as usual, and the press, led by the Murdoch-owned *Times* and *Sun,* began to attack the "power grabs" of the "unelected," "elitist," and "liberal" judges.

Over these years, the English judges took a more aggressive role toward civil rights. Sitting as judges in the Judicial Committee of the Privy Coun-cil, they impeded the enforcement of the death penalty in West Indian Commonwealth countries on the ground that delay "would constitute in-human punishment.[28] Indeed, such decisions hastened the end of appeals from such countries to London. At the same time, Britain adhered to, but never incorporated, the European Convention on Human Rights. The leading judges, including the two most recent chief justices (Lords Taylor and Bingham), lobbied for its implementation, but in the meantime, the judges shadowed its provisions.

The New Labour government has passed legislation to make the con-vention an integral part of English law, effective in 2000. Interestingly, this development was initially opposed by the Right on the ground that it would politicize the judiciary and by the Old Left on the ground that the judges are not to be trusted because of their conservative instincts. In the new legislation, violations of the convention will not entitle the judges to strike down statutes, but they will be able to certify the viola-tion, and this could lead to fast-track legislative change. The compromise enshrines competing notions: on the one hand, the persistent strength of parliamentary sovereignty, and on the other hand, deference to judicial independence. Lord Irvine, while welcoming the new legislation, also admits that it represents a considerable transfer of power to the judges.[29]

While the judges are now more circumspect in their political statements than they were even three or four years ago, issues have been raised that cannot now be ignored. If judges are to be a "third force" in British politics—perhaps part of the trendy but ephemeral third way—there may have to be a clearer demarcation of the judicial role. Over the last few years, judges have been pushing further at the boundaries. The English like to think of their constitution as growing organically. The organic may have to give way to the planned.

The current Liberal/Labour Committee on the Constitution may well push more rigorous thinking. Two Liberal Democrat peers, Lords Goodhart and Lester, who were primarily responsible for the sections on human rights and the judiciary in the 1991 draft constitution of the Institute of Public Policy Research (IPPR), argued in the Lords, in 1998, for a new constitutional court to hear such matters as devolution. This court would have a permanent membership rather than the ad hoc (and unsatisfactory) panel system traditional in Britain. Under the IPPR draft constitution, as in the U.S. Constitution, there would be a much clearer distinction between the branches of government. The lord chancellor would serve only in his judicial role, with a minister of justice responsible for what was formerly the lord chancellor's department; the judges of the final court of appeal would cease to be legislators; and all judges would be chosen by a Judicial Appointments' Committee.

The IPPR's recommendation for the choosing of judges was a judicial appointments commission, heavily dominated by the judges. It is an area in which the English have great difficulty. There is an increasing consensus that allowing one politician in the cabinet to choose judges is unacceptable, although the cause received a setback during the lord chancellorship of James Mackay, because he was immensely successful and imaginative in his choice of judges. The problem remains: if the judges are not chosen by the lord chancellor, then by whom? The idea of the judges as a self-selecting oligarchy, inherent in the IPPR's draft constitution, was unattractive to the Committee on the Judiciary, established by Justice (the British branch of the International Commission of Jurists) in 1991. In its report, it proposed a committee composed of a balance of lawyers (but no more than two judges) and laymen to advise the lord chancellor on appointments. Justice's advice was rejected by Lord Mackay and has now apparently been abandoned by Lord Irvine. The dilemma of judicial selection, however, remains.

Conclusion

The British traditionally prefer experience to principle. The situation may have changed with the New Labour government. Unlike its predecessor, it is thought to have clear policies, and it is obviously activist and image conscious, yet the judges have not thus far shown a willingness to abandon an independent stance. Lord Bingham, the new lord chief justice, is concerned about mandatory life imprisonment for murder and—at a different level—about efforts by the government to require disclosure of Masonic links. At the same time, the government continues to hand political tasks to the judges. In addition to the Human Rights Act, the Judicial Committee of the Privy Council determines disputes arising from having a devolved Parliament in Scotland.

Despite the new political responsibilities and irrespective of the need, Britain will not suddenly embrace three clear branches of government. The growth will be organic and will constantly be delayed by the tradition of parliamentary sovereignty. The Hague suggestion of a parliamentary veto on judicial appointments has yet to become official Conservative policy and will not therefore necessarily be the policy of the next Conservative government. But the argument at least concedes that it is legitimate, in the new millennium, to question the politics of the judiciary. Some form of judicial appointments committee, albeit advisory, cannot be far away.

Three centuries of parliamentary sovereignty will not, however, be lightly abandoned. Proportional representation, devolution, reform of the House of Lords, and even the Freedom of Information Act will help change the political scene. Only the frustrating belief in muddling through will prevent a public acceptance of the declining importance of parliamentary sovereignty, a formalized separation of powers, and an entrenched concept of the independence of the judiciary.

Notes

1. See Robert Stevens, *The House of Lords: Its Parliamentary and Judicial Roles* (Oxford: Hart Publishing, 1999), 107.

2. See Scotland Bill debate, *Hansard,* House of Lords, 28 October 1998.

3. [1998] 4 All E R 897 (H.L.).

4. House of Lords, *Judicial Business: Consideration of the 11th Report from the Appeal Committee (Petition of Senator Augusto Pinochet Urgate)* (1998) H.L.J. No 41 (Q.L.). The case is reported *sub nom R. v Bow Street S.N. exp Pinochet* (No. 2) [1999] 1 All E.R. 577 (H.L.).

5. See David Robertson, *Judicial Discretion in the House of Lords* (Oxford: Oxford Univ. Press, 1998).

6. See Robert Stevens, *The Independence of the Judiciary* (Oxford: Clarendon Press, 1993), 4–6.

7. The literature on the theoretical underpinnings is remarkably sparse. But see M. J. C. Vile, *Constitutionalism and the Separation of Powers* (Oxford: Clarendon Press, 1967).

8. See William Blackstone, *Commentaries on the Laws of England* (London: Maxwell, 1869), 322.

9. Robert Jackson, *The Chief: Biography of Gordon Hewart: Lord Chief Justice of England, 1922–40* (London: Harrap, 1959),126–44.

10. R. F. V. Heuston, *Lives of the Lord Chancellors, 1885–1940* (Oxford: Clarendon Press, 1964), 604.

11. Kate Malleson, *The New Judiciary* (Aldershot: Dartmouth, 1999), chapter 5.

12. Otto Kahn-Freund, "Labour Law," in *Law and Opinion in England in the 20th Century* (London: Sweet and Maxwell, 1959), 232.

13. *Parliamentary Debates* (5th Ser) H. C. Vol. 425, col. 1983 (23 July 1946).

14. See Brian Abel-Smith and Robert Stevens, *In Search of Justice* (London: Heinemann, 1967), 253–54.

15. Geoffrey Lewis, *Lord Hailsham, A Life* (London: Jonathan Cape, 1997), 277.

16. David Pannick, *The Judges* (Oxford: Oxford Univ. Press), 184–6.

17. Malleson, *The New Judiciary*, 51–52.

18. Memorandum, 31 January, 1943, P. R. O., L. C. O. 2/3630.

19. Robert Stevens, *Law and Politics: The House of Lords as a Judicial Body, 1800–1976* (Chapel Hill, N.C.: Univ. of North Carolina Press, 1978), chap. 2.

20. House of Commons, Home Affairs Committee, *Judicial Appointments Procedure,* 1996, paragraph 126.

21. John Griffith, "Human Rights, Legal Wrongs," *New Statesman* 12 (31 July 1998).

22. See Joshua Rosenberg, *Trial of Strength: The Battle between the Ministers and Judges over Who Makes the Law,* (London: Richard Cohen Books, 1997).

23. Robertson, *Judicial Discretion in the House of Lords*, chap. 6.

24. [1993] AC. 593.

25. *R. v Secretary of State for Unemployment,* [1995] 1 AC. 1 (1994).

26. *London Times,* 5 March 1994.

27. *R. v Secretary for Transport, ex p Factortame* [1991] 1 A.C. 604; [1992] A.C. 85.

28. *Pratt v A-G for Jamaica,* [1994] 2 A.C. (P.C.).

29. *New Statesman,* 6 December 1996, p. 12.

9

Judicial Independence in Australia

JOHN M. WILLIAMS

Australian political debate has euphemistically been described as robust. Political, as well as personal attacks, have not been out of place in an arena where the fainthearted rarely set foot. Recent High Court decisions, the court itself, and the justices have been labeled:

> "bogus," "pusillanimous and evasive," guilty of "plunging Australia into the abyss," a "pathetic . . . self-appointed [group of] Kings and Queens," a group of "basket-weavers," "gripped . . . in a mania for progressivism," purveyors of "intellectual dishonesty," unaware of "its place," "adventurous," needing a "good behaviour bond," needing, on the contrary, a sentence to "life on the streets," an "unfaithful servant of the Constitution," "undermining democracy," a body "packed with feral judges," "a professional labor cartel."[1]

There were many more epithets of a like character, many stronger.

Despite the above, throughout its history the Australian judiciary, and especially the High Court of Australia, has been deft in maintaining a safe political distance from the storm. This has been achieved despite the High Court bringing down what have been described as implicitly "political" decisions.[2] For instance, in 1948 the High Court held that the Labor government's attempt to nationalize the banks was unconstitutional.[3] Likewise, the attempt by the Liberal government of Robert Menzies to ban the Communist Party in 1950 suffered a similar fate at the hands of the High Court.[4] Notwithstanding the political irritation these and other decisions caused their respective proponents,[5] their reception could be described as positively good humored when compared to the recent attacks on the High Court of Australia. As one judge noted, "in adopting a more active role the High Court [has] move[d] to the eye of the storm of public affairs."[6]

This chapter is divided into three sections. The first deals with the structure of the judiciary in Australia as well as with the judicial appointment and dismissal procedures. The second explores the role, rationale, and function of the judiciary. The final section concentrates on some of the challenges facing the judiciary and the importance that a theory of judicial independence has for Australia.

Constitutional Foundations of the Australian Judiciary

The federation of the Australian colonies in 1901 was a difficult and sometimes ponderous task for citizens and framers alike.[7] Indeed, Alfred Deakin, the second prime minister of Australia, described it as being achieved only after a "series of miracles."[8] Notwithstanding the difficulty of the process, the constitution was not so miraculous in its production. The framers were, to a large degree, limited by their own history and imagination. The bringing together of the jealous colonies necessitated a federal system. Almost immediately, the U.S. Constitution was to prove the most amenable to the Australian experience.[9] However, the framers were not "slavish" in their adoption of the American template.[10] In particular, the framers designed the High Court to be a general court of appeal from both state and federal jurisdictions. Further, the High Court was granted a wider original jurisdiction than its U.S. counterpart had been granted.

As a federal nation, the Australian judiciary is divided into its state and commonwealth components. At the pinnacle of the federal judicial hierarchy is the High Court, which consists of seven justices. Within the federal jurisdictions, there are other federal courts (including specialized courts such as the Family Court of Australia). The structure of the state jurisdictions are similar. Each state has a state supreme court. Below this level are district, or county, courts, and finally, magistrate, or local, courts. However, a unique aspect of the Australian system is the power of the parliament to invest state courts with federal jurisdiction.

Appointment and Dismissal of the Australian Judiciary

The appointment and dismissal of federal judges is set out in Section 72 of the constitution. That section states that:

The Justices of the High Court and of the other courts created by the Parliament—

(i.) Shall be appointed by the Governor-General in Council:

(ii.) Shall not be removed except by the Governor-General in Council, on an address from both Houses of the Parliament in the same session, praying for such removal on the ground of proved misbehaviour or incapacity:

(iii.) Shall receive such remuneration as the Parliament may fix; but the remuneration shall not be diminished during their continuance in office.

The appointment of a Justice of the High Court shall be for a term expiring upon his attaining the age of seventy years, and a person shall not be appointed as a Justice of the High Court if he has attained that age.

Thus the appointment of a federal judge is by the governor general in council, which is the executive of the government of the day. The dismissal procedure is outlined in Section 72 (ii), that is by the governor general in council, on an address of both houses in the same session on the grounds of "proved misbehaviour or incapacity." The retirement of judges at the age of seventy was mandated after the successful passage of a referendum in 1977.[11] Before this, tenure was for life.

Section 122 of the Commonwealth Constitution empowers the Commonwealth Parliament to "make laws for the government of any territory." The tenure of Australian Capital Territory[12] and Northern Territory judges has been considered by the High Court, and it has been determined that the commonwealth can create such courts without the need to observe the requirements of Section 72 of the Commonwealth Constitution.[13] The territorial governments have however passed legislation that seeks to regulate the appointment (and in the case of the Northern Territory, the removal) of territorial judges. Briefly, the situation in the Northern Territory resembles that of the commonwealth, and the Australian Capital Territory is similar to the position of the states. However, territorial arrangements are subject to overriding commonwealth legislation.

The organization of the state judiciary is found in the various state constitutions. A brief outline of the constitutional and legislative schemes is contained below.[14] In all the states, appointment is by the executive, and apart from the requirement that the person meets certain professional standards, there are no limitations on who may be selected. In relation to their removal, there is some variation between the states. In Victoria,

Western Australia, and South Australia, the commission of a judge of the Supreme Court shall remain in force during their "good behaviour." This is subject to removal by the governor, who may remove any judge upon an address to Parliament.

In Queensland, judges of the Supreme Court also hold their commission subject to "their good behaviour." However, their removal may be by one of two methods: The first is by the governor in council acting alone on grounds other than those contained in the acts (that is other than a lack of good behavior). The second is by the governor in council upon an address to the Legislative Assembly on grounds not limited to "good behaviour."[15]

In Tasmania, it is unlawful to "suspend" or "amove" any judge of the Supreme Court "unless upon the address of both houses of parliament." However, there are no grounds prescribed.

After the passage of the Constitutional (Amendment) Act of 1992, the tenure of judicial officers in NSW is similar to that in the commonwealth. Thus they hold office subject to "an address from both houses of Parliament in the same session, seeking removal on the ground of proved misbehaviour or incapacity."

Method of Judicial Selection and Appointment

The selection and appointment of judges in Australia, as has been noted above, is exclusively in the hands of the executive, which, in real terms, is the government of the day. At the commonwealth level, there is a statutory requirement under Section 6 of the High Court Act 1979 that states: "Where there is a vacancy in an office of Justice, the Attorney-General shall, before an appointment is made to the vacant office, consult with the Attorneys-General of the States in relation to the appointment." It is by no means clear what obligations are created by the need to "consult" the state attorneys general. In practice, it may amount to little more than a request to the state attorneys to nominate an individual for consideration by the commonwealth attorney general.

The appointment of High Court justices has been at the center of political debate. After a number of controversial High Court decisions, and with a change of government, there have been calls for the High Court to retreat from its perceived judicial activism to a more "traditional" role. One of the most vocal advocates of this has been the then-deputy prime minister, Tim Fischer, who has called for the appointment of "capital C conservatives" to the High Court.[16] These calls were made at a time when the membership of the court was changing because of retirements. Thus they were interpreted by many to be an indication on the part of some members of the government of a willingness to shape the ideology of the bench.

In addition to a debate over the ideological composition of the High Court, a question remains of the geographical makeup of the court. The High Court bench has traditionally come from NSW and Victoria, while two states (Tasmania and South Australia) are yet to have a High Court appointment. Lastly, the issues of gender and ethnic composition of the Australian judiciary remain. As then-High Court Justice Lionel Murphy said in 1983, "When it comes to women judges we have not even reached the stage of tokenism."[17] That situation has improved on the High Court since Lionel Murphy spoke in 1983 but only by a factor of one: Justice Mary Gaudron was appointed in 1987. Many of these issues will be dealt with in greater detail below. However, it is enough to note that the current selection and appointment methods are in the hands of the federal government.

At the state level, the attorney general generally consults with interested parties such as the chief justice of the Supreme Court and the Bar Council. From these consultations, the attorney general makes a recommendation to the cabinet, which, in turn, recommends to the governor in council that a particular individual be appointed. As with the commonwealth appointments, much interest remains in the gender and socioeconomic backgrounds of the judiciary.

Testing Time for the Australian Judiciary

The role of the judiciary in a liberal democracy is often linked to two substantive functions. The first relates to the administration of justice and the critical role of the judge. As Shimon Shetreet notes, "The basic premise in a civilized society committed to social order and good government is that as a general rule self-help by force is excluded, and whoever has a claim and cannot resolve the dispute amicably must bring it before the courts, which try the claim and pass judgment."[18] Thus, for Shetreet and many others, the selection of the judge is critical to the ultimate quality of the judicial product. The judiciary has also been given responsibility for a more burdensome task: the safeguarding of the system of governance. In constitutional democracies such as Australia, the separation of powers and the rule of law have historically been associated with the protection of rights. As G. Winterton argued, in the Australian context, it can be conceived as an implied bill of rights.[19]

These twin aspirations of the judiciary, the administration of justice and the protection of rights, have renewed interest in Australia in the role and function of the third arm of government. The Australian Constitution, however, lacks a foundational mythology that is so integral to the history of other liberal democracies. Unlike the revolutionary moment of the United States or the rainbow optimism of the new South Africa, the Australian Constitution was not founded in adversity or struggle. Indeed, when encouraging the Tasmanian people to vote in favor of the constitutional bill in 1898, one enthusiast resorted to a plea that a vote for the constitution would mean the founding of "a great and glorious nation under the bright Southern Cross, and meat will be cheaper."[20] Yet within this wonderfully self-serving call to arms were deeper associations. The federation of the Australian colonies in 1901 was the completion of a sentimental union that had been imagined decades before. All Australians would, from that day forth, live under one commonwealth constitution "under the bright Southern Cross." Moreover, meat *would* be cheaper after the dismantling of the colonial customs barriers. This was one of the major practical reforms that came with federation. Thus the framers of the constitution harnessed imagination and practical politics.

However, one aspect of Australia's "myth" deficiency is a belief that ours is a practical constitution lacking theoretical underpinnings. While the framers may have been practical colonial politicians not given to theoretical pronouncements, their constitution does incorporate many theoretical assumptions. These assumptions are often lost in the immediacy of the constitutional text. Yet, as Cass Sunstein has noted when reflecting on the nature of constitutional agreements, what these agreements represent are "incomplete theorized convergence on an abstraction."[21] The Australian Constitution expressly incorporated many features associated with modern constitutional democracies, such as a written constitution, the separation of powers, constitutional guarantees, and federalism. Yet the functioning of these features of the constitution were left unexpressed by the framers. They were, in Sunstein's phrase, "incompletely theorized."

The task of adding theoretical flesh to the bare bones on the constitution has fallen primarily to the High Court of Australia. It is a task that some members of the High Court have often felt reluctant to undertake (or even to acknowledge). For instance, Justice Michael McHugh has argued that, in interpreting the constitution, its meaning "must be determined by the ordinary and natural meaning of the text" rather than by recourse to "some theory external to the Constitution itself."[22] Yet we know that the High Court has had to grapple with the meaning and operation of phrases and structures in the constitution that offer little by way of explanation from the text. For instance, the nature of the separation of judicial power from the other arms of government has been an exercise of unpacking theoretical precepts by the High Court since 1901.

One of the justifications for a theory of judicial independence in Australia is the lack of any theoretical transparency in the role and function of the courts (and in particularly the High Court) in relation to the constitution. It should be stressed that what is being advocated is not the development of a theory of interpretation (such as originalism or legalism). This is an entirely different task. Obviously, judges do not wish to be constrained by a single theory. Rather, the point is that theoretical development is an inescapable element in understanding the role and function of the judiciary.

Ironically, one explanation for the current tensions between the judiciary and the executive in Australia has been a move on the part of some members of the judiciary to articulate in greater detail their role and function. For instance, the former chief justice of the High Court, Sir Anthony Mason, has confirmed that courts have "moved away from the declaratory theory and the doctrine of legalism to a species of legal realism."[23] Such openness about the nature of the judicial process has yet to take hold in the political arena, and statements like Mason's are seen as evidence of an activism that is said to be inappropriate for the judicial branch of government. As Justice Ronald Sackville, a judge of the Federal Court, stated in defense of the judiciary:

> It is fashionable in some quarters to express yearning for the days when judges did not make law but merely gave effect to pre-existing, albeit undiscovered, rules. Like so many simplistic slogans, this view of the judicial process—particularly the appellate process—is not merely incomplete, but wrong and harmful. The slogan is harmful because it can be and is employed to accuse the courts of exceeding their legitimate functions when, in truth, judicial law-making lies at the very heart of that function.[24]

This public theorizing about the role of the judiciary coincides with a quantum leap in the judicialization of politics. This worldwide phenomenon, while always a part of the judicial process in Australia, has recently placed the courts in the center of controversial social and political issues. In the 1990s Australia's High Court became the target of unprecedented attack by political leaders and interest groups after the Mabo (No. 2) and Wik decisions.[25] Both cases dealt with the native title rights of Aboriginal and Torres Strait Islanders and acknowledged, at common law, the continued existence of indigenous title over traditional lands. Increasingly, individuals and groups are demonstrating a willingness to litigate for social and political change rather than agitate for parliamentary redress. As such, the courts have found themselves embroiled further in political debates. This phenomena offers a further justification, if one were needed, for developing a theory of judicial independence.

As Peter Russell notes, the role of the judiciary in a well-functioning democracy calls for both action and restraint. A better understanding of the role of the judiciary is important in drawing the boundaries between the judiciary and the other arms of government.

A further justification for the development of theoretical explanations of judicial independence, like the previous point, has to do with the internationalization of legal norms. Just as rights are said to be universal, increasingly the nature of governance is assessed on the basis of international standards. This was emphasized by chief justices of Australia's States and Territory Courts in their *Declaration of Principles on Judicial Independence*, issued on 10 April 1997. In it, the chief justices committed themselves to the *Beijing Principles of Independence of the Judiciary*. In a public statement that accompanied the declaration, the then chief justice of the High Court, Gerard Brennan, stated that:

> The Declaration is a timely reminder of the constitutional reality that the Courts are an organ of government separate from, and independent of, the political organs. The Courts are an important element in the system of checks and balances that preserves our societies from a concentration of official power that might otherwise oppress the people and restrict their freedom under the law. The Courts are an organ of Government but they are not part of the Executive Government of that country. Political issues must be debated, political fortunes must wax and wane, political figures must come and go according to the popular will. That is the nature of a democracy. But the apolitical organ of government, the Courts, are there continually to extend the protection of the law equally to all who are subject to their jurisdiction: to the minority as well as the majority, the disadvantaged as well as the powerful, to the sinners as well as the saints, to the politically incorrect as well as those who proclaimed in order to benefit the Judges; it is proclaimed in order to guarantee a fair and impartial hearing and an unswerving obedience to the rule of law. That is the way in which our people secure their freedom under the law.[26]

Issues of Judicial Independence

In any discussion of judicial independence, it is essential to consider the influences to which the judges are exposed. These influences, as Russell notes, may be categorized in terms of the *sources* of dependency (both internal and external) and the *targets* of influence or control (the individual justice and the "corporate" institution). Any discussion of judicial independence must concern itself primarily with *undue* influence. Any attempt to insulate the judiciary from all possible influences would be impossible and, indeed, counterproductive. If the courts are required to reflect "community values," it would be of concern if they were cut off from public debate or academic comment.[27]

It is the external influences on the judiciary that are most accessible to analysis. The nature and extent of any internal "judicial culture" and its effect on individual members of the judiciary are difficult matters to identify or quantify. Indeed, some elements of "judicial culture" are required to buttress individual judges from undue external influences.

Attempts to Remove Judges

As was noted in the first section of this chapter, the structural guarantees for the judiciary in Australia are reasonably robust. The federal judiciary enjoys constitutional protection. The terms of their appointment and method of removal are clearly codified.

The closest that Australia has come to the removal of a High Court judge for "proved misbehaviour or incapacity" under Section 72 of the constitution was the case of Justice Lionel Murphy. Murphy, a former Labor attorney general in the Gough Whitlam government, was appointed in 1974 directly from Parliament. Murphy's reputation as a political reformer and radical were well established before his elevation to the bench. In short, "Murphy polarized people."[28] In 1984 allegations surfaced that Justice Murphy had attempted to pervert the course of justice by influencing the outcome of the trial of solicitor Morgan Ryan.[29] These allegations were aired at various Senate inquires, committal hearings, and, ultimately, at the trial of the judge. At his first trial, Murphy was convicted. He appealed against the conviction, was retried, and ultimately he was acquitted. These events prompted the Commonwealth Parliament to appoint three parliamentary commissioners in May 1986 to an inquiry into the conduct of Murphy and whether or not it could constitute "misconduct" within Section 72 of the constitution. The inquiry, constituted by three retired Supreme Court judges (Sir George Lush, Sir Richard

Blackburn, and Honorable Andrew Wells) took a wide view as to the meaning of "misconduct." As Sir George Lush states, "the word 'misbehaviour' in s[ection] 72 is used in its ordinary meaning, and not in the restricted sense of 'misconduct in office'. It is not confined, either, to conduct of a criminal nature."[30] Despite these conclusions, some debate remains as to whether the constitution uses the term in its broad or narrow sense. In the end, the announcement that Justice Murphy was dying of cancer ended the parliamentary pursuit.

The events of the Murphy case serve to highlight the inadequacy of the procedure dealing with the removal of a judge from office. As Sir Anthony Mason has argued, it would be preferable to establish a special complaints tribunal for resolution of these disputes rather than to create an ad hoc tribunal each time there is a controversy.

As for the state judiciary, there has been only one successful attempt to remove a Supreme Court judge from office. That was the case of a justice of the Supreme Court of Queensland, who was removed by the state governor in June 1989 after an address of the Legislative Council. As with the Murphy case, a commission of inquiry was established to report on the judge's conduct.[31] The commission found no misconduct in the judge's conduct of his judicial office. It did, however, make findings of fact as to the judge's taxation transactions and defamation actions. The Legislative Assembly used these findings as the basis of its address to the governor.

Finally, in New South Wales in 1998, there was an unsuccessful attempt to remove Justice Bruce from the Supreme Court on the grounds of "incapacity." The judge suffered from a number of medical conditions, including severe depression, which caused unreasonable delay in his handing down of judgments. A report was placed before the houses of the state parliament, but a motion seeking his removal was not carried.

Removal by Restructuring

In terms of the structural integrity of the judiciary in Australia, the most disturbing aspect in recent times has been the reorganization of courts and nonreappointment of judicial officers. The reorganization of courts and tribunals can no doubt be necessitated by a need to accommodate changing community requirements or aspirations. Some restructuring in Australia has also been necessitated by constitutional requirements.[32]

However, the Australian public has witnessed the reorganization of a number of courts and tribunals that calls into question the motives of the executive. These cases include the nonreappointment of Justice James Staples to the new Commonwealth Industrial Relations Commission, as well as of magistrates in NSW; the abolition of the Law Reform Commission and Administrative Appeals Tribunal; the abolition of the Accident Compensation Tribunal in Victoria; and the abolition of the Industrial Court and Workers' Compensation Board in South and Western Australia.

The failure to reappoint to the new body after the abolition of a court or tribunal challenges what Justice Michael Kirby has described as a convention respecting the tenure of judicial officers.[33] The practice being, as Anthony Mason states:

> (1) that the judge of the old court would be appointed to a new court created to replace the old court or to a court of the same status; (2) that if such an appointment were not available, the old court would not be abolished until its judges cease to hold office and in the meantime the judge would be entitled to the emoluments and entitlements of the old office, notwithstanding that the jurisdiction of the old court is transferred to the new court.[34]

In those areas where deep ideological division exists between the political parties (such as industrial relations), there has been a tendency to dismantle the legislative and policy prescriptions of the previous administration. In pursuit of such outcomes, judicial officers sometimes find themselves in the middle of policy revolutions. Clearly, there are strong democratic arguments for allowing governments to implement policies for which they were elected. Yet Australia has witnessed some restructuring of the judiciary that may have a more sinister explanation. That is, a government displeased with the performance or capacity of the judicial officer may have used the restructuring and nonreappointment as a means of ridding itself of a troublesome judge.

Countering Activism by Ideological Appointments

The makeup of the judiciary is an area where judicial independence is often challenged or pressured. This has been the case in Australia with recent High Court appointments. As was noted above, the court has been asked to adjudicate on legal issues that involve major political controversies. This has been most evident in the thorny area of native title.

Some political actors have responded to these decisions by questioning the role (and by implication, the capacity) of members of the High Court. Some of the "heat" in the rhetorical broadsides directed at the court is to be expected in a robust democracy. Indeed, some of the criticisms of the court were founded on the democratic argument that any reforms in the law should be left to the elected parliament and not to unelected judges.

The prime minister, John Howard, made such comments when he declared that "the laws governing Australians ought to be determined by the Australian Parliament and by nobody else."[35]

However, when public comments are designed to shake public confidence in the judiciary, questions of independence are raised. Recent criticisms indicate a desire to reshape the High Court to conform with the government's ideology. The call by the deputy prime minister that appointments to the High Court should be "capital C conservatives" is a case in point. This situation was exacerbated with the appointment of a critic of perceived judicial activism and native rights to the High Court. The appointee, Justice Ian Callinan, further fueled the controversy by initially resisting a submission that he not sit on a case upon which he had given advice to the commonwealth government as barrister. The case involved a challenge to legislation that will have implications for controversial amendments to the Native Title Act.[36] Ultimately, the judge stood down from the case but not until the matter had become a hot political issue.

These events bring into sharp focus one of the major concerns relating to the appointment process: that is the search for an ideologically acceptable individual to fill a vacancy on the High Court. It would be foolish to suggest that Australia has not witnessed the appointment of overtly political individuals to the High Court. Sir Edmund Barton, the first prime minister, left politics to join the first High Court bench in 1903. So too other constitutional framers became members of the judiciary in the first few decades of the commonwealth. Perhaps the best known "political" appointments to the High Court were Garfield Barwick and Lionel Murphy, both of whom were ministers in the Liberal and Labor governments respectively.

While these individuals clearly had an articulated political position before their appointment to the High Court, it has never seriously been suggested that their appointment was an attempt by their political soul mates to stack the court. Indeed, it is arguable that given their political background, the degree of scrutiny they received was greater than that of other judges. What these incidents highlight is a failure to distinguish between political appointments and political pluralism. One of the "problems" with appointments (be they political in the partisan or ideological sense) to the bench in Australia is that there is a poorly developed sense of "political" or judicial pluralism on the bench. While Australia has witnessed ideological diversity on the High Court, there is a general unwillingness on the part of judges, politicians, and the media to acknowledge political pluralism amongst the judiciary. This reluctance is connected with a tradition of drawing a sharp line between law and politics. It is ironic that this myth continues at a time when the judiciary is acknowledging the demise of another myth—that is, that judges do not make law.

Judicial Communication with the Public

The defense of judicial independence has been taken up by the judges themselves. The last two chief justices of the High Court, Sir Anthony Mason and Sir Gerard Brennan, both sought to publicly explain the court system.[37] Chief Justice John Doyle of the South Australia Supreme Court has highlighted the active role the judiciary must take in using the media to disseminate to the public the role of the judiciary. As he says:

> The courts should promote the independence of the judiciary. They can do so by improving public understanding of their work and, in that way, improving public understanding of the independence of the judiciary. The time has come for the courts to accept a responsibility to inform the public of their work. In this way the courts can strengthen public confidence in their work and the public understanding of their work, upon which public confidence and understanding judicial independence rests.[38]

An advantage of appealing directly to the public is that it breaks through a journalism in Australia that (with few exceptions) has not developed beyond shorthand labels, such as "centralist" or "states' righters," when reporting on judges or their decisions to the public. The need to appeal to the public may have become more critical when Commonwealth Attorney General Daryl Williams broke with convention and refused to "defend" publicly the judiciary against political attacks. As he said, "The judiciary should accept the position that it no longer expects the attorney-general to defend its reputation and make that position known publicly."[39]

The above section paints a picture of increasing tension between the judiciary and forces external to it. While it would be alarmist to suggest that this represents cracks in the foundations of judicial independence, the precedent it sets does raise concerns for the future of judicial independence.

Proposals for Reforming Judicial Selection

The method of appointment of judicial officers has already been covered in some detail in this paper. However, there remain questions in Australia as to whether the current method of selection protects the judiciary from political manipulation or, indeed, whether it privileges particular sections of society to the exclusion of others.

The idea of removing the selection of the judiciary from the exclusive control of the executive is not new. However, the suggestion is often prompted more by concern about the judicial outcome than about the quality of the judiciary. This is particularly the case with respect to the High Court bench following its decisions relating to contentious issues of commonwealth-state relations and native title. Ironically, Sir Garfield Barwick, a parliamentarian elevated by his political colleagues to the bench as chief justice, floated the idea of a "judicial commission" to advise the executive of individuals, "Who by reason of their training, knowledge, experience, character and disposition, are suitable for appointment to a particular office under consideration." The commission would be made up of "judges, practising lawyers, academic lawyers and, indeed, laymen likely to be knowledgeable in the achievements of possible appointees."[40]

The idea of the commission has received support from another chief justice, Sir Anthony Mason. Mason, however, does not favor limiting the executive to names provided by the commission. This caveat is based on democratic concerns regarding the transfer of power to appoint from an elected body to an unelected commission. While the idea of a "Judicial Commission" has been raised at various times, and as Roberts Stevens reports in his chapter is now under consideration in the United Kingdom, in Australia no government has as yet displayed any serious intention to implement what Sir Garfield described as a fetter on an "element of patronage."

One last question with respect to the judicial selection is its representative nature. As the Senate Standing Committee on Legal and Constitutional Affairs reported in its investigation of gender bias and the judiciary: "membership of the judiciary in Australia is remarkably homogeneous. Judges are overwhelmingly male, former leaders of the Bar, appointed in their fifties, and products of the non-government education system."[41] The issue of representation raises, according to the report, two related issues. The first is public confidence in the judiciary, and the second is "substantive law reform."

The first issue relates to whether or not an "unrepresentative" judiciary effects public confidence in the judicial system as a whole. As Simon Shetreet argues, the principle is that the judiciary should "fairly reflect" the community it serves.[42] Clearly, it is desirable to have a judiciary that mirrors as closely as possible the general community. Against this aspiration must be weighed the fundamental principle of what are the capacities we wish to see in a judicial officer. These may include any number of intellectual and personal qualities,[43] but the most basic of these is the ability to perform the judicial function at the highest possible level. To weaken this central tenet by appointing merely on the basis of community representation would be as corrosive of public confidence as would be maintaining an unrepresentative judiciary. What the current lack of diversity in the Australian judiciary indicates is the advantages that white male lawyers have had historically. This being said, with a much more diverse bar, there now appears to be a commitment to greater diversity on the bench while maintaining merit as the overriding concern.

The second argument for greater diversity (especially gender diversity) relates to a change in the substance of judicial decision making. It was suggested by those giving evidence to the Senate Standing Committee that a change in the makeup of the judiciary would bring about changes in the nature of legal reasoning. This was characterized as providing a different "voice" from the traditional male one, on the assumption that as the composition of the judiciary approached gender equality, there would be a change in the process and views of the judiciary.

Professional Evaluation and Development

Judicial outcomes, and by logical extension, the judicial officer, are subject to evaluation in numerous ways. In those jurisdictions where judges are elected, the quality of their "justice" can be tested at the ballot box. However, in places such as Australia, where the judiciary is not subject to this overt (and often emotive) democratic scrutiny, the means by which judges are "tested" is left to less direct means. It is at this point that professional evaluation, accountability, and independence quickly merge into a series of moving variables in a complex equation. Australia does not have a systematic method of professional evaluation.

At one level, the criticism of courts and their judgments is a form of professional evaluation. Notwithstanding that some criticism may be strident, ill conceived, or even wrong, it has a part to play in maintaining the public dialogue essential to the evaluation of standards. Australia has witnessed a number of instances where public disquiet has arisen following comments made by judicial officers that have not been seen to be in step with contemporary standards.[44] Public comment and criticism of the judiciary in situations of this kind are now widely acknowledged to be essential to the accountability of the judicial process.

While public or academic criticism of decisions is one means of evaluation, it is a relatively blunt instrument. It is dependent on the message being correct and on its being heard and acted upon. A less haphazard means of establishing judicial consistency, and some form of professional assessment, is the system of judicial review and appeal. This is the common means by which superior courts scrutinize the decisions of lower courts and tribunals for legal imperfections. While appeal and review by higher courts may bring about a correction of the decision, it may do little to chasten the errant judicial officer. Indeed, some judges in Australia have appeared to revel in their dissent. Further, it is a mechanism mainly for inferior courts and does little for the evaluation of the activities of judges of superior courts.

As with professional evaluation, there has been little movement in Australia to mandate judicial education. The creation of a mandatory system obviously raises concerns as to its encroachment on the independence of the judiciary.[45] Initiatives that have taken place to date have been basically aimed at improving the administration of justice in Australia. One such vehicle through which judicial education is conducted is the Australian Institute of Judicial Administration. The institute is an independent national organization dedicated to improving the operation of judicial systems throughout Australia. Since 1976 the institute has offered numerous education programs to judicial officers, covering topics such as technological change to cultural and gender awareness. In 1986 the New South Wales government established, through the Judicial Officers Act, a judicial commission, whose functions are judicial education and examining complaints against judicial officers. As part of it operation, the commission reports on sentencing trends and has conducted numerous educational programs designed for members of the judiciary in NSW.

Judicial Administration and the Division of Powers

The administration of justice is, of course, not a question for the judiciary only. It is in this context that tensions often arise between external forces and the judiciary. For instance, the executive's budgetary concerns regarding the "cost" of justice and the judiciary's concern with access to the legal system have been continuing points of public dialogue. As the landmark Canadian Supreme Court case of *Valente v. The Queen* (discussed by Peter Russell in his introductory chapter) has articulated, at "the heart" of judicial independence there are three "essential conditions": security of tenure, "financial security," and the "institutional independence of the tribunal with respect to matters of administration bearing directly on the exercise of its judicial function." This last condition, according to Justice Gerald Le Dain, requires certain minimum standards: judicial control over the assignment of judges, sittings of the court, the court lists, and the administrative staff engaged in carrying out these functions. While indicating that these represent the minimum constitutional standards, the Canadian Supreme Court acknowledged that greater administrative autonomy (including financial independence) was desirable.[46]

In areas where the judiciary is governed by federal jurisdiction, the Australian High Court has been vigilant in policing any encroachment on the part of the executive or the legislature into federal judicial power. One of the striking features of Australian jurisprudence has been the strict separation of judicial power from the other arms of government. Since the Boilermakers' case,[47] the High Court has established the doctrinal position that prohibits the investing of judicial power in a body not established in accordance with Chapter 3 of the constitution. The outcome of the case has been criticized for enshrining formalism and frustrating the effective operation of the administration state.[48] Thus the federal judiciary has provided itself, through a strict separation of judicial power, a protection of many of those features mentioned in Valente that are critical to judicial independence.

At the state level, concerns have been raised about the degree of judicial autonomy. Because there is no strict separation of powers at the state level, the constitutional protection of judicial power similar to that at the commonwealth level does not apply. As the Fitzgerald inquiry in Queensland put it:

> Independence of the Judiciary is of paramount importance, and must not be compromised. One of the threats to judicial independence is an over-dependence upon administrative and financial resources from a Government department or being subject to administrative regulations in matters associated with the performance of the judicial role. Independence of the Judiciary bespeaks as much autonomy as is possible in the internal management of the administration of the courts.[49]

In Australia, the administration of courts by the judiciary has incrementally expanded. Three distinct models of judicial administration currently exist.[50] The first is the "traditional" model, with the Attorney General's Department having responsibility for the administration of the courts. The second is the "separate department" model, where the judiciary is a separate department of government. The advantage of this model is that it places some distance between the executive and the judiciary by creating administrative procedures associated with government. The last model is the fully autonomous governance model, where the court is responsible for its own administration. This last model reflects the current situation with the High Court, the Federal Courts, and the South Australian and the Northern Territory courts.

By far the most contentious question relating to judicial administration in Australia is the question of funding. As numerous authors have pointed out, any advance in administrative autonomy is subject to financial restraint. As the court system is further stretched and funds for legal aid and other services diminish, greater burdens are placed on judicial officers.

Conclusion

It is trite to say that the judiciary has a central place in modern liberal democracies. If, as James Harrington stated, we wish to live in a society governed by the rule of law and not by rule of an absolute ruler, then the judiciary will be crucial in enforcing those rules and adjudicating disputes between citizens and the state.[51] Checks and balances remain as important as ever.

It is thus important that Australia, like other liberal democracies, have a judiciary that is both fiercely independent and accountable. As with so many issues of competing policy claims, there is a balance to be struck. In forging this balance, a developed theory of judicial independence will not only be helpful but perhaps will also be critical in framing public debate as to the role and function of Australian judicial independence.

The Australian judiciary has been "in the eye of the storm."[52] It has been criticized in the parliaments and the press for its perceived activism. It is difficult to escape the conclusion that those who damn the courts as "activist" are in reality calling for the maintenance of the status quo. Whether or not the courts can, or should, right historical wrongs is another debate. Further, what are the limits of the judiciary's power to do so?[53] The recent Australian experience shows that attempts by the courts to reshape the Australian social and political landscape will rouse powerful forces.

One inescapable conclusion to be drawn from the recent Australian debates about the judiciary is that there is no going back to a condition of judicial quietism. The courts, and particularly the High Court, will continue to feel the expectations of those who seek to vindicate rights in court and the confrontation of those whose interests are challenged. The debate it has engendered has witnessed individuals and groups not only lining up to defend or attack the courts but also to address the fundamental issues ventilated in the judicial decision. In recent times, the courts have supported Australia's deliberative democracy rather than "plunging Australia into the abyss."[54]

The above discussion has primarily outlined the strengths and weaknesses of the structural aspects of judicial independence in Australia. These structural foundations in many ways merely facilitate judicial independence. Beyond these, there is a need for individuals of robust integrity and fierce independence. To date, the Australian judiciary has shown itself to be resilient and jealous of its reputation for independence. While the Australian judiciary may be the subject of unprecedented political attack, there is no indication it will retreat from its traditional stance.

Notes

1. Quoted in Justice Michael Kirby, "Attacks on Judges: A Universal Phenomenon," *Australian Law Journal* 72 (1998): 601.

2. See Brian Galligan, *The Politics of the High Court* (St. Lucia: Univ. Of Queensland Press, 1987).

3. *Bank of NSW v. Commonwealth* (1948) 76 CLR 1.

4. *Australian Communist Party v. Commonwealth* (1951) 83 CLR 1418.

5. See E. G. Whitlam, *The Constitution Versus Labor* (Sydney: Wilson Service Press, 1965).

6. J. J. Doyle, "Constitutional Law: 'At the Eye of the Storm,'" *Western Australian Law Review* 23 (1993): 32.

7. See J. A. La Nauze, *The Making of the Australian Constitution* (Melbourne: Melbourne Univ. Press, 1972).

8. A Deakin, *The Federal Story: The Inner History of the Federal Cause* (Melbourne: Robertson & Mullens, 1944), 166.

9. See J. Reynolds, "A. I. Clark's American Sympathies and His Influences on Australian Federation," *Australian Law Journal* 32 (1958): 62; and J. M. Williams, "'With Eyes Open': Andrew Inglis Clark and Our Republican Tradition," *Federal Law Review* 23 (1995): 149.

10. See Z. Cowen and L. Zines, *Federal Jurisdiction in Australia* (Melbourne: Oxford Univ. Press, 1978), 1.

11. Constitutional Alteration (Retirement of Judges) Act (1977).

12. *McGinty v. Commonwealth* (1996) 186 CLR 140, 230.

13. *Spratt v. Hermes* (1965) 114 CLR 226.

14. For a further discussion, see P. H. Lane, "Constitutional Aspects of Judicial Independence," in *Fragile Bastion: Judicial Independence in the Nineties and Beyond,* Judicial Commission of New South Wales (Sydney, 1997), 65–73.

15. Further discussed in Ibid., 69–70.

16. See the *Age,* 6 March 1997, p. A6.

192 John M. Williams

17. L. Murphy, "Address to the National Press Club," in *The Power of Speech* (Moorebank: Transworld Publishing, 1989), 97.

18. Shimon Shetreet, "Judicial Independence: New Conceptual Dimensions and Contemporary Challenges," in *Judicial Independence: The Contemporary Debate,* eds. Shimon Shetreet and Jules Deschenes (Dordrecht: Martinus Nijhoff, 1985), 591.

19. G. Winterton, "The Separation of Judicial Power as an Implied Bill of Rights," in *Future Directions in Australia Constitutional Law* (Sydney: Federation Press, 1994), 185–208.

20. Justice Nicholls, "The Struggle in Tasmania," in *Making of the Australian Commonwealth* (London: Longmans Green, 1913), 356.

21. Cass Sunstein, *Legal Reasoning and Political Conflict* (New York: Oxford Univ. Press, 1996), 170.

22. *McGinty v. Commonwealth* (1996) 186 CLR 140, 230.

23. Anthony Mason, "The Role of Courts at the Turn of the Century," *Journal of Judicial Administration* 3 (1993): 164.

24. Justice Sackville, "Speech to Launch Vol. 20 of the UNSWLJ," *UNSW Law Journal* 20 (1997): 478.

25. *Mabo v. Commonwealth (No. 2)* (1992) 175 CLR 1; and *Wik Peoples v. Queensland* (1996) 187 CLAR 1.

26. G. Brennan, "Declaration of Principles on Judicial Independence," *Australian Bar Review* 15 (1996–97): 175.

27. For further discussion, see J. Braithwaite, "Community Values and Australian Jurisprudence," *Sydney Law Review* 17 (1995): 352.

28. R. McMullin, *The Light On the Hill: The Australian Labor Party 1891–1991* (Melbourne: Oxford Univ. Press, 1991), 430.

29. Further discussed in A. R. Blackshield, "The 'Murphy Affair,'" in *Lionel Murphy: A Radical Judge* (Calton: McCulloch, 1987), 230–57; and D. Brown, "Themes in an Inquisition: Justice Murphy and the Liberal Press," *Univ. Of New South Wales Law Journal* 10 (1987): 60.

30. "Parliamentary Commission Inquiry: Re The Honorable Mr. Justice Murphy," *Australian Bar Review* 2 (1986): 209.

31. Parliamentary (Judges) Commission of Inquiry Act of 1988. See also Justice M. D. Kirby, "Judicial Independence in Australia Reaches a Moment of Truth," *UNSW Law Journal* 13 (1990): 200.

32. *R. v. Kirby; Ex parte Boilermakers' Society of Australia* (1956) 94 CLR 254.

33. Further discussed in Justice M. Kirby, "Abolition of Courts and Non-reappointment of Judicial Officers," *Australian Bar Review* 12 (1995): 181.

34. A. Mason, "The Appointment and Removal of Judges," Judicial Commission of New South Wales, *Fragile Bastion,* 27.

35. Quoted in the *Australian,* 25 February 1997, p. 4.

36. See *Kartinyeri v. Commonwealth* (1988) 195 CLR 337.

37. See Gerald Brennan, "Courts for the People—Not People's Courts," *Deakin Law Review* 2 (1995): 1.

38. J. J. Doyle, "The Well-Tuned Cymbal," in Judicial Commission of New South Wales, *Fragile Bastion*, 39.

39. Quoted in Gerald Brennan, "The State of the Judicature," *Australian Law Journal* 72 (1998): 41.

40. Ibid.

41. Standing Committee on Legal and Constitutional Affairs, *Gender Bias and the Judiciary* (Canberra: Australian Government Press Service, 1994), 91.

42. See Shimon Shetreet, "Who Will Judge: Reflections on the Process and Standards of Judicial Selection," *Australian Law Journal* 61 (1987): 776.

43. See Justice B. Malcolm, "The Appointment of Judges," in Australian Institute of Judicial Administration, *Courts in a Representative Democracy* (Melbourne, 1995), 159–61.

44. See *Nationwide News Party Ltd. v. Wills* (1992) 177 CLR 1.

45. See Standing Committee on Legal and Constitutional Affairs, *Gender Bias,* 110.

46. Further discussed in I. Greene, "The Doctrine of Judicial Independence Developed by the Supreme Court of Canada," *Osgoode Hall Law Journal* 26 (1988): 177.

47. *R. v. Kirby;* Ex parte Boilermakers' Society of Australia (1956) 94 CLR 254.

48. See L. Zines, *The High Court and the Constitution* (North Ryde: Butterworths, 1997), 168–70 and 212–18.

49. Commission of Inquiry into Possible Illegal Activities and Associated Police Misconduct, *Report of a Commission of Inquiry Pursuant to Order in Council into Possible Illegal Activities and Associated Police Misconduct* (Brisbane, 1989), 134.

50. See, T. W. Church and P. A. Sallmann, *Governing Australia's Court* (Melbourne: Australian Institute of Judicial Administration, 1991).

51. J. Harrington, "The Prerogative of Popular Government Book I," in *The Political Works of James Harrington* (Cambridge: Cambridge Univ. Press, 1977), 401.

52. Doyle, "Constitutional Law: 'At the Eye of the Storm.'"

53. For further discussion, see Peter Russell, "High Court and the Rights of Aboriginal Peoples: The Limits of Judicial Independence," *Saskatchewan Law Review* 61 (1998) 247.

54. Kirby, "Attacks on Judges: A Universal Phenomenon," 601.

10

Seeking Social Justice?

*Judicial Independence and
Responsiveness in a
Changing South Africa*

HUGH CORDER

"Our Constitution emphasizes the attainment of substantive social justice," in the words of South African Judge Edwin Cameron. "It asks us each: *to what extent will legal institutions and legal forms assist in attaining social justice in our new society?*"[1] South Africa's judges are under pressure. This is not something new, for the courts have been at the center of political struggles since the turn of the twentieth century.[2] What has changed is the source of the pressure, generated by the judiciary's heightened political profile and an urgent necessity to transform the institutions of both justice and society. Partly because of the extraordinary process of political change and partly because of the idealistic aspirations of those who wrote the constitution, expectations are very high. The challenge for the judiciary is to throw off the mantle of executive mindedness and sectoral loyalty, which dominated its past,[3] and to embrace the key values of the constitutional democracy now formally in place,[4] without sacrificing the critically independent role assigned to it by the constitution.[5]

Many of the difficulties facing the judiciary in steering a course between independence and accountability stem from its past complicity in the evils of racist segregation and apartheid. This history must not be forgotten, but I will suggest that it contains a significant pointer to the judiciary's possible success in the future.

Structures in Flux

The shift in the basic law of government in South Africa from a narrowly sectarian repressive oligarchy to an inclusive, participative constitutional democracy inevitably resulted in the redefinition of the role of the judiciary. Much of the formal restructuring of the courts has taken place, though several initiatives remain uncompleted. Still, it is widely accepted that it will be some time yet before the ravages of racism cease to affect negatively both the demographic composition of those who staff the courts and the disproportionate impact of the administration of justice on certain sectors of the population.[6]

The structure, jurisdiction, and nomenclature of South African courts have changed since 1994, chiefly because of the newfound power of judicial review exercised by superior courts under the constitution. There is one entirely new creation, the Constitutional Court—consisting of a president, a deputy president, and nine other judges—which is the final arbiter of all constitutional matters. As well as exercising a range of powers to decide disputes between governmental authorities in the (essentially federal) state, the Constitutional Court, located in Johannesburg, makes the final decisions on the constitutional validity of any legislative or executive act and must confirm any such decision made by a lower court before such a decision takes effect. While most matters reach the Constitutional Court after being heard in another court, direct access is possible.

What was formerly the Supreme Court of South Africa, consisting of an appellate division at its apex and six provincial divisions, continues to exist, as do the supreme courts of the "independent" homelands created by apartheid. But their names were changed. The highest court of appeal for nonconstitutional matters is now known as the Supreme Court of Appeal (SCA), whose seat is Bloemfontein, and each of the former provincial divisions and the homelands courts has become a high court. The SCA has only appellate jurisdiction, while it and the high courts enjoy general jurisdiction with respect to constitutional as well as nonconstitutional matters. As mentioned, however, an order of constitutional invalidity issued by such a court is of no force until confirmed by the Constitutional Court. The SCA is headed by the chief justice, while the administrative head of each high court is known as the judge president.

The constitution stipulates that all these superior courts have the "inherent power to protect and regulate their own process and to develop the common law, taking into account the interests of justice." By contrast, the magistrates' courts and any other inferior courts, as they are known, have only the civil and criminal jurisdiction that is conferred on them by statute. Magistrates are public servants who have only recently been divested of the administrative authority they customarily exercised. There are approximately four hundred and thirty magisterial districts in South Africa, as well as regional magistrates' courts in the larger cities, whose criminal jurisdiction extends to trials for murder and rape. No inferior court may exercise any form of constitutional adjudication. Should a question relating to the constitutionality of a legislative provision arise, it will be referred to the high court in whose geographical jurisdiction the court lies, and it will proceed from there to the SCA and, then, if necessary, to the Constitutional Court for final resolution.

Appeals in criminal matters are generally heard by a bench of three judges of appeal in the SCA, while civil appeals are heard by a bench of five such judges. Any matter in a high court is generally heard by a single judge, whereas appeals heard by a high court from a decision of an inferior court are heard by at least two judges. In certain circumstances, an appeal may be made initially from a decision of single high court judge to a three-judge bench of that high court, and thereafter to the SCA.

Appointment of Judges and Magistrates

The appointment of judges in South Africa used to proceed along the lines adopted in Britain and much of the Commonwealth, namely, the president made judicial appointments with the advice of the cabinet. The establishment of a Judicial Service Commission (JSC) in the 1994 interim constitution, however, brought about substantial changes. A distinction was drawn between the appointment of constitutional judges and all others, including the promotion of judges to the SCA and the offices of "judges president" and their deputies.

The president of South Africa appoints the president and deputy president of the Constitutional Court as well as the chief justice and deputy chief justice of the SCA. This power is only to be exercised "after consultation with" the JSC and leaders of political parties, but it still allows the president a relatively free hand in selecting these judges, while emphasizing the political importance of the appointment of constitutional judges.

This fact is borne out by the method prescribed for filling vacancies on the Constitutional Court. The JSC advertises for nominees and interviews those short-listed, after which it submits to the president a list of three more names than the number of vacancies on the court. After consulting with the president of the court and the leaders of political parties, the president of South Africa makes the required appointments. If appointments remain to be made and the president finds the rest of the nominees unacceptable, he must advise the JSC and explain his dissatisfaction. The JSC then must supplement the list with further nominees, from which the president must make any remaining appointments. Once more, the president has a fair degree of latitude, constrained by the fact that at least four members of the court at all times must have served as judges in the SCA or high courts immediately before their appointment.

The freedom enjoyed by the president in selecting members of the Constitutional Court is more circumscribed with respect to the appointment of superior court judges, who are named "on the advice" of the JSC. It is also the practice of the JSC to present only one nominee for each vacancy on the bench to the president, and thus its recommendation effectively determines the appointment. The JSC's composition and manner of acting, therefore, is of paramount significance.

The JSC is a relatively large body, chaired by the chief justice. Further members from the legal profession are the president of the Constitutional Court; a judge president designated by the judges president; two practicing barristers and two practicing attorneys (solicitors), nominated by and representing all advocates and attorneys respectively; one teacher of law designated by all South African law teachers; and, when a vacancy in a particular high court is filled, the judge president of that division—making a total of nine lawyers from the profession. In addition, there are at least fifteen members, who are likely also to be qualified lawyers, nominated by political bodies: the minister of justice, six members of the National Assembly (at least three of whom are drawn from the ranks of opposition parties), four permanent delegates to the National Council of Provinces (the house of Parliament, whose particular function is representation of provincial interests in the national legislature), and four other persons designated by the president of South Africa after consulting with the leaders of all political parties represented in the National Assembly (currently seven in number). When a vacancy in a particular high court is filled, the premier of the province in which the court is situated is also a member. There is thus a clear preponderance of politicians on the JSC, the majority of whom are usually sympathetic to the government in power.

As to its powers, the JSC advises the central government "on any issue relating to the judiciary or the administration of justice,"[7] and it is clear that this would include being the forum for complaints about judicial conduct as well as supervising judicial education. This is a critical function that may well assume greater prominence in the future, but at present the

JSC has focused on and attracted national attention for its central role in judicial selection and appointments.

The JSC has brought a fair degree of openness to the judicial appointment process, certainly when compared to the past practice of secretive informality based on the British model, under which the president of South Africa formally appointed all judges "on the advice" of the cabinet. That system produced an effectively closed shop for establishment-minded senior members of the bar—almost exclusively white males—and allowed political parties to manipulate judicial appointments to further their ends. By contrast, the JSC advertises all vacancies and then interviews the short-listed candidates in public, as if in open court. Discussion of the merits of the judicial candidates and voting on them takes place in secret, although there have been calls for this also to take place in public, and the JSC now gives an account of the debates over the selection of judicial nominees.

In selecting nominees (and effectively appointing all high court judges initially), the JSC has a wide mandate in formal terms. The constitution provides in Section 174 that:

> (1) Any appropriately qualified woman or man who is a fit and proper person may be appointed as a judicial officer. Any person to be appointed to the Constitutional Court must also be a South African citizen.

> (2) The need for the judiciary to reflect broadly the racial and gender composition of South Africa must be considered when judicial officers are appointed.

Although there are no official statistics, the JSC has certainly ensured in the late 1990s that female or black, or both female and black, South Africans have been appointed more frequently than white males and that nonadvocates have also been appointed. A rough head count shows that, of the 192 judges serving permanently as of September 1998, including the first 11 members of the Constitutional Court, 29 are black males, 6 are white females, and 3 are black females. Several attorneys and academics have been appointed as well.

One of the ways in which the pool of candidates from which judges can be drawn is deepened is the use by the minister of justice of his power to make acting appointments to the bench. The minister may appoint an acting judge for any court other than the Constitutional Court, for up to a month at a time, after consulting with the senior judge on the court concerned. It has become an unwritten rule of the JSC that no candidate will be recommended for a judgeship unless he or she has served as an acting judge at some point in the past. The appointment of acting judges is not new to South African practice, however, and has generally not been misused. In addition, it has had the benefical effect of allowing the candidate an opportunity to assess his or her suitablity for the rigors and relative isolation of judicial office.

With regard to magistrates, the constitution merely provides that they must be appointed in terms of an act of parliament, "which must ensure that the appointment, promotion, transfer or dismissal of, or disciplinary steps against, these judicial officers take place without favour or prejudice." In fact, the critical role is played by the Magistrates Commission, whose responsibilities and authority ensure a relative degree of independence and security of tenure for magistrates, as opposed to other public servants. Magistrates have traditionally been appointed from the ranks of public prosecutors, but there have been several high-profile appointments from outside those ranks. Although the overwhelming majority of magistrates remains male, there is a greater proportion of black magistrates than there is black judges, rather ironically resulting in part from the legacy of the justice systems of the "independent homelands" under apartheid. As of September 1998, of the 1,143 magistrates, 708 were white, 28 Indian, 34 colored, and 373 black; there were 259 females, of whom only 75 were not white.

Clearly, with regard to the selection and appointment of judicial officers, there have been substantial changes that have a marked and generally positive effect on the demographic composition and legitimacy of the judiciary. These developments have undoubtedly been conducive to producing a less partial and more accountable process of judicial appointments, which should also contribute to establishing a responsive judiciary.

Conditions of Service and Removal of Judges

As for the conditions of judicial service, the constitution merely provides that a Constitutional Court judge serves a nonrenewable term of twelve years but must retire at age seventy, while other judges remain in office until they are discharged from "active service," and that salaries and benefits of judges may not be reduced. The details are provided in two statutes, the Supreme Court Act of 1959, and the Judges' Remuneration and Conditions of Employment Act of 1989, the relevant provisions of which are as follows: No judge may hold any office or render any services for which he or she receives any form of remuneration, other than for holding judicial office, without the authorization of the minister of justice.

While holding office, no summons or subpoena in any civil action may be issued against any judge, except with the consent of the court. Judges are remunerated at a rate determined by the president of South Africa; in addition, they receive a small annual allowance and the use of a vehicle provided by the state.[8]

All nonconstitutional judges are regarded as on "active service" until the age of seventy, provided that at least ten years have been served or until such a period has been completed. However, a judge who has completed fifteen years of active service and has reached the age of sixty-five years may request that the president discharge him or her. Conversely, a judge who on turning seventy has not yet completed fifteen years of active service may continue in office until such period has been served or until he or she reaches age seventy-five. Judges continue to be paid after discharge from service and receive a nontaxable gratuity when they are discharged. Constitutional judges, however, receive much larger gratuities on leaving office but are not entitled to a salary thereafter.

One other aspect relating to conditions of judicial service needs to be noted. Any judge who has been discharged from active service remains eligible for "service" for a period of up to three months a year until reaching the age of seventy-five and may even serve beyond that age if requested by the chief justice or the judge president of the division on which he or she served. Such service may not be in an office of lower status than the one vacated by the judge concerned, but it may be in other capacities, such as chairing a commission or state body. Judges performing service of this type are entitled to the salary attached to the office in addition to the salary they receive as a result of their years of regular judicial service. Refusal to take on additional service, however, results in a small financial penalty deducted from the judge's salary. Such additional service is, thus, a relatively common practice.

Removal of judges has always been a possibility, but, in fact, has not occurred since 1897.[9] At present, the constitution provides that a judge may be removed from office only if the JSC finds that he or she suffers from an incapacity, is grossly incompetent, or is guilty of gross misconduct, and if the National Assembly calls for that judge's removal, with the support of at least two-thirds of its members. The president must formally remove such a judge after these steps and may suspend any judge under investigation in the above manner.

Striking a New Balance between Judicial Independence and Accountability

While no commentator argues seriously that "telephone justice"[10] has existed at any stage in South Africa, and while security of judicial tenure has been a feature of all South African constitutions since 1910,[11] it is now widely acknowledged that biased judicial appointments in particular periods,[12] selective composition of the benches to hear particular types of cases,[13] and the dominance of an executive-minded approach in most divisions of the Supreme Court from the late 1950s to the early 1990s[14] combined to produce a judicial culture closely attuned to the interests of white South Africans. This is not to charge the judiciary as a whole with deliberate racism (although there were such incidents), nor is it to deny that there have at all times been judges who have used their power to counter legislative and executive injustices.[15]

The judiciary and the bodies that are representative of various parts of the legal profession in South Africa have always proclaimed their independence from the government and been supported by successive ministers of justice, even during the most dismal times for civil liberty and the rule of law.[16] It is correct to state, too, that outside of the "political sphere" in its widest sense, judicial development of the common law relating to crime, contracts, and family relations, for example, has been at least as good as comparable courts in the Commonwealth. The problem, nonetheless, remains that centuries of race and class discrimination have resulted in a fundamentally skewed distribution of wealth, privilege, and power, such that the administration of justice almost always treats those who are poor and black more harshly than those who are rich and white. The superimposition of a demand for formal equality in the constitution and the use of measures to address equal opportunity at a substantive level cannot change such patterns instantly, and that poses challenges for both the appointment of judges and their independence on the bench.

Painfully aware of that history, those who drafted the constitution set a high price on judicial independence and impartiality. Section 165, for instance, reads in part:

(2) The courts are independent and subject only to the Constitution and the law, which they must apply impartially and without fear, favour and prejudice.

(3) No person or organ of state may interfere with the functioning of the courts.

(4) Organs of state, through legislative and other measures, must assist and protect the courts to ensure the independence, impartiality, dignity, accessibility and effectiveness of the courts.

(5) An order or decision issued by a court binds all persons to whom and organs of state to which it applies.

These direct injunctions send a powerful message: the judiciary should enjoy healthy protection and respect. In general terms, too, further provisions of the constitution and statutes reinforce this message: judges have a high degree of security of tenure, they are relatively well provided for in respect to remuneration and other conditions of service, they enjoy a degree of immunity from civil suits, and the method of their selection is relatively open and objective.

In light of this, it might seem as though the outlook for substantive judicial independence is uniformly positive in South Africa. That view, however, must be qualified by the impact of the past and the socioeconomic conditions in South Africa, as described above. In the changed political environment of the 1990s, it is no longer good enough for the judiciary to argue, as in the past, that the demand for accountability is satisfied by the hearing of almost all matters in open court, by the freedom of the media to report on such proceedings, by the critical views of academic commentators, and by the possibility of being overruled by higher courts.

Something more than that litany is required to satisfy the legitimate public interest in holding the wielders of judicial power in fact to account, and it seems that the JSC provides a good medium for that. First, the JSC has brought a refreshing degree of openness to the judicial appointment process. The JSC's limited transparency of operation, however, needs to be widened formally to encompass a measure of disclosure about the debates over judicial candidates' suitability for the bench.

Second, there is no reason the JSC should not provide a formal mechanism for the reception and investigation of allegations of judicial misconduct, both on and off the bench, in cases that are unlikely to lead to a recommendation for removal from the bench. In fact, such a task is already expected of the Magistrates Commission. Of course, if the JSC were to assume that task, it would have to walk a fine line between judicial accountability and independence.

Third, the JSC could report regularly to Parliament and the public on the discharge of its functions and the state of the administration of justice. That would in all likelihood strengthen judicial independence through greater public appreciation for the complexity and pressures of the judicial process.

Fourth, the JSC could facilitate greater judicial awareness of public opinion and developments in the law, both nationally and internationally, through the promotion of judicial education throughout the career of judges. That is not a novel idea, but it has yet to be fully embraced by the South African judiciary.

These are at least four avenues toward establishing a measure of judicial accountability through the JSC, none of which needs to negatively affect judicial independence. Indeed, it would appear that the traditions and ethos of the bar and the bench provide a firm foundation for the development of substantive yet responsive independence in the courts. The chief potential threats would come from the possibility of an overt pursuit of a political party's agenda by a majority of the JSC, and from an overambitious pursuit by judges of socioeconomic goals in an apparent bending of the rules of law in order to mitigate the harshness of the past.

Judicial independence may provide the key to an approach to the exercise of governmental power that, through its restraint, may foster democratic accountability. In assuming that mantle, the judiciary of the new millennium would be taking further the approach that, as I have argued elsewhere,[17] characterized the work of the newly founded appellate division after the Union of South Africa was formed in 1910. At that stage, the courts were seeking to encourage reconciliation between English- and Afrikaans-speaking white South Africans, while the present task is clearly the divination and strengthening of the common bonds between all in South Africa.

Central to attaining that goal is the willingness of the Constitutional Court to remain autonomous of the legislative and executive branches, while also being responsive to the needs of the ordinary South African "consumer."[18] Fortunately, the record of the court thus far gives cause for optimism, for it has been prepared to uphold the constitution in the face of both legislative and executive inroads, while also showing a clear appreciation for the practical socioeconomic constraints under which the government operates.[19] At the same time, the constitutional judges, like their counterparts on other superior courts in South Africa, have not hesitated to hand down separate concurring and dissenting opinions,[20] reflecting a healthy state of debate and diversity that can only foster judicial independence.

Conclusion

By setting out South Africa's constitutional and statutory provisions in some detail, I have indicated that the formal aspect of judicial independence is relatively secure. Substantively, however, challenges remain, rooted in the judicial record of the past, the urgent need to address socioeconomic needs and expectations, and, paradoxically, the very distance that exists between the constitutional ideals and the daily reality of life for most South Africans. While the task is enormous, there is cause for hope.

It is fitting, therefore, to conclude with the words of the first black chief justice of South Africa, delivering a lecture in memory of a white, Afrikaans-speaking advocate and politician who died while a prisoner for crimes committed against the apartheid state. Chief Justice Ismail Mahomed ended his address by referring to the pursuit of perfection that arises from an awareness of human imperfection in these words:

> But the excitement of this pursuit into the future is immeasurably enhanced by the truths absorbed from the past and the present. For lawyers these include the insistence, at all times, that the attainment of justice must be the rationale for all law; that law cannot be distanced from justice and morality without losing its claim to legitimacy; that the ethical objectives of the law contain the life blood of a nation; that justice must be seen to be fair in its impact on the life of the humblest citizen in search of protection against injustice; that the law is accessible, intelligible, visible and affordable; and that any retreat from these truths imperils the very existence and status of a defensible civilization, first by corrosively destroying within it the source of the energy which sustains it and second by provoking disdain, disorder and rebellion from those it seeks to discipline.[21]

Notes

1. Judge Edwin Cameron, "Academic Criticism and the Democratic Order," *South African Journal on Human Rights* 14:1 (1998), 108 (emphasis in original).

2. See H. R. Hahlo and Ellison Kahn, *South Africa: The Development of Its Laws and Constitution* (Cape Town: Juta & Co., 1960), chaps. 5 and 6; Hugh Corder, "The Judicial Branch of Government: An Historical Overview," in *Essays on the History of Law,* ed. D. P. Visser (Cape Town: Juta & Co., 1989), 60–78.

3. See Albie Sachs, *Justice in South Africa* (London: Chatto-Heinman, 1973); Hugh Corder, *Judges at Work: The Role and Attitudes of the South African Appellate Judiciary,*

1910–1950 (Cape Town: Juta & Co., 1984); David Dyzenhaus, *Hard Cases in a Wicked Legal System* (Oxford: Clarendon Press, 1991); and Stephen Ellman, *In a Time of Trouble* (Oxford: Clarendon Press, 1992).

4. The Constitution of the Republic of South Africa (Act 108 of 1996).

5. For a good history of the process of the adoption of the constitution, see T. R. H. Davenport, *The Birth of a New South Africa* (Toronto: Univ. Of Toronto Press, 1998).

6. At the time of the first free elections in 1994, of the approximately one hundred and sixty-five superior court judges, only one was not white and only two were female.

7. See constitution, Section 178(5).

8. See the Judges' Remuneration Act, Sections 2, 10A and 11.

9. The president dismissed Chief Justice Kotze for daring to assert the power of judicial review in *Brown v. Leyds* (1897), 4 Off. Rep. 17.

10. A phrase implying that undue influence is brought to bear on judges to decide cases over which they preside is further discussed in Jane A. Roth, "Judging in New-Born Democracies," *Ohio State Law Journal* 54 (1993): 1109.

11. The South Africa Act of 1909 and the Republic of South Africa Constitution Acts of 1961 and 1983 all provided for judicial removal only for gross incompetence and misbehavior.

12. From 1948 to 1960, particularly during the "constitutional crisis" in the mid-1950s over the removal of the "coloured vote."

13. See Ellman, *Time of Trouble,* for a discussion of this practice in the late 1980s.

14. See C. F. Forsyth, *In Danger for Their Talents* (Cape Town: Juta & Co., 1985).

15. The best-known example is Justice John Didcott, who served on the Supreme Court during the last twenty years of apartheid, and who was appointed to the Constitutional Court in 1994, serving until his death in October 1998.

16. See, for example, the angry response of the Department of Foreign Affairs to allegations of the failure to comply with the rule of law from the International Commission of Jurists in *Erosion of the Rule of Law in South Africa* (Geneva: International Commission of Jurists, 1968), in *South Africa and the Rule of Law* (Pretoria: Department of Foreign Affairs, South Africa, 1968).

17. Corder, *Judges at Work,* 237–41.

18. See the model proposed by Mauro Cappelletti, "'Who Watches the Watchmen?' A comparative Study on Judicial Responsibility," in *Judicial Independence: The Contemporary Debate,* eds. Shimon Shetreet and Jules Deschenes (Dordecht: Martinus Nijhoff, 1985), 574–75.

19. See *S. v. Makwanyane* (1995) 3 SA 391 (CC); *Ex parte chairperson of the Constitutional Assembly: In re Certification of the Constitution* (1996) 4 SA 744 (CC); see *Executive Council, Western Cape Legislature v. President of the Republic of South Africa* (1995) 4 SA 877 (CC), *Minister of Justice v. Ntuli* (1997) 3 SA 772 (CC); and *Soobramoney v. Minister of Health* (1998) 1 SA 765 (CC).

20. See Lynn Taylor and Jonathan Klaaren, "Constitutional Court Statistics for the 1997 Term," *South African Journal on Human Rights* 14 (1998): 217.

21. Ismail Mahomed, "The Bram Fischer Memorial Lecture," *South African Journal on Human Rights* 14 (1998): 217.

11

Between Two Systems of Law

The Judiciary in Hong Kong

JILL COTTRELL AND YASH GHAI

The judiciary in Hong Kong is passing through a period of transition from a British colony to a special administrative region (SAR) of the People's Republic of China (PRC).[1] As an SAR, Hong Kong enjoys considerable autonomy and is guaranteed the legal system and the independent judiciary it had at the transfer of sovereignty. In several respects, the role of the judiciary now is even more important than before, because its function is to enforce the constitution of Hong Kong, the Basic Law, as the supreme law within the SAR.[2]

Constitutional instruments during the colonial rule, the principal of which was the Letters Patent, contained few normative provisions that could form the basis for a challenge in court to legislation or policy(at least until 1991, when the International Covenant on Civil and Political Rights (ICCPR) was incorporated into Hong Kong law). The Basic Law, however, has a most impressive scheme for the protection of rights. Courts also have greater responsibility for adjudicating relations between the members of the legislature and the executive, which arises in part because of the control by the chief executive over the legislative process. Perhaps even more important, the courts now have the function of maintaining the autonomy of Hong Kong from the Chinese Central Authorities, which they exercise by ensuring that interventions by those authorities follow the procedures as well as the substantive limitations prescribed in the Basic Law.

These new tasks make the judiciary's role more difficult and controversial. Domestically, difficulties are aggravated because the government's commitment to rights is seen as, at best, lukewarm, and the legislature is, for all effective purposes, subordinated to an unelected executive. Hence many disputes that should be solved by the political process fall to the courts. But it is in relation to the judiciary's role of mediating Hong Kong's autonomy that the most serious difficulties have arisen.

It is not only that China is much too powerful for Hong Kong and that there are major uncertainties about the status of the Basic Law and its relationship to the PRC Constitution. There also are fundamental differences between the political and legal cultures of Hong Kong and China. Ultimate decisions on interpretation of constitutional and other laws are made on the mainland by political and legislative authorities, acting under the hegemony of the Communist Party, which stands as a constant threat to the independence of Hong Kong courts. Moreover, because Hong Kong does not have a democratically accountable political system, there is a tendency to convert political into legal problems, while the mainland, with weak legal institutions and dominant Communist political culture, tends to turn legal issues into political ones, or at least to deal with them politically.[3]

The Basic Law attempts to separate the legal systems of Hong Kong and mainland China. However, there are some points of interface between the two systems. It is at these points that the independence and effectiveness of the judiciary come under strain, because the Hong Kong judicial system is subordinate to the Standing Committee of the National People's Congress (NPCSC).

We explore the tensions that arise from this interface, which is largely a conflict between two different concepts of the judicial function and of the centrality of legality. First, though, we describe some aspects of the rule of law in the colonial period and then the formal position of the judiciary under the Basic Law.

The Judiciary in the Colonial Period

In recent years—before and after the return of sovereignty of Hong Kong to the PRC—the independence of the Hong Kong judiciary has been much vaunted by government: "A key element in the past success and continuing attraction of the HKSAR [Hong Kong Special Administrative Region] is that its judicial system operates on the principle, fundamental to the common law system, of the independence of the judiciary from the executive and legislative branches of government."[4] However, for most of Hong Kong's history, litigants had little guarantee of a "fair and public hearing by a competent, independent and impartial tribunal."[5] Judicial independence was not a hallmark of colonial rule. This was apparent as far back as 1847, when the governor suspended the first chief justice for alleged drunkenness, though an inquiry before the Executive Council had substantially exonerated him.[6]

In fact, it was not so much hostility between executive and judiciary that gave cause for concern, but rather excessive closeness, as underscored by the role of the chief justice as adviser to the governor. The career path of a member of the colonial legal service often involved periods as an ordinary administrator; a person might serve as such even after having served as an acting member of the judiciary.[7] As recently as 1978, the new chief justice of Hong Kong had once been attorney general and then had been chief secretary and also occasionally acted as governor.[8]

Although it would no longer be considered appropriate for an individual to move from bench to administration, the system of promotion within the legal service continues. In 1988 the government decided against raising the retirement age of magistrates to sixty-five, because this would slow down the process of localization of the judiciary, because magistrates formed "the basic entry ranks to the judiciary."[9] It is only with the 1997 appointment of the chief justice and the members of the new Court of Final Appeal that Hong Kong had an appellate court wholly composed of former private practitioners, in the English style. Of three appointees to the Court of First Instance bench in 1997, one had been a magistrate and then a district judge, another had been a prosecutor in the government and then had been in private practice, had returned to government as director of public prosecutions, and had gone back to private practice; only one had been at the private bar throughout her career.

Moreover, the procedure under which judges may review their own decisions smacks more of bureaucracy than judiciary. Until a court of appeal was appointed in Hong Kong, the only route of appeal, other than to the Privy Council, was to the full court, presided over by the chief justice, even if he had given the judgment appealed. At present, after a magistrate makes a decision in his summary jurisdiction, he may, on his own initiative or that of a party, reopen the case, and reverse, vary, or confirm his decision.[10]

Moreover, it has never been easy to recruit judges for Hong Kong. The reasons are various. To some extent, it must be that the practice of taking judges from the Legal Department, while the latter was notably slow in localizing, restricted the choice. The bar was, until relatively recently, dominated by foreigners. And in recent years, at least, the financial rewards of service on the bench have been so far inferior to those of private practice that few have been prepared to accept appointment. By the end of the

1980s, the reputation of the bench was not such that people would be encouraged to accept appointment. In part, this was a question of competence, in part of executive interference, and to a considerable degree a question of leadership.

The appointment and retirement of colonial judges was also remarkably devoid of constitutional safeguards. Appointment and dismissal were matters of discretion and pleasure. In 1976 a Judicial Service Commission (JSC) was established, with functions purely advisory to the governor over judicial appointments and other matters the governor might refer to it.[11] There was a good deal of criticism of the presence of the attorney general as a member of this body, especially in the light of the tendency to promote from the lower ranks of the judiciary.[12] Apart from the chief justice and the attorney general, the seven members of the JSC were appointed by the governor. Two of these JSC members had to be judges, one a barrister, one a solicitor, and (since 1990) three persons not connected in any way with the practice of law. In July 1997 this body was renamed the Judicial Officers Recommendation Commission (JORC), and the governor's powers of appointment devolved to the chief executive.

The modern processes for dismissal of judges other than magistrates have been invoked very rarely, and never in the case of superior judges. It is clear that, as in England, for example, judges whom it would be laborious to sack, have been leaned on to go quietly—which is not to say that their departure has been regretted. Worries about possible threats to independence of the judiciary have perhaps caused some incidents in the 1990s to receive more publicity than might earlier have been the case.

The Transition

The gradual development of a less bureaucratized system of justice, with greater safeguards for the independence of the judiciary, is familiar in most other British colonies, as is the retention of promotion models of appointment and various types of temporary appointment after independence. But Hong Kong's destiny was not, of course, to be typical. Since 1984, the general nature of that destiny, as a special administrative region of the PRC, was clear. The debate and the developments over the legal system and the judiciary generally were to be influenced by the nature of Hong Kong's future constitution (the Basic Law and those aspects of the constitution of the PRC that are applicable to Hong Kong) and by the politics as well as by the law of the transitional period.

The Basic Law aims to provide for the coexistence of capitalism and Communism within one sovereign state through the doctrine of "one country, two systems." Tensions between Communism in China and capitalism in Hong Kong as economic systems were somewhat muted by the early 1980s, as China began its long march to marketization. Indeed, this fundamental shift in Chinese economic policy made possible the principle of "one country, two systems," and concerns about the coexistence or interaction of opposed economic systems more or less faded away. However, as the transfer of sovereignty approached, concerns arose about the autonomy of Hong Kong—not over its function as a device to maintain Hong Kong's economic system, but to safeguard its way of life, to promote greater democratization, and to protect rights and freedoms.

Economic reforms in China had not sufficiently altered the state-administered nature of the economy. The political system has changed even less. It is based on the domination of the Communist Party. The function of state institutions, including the National People's Congress, formally the "highest organ of state power," is to implement policies of the Communist Party, itself under the control of a small cabal. There is no democracy. Nor is there an important role for law in the protection of rights. Despite recent improvements, there is no rule of law in mainland China as understood and supported in Hong Kong. There are differences between the mainland and Hong Kong, not only in the formal structures of law and constitution, but also in the use and purposes of the law.

Law on the mainland does not, for the most part, provide an autonomous framework for the relationship between the state and the people.[13] Courts cannot review the validity of legislation, and until recently, they could not review the legality of administrative acts. There have been doubts among some mainland lawyers whether judicial review of any kind would be permissible under the Basic Law, on the basis that the Basic Law, being Chinese law, must be subject to Chinese legal principles.[14] The practices of the law are subordinated to politics on the mainland in a way that would be regarded as unacceptable in Hong Kong.

Lawyers in Hong Kong were aware of this but were inclined to feel that it was irrelevant to them. A first reading of the 1984 Sino-British Joint Declaration and the Basic Law that turned it into law suggested that nothing much was to change. Hong Kong was to have "a high degree of autonomy," and the main bulwark of that autonomy was to be the common law. This common law was to continue, and according to Article 81, "The judicial system previously practised in Hong Kong shall be maintained except for those changes consequent upon the establishment of the Court of Final Appeal of the Hong Kong Special Administrative Region." Indeed, under the Basic Law, of all branches of the Hong Kong government, the judiciary is the most independent from the central government.

The Court of Final Appeal (CFA), which replaced the Judicial Committee of the Privy Council on July 1, 1997, has three groups of judges: the permanent judges, including the chief justice, a list of judges who have served in Hong Kong from whom the chief justice may invite any individual to sit on a case, and a list of distinguished foreign judges from whom one judge may be invited for any one appeal. The High Court (known until the handover as the Supreme Court) consists of the Court of Appeal and the Court of First Instance (CFI); it is presided over by the chief judge of the High Court (CJHC). The inferior courts include the District Court, with wide, first instance, civil and criminal jurisdiction,[15] and the magistrates courts, presided over by magistrates who are normally legally qualified,[16] with criminal jurisdiction only and appeals going to the CFI. The Labour Tribunal, for which members need have no legal qualifications, deals with employment cases, appeals going to the CFI. The Small Claims Tribunal, which is a civil court presided over by a legally qualified adjudicator, deals with small civil cases, with appeals going to the CFI. Lawyers may appear before all these bodies except the Labour Tribunal and the Small Claims Tribunal.

On the whole, the process for the appointment of judges has not changed. True, two members of the judiciary (the chief justice and the chief judge of the High Court) are now required to be of Chinese nationality, without the right of abode in any other country. But otherwise it is still possible for judges from "other common law jurisdictions" to be appointed—indeed, this language is wider in scope than the former provision about having held judicial office in other Commonwealth jurisdictions.[17]

The Basic Law, in Article 88, provides that appointments should be by the chief executive on the recommendation of "an independent commission composed of local judges, persons from the legal profession and eminent person from other sectors." Appointments of judges of the Court of Final Appeal and of the chief judge of the High Court also require an almost U.S.-style endorsement by the Legislative Council, and must be reported to the Standing Committee of the NPC. The renamed JSC (JORC) is still to be chaired by the chief justice, and the secretary for justice (effectively the new name for the attorney general) remains a member. For regular appointments (as opposed to postretirement-age appointments), the advice of the commission is not binding. The JORC thus continues some of the previously objectionable features, and it is doubtful whether its composition meets the Basic Law criteria. But in practice the recommendations of the JORC are treated as binding, as the Basic Law requires.

The Basic Law also continues fundamentally the existing procedure for the removal of judges. However, the process now takes place wholly within Hong Kong, save that it must be reported to the NPCSC. The grounds for removal remain inability or misbehavior; for the removal of the chief justice of the Court of Final Appeal, the tribunal must be appointed by the chief executive and must consist of no fewer than five local judges, and the chief justice "may" then be removed by the chief executive. In the case of other judges, the tribunal is to be appointed by the chief justice and must consist of no fewer than three local judges; removal is also by the chief executive. In the latter case, the English version does not indicate whether the chief executive has any discretion after the tribunal has reported.

The other issue is how far the Basic Law procedure extends. The Basic Law refers to "judges" as being appointed and dismissed by the procedure described. The JORC deals, as it has since its inception, with the appointment of magistrates and a wide range of other offices, such as the coroner, which are termed "judicial offices." They are clearly not all "judges"—they include the registrar of the High Court, for example. A distinction is drawn between "judges" and other members of the judiciary. The only way to make sense of this is to assume a continuation of the existing system and that "judges" refers to the higher judiciary—but the drafting is far from satisfactory.

Notably, the Legislative Council now has a role in the regulation of the judiciary.[18] As the council is required to endorse the appointment of certain judges, it is like the U.S. Congress, but there is no enthusiasm for the legislature to emulate the style of the Senate Judiciary Committee. However, legislators rejected the administration's suggestion that, in order to protect judicial independence, the council should be merely a rubber stamp.[19] In its provision on the role of the legislature in removal, the Basic Law echoes the situation in England, though there the potential role of Parliament is much greater.

The previous standing orders of the council provided that, "A question shall not reflect on the decision of a court of law or be so drafted as to be likely to prejudice a case pending in a court of law." This is reproduced in the new Rules of Procedure,[20] while it is still provided by Rule 41(8) that in speeches, "The conduct of Judges or other persons performing judicial functions shall not be raised." This perhaps needs to be altered in the light of the new powers of the council. It is hard to see how the removal of a judge, or even the promotion of an existing judge to the post of chief justice, could be discussed under the latter rule.

Until the 1990s, the Legislative Council was hardly a democratic body and was generally somewhat passive. The 1990s saw a significant increase in the democratic element and a corresponding growth in council activity. Among the initiatives this surge of democratic energy has produced has been a system of standing committees, or panels, including one entitled Administration of Justice and Legal Affairs. Its terms of reference include "to monitor and examine, consistent with maintaining the independence of the Judiciary and the rule of law." Its members include some of the members of the council most experienced in law and politics. Over the years, the panel has discussed a number of issues relevant to judicial independence, including the constitution of the JORC. There is nothing in the Basic Law that requires such an arrangement, but neither is it precluded, and the system has continued.

Article 85 says that "members of the judiciary shall be immune from legal action in the performance of their judicial function." This makes no distinction between higher and lower judiciary, between acts and words, and between acts within and outside jurisdiction, all distinctions that figure in the common law.[21] The corollary of what was said earlier about the meaning of "judges" and "judiciary" in the Basic Law must surely be to conclude that Article 85 must include the magistracy. The phrase "the performance of their judicial function" implies a protection either wider or narrower than under the existing law—or possibly both. Magistrates and district judges have some immunity under statute if they are acting within their jurisdiction when malice and absence of reasonable and probable cause must be proved; if they acted outside their jurisdiction, the burden of proof of these elements is reversed. These provisions may be narrower than Article 85, in which case they are presumably amended by it. Conversely, if "judicial functions" could be construed as referring only to acts within their jurisdiction, the common law immunity of higher court judges could be argued to go further than required by the Basic Law. If so, it might be argued that Article 85 actually cuts down that immunity, since the common law applies only if consistent with the Basic Law. However, perhaps the Basic Law provides a minimum level of safeguards, and the common law, if it gives greater safeguards, continues in force. In any event, since the interpreters of this article will be the judges themselves, one might predict that they would construe any ambiguity in favor of the wider immunity.

According to Article 85, "The courts of the Hong Kong Special Administrative Region shall exercise judicial power independently, free from any interference." Though financial security is usually considered to be an important factor in preserving judicial independence, the only specific reference to such security refers to those judges who continued as members of the judiciary from the colonial period: Article 93 guarantees them not only their seniority but their "pay, allowances, benefits and conditions of service no less favourable than before." It also guarantees them or their dependants "all pensions, gratuities, allowances and benefits due to them on terms no less favourable than before, irrespective of their nationality or place of residence."

In the final years of colonial rule, relations between London and Beijing became so fraught that it was almost impossible to agree on anything remotely sensitive.[22] The judiciary was one such area. The original intention had been to replace the Judicial Committee of the Privy Council with the new Court of Final Appeal well before the handover. But this plan foundered on the rock of the "foreign judge" issue. The Basic Law says, in Article 82, that the Court of Final Appeal may "as required invite judges from other common law jurisdictions to sit." The mainland government took the view that in any one case only one such judge could be invited to sit. Others, including the bar, argued that there should be the possibility of inviting more. At the heart of the latter lay the new fear that the Hong Kong judges would not be independent and that their backbones would be more effectively stiffened if more foreign judges sat. Some would have preferred as many as three foreign judges.[23] Eventually, the Court of Final Appeal Ordinance was passed in 1995, but it was not to come into operation until July 1, 1997.

The interaction between the Basic Law, the Judicial Service Commission legislation, and the political/constitutional imbroglio led to a remarkable series of events. It proved impossible for the outgoing and incoming administration to agree on all the members for the JORC, and it became clear that a new body would be appointed on 1 July. There were also doubts whether the existing judges would continue in office after the handover—it was rumored that there would be no judicial "through train."[24] If, as individuals, the judges were to continue, they would have to be reappointed by the JORC. But if the judges did not continue, there would be no judges to sit on the JORC, and thus it could not sit!

The colonial administration, with the cooperation of the outgoing Legislative Council, put in place a transitional provision in the JSC Ordinance providing that any judge in office on 30 June would remain in office for the purposes of the Judicial Service Commissions Ordinance for the next day, too.[25] Meanwhile, in April the chief executive (designate) appointed the members of the JORC. It could not lawfully sit until 1 July. However, it undertook some "preparatory work" of a rather significant nature: it considered the claims of one hundred and forty or so people meeting the requirements under the Court of Final Appeal Ordinance for being chief justice.

This zealousness was, of course, commendable. Its task was no doubt made easier by the fact that even before it sat on 15 April, the race was widely thought to have but two runners: Andrew Li, rumored to be preferred by the chief executive designate, and Justice Benjamin Liu of the Court of Appeal, believed to be the favored candidate of the Chinese Ministry of Justice, Supreme Court, and other mainland authorities. The new JORC consisted largely of the same people as the old JSC, still sitting until 30 June. Two new lay members were members of the Preparatory Committee (responsible for the overseeing the transitional arrangements[26]) who had supported Tung Chee Hwa in the chief executive race. The JORC unanimously selected Andrew Li—a choice that might indicate the mainland government was sincere in its declaration it would permit Mr Tung to choose his team (or that Justice Liu was not as far ahead in Beijing's preferences as some had thought). The choice received the enthusiastic support of the legal profession and produced a chief justice who, as we shall see, proved no lapdog of the chief executive!

On the other side of the Chinese border was sitting the Provisional Legislative Council (PLC), almost certainly unlawful, or at least unable to perform any act with lawful effect in Hong Kong, either before or after the handover. However, on 24 May 1997, in Shenzhen, the secretary for justice told the members of the PLC of the JORC decision. Enthusiasm was expressed by a number of speakers, and the motion that the council support the nomination was passed without any necessity for a vote. In the early hours of 1 July, following the various handover ceremonies, the JORC ratified its nomination of Andrew Li and the chief executive appointed him and reported the appointment to the Standing Committee of the NPC. At 2:45 A.M. the PLC convened and ratified its own approval by passing the Hong Kong Reunification Ordinance,[27] which specified the names of permanent judges on the Court of Final Appeal and of the chief judge of the High Court, and these judges were sworn in. In the event, the other judges were assumed to be riding a "through train" and no questions arose as to the validity of the new JORC.

After the Transition

As the handover approached, anxieties remained high. As Peter Wesley-Smith observed of the "through train" issue, "Can any judge now sitting who is desirous of keeping his job through 1997 dare to offend pro-China sympathies?"[28] The transition is not over, but this does not mean it is premature to contemplate how things have gone so far. Have the fears of those litigants who in the mid-1990s showed signs of shunning the courts in favor of arbitration, for fear of a post-1997 decline in judicial independence, or of the pessimists of the legal profession or of academics, nongovernmental organisations,[29] or the U.S. government, been in any way realized?

The new chief justice has been most circumspect in his administration of the system. He has invited one member of the panel of nonpermanent judges to sit on each full appeal of the Court of Final Appeal—and these judges are such distinguished jurists as Sir Anthony Mason of Australia, Lord Cooke of New Zealand, and Lords Hoffman and Nicholls from the United Kingdom. He has abolished the colonial link to the church by doing away with the service at the opening of the legal year. And, perhaps more significant, he has replaced the colonial military guard of honor at the legal year ceremony not with soldiers of the People's Liberation Army, but with Hong Kong police. He was able to move away from a heavy reliance on acting judicial appointments, although he has not granted extensions to judges who have reached retirement age.[30]

In the above account, the judiciary appears as a strong institution. The few changes from the previous period appeared to fit within the familiar framework of a common law system. However, in one respect it was not so easy to fit the new system within the old framework. This concerned principally the provisions for the interpretation of the Basic Law in Article 158. The article is a compromise between and a combination of two different constitutional traditions. In Hong Kong, the responsibility for constitutional interpretation would lie with the courts. In China, it lies with the NPCSC. The original draft of the Basic Law had provided for only the NPCSC to interpret it, while key Hong Kong members of the Basic Law Drafting Committee had wanted the Hong Kong courts alone to have this power, as the only basis for secure legal guarantees of autonomy.[31]

The Basic Law divides the responsibility for interpretation between the NPCSC and the Hong Kong courts, leaving the adjudication of cases entirely to the Hong Kong courts. Within the framework of overarching powers of the NPCSC to interpret any provision of the Basic Law, it authorizes the Hong Kong courts to interpret any provisions during adjudication. However, a court from which no further appeal is possible in a particular case cannot interpret provisions dealing with the responsibilities of the central authorities or the relationship between them and the Hong Kong SAR. If the interpretation of such a provision will "affect" the judgment, then that court must ask the NPCSC to provide an interpretation of the provision and then apply it in adjudicating the case.

The general rule is that when the issue concerns a matter within the autonomy of Hong Kong, it is left to the Hong Kong courts. When it concerns a responsibility of the central authorities or the relationship between them and Hong Kong, it is left, ultimately, to the NPCSC. But this neat division is not always followed. By virtue of Article 158(1) of the Basic Law, the NPCSC's overriding powers of interpretation may affect any provision of the Basic Law. The NPCSC notion of interpretation is broad and may extend to the modification of the law. We thus have a somewhat unsatisfactory bifurcation of function and methods. Some provisions are determined following the common law method through the agency of the courts. Others are determined by a more political process, presumably using Chinese law methods.

To some extent, these difficulties of interface are intended to be overcome or minimized through the establishment of the Committee on the Basic Law (CBL), which acts in an advisory capacity to the NPCSC.[32] The CBL consists of six mainlanders and six Hong Kong residents. The NPCSC must consult the CBL before, among other things, interpreting the Basic Law. In that regard, the role of the CBL might be regarded as quasi-judicial. In practice, the members of the CBL have openly expressed their views on legal issues that come have come to them in their quasi-judicial capacity, and some of them have criticized the Hong Kong judiciary in extremely strong language. In the eyes of many commentators, the CBL is seen less as an independent and expert body than as one subordinated to Beijing, especially after the attack on the CFA decision on the right of abode was first orchestrated by both its Hong Kong and mainland members.

Article 158 enables the NPCSC to effectively overrule the interpretations of the Hong Kong courts, and this was seen not only as detracting from the independence or standing of the courts, but also as a major threat to the rule of law. It could be used to negate many guarantees of rights and autonomy. Various proposals have been made to limit intervention by the NPCSC through conventions of self-restraint as well as to judicialize the procedures of the NPCSC when it does interpret the law.[33]

The judiciary did not start auspiciously. For many commentators, it seemed as though the battle for judicial independence was lost a month after the handover, though this assessment turned out to be premature. The Court of Appeal in *HKSAR v. Ma Wai Kwan David* decided that the Provisional Legislative Council, which many argued was invalid as not within the contemplation of the Basic Law, was valid.[34] This was achieved with the assistance of considerable judicial gymnastics. The court accepted without any probing all government arguments about the "necessity" of the Provisional Legislature or the impossibility of proper elections before or shortly after the transfer of sovereignty. More seriously, and even less necessarily for the decision, the court held that the HKSAR courts had no jurisdiction to review the compatibility of National People's Congress (NPC) decisions with the Basic Law. The court accepted the argument of the solicitor general that, as previously Hong Kong courts could not question the acts of the British government, it could not now question those of the NPC.

The second "unnecessary" ruling was to the effect that the PRC authorities have complete powers over Hong Kong by virtue of the PRC Constitution. As with the previous point, the court completely disregarded fundamental differences in the constitutional status of Hong Kong before July 1, 1997, and now. The court did not discuss the relationship between the PRC Constitution and the Basic Law, and it did not refer to an NPC Decision of April 4, 1990, in which it stated that the Basic Law was "constitutional"—which was made precisely to avoid the doubts to which the court's decision gave rise. This decision threw into doubt the validity of numerous sections of the Basic Law that are inconsistent with the PRC Constitution—thus denying the basic premise of "two systems."

Better—and perhaps worse—was to come. Courts began to retreat from the extreme position taken in *Ma*. The opportunity for this arose in the case of the right of abode of "children" of Hong Kong permanent residents. The issue this time was less the direct application of Chinese law than it was the compatibility with the Basic Law of Hong Kong legislation (the Immigration Amendment [No. 3] Ordinance of 1997), which purported to give effect to some consequences of Chinese law. The applicants argued that the restrictions imposed by the ordinance on the entry of those mainland residents who qualified for the right of abode in Hong Kong under Article 24(3) breached the Basic Law. Specifically, the ordinance provided that the right of abode was only enjoyed if the requirements of a "certificate of entitlement" scheme were satisfied. For those living on the mainland, the scheme required them to apply to the Exit-Entry Administration of the Public Security Bureau. The system thus became inextricably linked to the mainland exit permit system, and thus subject to the existing quota for migration into Hong Kong—currently fixed at 150 people a day. Essentially, this meant that the new scheme represented very little change from the system that had been operating for a long time and under which numerous people had waited for many years to join relatives in Hong Kong.

Not only did the Court of Final Appeal's decision that this scheme was invalid amount to a declaration of invalidity of a piece of Hong Kong legislation, but it involved the delinking of a piece of mainland legislation from the immigration process.[35] While accepting that mainland laws were not to be applied in Hong Kong, the government argued that mainland laws could not be ignored either. As summarized by Justice Brian Keith in his first instance judgment, the government's position was that, if "the laws of mainland China restricted the number of its nationals who could settle in Hong Kong, it would be wrong for laws to be enacted in Hong Kong for entry into Hong Kong, which would be inconsistent with the laws of mainland China on the topic."[36]

Effectively, this position was no different from the government's position in *Ma*, namely that a Chinese law could override the Basic Law. Justice Keith found this argument unattractive, as it would have meant that "people who were accorded the right of abode in Hong Kong by virtue of Article 24, needed the permission of the Chinese authorities before they could enjoy that right. . . . The implementation of Article 24(3) would therefore be in the hands of the Chinese authorities." There was, however, a further issue: Article 22 (4) of the Basic Law states that "For entry into the HKSAR, people from other parts of China must apply for approval." Justice Keith held that this had the effect of validating the restriction in the Immigration Ordinance. Thus a direct "challenge" to the authority of the Chinese legislature was averted, though an indication of a more robust judicial attitude toward the enforcement of the Basic Law was flagged.

When the case reached the Court of Appeal, Chief Judge of the High Court Patrick Chan said that the analogy he had drawn in *Ma* with colonial courts might not have been entirely appropriate.[37] And the Court of Final Appeal asserted the jurisdiction of the HKSAR courts to review any legislative acts of the NPC or NPCSC for consistency with the Basic Law and to declare them invalid if found to be inconsistent, as a right and a duty. The court reached its decision, first, by a declaration of a general constitutional principle, and second, by reference to specific provisions of the Basic Law.

The general principle is one that it claims applies to all constitutions—that laws inconsistent with it are void and of no effect and that it is for the courts to determine questions of inconsistency and invalidity (thus ignoring a fundamental principle of Chinese constitutional law excluding judicial review). In the case of the Basic Law, it is the regional courts that have been given that responsibility. This responsibility extends to the review of acts of the NPC or its standing committee.

Having assumed jurisdiction, the court went on to decide that the right of abode under Article 24(3) was not qualified by Article 22 (which it held applied to those mainlanders who did *not* have the right of abode). Therefore, the Chinese law requiring exit permits for those with the right of abode could not be enforced, and the ordinance applying that restriction was unconstitutional.

The court also held that it was not necessary to refer the question to the Standing Committee of the NPC for interpretation. It was for the Court of Final Appeal to decide whether the conditions requiring a reference to the standing committee were satisfied; those conditions were that the provisions of the Basic Law in issue were "excluded provisions"—that is, they fell within those that are the responsibility of the central government of the PRC or concern the relationship between the central authorities and Hong Kong and that the decision *required* the interpretation of such a provision (the "necessity condition"). Because the court had held that the governing provision was Article 24 of the Basic Law, it was *not* necessary for the court to interpret Article 22, even if the latter was an excluded provision.

The foundations of the judgment were carefully crafted. The court sought the basis of its jurisdiction from the authority vested in it through the Basic Law by the National People's Congress, "the highest organ of state power," that is, of the sovereign. In other words, the court was saying that in the broad view it took of its jurisdiction, it was not engaged in any act of usurpation. Rather, it was carrying out the will of the NPC as laid down in the Basic Law.

Immediately after the judgment, one of the authors wrote:

> The Court of Final Appeal lays a broad and powerful base for constitutionalism. Its constant emphasis on rights and freedoms (described at different points as 'the essence of Hong Kong's civil society' and lying 'at the heart of Hong Kong's separate system') and its own broad jurisdiction, combined with guarantees of judicial independence, create an infinitely more effective base for the rule of law than during the colonial period, which under the doctrine of British sovereignty was incapable, notwithstanding the colonial rhetoric, of providing a true foundation for the rule of law. While taming sovereignty, the Court of Final Appeal decision makes even sharper the difference between legal traditions and approaches of the SAR and the Mainland, for it increases exponentially the constitutionalist factor in Hong Kong's system.

The Court of Final Appeal is also seeking to impose on the NPC, as regards its relation with Hong Kong, principles and restraints of constitutionalism that are alien to the PRC constitutional system. It is unthinkable that at present any judicial or other body on the Mainland would take a similarly restricted view of the law-making or other powers of the NPC. Is the Court of Final Appeal inaugurating a new constitutional jurisprudence for Mainland, or is it setting the stage for a show down with the mainland?[38]

Showdown there was, though it was through the proxy of the Hong Kong Department of Justice. The Court of Final Appeal was criticized by Hong Kong deputies to the NPC as well as by both Hong Kong and mainland members of the Basic Law Committee. Four leading Chinese lawyers called the decision "wrong."[39] The language used by some was little short of abusive. The chief justice was accused by one member of the Basic Law Committee of being a child who did not consult his parents' views.[40]

Although it was not clear initially which aspect of the decision most exercised the mainland legal authorities, it soon became clear that their discontent focused on the issue of the power of the court in relation to the NPC: "No organisation or department can challenge or deny NPC legislation and decisions," a Basic Law Committee member said.[41] It was reported that the chief executive had discussed the case with the authorities in Beijing. The secretary for justice went to Beijing—to listen, not to persuade, she said[42]—and Hong Kong members of the National People's Congress wanted the issue raised at the annual sitting of the congress.

Finally, in a most unusual procedure, the government asked the court, and it agreed, to "clarify" that part of its judgment relating to the NPC and its standing committee. In the run-up to this application, the secretary for justice had two private conversations with the chief justice on the issue, which elicited more critical comment. The court said,

> The Court's judgment on 29 January 1999 did not question the authority of the Standing Committee to make an interpretation under Article 158 which would have to be followed by the courts of the Region. The Court accepts that it cannot question that authority. Nor did the Court's judgment question, and the Court accepts that it cannot question, the authority of the National People's Congress or the Standing Committee to do any act which is not in accordance with the provisions of the Basic Law and the procedure therein.[43]

The court described the situation as "exceptional" and its course of action likewise. It did not discuss its power to reopen a decision once delivered, and it refused the bar association permission to appear as *amicus curiae*.

In Hong Kong at least, the "clarification" was generally seen as an act necessary to placate the mainland authorities rather than as an exercise in elucidation. It did not detract from the court's conclusions in the original judgment. The authority of the NPCSC to interpret the Basic Law was not an issue in the case. What was at issue was whether the court was required to refer Article 22 to the NPCSC for an interpretation under Article 158 (3). The court's decision that it did not have to refer the matter to the NPCSC was less contentious (or perhaps not noticed or understood) than the ruling that Hong Kong courts could review and, if necessary, refuse to apply mainland legislation if it was deemed inconsistent with the Basic Law. On the latter point, the court reaffirmed its position in its "clarification," albeit in more palatable language. The secretary for justice asserted that the crisis was over once the clarification had been issued. This, as we shall see, was premature.

Two basic views were discernible within Hong Kong. Some were optimistic, observing that the court did not water down its judgment. The optimists would take the view that Hong Kong's autonomy was not any the weaker for the clarification—indeed, it was stronger, because the court had reaffirmed it even when under strong pressure to be conciliatory to the central authorities. In this view, the independence of the judiciary was stronger rather than weaker. The matter had been resolved internally without intervention by the NPC. Also, the many positive rulings in the Court of Final Appeal judgment had been preserved.

The other view, held equally strongly, was that the independence of the judiciary had been compromised and that there is no doubt the Court of Final Appeal acted under political pressure, directly from the HKSAR government and indirectly from the central authorities. The case sets a bad precedent under which those who are dissatisfied with a judicial decision for political reasons can put pressure on the court for "rectification." It was not true to say that the matter has been resolved internally. The government was responding to pressures from the central authorities. No one in Hong Kong (including the Department of Justice) had any doubts about the meaning of the first judgment. Most lawyers thought that the judgment was correct. In this view, Hong Kong was merely using internal procedures to appease the central authorities, and its long-term consequences will be extremely negative.

Those who sat in the court the day it gave its clarification were conscious of a marked difference from the atmosphere the day the first judgment was delivered. On the first occasion, the chief justice delivered the judgment in a confident style, assured of the authority and prestige that we confer on or recognize in the judiciary. On the occasion of the clarification, the impression was of a court and counsel trying to avoid getting to grips with the real issue at stake. The judges appeared ill at ease throughout the case, as if unsure of their authority. The judgment, delivered after a short break, lacked the flow of the earlier decision, its prose somewhat convoluted, and its reasons scanty. There was a strong sense that the court was acting at the indirect behest of the mainland government.

The morale of the judiciary was believed to be at a low ebb after this "clarification." Naturally, the concern was whether this would affect the attitude of the judiciary in future cases. Soon another sensitive case reached the Court of Appeal—but the court defied fears that it might succumb to the temptation to mollify the mainland authorities.[44] The court declared invalid Section 7 of the National Flag and National Emblem Ordinance 1997, which criminalized the conduct of defacing the national flag, for incompatibility with the freedom of expression guaranteed by the ICCPR under Article 39 of the Basic Law. Although this too was a local ordinance implementing national legislation, it differed from the immigration ordinance in that the national legislation it implemented is extended to Hong Kong through the mechanism of Article 18 of the Basic Law and appears in annex 3 as one of the National Laws applying to Hong Kong.

Within Hong Kong, the judiciary is the subject of considerable fascination and, no doubt, some ambivalence. On the one hand, the substance of some of its more notable decisions may not have the support of the majority of the Hong Kong people. The apprehension of the size of immigration influx that is likely to be generated as a result of the "right of abode" cases is considerable. Nor is it likely that many Hong Kong people have a great deal of sympathy with the mutilation of flags. On the other hand, some, at least, of the courts' decisions will strike a chord among those many Hong Kong people who were, and remain, concerned about the erosion of Hong Kong's autonomy under the Basic Law. There seems little prospect that the reasons for public discussion of the courts will disappear in the new future. When the "flag" case comes to the CFA, it may be that the court will be able to reach a decision more palatable to the mainland authorities, but can it do so without exposing itself to suspicions of wishing to placate those authorities? Or will the chief justice, as one commentator has predicted, find his court faced with another case that should arguably go to the NPCSC and have to choose between eating his words or "causing another constitutional crisis"?[45]

Epilogue

Even before the CFA could hear the appeal on the flag case, the government itself precipitated a constitutional crisis. Fearing that the right of abode decision would open the "floodgates" to migration from the mainland, it did all it could do to obstruct implementation of the decision, while the courts tried to prevent the worst excesses of bureaucratic arbitrariness in dealing with those who claimed the right of abode under the decision. The government responded by whipping up public discontent with the decision, painting misleading and alarming pictures of the numbers of persons under the CFA's decision to enter Hong Kong (the government's estimate, challenged by many, is that 692,000 have an immediate right of abode and that their offspring, who will acquire the right seven years after the first wave arrives, number 983,000) and of the pressure they would impose on public services and employment. The government claimed, on the most flimsy of evidence, that Hong Kong would have to spend HK$710 billion on capital projects and, by 2009, another HK$33 billion to absorb the migrants. Surveys showed rising public anxiety at the implications of the decision, and many respondents declared they considered the prosperity of Hong Kong more important than rights. Having thus prepared the public, the government announced various options to overturn the CFA decision: to ask the CFA to reconsider its decision, to seek the amendment of the Basic Law, and—its preferred choice—to secure the assistance of the NPCSC to reinterpret the Basic Law to overrule the CFA.

In May 1999 the secretary for justice traveled to Beijing to discuss the procedure for such a request (although the Basic Law makes no provision for this kind of request, which would effectively make the NPCSC an appellate court from decisions of the CFA). The proposal drew considerable support from those concerned about the threats to Hong Kong's prosperity, but it was severely criticized by those who saw in the proposal the most fundamental challenge to the autonomy of Hong Kong and to the rule of law since the transfer of sovereignty. The government seemed determine to seek an interpretation from the NPCSC, which implied that the CFA was wrong and would be corrected by it. The government's intention may not have been to downgrade the CFA, but the general criticism of the CFA for having precipitated a major social and economic crisis—and for having been "wrong"—had the effect of downgrading the judiciary in the eyes of the public. This result, in turn, precipitated a major constitutional crisis in which the independence of the judiciary would be compromised, as the logic of Article 158, the Achilles heel of Hong Kong's autonomy and judicial independence, unfolded—although it should be noted that it was not China, but the unwillingness of the Hong Kong government to accept the CFA ruling, that may ultimately lead to the demise of judicial independence.

The denouement took place when the NPCSC accepted the request of the chief executive to overrule the CFA. Adopting the chief executive's argument, the NPCSC's interpretation chastised the CFA for its errors without giving any reasons and stated that the court had misunderstood the intention behind Article 24. The standing committee also stated that the CFA should have sought NPCSC interpretation of the validity of the exit permit requirement, because that concerned the responsibility of the central authorities. But the standing committee did not engage with the elaborate discussion of the CFA's reasoning on this point.[46]

The standing committee's action highlighted a major defect in the Basic Law with regard to the rule of law. It had been confidently but naively assumed that the committee would use its powers of interpretation only on reference from a court. The exercise of this power at the request of the Hong Kong government was widely interpreted as an executive overruling of the decision of the highest court, since it was clear that once the government request was made, it would be acceded to. Even if the standing committee had made up its own mind, the procedures it followed are totally inconsistent with the rule of law: lawyers for the children had no right of reply, legal arguments were not allowed, and no reasons were given for the decision.

Another blow to the common law lies in the rule that the decisions of the standing committee are binding on Hong Kong courts. Yet this decision provides no guidance on interpretation, and the courts have no idea of the mysterious ways by which the standing committee reaches its decisions (other than that senior officials of the Communist Party play the leading role). The CFA had itself expounded at great length the principles of constitutional interpretation that must guide the courts. The status of those guidelines is now in doubt. Can the common law survive or develop without its established rules interpretation?

The decision of the standing committee generated a huge public debate on the rule of the law and the independence of the judiciary. The bar association conducted a vigorous campaign against the government's reference to the standing committee. The solicitors, always more timorous than barristers, supported the government through the Law Society. The public was ambivalent, valuing judicial independence but worried about the effects of mainland migration on its welfare, indicating that there were limits to its support for the rule of law.

Both before and after the interpretation, the government and its servants have argued with great force in favor of their own view of the legality and propriety of the government's course of action. A senior member of the Department of Justice—since made acting solicitor general—insisted that the government could at any time ask for an interpretation by the SCNPC, "before, during or after a case."[47] The secretary for justice seems to have accused dissenters of being unwilling to learn about Chinese law.[48]

The judiciary kept its head down (save for a senior judge of the Court of Appeal, Mr. Justice Gerald Godfrey, who broke with precedent and wrote to the press implying that the government did not understand the rule of law.[49]) And in September 1999 at a meeting of Asian judges in Seoul, the chief justice said:

> The Judiciary has a vital constitutional role to ensure that the Executive and the Legislative act within the constitution and the law, that there is no abuse of power and that the fundamental rights and freedoms of citizens are safeguarded. . . . The effective discharge of this constitutional role is a difficult task for the courts. . . . Court decisions are and should be vigorously exercised in a free society. Further, such public debate would have the benefit of informing and educating the public about the judicial system and the issue at stake. But to maintain the independence of the Judiciary, it would not be acceptable or desirable for judges to have to defend their judgments in the political arena. It is therefore important that the right to scrutinize court judgments should be responsibly exercised.[50]

But the CFA was soon called upon to react to the NPCSC's interpretation, in *Lau Kong Yung v. Director of Immigration*.[51] Capitulation, as many commentators have remarked, was total. The respondents argued that the NPCSC had the power to make an interpretation only on a reference from the CFA, and even then it could only interpret an "excluded" provision. The court rejected the argument, holding that the NPCSC had plenary powers of interpretation under Article 158(1) of the Basic Law. Since the court could have reached its decision on Article 158(1) alone, it is unfortunate that it went on to rely also on Article 67(4) of the Chinese Constitution. This approach denies the self-contained nature of the Basic Law and raises considerable doubts about status and effect of the Basic Law in the face of several contrary provisions of the constitution.

The second issue was the effect of the interpretation. The court had little difficulty in demonstrating that the NPCSC had seen a link between Articles 22(4) and 24(2)(3), although this was not explicitly stated in the interpretation, and the court held that an exit permit was essential to the exercise of the right of abode, thus accepting the reversal of their own decision in January.

The Basic Law does not explicitly deal with the effect of an NPCSC interpretation under Article 158(1). The court held that the "general power of interpretation of the Basic Law vested in the Standing Committee by Article 158(1) is plainly a power to give an authoritative interpretation of the Basic Law binding on all institutions in the Region. There is no occasion to spell out the obvious in the Basic Law."[52] This left the question of the effect of such interpretations on existing rights and obligations. Sir Anthony concluded that the vesting of judicial power in the Hong Kong courts meant that the interpretation could not affect parties to the litigation, and the interpretation itself also makes this point explicitly.

Precisely whose right to a permanent residency would be governed by the January 1999 decision was left open by the CFA. In June 2000 this issue was being litigated at the instance of over five thousand people who argued that they were entitled to the benefit of the earlier decision.

Another question the CFA did not go into is the right of the chief executive to ask the NPCSC for an interpretation. The chief executive relied on Articles 43 and 48(2) of the Basic Law as the basis for his request to the State Council "seeking the assistance of the central government in resolving the problems encountered in the implementation of the relevant provisions of the Basic Law." In our view, neither of these provisions justifies the request or the subsequent action of the State Council in requesting an interpretation from the NPCSC. The CFA, however, implicitly approved of the conduct of the chief executive and the State Council and opened the way to future references. By evading the issue of the legality of the chief executive's request, the CFA has abandoned the attempt to circumscribe the powers of the chief executive and the central authorities that had characterized its January decision. The court has also hinted that it is poised to abandon its criterion of the "predominant provision" for deciding on judicial references.[53] A more liberal approach in making judicial references to the NPCSC will reduce pressure on the government to invoke Article 158(1), but at the expense of undermining the autonomy of the courts that is one important purpose of Article 158(3). If the December decision is a clue, the CFA is unlikely, contrary to its promise in January, to scrutinize the conduct of the central authorities and give effect to it only if it is consistent with the law and procedure of the Basic Law.

The flag case followed hard on the heels of the right of abode case, and here again, for whatever reason, the decision was no doubt palatable to the central authorities, the CFA upheld the criminalization of the desecration of the national and regional flags, again in unnecessarily broad language.[54]

At the opening of the legal year in January 2000, the chief justice made what most commentators saw as a criticism of the government: "where the courts come under unwarranted attack, it is the constitutional responsibility of the Government, that is the executive authorities, to explain and defend the fundamental principle of judicial independence, whether or not the decision in question is in its favour."[55] Though the administration puts a brave face on it, it seems that the government realizes that the right of abode episode has been somewhat demoralizing for the judiciary as well as a poor advertisement for the rule of law and the autonomy of Hong Kong. Faced with critical comment from the press and the profession at home as well as concern internationally,[56] the administration has embarked on a damage- limitation exercise or, to put it more positively, a series of "Measures to promote the rule of law and judicial independence, and to enhance confidence in Hong Kong's legal system."[57] The Department of Justice has skillfully turned the chief justice's statement to its advantage, pointing out that he did go on to say that the government accepted its responsibility.

We can see signs of this concern on the part of the government in the publicity given to statements of retiring judges that they are satisfied that judicial independence has been preserved; in the posting on the Internet of statements by two retiring judges of the CFA that they are simply leaving because they have reached retiring age, or want to spend more time with their families;[58] in the suggestion mentioned earlier that the Legislative Council should simply rubber-stamp the replacement of these judges; and, above all, in the insistence that interpretations of the Basic Law would be sought only in "highly exceptional circumstances." "The Department of Justice hopes that the Administration will not again be faced with a problem of the magnitude of the right of abode issue, and that another request by the Chief Executive for a SCNPSC Interpretation will not be necessary."[59]

Notes

1. See, generally, Yash Ghai, *Hong Kong's New Constitutional Order*, 2d ed. (Hong Kong: Hong Kong Univ. Press, 1998).

2. See Article 11 of the Basic Law.

3. See Yash Ghai, "Litigating the Basic Law: Jurisdiction, Interpretation and Procedure," in *The Constitutional Debate: Competing Paradigms of Legality and Interpretation,* eds. Fu Chan and Yash Ghai (Hong Kong: Hong Kong Univ. Press, 1999).

4. Annual Report of the Government of Hong Kong, *Hong Kong: A New Era;* see also the chief executive's policy address, delivered to Legislative Council (7 October 1998).

5. The phrase is from the International Covenant on Civil and Political Rights (ICCPR) and is reproduced in Article 10 of the Hong Kong Bill of Rights of 1991.

6. J. W. Norton-Kyshe, *The History of the Laws and Courts of Hong Kong from the Earliest Period to 1898* (1898; reprint, Hong Kong: Vetch & Lee, 1971), 156.

7. See Eric Barnes, "The Independence of the Judiciary in Hong Kong" *Hong Kong Law Journal* 6 (1976): 7.

8. Bernard Downey, "The Next Chief Justice," *Hong Kong Law Journal* 8 (1978): 282.

9. Chief secretary during the second reading debate on the Pension Benefits (Judicial Officers) Bill, *Official Proceedings of the Legislative Council* (23 November 1988), 748.

10. Section 104 of the Magistrates Ordinance.

11. Judicial Service Commission Ordinance No. 65 of 1975.

12. See, for example, Henry Litton, "Editorial: The Judicial Service Commission and the Attorney-General," *Hong Kong Law Journal* 13 (1983): 129.

13. Generally on the Chinese system, see Hung-yee Albert Chen, *An Introduction to the Legal System of the People's Republic of China,* 2d ed. (Hong Kong: Butterworths Asia, 1998).

14. Zhou Wei, "The Sources of Law in the SAR," in P. Wesley-Smith, ed., *Hong Kong's Transition: Problems and Prospects* (Hong Kong: Faculty of Law, Hong Kong Univ., 1993).

15. Ordinance No. 29 of 2000 raised the civil jurisdiction of the District Court from HK$120,000 (US$15,380) to HK$600,000 (US$76,920). It is estimated that 50 percent of the civil actions that would have been started in the CFA will now be started in the district court. *Legislative Council Paper No. CB(2) 1908/99–00 (01).*

16. This is not required by the ordinance, but permanent magistrates, of whom there are about ninety and who are always lawyers, and special magistrates with more limited powers, of whom there are ten and who may be lay justices of the peace, no longer have any judicial functions.

17. Article 92. The various pieces of legislation were amended in 1997 by the Administration of Justice (Miscellaneous Provisions) Ordinance No. 14.

18. The council had been given one role in connection with the judiciary in 1998 when the Pension Benefits (Judicial Officers) Ordinance Section 37 required that the council approve any exemption or modification of pension rights as they affected a judicial officer.

19. Kong Lai-fan, "LEGCO Rejects Rubber-stamp Role," *South China Sunday Morning Post,* 4 June 2000.

20. These can be found on the Internet at <http://www.legco.gov.hk/yr99-00/english/procedur/content/rop.htm>, accessed 6 June 2000. They were published as Legal Notice 265 of 1998.

21. There is no space here to elaborate on these issues See further, for example, the work of Abimbola A. Olowofoyeku, *Suing Judges: A Study of Judicial Immunity* (Oxford: Clarendon Press, 1993), and *Law of Judicial Immunities in Nigeria* (Ibadan: Spectrum Law Publishing,1992).

22. For an account, see Jonathan Dimbleby, *The Last Governor: Chris Patten & the Handover of Hong Kong* (London: Little, Brown, and Company, 1997).

23. See Ghai, *Hong Kong's New Constitutional Order*, 324.

24. See P. Wesley-Smith, "Judges and the Through Train" *Hong Kong Law Journal* 25 (1995): 1.

25. Judicial Service Commission (Special Provision) Ordinance No. 78 of 1997, Section 2.

26. See Ghai, *Hong Kong's New Constitutional Order*, 260.

27. The report of that nocturnal Legislative Council meeting is available on the Internet at <http://www.legco.gov.hk/yr97-98/english/counmtg/hansard/970701fe.htm>, accessed 6 June 2000.

28. Wesley-Smith, "Judges and the Through Train," 2.

29. See, for example, the Hong Kong Monitor, "Threats to the Rule of Law at the Handover," written in June 1997, published in *Newsletter* August 1997, and available on the Internet at <http://hkhrm/org.hk/english/reports/enw/enw0897c.htm>, accessed 4 June 2000.

30. Though this did not prevent some (if only mild) speculation as to why in 1998 Justice Sears, who had been somewhat outspoken on some issues, was refused a second extension. See Cliff Buddle, "'People's Judge' Forced to Retire" *South China Morning Post,* 20 September 1998.

31. Martin Lee, "A Tale of Two Articles," in P. Wesley-Smith and A. Chen, eds., *The Basic Law and Hong Kong's Future* (Hong Kong: Butterworths, 1998).

32. NPC Decision of 4 April 1990 and Articles 17, 18, 158 and 159 of the Basic Law.

33. Ghai, *Hong Kong's New Constitutional Order*, chap. 5.

34. [1997] 2 *Hong Kong Cases* 315.

35. *Ng Ka Ling v. Director of Immigration* [1999], 1 HKC 291 (three cases were dealt with together).

36. *Cheung Lai Wah v. Director of Immigration* [1997], HKLRD 1081, 1090.

37. *Cheung Lai Wah v Director of Immigration* [1998], 1 HKLRD 772, 779.

38. Y. Ghai, *South China Morning Post,* 3 February 1999.

39. See No Kwai-Yan, "Concern for Judicial System," *South China Morning Post,* 8 February 1999.

40. May Sin-Mi Hon, "Personal Attacks 'Must Stop,'" *South China Morning Post,* 12 February 1999.

41. Beijing University Professor Xiao Weiyun, reported in the *South China Morning Post,* 8 February 1999.

42. Chris Yeung, "Justice Chief's Trip 'Mainly to Listen'" *South China Morning Post,* 12 February 1999.

43. *Ng Ka Ling v Director of Immigration (No. 2)* [1999], 1, *Hong Kong Cases,* 425, 427; and (1999) 2 *Hong Kong Court of Final Appeal Reports,* 141.

44. *HKSAR v Ng Kung-Siu* [1999], 1, *Hong Kong Law Reports and Digest*, 783.

45. Danny Gittings, "Judgment Flagged for Controversy" *South China Sunday Morning Post*, 18 April 1999.

46. *The Interpretation of the Standing Committee of the National Peoples Congress of Articles 22(4) and 24(2)(3) of the Basic Law of the Hong Kong Special Administrative Region of the People's Republic of China*, Legal Notice 167 of 1999, in *Gazette of the Hong Kong Special Administrative Region, Second Supplement*, 28 June 1999.

47. Ng Kang-chung, "Tung 'Can Appeal for NPC Auling Anytime,'" *South China Sunday Morning Post*, 13 June 1999.

48. Angela Li, "More Heat for Law Chief over Letter," *South China Morning Post*, 9 June 1999.

49. *South China Morning Post*, 12 May 1999; Justice Godfrey quoted a justice Wilson of the Canadian Supreme Court in *Re Bachand v. Dupuis* [1964], 2 DLR 641, at 655 in a passage that nicely captures the essence of what seems to have happened when the secretary for justice went to Beijing to sort out the reference to the NPCSC, as follows, "The whole value of the legal system—the integrity of the rule of law—is at once destroyed if it becomes possible for officials by arbitrary decisions made, not in the private office of officialdom, without hearing the parties, without taking evidence, free of all obedience to settled legal principles, effectively to overrule the Courts."

50. "Administration of Justice in the 21st Century," at the sixteenth biennial Law Association for Asia and Pacific (LAWASIA) conference, to be found on the Internet at <http://www.info.gov.hk/jud/whatsnew/html/speech/speech_cj.htm>, accessed 6 June 2000.

51. [1999] 2 *Hong Kong Court of Final Appeal Reports*, 300.

52. Ibid., 324.

53. Ibid.

54. *HKSAR v. Ng Kung Siu* [1999] 2 *Hong Kong Court of Final Appeal Reports*, 442.

55. Cliff Buddle and Magdalen Chow, "Top Judge in Plea to Government," *South China Morning Post*, 18 January 2000.

56. Including the Seventh Report of the Speaker's Task Force on the Hong Kong transition (U.S. Congress), presented to the House of Representatives by Doug Bereuter on 7 February 2000, available on the Internet at <http://www.house.gov./international_relations/ag/hongkong7.htm>, accessed 7 June 2000.

57. "Measures to Promote the Rule of Law and Judicial Independence," Legislative Council Paper No CB(2) 1698/99–00(03), which can be found on the council's web site at <http://legco.gov.hk/yr99-00/english/panels/ajls/agenda/ajag1804.htm>, accessed 7 June 2000

58. <http://www.info.gov.hk/jud/whatsnew/index.htm>, accessed 7 June 2000.

59. "Measures to Promote the Rule of Law," paragraph 20.

12

The Critical Challenge of
Judicial Independence in Israel

SHIMON SHETREET

The Israeli judiciary has long enjoyed independence—that is, the independence of the individual judge's security of office and independence in adjudicating cases. However, the constitutional position of the judiciary remains inadequate. The opportunity for providing constitutional protection was unfortunately missed in 1980, when the Basic Law: Adjudication was passed in the Knesset. The minister of justice at the time, Moshe Nissim, decided on grounds of principle to refrain from introducing into the Basic Law a provision requiring a special majority for its amendment. The judiciary failed to convince the minister and the Parliamentary Constitution and Justice Committee to include in the law a requirement for a special majority for its amendment equivalent to the provision included in the Basic Law for the Knesset. Subsequent attempts to provide constitutional protection for judges were not successful.

Although the role of the judiciary in Israel has increased significantly, the constitutional position of the judiciary remains inadequate. A simple legislative majority could change every provision relative to the judiciary. The challenge has become much greater since 1992, when the Knesset passed two very important constitutional pieces of legislation: the Basic Law: The Dignity of Man and his Freedom and the Basic Law: Freedom of Occupation. These two Basic Laws opened a new era in the Israeli legal system. They established constitutional standards that cannot be violated by ordinary legislation. Thus, by implication, they gave the courts the power to invalidate legislation found to be contrary to the Basic Laws. In effect, they constitutionalized the Israeli legal system.[1]

The anomaly of the Israeli judiciary led by a supreme court, which had a strong role in governance long before 1992 and which was made even wider through the mini constitutional revolution of 1992, remaining unprotected constitutionally is not merely a theoretical concern but is a very practical and critical challenge. The court has been asked to rule on numerous politically charged issues. These rulings often bring about threats to the collective independence of the judiciary, which Peter Russell in his introductory chapter classifies as "structural" in nature: proposals to limit the jurisdiction of the courts or to change the terms of office of judges. In the absence of adequate constitutional protection, such changes require only a simple majority vote of the Knesset. At the same time, amendments of the Basic Laws require a special majority, thus putting much greater pressure on the courts in their adjudication of constitutional cases. Whereas in the past legislative measures amending judicial rulings required a simple majority, they now require a special majority. Only once has such a majority been mobilized in the Knesset—in the Meat Import Cases.[2]

This chapter analyzes judicial independence in Israel and proposes the components of adequate constitutional protection of judicial independence. The opening sections examine the increasing judicial role in Israel and public attitudes toward the judiciary. It then turns to the judiciary's efforts to fine-tune its role and moves on to review interventions by the political branches in judicial affairs. The final section concludes with a discussion of the constitutional reforms needed to secure judicial independence in Israel.

Increasing Role of the Judiciary

While most of this chapter deals with the Supreme Court of Israel, it bears emphasizing that this court sits at the top of a hierarchy of courts. Immediately below it is the district court, a court of general jurisdiction over civil and criminal matters. Below that is the magistrates court, with jurisdiction in civil suits with a monetary value of up to a million shekels ($250,000) and criminal jurisdiction over lesser offences. The Supreme Court, as the court of last resort, hears appeals from the district court. In addition, the Supreme Court has an important original jurisdiction in administrative matters; it, for example, entertains petitions against government agencies and ministers for violating laws, including common law duties binding on them.

In recent decades, a trend toward an expansion of the Supreme Court's role, on the one hand, and a decline in the power of the executive, on the other, has taken place as a result of a growing tendency to bring politically charged issues before the court. At the same time, the High Court of Justice has demonstrated a willingness to adjudicate these issues on the merits and to interfere with the authorities' decisions. By adopting a more liberal approach to the rules of justiciability and standing, the court has opened its doors to many issues that were not adjudicated in that court in the past.

The public has resorted to the courts for settlement of problems the political authorities failed to resolve. Thus the courts adjudicated the validity of non-Orthodox conversion conducted in Israel, the closing of streets on Sabbath, the validity of the General Security Service interrogation practices, the introduction of summer daylight savings time, the exemption from conscription of *yeshiva* students, the constitutionality of allocating broadcasting time for election propaganda, the retroactive increase in allocation of funds to political parties for financing campaigns, and the immunity of Knesset members. The Supreme Court adjudicated cases regarding the rights of a one-man faction in the Knesset, the validity of a pardon granted to the heads of the General Security Services in the midst of a heated public debate, the power of the minister of justice to refuse to surrender a criminal fugitive declared extraditable by the courts, and even the time when a speaker of the Knesset ought to put a motion of no confidence to a vote.

Sometimes the executive intentionally diverted the onus of making decisions from itself to the judiciary to avoid paying the political price involved in making the decision itself. The increasing role of the courts has also been manifested by the greater willingness to review substantive decisions, and specifically security considerations.[3] The supervision the High Court of Justice exercised when Israel administered the territories in Gaza and the West Bank is another illustration of a broadening of the judicial function.

Changing the Rules of Justiciability and Standing

In a democratic society, greater recourse to the courts to solve political questions can be paradoxical. People turn to the judiciary because it is independent of politics, but in so doing, they inevitably immerse the judiciary in politics. The court has reacted by developing procedural barriers to filter out petitions, thus restraining this phenomenon to a certain degree. The clearest example of such an instrument is the development of the doctrine of justiciability.

Literally speaking, a dispute is justiciable in its normative meaning if there exists a yardstick for its resolution.[4] This formulation emphasizes the objective element of the concept but conceals more than it reveals. It focuses on the courts' ability to adjudicate a conflict rather than on the desirability of a judicial decision. The court no longer accepts the view that certain activities of public authorities are not subject to adjudication by legal standards. On the contrary, the court has held that the law governs every action (i.e., normative justiciability), but noninterference may result from exercise of the court's discretion (i.e., institutional justiciability).[5]

Another important test that determines whether or not the court will take up the case is the test of *locus standi,* or standing to sue. On this issue, the Supreme Court abandoned altogether the traditional approach, according to which a public petitioner lacking a direct interest in the petition would be deemed to lack *locus standi.* The court formulated a more liberal approach, based on a pragmatic balancing between two competing considerations: the importance of recognizing public petitions as safeguards for the rule of law and the fear of overburdening the court with petitions. The court held that a proper balance between these two considerations would be struck by granting standing to a petitioner who was able to point to an issue of special public importance, or to a seemingly serious fault in the action of the authorities, or to the fact that the act in dispute is of special constitutional importance. The court stressed that these categories did not constitute a closed list, but were markers for sorting out the competing interests. Moreover, in the Becker case, the court pointed out the functional link between *locus standi* and justiciability: "The stronger the right of standing which the petitioner can show . . . the greater will be the court's willingness to overcome its reluctance to interfere in political matters, and vice versa: a weak right of standing strengthens this reluctance."[6]

Debate over the Judicial Role

When confronting an ideologically charged issue directly, the judges tend to conceive their role as one of identifying and applying, rather than creating, the principles and norms applicable to the case. They have not viewed themselves as authorized to express "their very own personal inclinations and predilection." On the contrary, "when we confront an issue whose true nature is social rather than legal, we, as judges, are obliged to express what appears to us to reflect the community's opinion rather than a private opinion."[7] In practice, however, the judicial role has not always been limited to identifying prevailing public opinion. In certain cases, judges have referred to the educative, molding nature of the judicial decision.[8]

Criticism has been voiced against ideological and constitutional judg-ments on the grounds that in a democratic regime the legislative function is carried out by an elected body, which expresses the majority's will. Since judges are neither elected by the public nor answerable to it, the public cannot express dissatisfaction with the judges' decisions by replacing them with others.

In response to this criticism, Justice A. Barak has offered a theoretical basis to guide the adjudicative process that addresses this challenge to the democratic legitimacy of the judiciary.[9] He suggests that when a judge decides a case in a democratic regime, he should be aware of the values of the society within which he is adjudicating. When judges have to interpret the meaning of ambiguous statutes, and where the legislative intent cannot be ascertained, Barak suggests that such legislation be interpreted by using the basic values of the system as "background assumptions." The basis for these values in Israel may be found in the Declaration of Independence and includes principles of equality and justice, the existence of the state and its Jewish and democratic character, public order and security, the separation of powers, and the basic rights of individuals.

Security Considerations and Emergency Situations

Since its establishment in 1948, existence of the State of Israel has been constantly threatened, with recurrent wars followed by periods of relative quiet and stability. This situation is reflected in the Israeli legal reality in which an official and continuous state of emergency has existed without any relaxation even during periods of relative calm.[10]

In the first years of the state, the Supreme Court annulled security decisions where it was proven that the public officer exceeded his authority or did not fulfil procedural requirements laid down by law. Until the end of the 1970s, the court refused to intervene where the argument was not one of excess of jurisdiction or procedural defect but an attack against the decision itself. If the argument was that security considerations did not justify the decision, the court would dismiss such an argument if the minister or the military commander could prove that two conditions were fulfilled: that he acted within his jurisdiction and that he acted in good faith.

In later years, the courts have shown a greater willingness to review substantive decisions of the executive. In the Elon Moreh case,[11] the court undertook an examination of the motives of the authorities and concluded that the government had acted from general security motives and not to serve military needs. The judgment established the ruling that security considerations are subject to substantive review even when the authorities are operating within their powers. This trend of increasing the scope of judicial review of security considerations was explicitly emphasized by Justice Barak in the Schnitzer case,[12] where the court overturned the military censor's decision banning the publication of sections of an article about the Mossad (Israeli intelligence) in a Tel Aviv newspaper.

Judges as Chairmen of Commissions of Inquiry

The important role judges play in Israeli public life is by no means confined to adjudication on the bench. Judges are frequently appointed to lead inquiries into major public controversies and matters of the highest national importance. These commissions are instituted by law, and their terms of reference are defined by the government. But the president of the Supreme Court determines the composition of the commission. In addition, judges have been asked to chair nonstatutory governmental committees for the investigation of various matters, some of which were very sensitive, such as the task of reviewing the structure and function of the Israeli secret services, or the remuneration of teachers.

Commissions of inquiry chaired by judges have investigated a long series of matters, including the Wadi Salib ethnic riots in 1959 in Haifa (Justice Moshe Etzioni), corruption in soccer games and soccer organizations and clubs (Justice Etzioni), corruption in the government in the Raphael Affair (Judge Golan), oil drilling operations in Sinai in the Netivei Neft Affair (Justice Alfred Witkon), the fire at the El-Aksa Mosque (Justice Yoel Sussman), and the killing of a civilian by the police in the Kfar Shalem Inquiry.

Perhaps the most significant inquiries conducted by judges have been those related to war. Shimon Agranat, president of the Supreme Court, for instance, chaired a commission on the Yom Kippur War of 1973. Following the commission's report, Prime Minister Golda Meir and Minister of Defense Moshe Dayan were forced to resign under popular pressure, even though the report had placed the responsibility for the neglect and misjudgment of the projected plan of the enemy on the military, rather than the political, level. Subsequently, other justices have headed controversial commissions.

There is, of course, a division of opinion on the legitimacy of appointing judges to chair commissions. But it would appear that in times when there is a loss of public confidence in the political branches, such an appointment is generally accepted as justified.[13]

Public Confidence in the Courts

The courts can only perform their function as an institution to resolve disputes in society if they enjoy public confidence. Research on the status of the Supreme Court in the public eye indicates that the judiciary, and especially the Supreme Court, enjoys tremendous public support and legitimacy. This broad legitimacy has various expressions, such as: the ascription of superior traits amounting to a mythic image of the court; regarding courts as neutral nonpolitical bodies; and looking upon the court as guardian of democracy in Israel. All of this is manifest in the public's readiness to accept the court's judgments, even when these judgments contradict personal opinions and expectations.

Although there is broad general support for the Supreme Court, support rates vary significantly from one decision to another. When the judgment is a criticism of the army authorities, support for the decision declines. This phenomenon is a result of the Israeli public's conception of security matters as "veto-areas" in which the civil authorities should not interfere.

In this context, the new Basic Laws allegedly contributed to the legitimacy of the Supreme Court's review of the other authorities. However, analysis of developments since the introduction of those Basic Laws reveals that public criticism of the judiciary has increased and that this phenomenon has found a political expression: political actions aimed at eliminating the results of court decisions and attempts to initiate reforms that would limit the power of the court.[14]

In this politically charged environment, the Supreme Court has followed a number of principles and practices aimed to ensure that justice will not only be done but also will be seen to be done.[15] These include the "open court" principle, which is one of those fundamental principles of the legal system with a basis in statutory law,[16] and a court's duty (again grounded in statute) to state reasons for its decisions. The importance of public confidence in the courts is further reflected in the rather strict tests applied for self-disqualification of judges for bias.[17] The test does not require proof that bias has actually influenced the judge, but rather that there is a real likelihood that it will influence the judge. The traditions of the bench go even further than the strict requirement of the law of bias.

Concern for maintaining public confidence is also evident in guidelines issued by the president of the Supreme Court on the assignment of cases. No specific guidelines govern how the president is to choose particular judges to sit on any case. There is a guideline governing the choice of judges in the district and magistrate's courts, but its legal validity is doubtful, since it was issued by the president of the Supreme Court, in spite of the legal arrangement that case allocation in those courts is within the jurisdiction of the presidents of each of those courts. The guideline provides that court presidents may base their selection on specific considerations for each case or on an automatic system based on file numbers or alphabetically according to the names of the parties. The assignment method could combine both methods. Although the president of the Supreme Court's authority to issue such a guideline is doubtful, it reflects the law and practice concerning the powers of the presidents of courts regarding case assignment.

The desirability of an assignment based on a judge's particular specialization in a certain area has been questioned. Such a deliberate assignment may harm judicial independence if all decisions in one area are based on the views of one judge rather than incorporating the views of the whole court. The Supreme Court Working Guidelines support rotation of judges, so that judges decide all sorts of cases, thereby gaining broader experience and knowledge. Nonetheless, this has not prevented some judges from gaining a strong reputation for their expertise in certain areas of the law. Another point to be taken into account in the assignment of cases is consideration of a fair reflection of social classes, ethnic and religious groups, and ideological inclinations. It is particularly important in sensitive cases for panels to be either altogether neutral or balanced.[18]

In the open society of our modern age, the press plays a very important role in checking public institutions. Courts and judges, like all other social and governmental institutions, are subject to public criticism and the watchful eyes of the press.

Resolution of the Controversy on the Judicial Role: Fine-Tuning

The Supreme Court of Israel has made a significant contribution to the democratic system of government of Israel, to the protection of civil rights, and to the fair and proper administration of government. The court's contribution was especially important in the crisis period the Israeli political system experienced in the mid-1990s. But having said this, it seems clear that the time has now come for some fine-tuning of the judicial role in Israel.

Fine-tuning the borderlines between the judiciary and the other branches is essential because of the ever-increasing critical voices on the scope of the judicial role in Israeli society. Many have claimed that the borderlines have been pushed into territory that lies beyond the appropriate domain of the judiciary. This claim reflects a widely held public sentiment, and the court, which cannot operate in disregard of public sentiment, must take careful note of this concern.

The fine-tuning of the judicial role in society and the adjustment of the boundaries between the judicial branch and the other branches has to be established by the courts themselves, just as the dramatic broadening of judicial review was established by the judges themselves. And when should this remarking of the demarcation lines between the judiciary and the other branches take place? I think that when judicial intervention in a certain area has brought about substantial disruption in the balance between the judiciary and another branch, then the court has to redefine the boundary and then withdraw from the area in question.

The court itself must determine whether a substantial disruption or imbalance has occurred. Just as the court has extended its role by employing such tests as "substantial harm of the rule of law" or "adverse impact on the parliamentary government" to broaden standing (the right to sue the court), so must it develop the proposition of preventing substantial disruption or imbalance of the relations between the branches of government as the doctrinal rationale for adjusting the demarcation line between the judiciary and the other branches of government.

The task of charting newly defined boundaries between the judiciary and the political branches is no less challenging than the task of broadening judicial jurdistiction. The challenge is to avoid unnecessary judicial withdrawal from vital areas that need judicial supervision, while at the same time removing or reducing the judiciary's presence in areas where it has substantially disrupted relations between the judiciary and another branch.

The court has developed a number of judicial strategies for this task. One pattern is to rule on the case but to postpone the operative order to a later date to allow the executive and the legislature to respond to the court decision. This pattern was followed in the 1993 case of Pessaro-Glodstein,[19] in which the Supreme Court declared that non-Orthodox conversion in Israel was legitimate and state authorities exercising civil powers (as distinguished from religious halacha on marriage and divorce) could not refuse recognition of such conversion. The court postponed operative application, giving the executive and the legislature a grace period to respond to the ruling. The government has repeatedly asked for extension of the period and the matter has been pending now for about six years. The court followed the same strategy in 1999, when it declared as unlawful the administrative policy on *yeshiva* students' exemption from army service.[20]

To avoid clashes with certain segments of the community, sometimes the court strikes the balance of interest in a way that gives more weight to certain social interests. This was done in the Lior Horev Case on the closing of Bar Ilan Street in Jerusalem.[21]

Executive and Legislative Intervention in the Justice System

The change in the role of the Israeli Supreme Court is evident in the tone of its reaction to executive action aimed at frustrating the results of court decisions. The executive has on occasion used physical action to render judgments ineffective. More often, judicial rulings invalidating executive action were overcome by retroactive parliamentary legislation and at times even by resorting to administrative emergency legislation.[22]

The Supreme Court has reacted very strongly to any attempt by the executive to avoid the result of judicial decisions by physical action. Thus, for example, the deportation of persons before they had an opportunity to file a petition in the High Court of Justice, or while a petition was pending or being filed, has been met by a strong rebuke from the court. Indeed, the court seriously reprimanded the legal adviser to the government in 1975 when an order for deportation was carried out while the petition to the High Court was being filed. The Supreme Court has also insistently required strict executive obedience to court orders and has reacted fiercely to any attempt by the executive to deviate from commitments given to the court by state attorneys.[23]

The status of the Israeli judiciary is, thus, not entirely unassailable. Governmental and legislative intervention often occurs in various spheres of the judicial activity and takes many forms. As can be seen from the ensuing analysis, different patterns of intervention have been discerned during different periods in the history of the state.

The weakest form of intervention by political elements in the judicial system is that of political debates of matters concerning the courts, particular judges, and their decisions. In general, it is the view of this author that there is nothing wrong with such intervention. The modern concept of the doctrine of separation of powers requires a system of "checks and balances," and one expression of this system is the right of the executive and legislative branches of government to be at liberty to discuss the way in which the judicial branch is functioning. Respect for the judiciary would suffer if judges themselves aroused public debate on the issues dealt with in their decisions. Therefore, it is the function of the executive and the Knesset to bring the issues to the attention of the public. Indeed, such discussions may very well further the interests of the judiciary.

A somewhat more serious pattern of intervention is that of executive supervision of the judicial system. This pattern is also basically acceptable.

Legislative intervention in the administration of the judiciary occurs in relation to the sensitive issue of judicial salaries. To ensure that the Knesset does not use financial measures as a means of "punishing" judges, the law prohibits any decrease in judges' pay alone, in the absence of an across-the-board pay cut of civil service employees. This statutory protection is, however, insufficient, since there is no legal bar to the reduction of judicial pay for reasons other than general economics.

Another sensitive form of intervention is the appointment of judges. It is generally accepted that political intervention in this area is legitimate. Indeed, in the opinion of this author, it is a positive phenomenon, because it is important to ensure that the judiciary reflects the whole spectrum of political opinion in the state.

The existing situation, whereby judges are appointed by a collegial committee consisting of three judges, two representatives of the bar association, two representatives of the executive, and two from the legislature, is entirely satisfactory, because although the Judicial Selection Committee is chaired by the minister of justice, the majority of its members are drawn from the ranks of the legal profession and not from those of the politicians.

However, regarding appointments to the bench, it is regrettable that legislative intervention in this area has gone beyond mere representation on the committee. An example of this intervention was the passing of the "Rabbi Assaf Law." The sole purpose of this law was to grant retrospective legitimacy to the appointment of Rabbi Assaf to the Supreme Court, notwithstanding his lacking the qualifications required by law for such an appointment. Another example of this phenomenon is the "Binyamin Halevi Law."[24] This law was designed to prevent Binyamin Halevi, president of the district court, from appointing himself to preside over the bench in the Eichmann trial. Judge Halevi had expressed strong sentiments against Eichmann in another case, and it was felt that it would be politically damaging to allow him to preside over the trial. The attempts made to change the law regarding the retirement age of judges in order to allow the president of the Supreme Court, Yizhak Olshan, to remain at his post for several more years, is yet another example of illegitimate intervention on the part of the legislature. Although there are only a few examples of this type of intervention, they are sufficient to alert us to the dangers of unfettered political intervention in the administration of the court system in Israel.

A much more serious form of intervention is direct and unmediated political interference in matters pending in court. Unfortunately, there are a number of cases of intervention of this type on record in the history of Israeli law. Such cases tend to occur in relation to issues of profound public concern and controversy. Particularly serious was the pressure brought to bear on the judges in the Shalit case, which involved the definition of Jewish identity under the Law of Return. Justice Sussman made explicit reference to this pressure in his written opinion. Nor has this been the only instance of such pressures being brought to bear on Israeli judges.

Even more serious is intervention aimed at preventing justiciable matters from coming to court. Most of the cases in this category involved hasty government measures designed to "create facts on the ground" in such a way that either the individual has no time to petition the High Court of Justice for relief or the issue becomes moot. An example of this form of intervention was the expulsion of Dr. Soblen in the 1960s and of two deportees from Hebron in the 1970s immediately before a judicial hearing against the order. In effect, the executive rendered the legal proceedings moot and prevented the hearing from taking place. Intervention in the same form was used in the expulsion of Fahad Khawasmeh, which was implemented too quickly to allow him to petition the High Court of Justice for relief. It should be noted that a petition by Mrs. Khawasmeh eventually brought the matter before the court, and the executive was the subject of judicial criticism.[25]

The Knesset has also used legislation as a form of intervention to nullify the effects of legal decisions. The first such case involved legislation passed by the Knesset in 1955 in the wake of the court's ruling that the appointment of Rabbi Nissim as the Sefardic chief rabbi of Israel was invalid. The Knesset issued an act changing the qualifications for the office of the chief rabbi, thereby nullifying the court's decision. Similar improper legislative interventions have occurred in more recent times. Following a court ruling that a municipal bylaw restricting the opening hours of factories and recreational facilities on the Sabbath and religious holidays was invalid, the Knesset passed a law permitting municipalities to make bylaws of precisely this nature. The objectionable intervention was the retrospective provision in the law stating that all bylaws relating to this issue are to be regarded as if they had been made in accordance with its provisions.[26]

The most blatant form of intervention of this sort consists simply of ignoring the courts' decisions and failing to execute judgments. The enforcement of legal decisions is always dependent on the executive. It is also accepted, even by the courts, that, given limited resources, it is not possible to enforce every single legal decision.

The greatest temptation to adopt this blatant type of strategy arises in cases involving major public controversies. However, it is in these very cases where preservation of the honor and independence of the judiciary is at stake that strict enforcement of its decisions is of utmost importance. It is to the credit of Israeli governments that they have never refrained from enforcing a legal decision on the grounds of public pressure. The Elon Moreh case involved an order of the Supreme Court requiring the dismantling of a settlement and the restoration of land to its legal owners.[27] There was no declaration on the part of any person or body that the court's decision ought to be ignored. In fact, however, the government waited ten weeks before commencing with the evacuation of the property, thereby indicating a most execrable tendency to view legal decisions as neither final nor binding.

It appears from the preceding analysis that there are many diverse forms and patterns of government and legislative intervention against the independent functioning of the judiciary. It must be emphasized that it would be incorrect to claim that such intervention is the norm in the State of Israel. The norm is that judicial independence is maintained. But the many examples cited above of such intervention indicate a real danger to the standing of the judicial system and the need for action to ensure that these exceptional cases are not repeated.

Constitutional Protection of the Judiciary

The judiciary is one of the three constitutional branches of the state. It is, therefore, vital that the judiciary receive the constitutional protection necessary for maintaining its independence. At present, the status and jurisdiction of the judicial branch is anchored in the Basic Law: Adjudication. This law, however, fails to provide sufficient protection for the judiciary in terms of its specific provisions, and more generally in terms of the binding nature of the law itself.[28] Proof of its inadequacy is afforded by the many cases over the years in which its ideal of judicial independence has been compromised.

From the normative standpoint, it is desirable that the protection of judicial independence take place at the constitutional level. However, the constitutional status of the Basic Law is no different from any other, except insofar as it remains unaffected by orders made under the emergency regulations.[29] Indeed, this exception protects the judiciary against orders issued by the executive under the emergency powers. However, there is no provision that would shield the Basic Law: Adjudication from amendment by ordinary parliamentary legislation, even if such an amendment is not explicitly stated.

Proper constitutional protection requires that certain principles be entrenched in the law to protect basic norms. The first principle should be a prohibition against setting up special tribunals to hear specific disputes. In the absence of such a prohibition, it is possible to circumvent the judiciary by creating a whole system of special tribunals. Section 1 (c) of the Basic Law: Adjudication does indeed contain this prohibition.

The second principle requiring constitutional protection is that of proper execution following the rendering of a legal decision. The importance of this principle cannot be emphasized too strongly, because it deals with one of the points at which the judicial system is at its weakest. This vital principle is nowhere to be found in the Basic Law: Adjudication. It is true that Israel has a tradition of obedience to legal decisions. However, a tradition is not enough to ensure adequate protection, especially since the tradition itself has not always been followed, as is evident from many of the cases discussed in this chapter.

The third principle in connection with constitutional protection of the judiciary is that of strict separation between the judiciary and the public service. This separation ought to apply at the personal level, that is, judicial officials may not serve in any political capacity or occupy any position in the public service. It should also apply at the institutional level, that is, the status of the judges must be clearly defined in terms absolutely distinct from those of public service employees. There is no constitutional protection of this principle in the State of Israel, though it has been mentioned in the Landau Committee Report on Judicial Ethics.[30]

The fourth principle is the prohibition on detrimental changes in the terms of office of judges. This does not mean that every aspect of judicial terms of office must be entrusted to the judiciary, because such a situation would contravene the doctrine of "checks and balances." The prohibition should be limited to those judges who are currently serving on the bench. The dangers inherent in any deviation from this prohibition are clearly evident. Changing judicial terms of office might be used by the political branches of the state as a means of indicating to the judges that their decisions are not politically acceptable. It might also be used as a means of attempting to influence actual legal decisions. The Basic Law: Adjudication (Section 10(b)) provides that judges' pay may only be cut if the wages of another sector of officers or workers are also reduced. But this provision, as indicated earlier, needs to be strengthened, as it leaves open the possibility of reducing judges' pay for reasons that have nothing to do with economics, provided that another group is also subjected to a wage reduction.

The fifth and final principle is that of "the natural judge." This principle requires that courts be constituted before trials are announced so that in judicial assignments there is no possibility of one judge being preferred over another to produce a desired outcome. The application of this principle ensures absolute neutrality and randomness with respect to the composition of the judicial panel in any particular case. Though the "natural judge" principle is accepted in countries in continental Europe, Anglo-American and Israeli laws content themselves with the rule that a particular judge may be rejected on the grounds of a suspicion of bias. I find this rule insufficient, because it is a negative one and applies only where there is some suspicion of judicial bias. The "natural judge" principle goes further and guarantees fairness and neutrality from the very beginning. Needless to say, if by pure chance a judge who is suspected of being biased is selected, then there is always provision for her or his removal from the case based on a well-defined procedure.

It is by now fairly evident that there is still a long way to go before Israel achieves proper constitutional protection of the independence of its justice system. One of the reasons for this lack of constitutional protection is the inability of the judges to organize themselves effectively and to defend their status. A major factor contributing to this lack of effectiveness undoubtedly is the judicial tradition of avoiding any type of conflict or protest in the political arena, especially if it takes place in public.

Strengthening the Institutional Independence of the Judiciary

In the area of court administration, when control is vested in the hands of the executive, as is the case in Israel, any number of challenges to judicial independence arise. The minister of justice is responsible for the administration of the courts and, with the consent of the president of the Supreme Court, appoints the director of courts. The director is responsible for managing the courts and is accountable to the minister. The minister of justice is vested with wide additional powers: he has the authority to establish courts, he enacts regulations governing court administration and court procedure, and he chairs the Judicial Selection Committee. He also has the sole authority to initiate disciplinary proceedings against judges.

Other powers held by the minister must be exercised with the consent of the president of the Supreme Court. In addition to appointing the director of courts, these include the power to temporarily appoint a judge to a superior or inferior court, to appoint the president of the district and magistrate courts, and to transfer judges from one court to another on certain conditions. Before a 1992 amendment to the Courts Law, the minister was required only to consult with the president in these cases. While the amendment is welcomed as is the custom whereby the minister consults with the president with any of his powers in relation to the courts, these developments, I submit, do not go far enough.

The main responsibility for court administration should be vested jointly in the president of the Supreme Court and the minister of justice. I have proposed a model that accords with the principle of the minister of justice being responsible to the Knesset for the courts as required in a parliamentary system such as Israel's. At the same time, this model strengthens the position of the judiciary in the administration of the judicial system as required by the principle of judicial independence.

My model for shared responsibility, which included the proposal that the director of courts shall be appointed jointly by the minister of justice and the president of the Supreme Court, was basically adopted by the amendment to the Courts law. But the model also proposed that the court budget should be separated from the ministry's budget and be prepared jointly by the minister of justice and the president of the Supreme Court.[31] Another change needed is separation of court employees from the civil service (which is the current situation as regards the employees of the State Comptroller's office). In addition, authority to enact regulations should be vested jointly in the president of the Supreme Court and the minister of justice on the basis of proposals from a committee set up by law. Although I have proposed that responsibility for administration of the courts be vested jointly in the minister of justice and the president of the Supreme Court, some administrative matters that bear directly on adjudication should be the sole responsibility of the president of the Supreme Court. These would include the transfer of judges from one locality to another, the appointment of replacement judges, supervision of judges, and the determination of their hours of work.

Conclusion

The preceding analysis shows that it is critically important that the Israeli legal system meet the challenge of providing constitutional protection for judicial independence, the position of the courts, and judicial terms of office. There is an express commitment of the new Israeli government under the leadership of Prime Minister Ehud Barak to complete the constitution. I hope that in this climate, which is favorable to constitutionalism, the provision of constitutional protection will come within a reasonable period.

Notes

1. See A. Barak, "Constitutionalization of the Israeli Legal System," *Israeli Law Review* 24 (1994): 4.

2. See the *Mitrael Cases*, HC 3827/93; HC 5009/94; and Shimon Shetreet, *Between Three Branches of the Government—The Balance of Human Rights in Matters of Religious Liberty* (Jerusalem, Israel: Floersheim Institute of Policy Studies, 1999).

3. Further discussed in Shimon Shetreet, "Developments in Constitutional Law: Selected Topics," *Israeli Law Review* 21 (1990): 368.

4. See Shimon Shetreet, "Standing and Justiciability," in *Public Law in Israel*, eds. I. Zamir and A. Zysblat (Oxford: Oxford Univ. Press, 1997), 265–74.

5. See A. Ben-Dor, "Justiciability in the High Court of Justice," *Mishpatim* 17 (1987): 592.

6. H.C. H 40/70, *Becker v. Minister of Defence & Others*, 24(1) P.D. 238.

7. H.C. 47/82, *The Movement for Progressive Judaism Foundation, et al. v. Minster of Religion, et al.*, 43(2) P.D. 661.

8. Ibid., 721.

9. A. Barak, "Constitutional Law without a Constitution," in *The Role of Courts in Society*, ed. Shimon Shetreet (Dordrecht, Netherlands: Martin Norjhoff, 1988), 448.

10. See Shimon Shetreet, "A Contemporary Model of Emergency Detention Law: An Assessment of the Israeli Law," *Israeli Yearbook on Human Rights* 14 (1984): 193.

11. H.C. 390/70, *Duwikat v. Government of Israel*, 34(1) P.D. 1.

12. H.C. 680/88, *Schnitzer v. Chief Military Censor*, 42(4) P.D. 617.

13. For further discussion, see Shimon Shetreet, "The Yom Kippur War Commission of Inquiry: The Overall Judgement,—Favourable," *Mishpatim* 8 (1977): 74.

14. See Y. Dotan, "A Constitution for the State of Israel—The Constitutional Dialogue after the 'Constitutional Revolution,'" *Mishpatim* 28 (1997): 149.

15. For further examples, see Shimon Shetreet, *Judges on Trial: A Study of the Appointment and Accountability of the English Judiciary* (Amsterdam: North Holland Publishing Co., 1976), 204.

16. Section 3 of the Basic Law: Adjudication states that, "A court shall sit in public unless otherwise provided by Law or unless the court otherwise decides under Law."

17. See Shimon Shetreet, "The Administration of Justice: Practical Problems, Value Conflicts and Changing Concepts," *Univ. Of British Columbia Law Review* 13 (1979): 52.

18. See Shimon Shetreet, *Justice in Israel: A Study of the Israeli Judiciary* (New York: Klewer, 1994), 303–305.

19. H.C. 1031/93, *Pesaro v. The Minister of Interior*, 49(4) PD 661.

20. H.C. 3267/97, *Rubinshtein v. Minister of Defence*, (1997).

21. H.C. 5016/96, *Horev v. The Minister of Transport*, (1996).

22. See J. Freudenheim, "The Laws of Validation and the Rule of Law," *HaPraklit* 23 (1967): 381.

23. See *Kawasme v. Minister of Defence*, 35(3) P.D. 113, 119.

24. H.C. 58/68, *Shalit v. Minister of Interior*, 23 (2) P.D. 447, 505.

25. Further discussed in Shetreet, *Justice in Israel,* chap. 20.

26. H.C. 291/55, *Rabbi David Dayan v. Minister of Religion and the Chief Rabbinical Council of Israel,* 9 P.D. 997; and Municipalities Law Amendment (no. 40) (1990).

27. H.C. 390/79, *Dwikat v. Government of Israel,* 34(1) P.D. 1.

28. Further discussed in Shimon Shetreet, "Judicial Independence: Conceptual Dimensions and Contemporary Challenges," in *Judicial Independence: The Contemporary Debate,* eds. Shimon Shetreet and Jules Deschenes (Dordrecht, Netherlands: Martin Norjhoff, 1985), 590.

29. See C. Klein, "The Founding Authority in Israel," *Mishpatim* 2 (1970): 51.

30. The Committee for Examining the Subject of the Professional Ethics of Judges, *The Judicial System Brochure* No. 6 (September 1985).

31. Further discussed in Shetreet, *Justice in Israel,* chap. 15.

13

Judicial Independence and Instability in Central America

J. MICHAEL DODSON
AND DONALD W. JACKSON

Writing in 1984, Joel Verney offered this assessment of the independence of twenty Latin American supreme courts: the "general consensus" of the literature was that Latin American supreme courts were "politically dependent and dominated by the political environments in which they were embedded."[1] From all of Latin America's supreme judicial bodies, only the Supreme Court of Costa Rica was deemed an "independent and activist court."[2] Concerning Central America specifically, apart from Costa Rica, the rest of the region included three "minimalist" courts, that is, ones that had "institutional continuity" but that exhibited little independence vis-à-vis other governmental agencies (in El Salvador, Guatemala, and Honduras), and one "personalist" court (subordinate to the Somoza dictatorship) in Nicaragua.

Political change in the 1980s and 1990s altered somewhat the conditions that gave rise to Verner's analysis as it pertained to Central America. For example, the Nicaraguan revolution of 1979 reduced the influence and legacy of Somoza in all aspects of politics and government, including the judiciary, albeit without achieving judicial independence. However, the "minimalist" category still seems to describe Honduras. A 1993 report of the United States Agency for International Development (USAID) on the Honduran legal system found that, while Honduras never matched Guatemala or El Salvador in its record of human rights violations or in the pervasiveness of impunity, its performance left much to be desired. Over "the past decade, crime in Honduras has increased, and the courts, shorthanded of staff and resources and burdened with antiquated judicial procedures, have not been able to cope with a burgeoning backlog of cases."[3] Surveys taken among public and judicial officials in the late 1980s revealed a widespread view that the justice system was subject to rampant corruption. The USAID report concluded that "the credibility of the judicial system is frequently compromised by the public perception that the powerful and privileged can turn judicial proceedings to their advantage through political connections and bribery" and that the Honduran "Supreme Court has little autonomous power vis-à-vis the other major actors in the political system."[4]

Costa Rica remains the exception to the rule in Central America when it comes to judicial independence. Yet two of the most interesting countries in the region are El Salvador and Guatemala. Despite their troubled, authoritarian histories, these two countries are presently striving to achieve a "democratic transition" to institutionalize the rule of law.

Samuel Huntington's description of the "third wave of democracy,"[5] a phenomenon that began in the early 1980s, has spurred considerable research on democratic transitions in Central America and in South America. Several South American countries led the "third wave" by rejecting military rule and deposing the so-called bureaucratic authoritarian regimes that were associated with it. Elected civilian governments emerged when the relevant political actors, especially the armed forces, began to accept the legitimacy (or necessity) of electoral politics.

However, enthusiasm about democracy's prospects was soon tempered by experience. It became clear that students of democracy in the region needed to avoid the "fallacy of electoralism,"[6] that is, of confusing elections with democracy. Instead, scholars evinced growing concern for what Manuel Antonio Garreton has called "democratic survival." Garreton's vivid phrase refers to an incomplete state of transition. The institutions of democracy exist formally but, in practice, judicial independence and the rule of law remain especially weak. One danger in such circumstances is that the citizenry becomes skeptical, or even cynical, about the legitimacy of democratic institutions.[7]

Rather than reviewing the abundant literature on democratic consolidation,[8] we take the widely shared view that most of Latin America's transitional regimes are "nonliberal democracies" that have not effectively institutionalized either judicial independence or the state's accountability before the law. As Juan Linz pointed out, liberal democracy presumes "a state bound by law,"[9] which, in turn, requires an independent judicial system. Therein lies one of the great challenges to democratic consolidation in Central America and in Latin America as a whole. Consider the magnitude of the problem. As Larry Diamond points out, establishing the rule of law

> requires more than independent and professional judges (which in turn require good pay, a substantial and secure term in office, and depoliticized procedures for selection). It demands that those judges have the staffing and financial resources to be effective and that they be served and petitioned by a dense infrastructure of institutions that compose an effective legal system: prosecutors, public defenders, police, investigators, legal aid programs, bar associations, law schools, and so on.[10]

In El Salvador and Guatemala, for instance, the independence and professionalism of judges are the immediate goals yet to be achieved. But all else that Diamond mentions is at best a long-term aspiration fraught with difficulties.

Central American countries also face the challenge of altering the existing legal and political culture, a task that requires a thoroughgoing attack on the "plague of corruption."[11] Citizens throughout the region express very low opinions of their judicial systems. Evidently, public awareness of the predatory and "rent-seeking" propensities of judicial functionaries is quite high.

Historical Background of Judicial Reform in Central America

According to a 1998 article in the *New York Times*, "There is an argument to be made that the favorite pastime of Latin American politicians is neither soccer nor baseball, but tinkering with their countries' constitutions."[12] As this pertains to Central America, for example, El Salvador has had fourteen constitutions since successfully rebelling against Spanish rule in 1821. Typically, most constitutional "reforms" of this type have served the interests of those who have seized political power or who seek to retain it. The constitutional and other reforms that were embraced in the internationally mediated peace agreements signed in El Salvador (1992) and Guatemala (1996) were of a different nature, however. The peace agreements brought some closure to decades of political repression and organized rebellion. In both countries, the immediate precedent to peace was a brutal counterinsurgency war that caused vast loss of life, extreme displacement of populations, and systematic, large-scale violation of human rights.[13] The absence of civil freedoms, arbitrary and repressive exercise of state power, and the often wholesale assault on human rights by state security forces were major causes of these internal wars. As John Booth and Thomas

Walker have aptly observed, the overriding aim of authoritarian governments in that period was to "demobilize" a populace that was seeking a greater degree of participation in political life.[14] Accomplishing that goal required extreme political repression, with the result that systematic violation of human rights was a mainstay of authoritarian rule in pre–peace accords El Salvador and Guatemala. In neither country did the judicial system function to check these abuses. In that respect, the judiciary was complicit in the total breakdown of the rule of law.[15] Hence broad judicial reform was clearly a necessary element of democratic transition and consolidation in both countries.[16]

A number of excellent studies document the military's role in undermining the most basic foundations of a liberal democracy in Central America.[17] Complementary research has examined the role of antidemocratic elites, especially rural elites, in repressing earlier efforts to promote democratization.[18] Much less notice, however, has been taken of the complicity of the judiciary in the breakdown of the rule of law. Whether through active collaboration with an authoritarian executive or through passivity, all across the region the judiciary has failed to distinguish itself by defending human rights during periods of authoritarian rule. The pattern was very pronounced in El Salvador and Guatemala.

In a valuable new study,[19] Rachel Sieder concluded that, with the single exception of Costa Rica, Central American judiciaries have long been characterized by a high degree of politicization and extreme dependence on the executive branch. This profound lack of independence was typically compounded by extraordinary institutional weakness, as reflected in a lack of resources and trained personnel, low salaries (which invited corruption), and secretive procedures for handling cases.

In the specific case of El Salvador, Sieder found that before the peace accords, the judiciary had never functioned as a government authority independent of the other branches, that the judiciary itself concentrated and centralized authority in a highly authoritarian manner, and that "throughout the civil war the judicial system consummately failed to challenge the impunity of the military, which refused to submit to the rule of law." Indeed, the Supreme Court actively promoted impunity by shielding the armed forces from investigations into egregious cases of human rights violations.[20] Nor did the courts resist the imposition of states of emergency under which the Salvadoran state managed to routinize the coerced or "extra-judicial confession."

Sieder's description of Guatemala parallels that of El Salvador, but the weakness of the rule of law is compounded in Guatemala by the fact that, historically, the judiciary there has been alienated from the indigenous population. In other words, both law and judicial process are organized according to *Ladino* precepts, norms, and customs, and thus the legal system has been used to subjugate the indigenous population. Under the counterinsurgency regime that was installed after the 1954 coup ousting Jacobo Arbenz, the military became so heavily involved in the investigation and punishment of crime that the distinction between executive and judicial functions became blurred beyond recognition. The problem again became acute in the early 1980s, when the executive summarily dismissed the magistrates of the Supreme Court, suspended the constitution, and created special tribunals that held summary trials devoid of due process. During this period, the military established direct political control over the rural and indigenous populations and systematically deprived these sectors of their civil and human rights without objection from the judiciary. In short, in Guatemala the state's actions obliterated any pretense of separation of powers, leading to the subordination and marginalization of the judiciary as a force for protecting human rights and preserving the rule of law.

The Ideal of Judicial Independence

Institutional reform in Central America must foster greater trust in public institutions, because such trust is a necessary underpinning of the rule of law. A first step toward achieving that trust is strengthening the justice system, including the genuine independence of the judiciary. In discussing judicial independence, we follow Owen Fiss's analysis, dividing judicial independence into three closely related concepts: "party detachment," "individual autonomy," and "partisan (or political) insularity."[21] Peter Russell's cogent conceptualization in this book combines these three concepts into a single concept of "relational autonomy," that is, the "autonomy of judges—collectively and individually—from other individuals and institutions." Russell also proposes a second meaning of judicial independence, one in which independence becomes a reality whenever judges actually make decisions that exhibit their independence. Since such manifestations of judicial independence are rare, and because of the many violations of relational autonomy that occur, for Central America, Fiss's conceptualization is more useful.

First, party detachment requires judges to be neutral with regard to the litigants who appear before them in court. This idea is at the core of the judicial role: that a judge be impartial with respect to the interests of the parties he or she is required to adjudicate. A bribe, or any claims of kinship or personal friendship, violate the principle of party detachment. The principle also is violated if a judge's decisions in cases involving the government are dictated by the government responsible for her or his appointment. In short, whenever a judge favors one party over another without regard to the facts or the law, the principle of party detachment is violated.

"Individual autonomy" relates to "collegial relationships," or the power of one or more judges over another.[22] Peter Russell refers to this as the "internal" dimension of relational autonomy. Certain instances of vertical authority within the judiciary are legitimate. For example, appellate courts reviewing the decisions of a trial judge. However, the individual autonomy of a judge is violated by the exercise of power by one judge (or group of judges) over another to mandate a decision that, in the estimation of the subordinate or collegial judge, is not required by precedent or by a reasonable interpretation of substantive or procedural rules of law. This kind of interference in the decisions of lower court judges is a serious problem in nonliberal regimes.

Third, judicial independence points to relations between the judiciary and the other branches of government, that is, to the separation of powers. Peter Russell refers to this as the "external dimension" of relational autonomy, and according to Fiss, a court—as a governmental institution—is supposed to be free of "influence or control" from other governmental institutions. However, some kinds of government influence may be appropriate, as in the case of the solicitor general of the United States, for example, presenting briefs and arguments before the Supreme Court. Judges, however, should be free of improper or illegitimate forms of influence, particularly partisan influence. Partisan insularity suggests that judges should be free of the influence of other governmental institutions or officials on grounds of partisan loyalty or ideology, or of any form of coercion aimed at achieving an outcome favored by political interests but not dictated by law.

In short, genuine judicial independence requires judges who are detached and neutral as to the parties before them, who have sufficient individual autonomy to make their decisions based on the law and facts in a case, and who are insulated from any form of partisan influence and control.

Achieving such judicial independence in nonliberal regimes undergoing transition requires a broad range of reforms, including:

(1) Methods of selection that seek to transcend, as much as possible, the intrusion of direct partisanship into judicial appointments. Merit selection based on nonpartisan, bipartisan, or multipartisan assessment of objective qualifications is probably the best available option.

(2) Tenure of office should be relatively long, carry an adequate remuneration, and be protected by legal safeguards against retaliatory removal for unpopular decisions.

(3) Removal for official misconduct (bribery, extreme professional incompetence, personal disability) should be well grounded in procedures that guarantee due process.

(4) Courts must have adequate resources in the form of professional staff support, facilities, and finances to accomplish their duties.

(5) Finally, it is essential that there exist a legal and political culture supportive of the rule of law. All the above elements may be inadequate if there is no broad cultural agreement that *all* individuals and groups are under the law and will abide by judicial decisions.

Understanding the concepts of judicial independence and identifying the essential elements for achieving independence provides the necessary background for an analysis of judicial independence in El Salvador and Guatemala.

Peace Accords and Judicial Reform in El Salvador

The Chapultepec Accords in El Salvador (signed January 1992) prescribed specific changes in the justice system that were intended to "depoliticize" the administration of justice. These changes included: (1) the election of Supreme Court justices, from a list of nominees submitted by the National Council of the Judiciary, by a two-thirds majority of the legislative assembly; lengthening the terms of Supreme Court justices to nine years and staggering their terms so that no assembly, save the first one, could elect all the members of the court; (2) a decentralization of power within the judiciary, chiefly by transferring the power to select and discipline lower court judges from the Supreme Court to the National Council of the Judiciary; and (3) a constitutional guarantee that the judicial branch receive 6 percent of the national budget in order to enhance its independence of the executive and legislative branches.[23]

The Peace Accords also provided for the Truth Commission, which was charged to review and examine the most serious acts of violence committed during the civil war and assign the appropriate moral responsibility.

The commission's March 1993 report, *From Madness to Hope*,[24] sharply criticized the existing Supreme Court, and the Salvadoran judicial system as a whole, for its failure to protect human rights throughout the war and also for obstructing the work of the commission. The Truth Commission called for a purge of the judges responsible. From the standpoint of democratic transition, the Truth Commission was critical to the peace process, because it established a "baseline" of government (and guerrilla) accountability, which was seen as an essential step in establishing the rule of law.

The Judicial System before Reform

The key word in describing the Salvadoran judiciary before the recent reforms is *impunity*. Before the constitutional reforms of 1991, the judiciary was structurally dependent on the other branches of government in two critical respects. First, the selection of Supreme Court justices was based strictly on party loyalty and was guided by the preferences of the chief executive, "who was always looking for friends and loyalists of the governing party."[25] Second, funding for the court was controlled by the Ministry of Hacienda, which meant it was subject to executive control. The law of the judiciary concentrated the power to administer the courts at all levels in the hands of the president of the Supreme Court of Justice.

These structural features assured the politicization of the administration of justice and allowed the chief justice to personalize the exercise of judicial authority. Lower court judges were thus named on the basis of personal friendship or political ties, and the entire judiciary reflected the hegemony of the party in power. Indeed, justices of the peace were "a species of political promoters," who devoted most of their time to doing political party work in concert with mayors, governors, and local military commanders.[26] During this era, Salvadoran society was heavily militarized. Police functions, including criminal investigations, were carried out under military control. Arraignments typically occurred in the police station, and extrajudicial confessions, produced through intimidation or torture, were the norm.[27] This criminal justice system made a mockery of the presumption of innocence, and its functioning affected the poor almost exclusively.

In sum, before the peace accords, the Salvadoran judicial system did not protect the rights of ordinary citizens. At the same time, government officials and social elites enjoyed immunity from punishment for committing crimes or abusing power. Political power dominated the Supreme Court, and the Supreme Court was in a position to dominate or intimidate the balance of the judiciary.[28] To top it all, the judicial system received only about 2 percent of the national budget.[39] Hence:

The judicial system was so debilitated that it became imprisoned by intimidation and vulnerable to corruption. Given that the justice system has never enjoyed true institutional independence from the executive and legislative branches, its inefficiency only increased until it became, either because of inaction or an unfortunate attitude of subservience, a contributing factor to the tragedy that the country has suffered.[30]

The Truth Commission called for the resignation of the entire Supreme Court and specifically accused the court's president, Mauricio Gutiérrez Castro, of misconduct. During the time he remained in office (until mid-1994), Gutiérrez Castro actively opposed efforts to reform the judicial system.

Judicial Reform under the Peace Accords

Given the Supreme Court of Justice's importance in determining the character of the justice system in El Salvador, let us turn first to reforms affecting this court. "The very first objective of judicial reform here was to reconstitute the Supreme Court of Justice and the method of electing justices."[31] These words of the first chief justice elected under the reform laws go to the heart of the matter. Broad agreement existed that constituting a professional and independent Supreme Court was a necessary first step to creating a competent, nonpartisan judiciary. Reforms enacted in December 1991 provided for the election of Supreme Court justices for terms of nine years by a two-thirds majority of the Legislative Assembly. The assembly is required to elect candidates from a list prepared by the National Council of the Judiciary, and one half of the candidates must be nominated by bar associations. Although this method of election does not entirely remove partisanship from the process, its aim was to require consensus among diverse parties in order to elect justices of diverse backgrounds to the court, thus making the court more pluralistic in political terms—and presumably less beholden to the majority party as well as less vulnerable to political manipulation by the chief executive.

Critics had also urged that the administrative powers of the Supreme Court be dispersed to assure greater independence on the part of lower court judges. The major reform that has been implemented in this regard involves the role of the National Council of the Judiciary (CNJ), which is further discussed below. In the main, however, the centralized nature of judicial authority has not been altered by reform. The Supreme Court retains the power to appoint and remove lower court judges; the power to promote, transfer, or discipline them; and control over their budgets. The

Supreme Court also licenses lawyers and notaries and can suspend or dismiss them.

Some observers in El Salvador argue that the election of an entirely new Supreme Court in July 1994 resolved the most serious defect of the existing justice system, thereby lessening the urgency of further structural reforms. That argument rests on two key points. First, the financial dependence of the judiciary was overcome by a 1991 reform that gradually increased the judiciary's share of the national budget from 2 percent to 6 percent over a five-year period.[32] In 1994 the allocation was amended by law so that 4 percent of the budget will go to the judiciary per se, while 2 percent will go to the Public Ministry, which includes the Attorney General's Office, the State Counsel's Office, and the Office of the Procurator for the Defense of Human Rights.[33] As the current vice president of the Supreme Court put it, "the process of selecting judges has been invested with democratic guarantees."[34] Even stout critics of the judiciary, such as two former heads of the Human Rights Division of the United Nations Observer Mission in El Salvador (ONUSAL), agreed that the initial reformed Supreme Court was a great improvement, and the current CSJ president, Dr. José Domingo Méndez, agreed, observing that "we no longer have a partisan court in the traditional sense."[35] Nonetheless, the structural conditions for a reimposition of authoritarian administration of the courts remain in place.

The second key element in the reform of the Salvadoran justice system was the establishment of a National Council of the Judiciary, which was created by law in 1989. The enabling legislation provided that five of the ten members of the council must be sitting members of the Supreme Court. The other five members of the council are made up of three representatives of the Lawyers Federation and two lawyers elected by the law faculties of Salvadoran law schools. The power to cast tie-breaking votes was given to a council member representing the Supreme Court. Clearly, these structural features minimize the Council's real independence from the Supreme Court.

Proponents of more extensive reforms wanted a council independent of both the Supreme Court and the political branches of government. But a compromise version of the law was adopted by the assembly in December 1992. The compromise legislation defined the council as an independent institution composed of eleven members, chosen as follows: two lawyers (not justices) proposed by the Supreme Court, one appellate (second instance) judge, one trial judge (first instance), three practicing lawyers, one law professor from the University of El Salvador, two law professors from private universities, and one member from the Public Ministry. The council members are to be elected by a two-thirds vote of the National Assembly from among three nominees for each position. The council is charged with two crucial responsibilities: evaluating the performance of judges and magistrates and training professionals within the justice system, including judges. The council's evaluations of sitting judges are to be the basis on which the Supreme Court makes promotions or takes any disciplinary action such as suspension or dismissal. In short, the law intends the CNJ to play a crucial role in the process of *"depuración,"* or the cleansing of the Salvadoran judiciary.

The 1991 reform put the Judicial Training School (ECJ) under the authority of the council. The law was broadly written so that the ECJ was charged with training not only judges but prosecutors, public defenders, procurators, and other personnel in the justice system. Providing such training might well enhance the quality of justice, but it clearly strains the resources of the National Council. Within the limits of its resources, the ECJ has addressed its twin tasks of training and purification in a systematic way. All sitting judges are being reviewed as to their "technical and administrative competence" and their "ethical qualities," and candidates for new appointments must pass a competitive review of their curriculum vitae.[36]

On paper, the goals and procedures described above make perfect sense. The Judicial Training School is clearly working to raise the level of technical competence within the judiciary. The National Council and the Supreme Court are, however, proceeding with considerable caution when it comes to purging judges from the system. In October 1994 the Human Rights Division of ONUSAL presented a list of fifty-two judges against whom serious complaints of corruption or incompetence had been made. When the ONUSAL chief of mission, Enrique Ter Horst, subsequently pointed up the report's finding of "shameless and corrupt judges in El Salvador," his comments generated an intense nationalistic outcry.[37] Yet the report was consistent with the findings of the Truth Commission, which suggested that a large proportion of the judiciary had been involved in obstructing justice and fostering impunity.[38] As of January 1997, the Supreme Court had sanctioned a total of fifty-seven judges, including removing twenty-nine, suspending twelve, censuring four, and transferring twelve.

Despite that record, the most recent report of the UN secretary general found the process of cleansing the judiciary to be slow and inadequate. Of equal interest is the fact that none of these sanctions was based on findings of corruption! It would seem, then, that the reformed Salvadoran judiciary is serious about reviewing judicial performance from the standpoint of competence or efficiency, but it has less zeal for the politically more charged task of rooting out corruption. Because the effort to strengthen the judiciary involves the complementary processes of training and disciplining, it is too soon to judge success.

The Peace Accords and the Framework
for Reform in Guatemala

Unlike El Salvador, where the peace process was hastened by military stalemate, the Guatemalan army effectively defeated the guerrilla forces of the Guatemalan National Revolutionary Unity (URNG) militarily. From a position of strength, the armed forces presided over a transition to civilian rule that began with elections in 1985. Still, serious negotiations with the guerrillas, leading to formal peace agreements, did not begin until the early 1990s and were not concluded until 1996. Thus the democratic transition preceded the peace process in Guatemala, albeit with quite limited results in terms of achieving the reforms that would lead to liberal democracy. Indeed, several coup attempts in the late 1980s and the failed *autogolpe* (or "self-coup") of President Jorge Serrano in 1993 demonstrated that authoritarian enclaves persisted and reform had not proceeded very far. The crisis of May 1993 showed that:

> The president of the Supreme Court compromised the independence and integrity of the judicial system by using his position to make political deals with legislators. The executive engaged in clientelism and entered into the deal making prevalent in Congress and the Supreme Court. In short, instead of an established separation of powers between the three branches of government, there was blatant disregard for institutional procedures and the rule of law, open deal making within and among the three branches, and officials' unwillingness to reform.[39]

Serrano's *autogolpe* failed, because after eight years of minimalist democracy, Guatemala's newly mobilized civil society actively coalesced against it. Serrano was forced into exile, and the interim president, Ramiro de Leon Carpio, who was installed by Congress, moved to purge both Congress and the Supreme Court. In early 1994 (coincidentally almost simultaneously with similar developments in El Salvador), early elections were held for Congress, which, in turn, selected a new Supreme Court under reformed procedures.[40] At the same time, the peace negotiations that had bogged down during the May crisis suddenly began to bear fruit.

As in El Salvador, the peace process produced a series of agreements on a range of issues and also authorized the UN to set up the United Nations Verification Mission (MINUGUA), which took up the functions both of verifying compliance with the human rights accord and of initiating institutional strengthening projects. The final substantive accord, signed in September 1996, prescribed reforms in all three branches of government to address the problems of separation of powers outlined above.

The Judicial System before Reform

Historically, the judiciary in Guatemala was plagued by the political and technical problems found elsewhere in Central America, but it had the additional burden of barely functioning at all for the vast majority of the population. More than one hundred years ago, in an effort to secure a controlled system of labor for the coffee plantations, the so-called *mandamiento* (or "forced labor system") was imposed on rural workers. The enabling legislation, or *reglamento de jornaleros,* authorized farm owners to exert almost total control over landless rural workers. Under these conditions, the coffee plantations became "separate judicial spaces," with their own authoritarian and discriminatory legal regime. In the Guatemalan countryside, the landowner "represented absolute law within the farms; he imposed fines, incarcerated workers, measured and valued work and effectively constituted judge and jury."[41]

The draconian labor laws of the 1930s only served to reinforce this system of separate and essentially private justice in the countryside. As to the justice system more generally, President Jorge Ubico (1931–44) imposed an extreme degree of executive control that completely subordinated the judiciary to executive will. The president assumed the power to appoint not only the members of the Supreme Court but even local justices of the peace.

Any expectations that Guatemala might move toward greater separation of powers following the October Revolution of 1944 were disappointed following the overthrow of the Arbenz government in 1954. The new head of state, Colonel Castillo Armas, restored the practice of directly nominating judges down to the local level, thus continuing a long tradition of politicizing and subordinating the judiciary. As the ensuing counterinsurgency state began to take shape, additional measures, such as the appointment of military commissioners to "police" rural areas, had the effect of militarizing the police function throughout the country. This phenomenon reached its logical extreme in the system of civil patrols that was set up under the dictatorship of General Efraín Ríos Montt (1982–83).[42] The silence of the judiciary in the face of massive abuse of human rights in the days just before the democratic opening of 1985 indicates the degree to which the Guatemalan judiciary was marginalized and demoralized in a political system that was heavily militarized and that deeply distrusted the liberal concepts of separation of powers and judicial independence.

Judicial Reform under the Peace Accords

It would be difficult to overestimate the importance of the peace accords to the task of judicial reform in Guatemala. Following the 1985 election of a civilian president, considerable development aid flowed into the country. In cooperation with USAID, Harvard Law School embarked on an ambitious program of training and reform, particularly focused on the criminal justice system. The results of these projects, though, were so meager that USAID withdrew after several years. Indeed, "Guatemala holds the dubious distinction of being the only country in Latin America where USAID has decided to terminate a judicial reform project because of manifest lack of progress."[43] According to Rachel Sieder, a major reason why these early reform efforts failed is that they addressed only technical deficiencies, not the structural and political problems that facilitated "continuing involvement of the executive and military at the heart of the judiciary."[44] Addressing these issues required a comprehensive peace agreement and international verification.

Nonetheless, prospects for democratic consolidation are enhanced in Guatemala, as they were in El Salvador, by the fact that the peace accords specified guidelines for reform, and the formerly warring elites have embraced these guidelines publicly. In that sense, a legal framework for establishing the rule of law now exists. The challenge is to get from theory to practice, to operationalize the guidelines both in structural reforms and in the behavior of judges and other key actors in the justice system.

Under the stimulus of the peace accords, a number of important structural changes were adopted that aim at restoring the separation of powers and establishing judicial independence. The Accord on the Strengthening of Civil Power and the Function of the Army in a Democratic Society, signed in September 1996, acknowledges that the administration of justice is "one of the major structural weaknesses of the Guatemalan state."[45] Pursuant to this accord, President Álvaro Arzú appointed a commission to study and make recommendations for reform. The commission began its work in March 1997 by organizing extensive sectoral participation in a series of public forums designed to ascertain the complaints and concerns of employees within the justice sector and the public.

In its interim report, issued in August 1997, the commission identified the following three broad reform goals: (1) separation of the jurisdictional function from the tasks of judicial administration, and streamlining the latter; (2) promoting judicial independence; and (3) increasing public access to judicial remedy, with special attention to the needs of the indigenous majority. A parallel initiative has emerged within the Supreme Court itself in the form of the Commission to Modernize the Judicial Organ, which is assessing the technical requirements for modernization of the judiciary. Evidently the findings of this latter commission are being shared with the presidential commission and will serve as the basis for developing a "strategic plan" for justice system reform.[46]

The Guatemalan judiciary is characterized by extreme centralization in every aspect, from the physical concentration of judges in a single location in Guatemala City to the placing of virtually all administrative responsibilities in the hands of the CSJ (Corte Suprema de Justica). The CSJ is both the highest court in the land and the administrator of the entire court system, a design feature that leads to confusion of administrative and jurisdictional functions and that compromises the independence of lower judges within the "verticalist," or hierarchical, system. Administration is carried out through the Presidency of the Judicial Organ (POJ), a body that has responsibility for hiring, firing, and evaluating all judicial system personnel, both professional and administrative. Within the POJ, the entity charged with evaluating all judicial personnel is the General Supervisory Body of Tribunals (GSBT), a body that has been sharply criticized for inefficiency and authoritarianism. The GSBT is poorly staffed, keeps no statistical data on the cases it handles, is more reactive than proactive, and is given to interfering in judicial decision making by rendering public assessments of the way judges apply the law to specific cases. As a consequence, the "Supervisory is seen as an expression of power, not as an objective and transparent mechanism" used by the POJ to evaluate and control judicial personnel.[47] The low degree of professionalism that characterizes this body renders it ineffective in combating corruption within the judiciary.

A principal goal of the presidential commission is to introduce a more modern and efficient management system into the judiciary. A critical first step is to separate the jurisdictional and administrative functions, reserving the former to the CSJ and creating a new body, a council of the judiciary, "composed of judges, magistrates, lawyers, and representatives of the law faculties," which would be responsible for screening applicants, recommending judicial appointments, and disciplining judges.[48] To be effective, such a body will need to administer a judicial career law, which is not yet on the books. Indeed, despite the fact that the 1985 constitution mandated that Congress establish such a law, it has not yet done so. Hence there is no legally established standard on which to base judicial selection or evaluate judicial performance, a situation that clearly undermines judicial independence inasmuch as it opens the way for politically motivated appointment, promotion, or dismissal of judges.

In October 1998 the Congress finally approved a number of reforms concerning the administration of justice (along with other constitutional reforms—fifty in all). A popular referendum on these reforms was held on May 17, 1999. The results were dismaying indeed for the prospects of democracy in Guatemala. The modal response was not to vote at all; the abstention rate was 81.4 percent.[49] But the few who did vote did not provide a majority in favor of any of the reforms. Only 41.8 percent of those voting approved the proposed reforms of the judicial system.[50]

With the failure of reforms, even the independence of Supreme Court magistrates remains problematic because of the existing system of appointment in which Congress elects the magistrates to five-year terms, and all at the same time. In reaction to the problem of centralized authority, a 1993 reform limited the chief justice to a one-year term with no reappointment. The presidential commission found this feature to be disruptive to strategic planning and continuity of administration and recommended a three-year renewable term.

Modernization of the judiciary in Guatemala is a task that requires a significant reallocation of resources to the justice system. Currently, the constitution requires that no less than 2 percent of the national budget be allocated for the administration of justice. In practice, that figure of 2 percent has defined the budget, a figure that is profoundly inadequate apart from problems of mismanagement. That figure is supplemented through fines and assorted fees. There is no strategic plan for using the financial resources the judiciary does have available. The most pernicious consequences of this lack of financial support are grossly inadequate judicial services throughout the country and an open invitation to corruption. Cases may often come before a judge either through outright bribery of the judge, or through bribes offered to the court personnel who "process" the cases and, in effect, control the docket. The most prominent proposed remedy is to increase the constitutionally mandated allocation to 6 percent of the national budget. Yet it remains to be seen whether that amount would be sufficient to sustain adequate judicial salaries and court budgets, maintain a dynamic and effective judicial training school, *and* provide for the dramatic expansion of the court system that is needed to bring justices of the peace to the 34 percent of municipalities that do not have them.

Still unaddressed, the greatest challenge the system faces is providing judicial access and remedies in the language and culture of Guatemala's indigenous majority. Two key recommendations designed to broaden access are the provision of translators and the adoption of alternative conflict resolution mechanisms, both of which would add further financial burdens to the justice system. Modest reforms to accomplish such goals were adopted in 1998, but the failed referendum represents a serious obstacle to reforms.

Conclusion

The reform goals set forth above, and the concrete proposals for meeting them, represent a daunting challenge to the citizens, the government, and external donors. The present state of the judiciary is manifestly one of weakness, inefficiency, and corruption. In the eyes of the public, the judiciary is characterized by "corruption and impunity." The people in both countries have little trust or confidence in their governmental institutions —or indeed in their fellow citizens. The May 1999 referendum stands witness to the alienation of voters and to their lack of confidence in the present system.

The findings of our own survey research, carried out in El Salvador (August 1996) and Guatemala (October 1997), put this point in especially stark relief.[51] We posed the question: "Some say that you can usually trust other people. Others say you must be cautious and wary in your relations with other people. Which is your view?" In El Salvador only 6 percent of respondents said you could trust others; an astonishing 94 percent expressed the need to be wary. Our findings in Guatemala were only slightly less extreme, with just under 12 percent expressing trust, while 88 percent voiced caution and wariness.

These dramatically Hobbesian findings may be put into perspective by comparing them to the results of surveys conducted in East Germany. In a nation accustomed, until recently, to living under the shadow of the secret police, 26 percent of citizens stated that "people can be trusted."[52] That citizens of the former East Germany are four times more likely to trust in others than are the citizens of El Salvador underscores the challenge the latter nation faces in consolidating democracy.

With respect to the United States, the General Social Survey conducted by the National Opinion Research Center at the University of Chicago asked "trust" questions in the United States for most of the years between 1972 and 1994. The average over the entire sample for those years is that 41 percent of Americans believe that most people can be trusted. Higher levels of trust were reported in early years (47 percent in 1973, 49 percent in 1984). The lowest level of trust was in 1994 (34 percent), the last year reported.[53] Despite the downward trend, the results in El Salvador and Guatemala are striking compared to the relatively stable liberal democracy of the United States. As political scientist Richard Rose has insisted, public trust is "a necessary condition for both civil society and democracy,"[54] but it appears to be a scarce and fragile commodity in post–peace accords El Salvador and Guatemala.

The cumulative effect of authoritarian government in El Salvador and Guatemala was to undermine the rule of law in two critical ways: (1) by making a mockery of judicial independence and (2) by creating a climate of extreme mistrust within the political culture. These two features of the current transitional process stand as significant potential barriers to the development of the rule of law and to democratic consolidation.[55]

In sum, achieving the elements of judicial independence, such as partisan insularity, extending access to judicial remedies to the indigenous communities, and eliminating political corruption and impunity, are goals that will take political will on the part of Salvadoran and Guatemalan elites. These elites face many competing demands for the scarce resources they have to allocate. Judicial reform must compete with the demands for reform throughout the justice system, including police reform, strengthening public prosecutors and public defenders, and the like—all in the face of rising crime and growing public demand for "law and order." And these are formidable challenges, indeed.

Notes

1. Joel G. Verner, "The Independence of Supreme Courts in Latin America: A Review of the Literature," *Journal of Latin American Studies* 16 (1984): 463. The evidence consisted of Verner's assessment of what scholars had written about the courts of each country and, to a lesser extent, on the collective judgments of scholars previously reported by Kenneth Johnson in 1975. See Kenneth F. Johnson, "Scholarly Images of Latin American Political Democracy (1945–1970)," in James W. Wilkie, ed., *Statistical Abstract of Latin America* 17 (1975): 347.

2. An "Independent-Activist" court is one that has "consistently and successfully resisted encroachments on its independent authority and has been able to say "no" to

other governmental agencies and to "make it stick" in the post-1948 period." Verner, "The Independence of Supreme Courts in Latin America," 479.

3. United States Agency for International Development, *A Strategic Assessment of Legal System Development in Honduras,* AID Technical Report No. 10, 1993, 15.

4. Ibid., 18.

5. Samuel P. Huntington, *The Third Wave: Democratization in the Twentieth Century* (Norman, Okla.: Univ. of Oklahoma Press, 1991).

6. Terry Lynn Karl, "Dilemmas of Democratization in Latin America," *Comparative Politics* 23 (1990): 1.

7. Manuel Antonio Garreton, "Political Democratization in Latin America and the Crisis of Paradigms," in *Power and Popular Protest,* ed. Susan Eckstein (Berkeley, Calif.: Univ. of California Press, 1989).

8. For recent works that focus on Latin America, see Joseph S. Tulchin, *The Consolidation of Democracy in Latin America* (Boulder, Colo.: Lynne Rienner Publishers, 1995); Larry Diamond, "Consolidating Democracy in the Americas," *ANNALS, AAPSS* 550 (March 1997): 12; Andreas Schedler, "What Is Democratic Consolidation?" *Journal of Democracy* 9 (April 1998): 91; and William C. Prillaman, *The Judiciary and Democratic Decay in Latin America: Declining Confidence in the Rule of Law* (Westport, Conn.: Praeger, 2000). Prillaman is pessimistic about the efficacy of judicial reforms in Latin America, with the possible exception of recent efforts in Chile.

9. Juan J.Linz, "State Building and Nation Building," *European Review* 1 (1993): 355.

10. Diamond, "Consolidating Democracy," 32.

11. William Ratliff and Edgardo Buscaglia, "Judicial Reform: The Neglected Priority in Latin America," *ANNALS, AAPSS* 550 (March 1997): 63.

12. Larry Rohter, "In Latin America, 'The Constitution Is What I Say It Is,'" *New York Times,* 30 August 1998.

13. William Stanley, *The Protection Racket State: Elite Politics, Military Extortion, and Civil War in El Salvador* (Philadelphia: Temple Univ. Press, 1996); David Stoll, *Between Two Armies in the Ixil Towns of Guatemala* (New York: Columbia Univ. Press, 1993).

14. John Booth and Thomas W. Walker, *Understanding Central America,* 2d ed. (Boulder, Colo.: Westview Press, 1993).

15. Rachel Sieder, *Central America: Fragile Transition* (New York: St. Martin's Press, Inc., 1996).

16. Thomas Buergenthal, "The United Nations Truth Commission for El Salvador," in *Transitional Justice: How Emerging Democracies Reckon with Former Regimes,* Vol. 1, ed. Neil J. Kritz (Washington, D.C.: United States Institute of Peace, 1995); Neil J. Kritz, "The Rule of Law in the Post-Conflict Phase: Building a Stable Peace," in *Managing Global Conflict,* eds. Chester Crocker, Fen Osler Hampson, and Pamela Aall (Washington, D.C.: United States Institute of Peace, 1997).

17. Ricardo Falla, *Massacres in the Jungle: Ixcán, Guatemala, 1975–1982* (Boulder, Colo.: Westview Press, 1994); Beatriz Manz, *Refugees of a Hidden War: The Aftermath of Counterinsurgency in Guatemala* (Albany, N.Y.: State Univ. Press of New York, 1988);

Americas Watch, *El Salvador's Decade of Terror: Human Rights since the Assassination of Archbishop Romero* (New York, 1991).

18. Enrique Baloyra, *El Salvador in Transition* (Chapel Hill, N.C.: Univ. of North Carolina Press, 1982); Susanne Jonas, *The Battle for Guatemala: Rebels, Death Squads, and US Power* (Boulder, Colo.: Westview Press, 1991); James Dunkerly, *Power in the Isthmus: A Political History of Modern Central America* (London: Verso, 1988).

19. Sieder, *Central America.*

20. Mark Danner, *The Massacre at El Mozote* (New York: Vintage, 1994).

21. Owen M. Fiss, "The Right Degree of Independence," in *Transition to Democracy in Latin American: The Role of the Judiciary,* ed. Irwin P. Stotzkey (Boulder, Colo.: Westview Press, 1993). We are indebted to Christopher Larkins for first calling our attention to Fiss's three-part definition of judicial independence. See Christopher M. Larkins, "Judicial Independence and Democratization: A Theoretical and Conceptual Analysis," *The American Journal of Comparative Law* 44 (1996): 605.

22. Ibid.

23. Margaret Popkin, *Justice Delayed: The Slow Pace of Judicial Reform in El Salvador* (Washington, D.C.: Washington Office on Latin America, 1994).

24. Commission on the Truth for El Salvador, *From Madness to Hope: The 12-Year War in El Salvador,* United Nations Publications, S/25500, 1993.

25. Author's interview with Rene Hernandez Valiente, vice president of the Supreme Court of Justice, 6 June 1995.

26. Author's interview with Dr. José Domingo Méndez, president of the Supreme Court of Justice, 14 June 1995.

27. Author's interview with Jorge Obando, director of the Agency for International Development's Judicial Reform Program, in San Salvador, 9 January 1995.

28. Francisco Díaz of the Center for the Study of Applied Law (CESPAD) has repeatedly pointed out the problem of concentration of judicial power in the Supreme Court. Author's interview with Francisco Díaz, 12 January 1995.

29. Gary Bland, *El Salvador: Sustaining Peace, Nourishing Democracy* (Washington, D.C.: The Latin American Program, Woodrow Wilson Center, 1993), 33.

30. El Salvador Truth Commission, *From Madness to Hope,* 190.

31. Author's interview with Domingo Méndez, 14 June 1995.

32. Author's interview with José Albino Tinetti, director of the Judicial Training School, an organ of the National Council of the Judiciary, 6 June 1995.

33. Popkin, *Justice Delayed.*

34. Author's interview with Hernandez Valiente, 6 June 1995.

35. Author's interviews with Dr. Felipe Villavicencio, 11 January 1995; Reed Brody, 10 January 1995; and Domingo Méndez, 14 June 1995.

36. Author's interview with Domingo Méndez, 14 June 1995.

37. Reed Brody, "The United Nations and Human Rights in El Salvador's 'Negotiated Revolution,'" Unpublished report, 1995, 14.

38. Author's interview with Nidia Díaz, FMLN deputy and president, Commission of Justice and Human Rights of the Legislative Assembly, 12 June 1995.

39. Rachel M. McCleary, "Guatemala's Postwar Prospects," *Journal of Democracy* 8 (April 1997): 134.

40. David Holiday, "Guatemala's Long Road to Peace," *Current History* 96 (February 1997): 74.

41. Rachel Sieder, "Customary Law and Local Power in Guatemala," Unpublished paper, 1997, 3.

42. Americas Watch, *Civil Patrols in Guatemala* (New York, 1986).

43. Seider, *Central America*, 196.

44. Ibid., 197.

45. "Agreement on the Strengthening of Civilian Power and on the Role of the Armed Forces in a Democratic Society," available at Internet web site <http://www.un.org/Depts/minugua/paz9.htm>, accessed 3 July 1997.

46. In August 1997 the commission published a five-year plan for modernization entitled "Plan de Modernización del Organismo Judicial 1997–2002." (Guatemala City: Comisíon de Modernización del Organismo Judicial). The authors have drawn on that document for the analysis provided in this section of the chapter.

47. Ana Montes Calderon, *Diagnostico del Sector Justicia in Guatemala* (Guatemala: Interamerican Development Bank, 1996), 16.

48. The Myrna Mack Foundation, a human rights nongovernmental organization working closely with the judicial reform project, has recommended creating a "Directing Council of the Judicial Career." While the name varies, the essential thrust of this recommendation is the same—to professionalize and depoliticize judicial administration and practice. Their proposal differs from that of the presidential commission primarily in that it would include in the council a representative of Congress and of civil society.

49. Early attempts to explain the referendum results stressed the lack of political leadership in a party system that is badly fragmented and opportunistic as a result of decades of military rule. See, for example, Rene Poitevin, "Guatemala, la Democracia Enferma," *Dialogo* (FLACSO, Facultad Latinoamerica de Ciencias Sociales), available at Internet web site <http://www.geocities.com/Athens/Rhodes/9162/FLACSOdialogo.html>, accessed 6 June 2000.

50. Association of Research and Social Studies (ASIES), Monthly Report for May 1999, available at Internet web site <http://www.asies.org.gt.analisis.html>, accessed 6 June 2000.

51. The Salvadoran survey was conducted by the Institute of Public Opinion of the Universidad Centroaméricana José Simeón Cañas (IUDOP-UCA) during July and August 1996 with a sample of 1,199, selected consistent with the proportions disclosed in the most recent national census, with a margin of error of + or −4 percent. The Guatemalan survey was conducted by Gallup de Centroamérica in October 1997

with a sample of 1,214, representative of the adult population according to the most recent national census (including indigenous people), with a margin of error of + or − 2.8 percent.

52. Claus Offe, "How Can We Trust Our Fellow Citizens?" unpublished paper, 1997, 12.

53. National Opinion Research Center, "General Social Survey: Trend Table— Trust," available at Internet web site <http://www.icps.umich.edu/ GSS99/trend/ trust.htm>, accessed 6 June 2000.

54. Richard Rose, "Postcommunism and the Problem of Trust," *Journal of Democracy* 6 (January 1994): 65–78.

55. Chiefly after considering the cases of Argentina and Chile, Larkins agrees that "nurturing . . . judicial independence during the process of democratization is no easy task," "Judicial Independence and Democracy," 625.

14

The European Court of Justice

MARTIN SHAPIRO

This chapter presents an empirical theory of successful "higher-law" judicial review courts. In short, courts and in particular the European Court of Justice (ECJ), succeed in striking down statutes or other acts of government on the grounds that they are in conflict with laws of higher status. The theory is extremely incomplete. It seeks to specify only some of the conditions under which such courts will be successful and some of the causes of certain polities choosing to attempt to establish such courts. The theory treats not only the causes and success of higher-law judicial review courts but also their relationship to democracy. The theory is built up from a number of blocks of argument that will be presented separately here before being combined. None of the blocks is new. No originality is claimed for the theory, except perhaps that it resembles the originality found in so-called "combination patents," that is, patents that combine a number of already-known elements to achieve a useful result not previously achieved.[1]

Building Blocks of a Theory of Judicial Power

Block one is lifted from my book, *Courts*.[2] Courts enjoy a basic social logic that accounts for their creation and success as an institution in nearly all polities. Where two persons fall into a dispute, if they cannot resolve their differences themselves, seeking assistance from a third party makes obvious sense. Third-party conflict resolution is, however, inherently unstable, because at its very culmination, when the third party announces which of the two disputants should prevail, the triad of equals will appear to the loser to have resolved itself from the height of fairness to the most basic of all unfairnesses-two against one. The institutional nature of the triadic conflict resolver is determined by this dynamic. The triadic resolver must avoid, excuse, or disguise two against one. Thus the great bulk of triadic conflict resolution is provided in the form of a range of forms of mediation in which things are managed so that there appears to be no winner or loser but, instead, there appears to be an agreed-upon intermediate solution.

Where triadic conflict resolution is going to yield a winner and loser, it will attempt one or another device for mitigating the appearance of two against one. The most fundamental is consent. The triadic figure is mutually chosen by the two parties. Having himself chosen the triadic decider, the loser then cannot claim two against one. Moreover, the triadic figure may announce in advance that he will only resolve the conflict by the application of a preannounced rule consented to by the disputants. Having chosen the rule under which a decider also chosen by himself has decided, the loser is doubly estopped from claiming two against one.

At some point in the evolution of most legal systems, office and law are partially, but only very partially, substituted for consent, that is, disputants must in some disputes under some circumstances submit their dispute to a dispute resolver chosen not by themselves but the state and to a rule enacted by the state not specifically chosen by themselves.

The key point is that even where no preexisting legal rule actually exists, where no law has previously been made, the triadic conflict resolver will pretend he is deciding according to a preexisting legal rule, because to do so assists his authority in solving the most fundamental of his institutional problems—two against one. Moreover, having announced such a legal rule once, the judge, and his fellow judges, will necessarily proclaim the same rule again in the future, lest their inventions be unmasked. They can hardly keep announcing different rules in successive similar cases and hope to be believed in their claim that the rule they are applying preexisted. Thus courts make law not as an independent activity but as an integral and inescapable aspect of their fundamental social logic as conflict resolvers.

The second block of argument is drawn from existing bodies of constitutional theory and applications of public choice to that theory. Taking a democratic constitution essentially to be a contract between the demos and a government acting as its agent, a long-recognized problem is that of enforcement. Problems of contract enforcement typically are met by self- or reflexive-enforcement arrangements or by self-help rights vested in the parties. In a sense, the ideal contract is self-enforcing. Constitutional contracts seek to place limits on the political authority contracted to an agent.

The standard self-enforcement device to police those limitations is division of powers either between a central and territorial segments of government or between branches. In theory at least, such devices provide automatic self-enforcement of the limitations in favor of the principal but without any need for action on his part because each part of government will jealously check and balance every other part.

An expansion by one part of government beyond its prescribed limits will usually be an invasion of the prescribed authority of another part. As each part of the agent acts to protect its own authority, the contract is automatically enforced. Of course, the demos need not resort to such self-enforcement clauses. Instead, it may depend on the principal acting as its own enforcer through elections or revolution.

Should the demos choose division of powers, however, as one of its enforcement mechanisms, it necessarily has established a situation of high potential constitutional conflict. Almost inevitably, the pieces of government will fall into conflict with one another. Referring back now to my first block of argument, a standard response to conflict is the establishment of triadic conflict-resolution structures. Thus the demos need not necessarily include, but is likely to include, such a structure in the constitution if it chooses division of powers as a mechanism for contract enforcement. For these reasons, higher-law judicial review courts are likely to be encountered in democratic constitutions that choose division of powers as a contractual self-enforcement device.

Now comes the third block of argument, which may be labeled "the junkyard dog." There is an old American lead-in to various expressions: "If you buy a junkyard dog . . ." The junkyard is an outdoor facility where scrap metal is bought, sold, and stored. Typically, it covers a good deal of ground in a crime-prone part of a city and is surrounded by a fence or wall to deter thieves. The fence rarely proves sufficient deterrent, and a large area full of huge piles of junk is not easily kept under human surveillance. Particularly before the age of electronic surveillance, the solution was the junkyard dog—a large, fierce, ever-hungry and angry dog kept chained during business hours and left free to run loose within the fence at night. There was, of course, the difficulty of getting the dog rechained the next morning, and so the junkyard operator, as well as the thief in the night, might well get bitten. The junkyard operator, however, was hardly in a position to complain. "If you buy a junkyard dog . . ."

If the demos constitutionally chooses division of powers and constitutionally chooses a higher-law judicial review court to resolve conflicts that arise out of that division, it has chosen judicial lawmaking, because judges cannot resolve conflict without making law. "If you buy a junkyard dog . . ."

The demos that has bought the dog to bite the parts of government must expect to sometimes be bitten itself, that is, to become subject to laws that have not been made democratically but by judges acting outside the prescribed process for constitutional amendment and statutory enactment. The demos may choose not to buy the dog in the first place or may later get rid of it, but so long as it keeps the dog, quibbles about the antidemocratic or nondemocratic character of judicial review are beside the point. Thus the seeming paradox that higher-law judicial review may constrain the policy-making power of other parts of government, but only by increasing the policy-making powers of courts, is unavoidable. If you buy the court, you buy judicial lawmaking. Courts make law, just as dogs bite.

To this simple third block, I wish to add two bodies of supplementary argument. One has to do with areal division of powers,[3] the capital division of powers and human rights, and the other has to do with "interpretation."

A higher-law judicial review court that deals with areal division of powers, that is, the kind of division we find in confederations, federations, and such like, is in a particularly good situation for success, or so I would argue. The reason is the "second best" phenomenon. For each participant in a rule-governed process, the best situation is that all other participants obey the rules while he is free to disobey. Yet it is highly unlikely that this highly desirable state of affairs can be achieved or, if achieved, can long remain stable. The second best resolution for each participant is that all participants, including himself, always obey the rules. Thus in an areal division of powers system, while each government constantly will be tempted to disobey the rules and will sometimes do so, it will both be anxious that all other governments be called to account for rule breaking and not be too upset if it itself is called to account. It follows that even when a higher law judicial review court decides in favor of the common government and against one of the members, the other members are not likely to see the decision as one against their own interests but rather as one contributing to the "second best" of all possible worlds.

This second best phenomenon explains why even where the higher-law judicial review court is embedded within the common government, as it typically is, even its decisions in favor of the common government will not be seen by the members as involving that most fundamental of unfairnesses—being judge in its own case. It also explains why a higher-law court deciding against one member and then another usually does not generate over time a coalition of members against it but rather is able to knock off one member at a time on one question at a time.

All this, of course, does not mean that a higher-law review court in an areal division of powers system is guaranteed success even in the face of massive stupidity on its side. Such a court can engender a multimember coalition against it if it offends too many members too frequently or too obviously serves as a tool of the common government.

Higher-law judicial review courts are less well placed when they act in the other division of powers arena, division among the branches of a central or common government. The second best phenomenon is still there but is greatly weakened because the number of participants is small. The appearance of two against one is difficult to avoid where only a single legislature and a single executive are the relevant constitutional parties in conflict and the reviewing court is the third party. Partisan party politics are more likely to be more dramatically at play in such confrontations within a single government than in areal division of powers disputes.[4]

Finally, a higher-law judicial review court acting solely in the context of individual rights threatened by some governmental action is in the weakest position. It is deprived of "second best." From the point of view of all government organs, it would be best if the court never interfered in their dealings with the citizens, and it would also be second best and third best if the court never interfered. To be sure, there may be times when it is politically expedient for one part of a divided government to back the court against another branch accused of rights violations. So a human rights court generally is better off in a constitutional regime of divided powers than one of nondivided powers. But such situations are likely to be fortuitous. A court defending human rights will often find itself with no government defenders. Thus a higher-law judicial review court is most likely to be successful in areal division of powers cases, less likely in capital division of powers cases, and least likely in individual rights cases.

The second supplementary argument concerns interpretation. Higher-law judicial review courts are engaged in constitutional interpretation, in general statutory interpretation, and in a peculiar form of statutory interpretation in which statutes are interpreted so as to bring them into harmony with the relevant higher law to "save" their constitutionality.

The fourth block in the argument consists of pointing out a number of interrelated features of judicial decision making and their effect on judicial relationships with nonjudicial actors. Judicial lawmaking necessarily is case-by-case lawmaking in both common and noncommon law systems. While logically it is possible to conceive of a case-by-case judicial lawmaking system that vigorously refuses any form or degree of *stare decisis* or of incrementalism (perhaps the Delphic oracle), in fact where there is case-by-case judicial lawmaking, *stare decisis* practices are likely to arise, because there is enormous utility in stability and predictability in law. For the same reason, judicial decision or policy or lawmaking will be incremental, for incrementalism is the best method of making new policy while maintaining stability and predictability. Moreover, incrementalism is the best solution to the principal institutional problem in courts: that they must make law but must appear not to be doing so.[5]

Inherent to incremental judicial lawmaking as a discourse is a special dynamics of the general and the particular. General legal rules or doctrines are announced in the course of applying them to a particular fact setting. Moreover, inherent in the very course of the particularized announcement is the message that the same rule will be applied, indeed the court is bound to apply, in future, similar, particular fact situations. Judges become expert at manipulating this general-particular dynamic so as initially to embed policy changes of great long-term significance in what appear to be minor, insignificant decision-making occasions. The new law is established in a series of minor, esoteric, technical cases.

By the time its full policy impact is perceived by others, the new doctrine is well established and the judges and their supporters are asking why others are complaining now about a long-established, long-accepted law. Reenforcing this tactic is the ability of the judges to disguise even the initial introduction of the new law by emphasizing its particularity, that is, by depicting it as only a special rule for the special facts of the case in which it is introduced, leaving it to later cases for the rule slowly to float free of the special facts that purportedly engendered it. Here is a description of the Court of Justice itself.

> A common tactic is to introduce a new doctrine gradually: in the first case that comes before it, the Court will establish the doctrine as a general principle but suggest that it is subject to various qualifications; the Court may even find some reason why it should not be applied to the particular facts of the case. The principle, however, is now established. If there are not too many protests, it will be reaffirmed in later cases: the qualifications can then be whittled away and the full extent of the doctrine revealed.[6]

In many polities, constitutional review judiciaries are established as nonelected, relatively long-term-of-service officials, where legislatures and executives are elected and for relatively short terms. The capacity of courts to introduce new policy by long-term incremental implementation allows judges to manipulate the "not on my watch" proclivities of elected politicians. Even where those politicians manage to be sufficiently alert and knowledgeable to spot the greater significance of the little judicial decision lurking in the technical legal brush, they will be much inclined to leave it right where they found it if the real trouble over it is going to come after the next election. Moreover, the very role of constitutional judges is to concern themselves with basic constitutional values or fundamental rights while deciding particular cases. Thus, while judges are incrementing to long-term goals, the politicians with whom they must deal and who constrain them are concerned largely with immediate electoral survival. Where a court is moving toward big long-term change, most politicians will be happy to join the judicial pretense of legal stability now.[7]

Finally, case-by-case, incremental policy change in law is part of a technical discourse that contains no real rules at all for when or how fast or how often or how big change shall be. Thus the very technical discourse that protects judges constrains them relatively little in varying the pace of legal change in order to take advantage of both momentary circumstances and the short time frames of other politicians. At the extreme, a court that dramatically reverses its own previous decisions frequently and over short time periods will suffer loss of lawyers' face. For the most part, however, the rules of the law incremental game are very unspecified as to how many yards to a first down, how many bases to a run, or how many inches in a regulation step. Judges may constantly vary the length and speed of their policy steps to conform to the intermediate political terrain they are traversing toward their policy goals.

The fifth and final building block has to do with text. Most judicial lawmaking occurs through the "interpretation" of text written by others. I hope I do not need to go through the whole postmodern fish story to demonstrate that those who interpret text make text, particularly because I do not need to insist that the text itself has absolutely no meaning of its own. In politics, this literary tale has been public choiced and comes out as follows: the more efficient the legislative process is in producing new statutes or amendments to old ones, the less powerful judicial review is.[8]

Constitutional judicial review is, of course, a somewhat special case. It is unlikely to flourish in one-party states, because the single party need pay no attention to the constitution. Similarly, where one party in a two-party state enjoys overwhelming electoral advantage over the other party for a long period of time, the advantaged party need pay no attention to the constitution. Witness the New Deal. Even where parties are strong and competitive, constitutional judicial review may be weak if the constitutional amendment process is quick and easy as it is in some American states. Thus California once experienced a constitutional review crisis in which three state supreme court justices were deselected because they had persistently refused to implement a constitutional amendment adopted by popular electoral mandate. Most constitutions are relatively hard to amend both because their formal amendment processes are difficult and because their basic provisions are enshrined in popular or elite political cultures. Thus constitutional review is likely to flourish in competitive party states where party discipline is weak or where there are multiple parties.

The issue of judicial independence is implicated in the model through a basic paradox in the nature of judicial independence. We expect courts to be independent at retail, not at wholesale. That is, we expect that other political actors will not seek directly to influence the outcome of particular cases, except through open participation in the litigation process. But courts are courts of law. We expect them to make their decisions according to law. We do not expect them to be independent of law. And most of the law is made by other political actors. The courts are supposed to be not independent, but servants of the lawmakers.

It follows that judges are most independent when they are their own lawmakers. To the extent that constitutional courts "interpret" their own constitutional texts that are difficult to formally amend, they are considerably more independent at wholesale than courts that "interpret" statutory texts that are easily amended by legislators.

The ECJ and the European Union

Against this model we may now turn to the European Court of Justice about which a number of tales may be told. The multiplicity of tales results because each ECJ story is a subplot of a different story about the European Community (EC), or European Union (EU), as a whole.

The two stories of the EC have been so often told that they need only be briefly outlined here. The first is "intergovernmental." The various member states of the EU have formed a series of treaty alliances with one another. New EU policies are initiated through bargaining among the member states. To some degree, and always reserving final options to themselves, the member states have created international institutions as agents to formulate and implement such policies, but those institutions always remain agents subject to the will of their principals.

The ECJ and Intergovernmental Relations

Specifically in relation to courts, this model is capable of recognizing that sovereign states that enter into an agreement, any kind of agreement, with one another may choose to create a third-party conflict resolver for disputes between members that arise over differing interpretations of the agreement. Where all agreeing states have sufficient long-term interests in the continuing stability of the agreement, each will comply with the judgments of the third-party conflict resolver even when such a judgment runs against its own short-term interests, and each will exert pressure on the others to comply in such circumstances. Thus, while all power remains in the member states, an international court may become sufficiently institutionalized that its judgments against states that are parties to the agreement will be routinely obeyed by losing as well as winning states on rational-state self-interest grounds. Such courts are particularly likely to arise in connection with international and regional trade agreements in which all parties realize substantial gains from trade in both the short and long run, and either the national costs of those gains are diffused over the various sectors of each national economy, or special steps have been taken in the agreement to ameliorate concentrated national sectorial costs.[9] The ECJ is such a court.

The ECJ consists in fifteen judges—one selected by each member state but appointed by the common agreement of all the member states. They serve six-year, staggered terms, with a partial change in membership every three years. There are also nine advocates general, who play an important role in the court's deliberations and who also serve six-year, staggered terms. Five are selected by the five largest member states and the remainder in rotation by the other members. The court sits in three- and five-judge chambers and in plenary sessions. Only a single opinion appears for the court in each case, but it is accompanied by an analysis of the case by one of the advocate generals. Judges may not hold other offices. They may be removed only by the unanimous vote of their fellow judges and advocates general. The treaties provide that they must be "persons whose independence is beyond reasonable doubt" and who possess the qualifications required for appointment to the highest courts in their countries or "jurisconsults of recognized competence."

A mixture of senior national judges, professors, and former national office holders with legal qualifications have been appointed. There is little evidence of member-state governments seeking to lobby their "own" judges. Because votes are not recorded, there is no way of knowing whether judges have favored their own country of origin.

The tellers of this tale tend to be international relations specialists and are rather naive about the nature of courts and law. They see courts as solely conflict resolvers that occasionally engage in necessary "interpretation" of the contracts of governance or international agreements that they "implement." They buy the age-old judges' lie that we "discover," we do not make the law. They deny the independent lawmaking capacities of courts. This denial is particularly crucial to the intergovernmental view of the EU, for clearly the EU has gone further than any other international organization in institutionalizing central, long-term organs with apparently self-contained policy-making authority binding on the member states.

At least until 1992, however, the basic lawmaking process of these organs could be seen as intergovernmental, because the ultimate lawmaking authority was the European Council, on which each member state had a seat and which enacted legislation under a unanimity rule. Such a member-state veto system ensured that even the institutionalized center remained intergovernmental.

To the extent that the ECJ exercised lawmaking as well as mere implementing powers, this intergovernmental interpretation of EU institutionalization was threatened, because no such member-state veto existed for the litigation process. Thus the naivete of the intergovernmentalists about courts was reenforced by their self-interest.

When this naivete is forcibly pointed out to intergovernmentalists, they tend to retreat to the last refuge of all political science scoundrels, the rule of anticipated reaction. They argue that while indeed the ECJ may make some little law, that is policy, on its own and that law is then by and large obeyed by the member states without the possibility of veto, nevertheless the ECJ will only make such law as it anticipates all the member states are willing to obey. Such a hypothesis is, of course, scientifically extremely weak because it is completely impossible to falsify no matter what data is collected. Any lawmaking act of the court, no matter how extreme or innovative, or seemingly contrary to the interests of one or more of the member states, will be a confirmation of the anticipated reaction hypothesis so long as the member states obey. It will be impossible to offer any instance in which one or more of the member states was forced to eat humble pie rather than being judicially served the pie it was already known to be prepared to eat. And if in some instances pie is actually refused, that even further confirms the hypothesis of ultimate state power.

Also, some attention must be payed to domestic political orders. The members of the EU are all rule-of-law states. One of the peculiar features of the EU treaties is their Article 177 procedures.[10] Under these procedures, a citizen of a member state who is engaged in litigation in the domestic courts of his own state may request that a national judge make reference to the ECJ on a particular point of EU law on which the ECJ will render a judgment. The case is then returned to the referring court, which renders a final judgment on the case as a whole, guided by the ECJ pronouncement. Frequently, the ECJ judgment is that a national law or decision at issue is in conflict with EU law, that the national court is legally obligated to treat EU law as superior, and that, as a result, the individual litigant prevails over the member-state litigant or over the private litigant protected by member-state law.

Thus in proceedings taken under Article 177, it is the court of the member state acting within the domestic legal system of the member state, not the ECJ, that orders the state to obey the EU law that has now become the domestic law. For the member-state government to disobey its own court would violate its own national rule of law norms.[11] For intergovernmentalists to argue that the ECJ has no lawmaking authority that the member states must obey, they must now argue that domestic courts have no independent lawmaking authority that the rest of their domestic governments must obey. Such a position would appear nonsensical to students of law and courts save those few of the most blindly orthodox who still assert that courts only interpret not make law, if any such students still survive.

The ECJ and the Development of Quasi-Federalism in the EU

The alternative story to that of the intergovernmentalists is often labeled neofunctionalist, but in the context of the EU, it better might be called quasi-federalist. This story tends to be teleological, seeing the ultimate destiny of the European Communities, then community (EC), then union (EU) to be a United States of Europe. The ECJ itself has been one of the principal proponents of a discrete and discreet version of this story. This story emphasizes that the member states not only entered into a customs union, that is an international agreement, but into a series of agreements that progressively institutionalized a number of transnational organs and a transnational lawmaking process. In doing so, it is claimed, they transferred portions of their sovereignty to these organs and processes, thus transforming a treaty regime into a new, constitutional order of shared sovereignty, into what might well be called a federal union.

Whatever it once may have been, the formal lawmaking process of the EU is now largely federal and majoritarian. On most issues, there is no longer an individual state veto; voting is by a "qualified" majority voting rule under which more populous states have more votes, and the European Parliament, which is popularly elected and in which individual members, not state delegations, cast votes, plays an increasingly important role. Moreover, the ECJ makes the constitutional law of this federal union case by case and successfully imposes that law on the member states. Only the fact that the European Council, the ultimate lawmaking body of the EU, consists of instructed delegates of the member states' governments rather than directly elected representatives of the people of the EU keeps the organization closer to the confederal than the federal end of the divided sovereignty spectrum. Particularly with the new European monetary policy, the division of spheres of policy making between the member states and the transnational institutions more and more favors the EU sphere.

The difficulty with the quasi-federalist story is that it is still very quasi. The European Council does remain the ultimate lawmaking authority, even if the lawmaking activities of the ECJ are fully acknowledged. And the council continues to consist of cabinet ministers of the member-state governments, who are bound by the internal discipline of those cabinets and instructed by those governments.

In the late 1980s, after many years in which political integration was in the doldrums, the Single European Act (1987) signaled new great expectations of a revival of progress toward federalism. The subsequent mixed public response to the further integrative steps of the Maastricht Treaty (the Treaty on European Union, 1992) and the very mixed messages of the Amsterdam Treaty (1997) have led to a retreat from assertions of a federal telos to the proclamation of the EU as *sui generis,* a unique political arrangement constituting its own evolutionary line. This development in the real world runs parallel to some of the latest fashions in political science, particularly the new institutionalism, with its sensitivity to "path dependency" and the "rules of the game."[12] This approach is reflected in my earlier block of argument labeled "junkyard dog." In general, the argument runs that, once created by political forces, political institutions not only have a certain independent survival capacity but also they themselves to some degree reconstitute the political forces that created them. Thus institutions defined either as persistent complexes of values or organizational entities are both the victims and beneficiaries of path dependency. Once created, their very existence to some degree both constrains and enables political actors to choose among various ranges of alternative actions.

The EU institutions are indeed *sui generis.* They neither are drawn on by a federal telos nor are they a mere facade for the ever-constant sovereignty of the member states. Having created the institutions, the member states have set in motion a chain of interactions between those institutions and themselves, including further evolution of those institutions the members can neither entirely foresee nor entirely control. More specifically, having created the ECJ as a third-party conflict resolver to deal with incomplete contract problems among themselves and with principal agent problems between themselves and other EU organs, the member states have bought the lawmaking (policy) powers of that court, which are institutionally inherent in courts, whether they knew it or not and whether they like it or not.

Even if this general institutional approach were to be universally accepted, there would remain a debate about how much in fact the ECJ has imposed law on member states that they would not have imposed, or would have not been prepared to impose, on themselves in a multinational bargaining process devoid of lawmaking organs. Essentially, the court's jurisdictional authority rests on three factors. The first is the power to engage in judicial review of both EU norms and member-state norms said to conflict with EU norms. The member states explicitly agreed to this judicial review in the treaties themselves and have generally continued to agree to it. The second is the supremacy of EU legal norms over member-state legal norms. The member states clearly agreed and continue to agree in general to the supremacy of those EU norms, including judge-made ones, that facilitated the single European market. The German Constitutional Court denies the total and complete supremacy of EU law, but only when such law might infringe on fundamental human rights guaranteed by the German constitution. No member state seems inclined to deny that there has been some surrender of sovereignty to the EU.

The third factor is "direct effect," the doctrine that both provisions of the treaties themselves and the legislation enacted by the European Council (and, therefore, the case law of the court "interpreting" them) become a part of the domestic law of each member state enforced by the courts of each member state. Direct effect is at the very core of the arguments against the intergovernmental model. This is because, under the direct effect doctrine, laws made by the EU become directly binding on the citizens of each member state and on the judges of those member states without any action of the member-state governments incorporating those laws into their own law and hence without any possibility of the member-state governments vetoing EU laws. Indeed, as we have already noted, under direct effect, if a member-state government violates an EU law, it is violating the laws of its own country and thus offending the most basic norm of the rule of law.

While there is a bit of evidence that the member states knew and to some small degree intended some direct effect, it is pretty clear they did not foresee either its ultimate scope or its ultimate potential for expanding

ECJ judicial review power over domestic legislation. Indeed, there is much evidence that the members expected most apparent conflicts between national and European Community law to be resolved by direct political negotiation between member-state governments and the commission or interstate negotiation in the council rather than by litigation culminating in ECJ final declarations of "what the law is." By institutionalizing the direct effect doctrine on its own initiative, the court has invented most of its own bite.

Have these partially self-invented court powers actually been used to impose policies on the member states that they oppose or at least would not have imposed on themselves *sua sponte?* The ECJ has struck down a large number of state laws, administrative regulations, and individual decisions as contrary to EU law. Inevitably, many of these ECJ judgments were brush-clearing operations to purge member-state statute and regulation books of old laws the states simply had not bothered to winnow for violations of the new treaties. Given the nature of the Article 177 proceedings in which many of these laws were struck down, the member states often had not even made a conscious decision to defend them before the ECJ.[13] Even where the state was technically a party, sometimes one of the entrenched state bureaucracies was attempting to defend its turf against new EU rules that the elected political leadership of the state probably approved or to which it was indifferent.

In the intergovernmental story, the very occasional obduracy of violating member states against ECJ judgments is emphasized, and it is claimed that, for the most part, the ECJ only strikes down state norms that it knows the states are not committed to defending. As usual, claims of this nature are impossible to falsify. All that the opposing sides can say is that the ECJ itself routinely strikes down state laws and even more routinely delivers judgments in Article 177 references that lead member-state courts to rule against the laws of their own states. And member-state governments routinely acquiesce in these judgments. Very rarely do the member states reverse the ECJ by treaty amendment or revision of European Council legislation, but these very episodes show that the ECJ indeed does sometimes attack member-state laws the states are committed to defending and that the member states typically respond not by attacking the court but by the quite routinely legal means of changing the treaties.

Conversely, there have been episodes in which certain member-state governments, most notably the German government, do seem to have been waging campaigns of intimidation against the court, and there are pretty reliable reports that the court has sometimes actually been intimidated.

All of this seems to add up to the new institutionalist conclusion that the court, in fact, does sometimes bite and usually, but not always, gets away with it.

If the ECJ only successfully struck down member-state laws from time to time and occasionally enforced the constitutional separation of powers on its fellow EU organs while making a bit of new constitutional law from time to time, it would be worthy of our attention. There is, however, a larger, and as usual contested, set of stories to be told. I take up three of those stories here and prognosticate about a fourth.

The first is a quite grand story. After the initial flurry of integrationist activity resulting in the Coal and Steel Community Treaty (Treaty of Paris, 1951) and the European Economic Community Treaty (Treaty of Rome, 1957), forward integrationist movement in the EC bogged down. In 1966 the European Council adopted a unanimity rule that effectively ended any chance of its being a source of further integration, and it is both the chief legislator and chief executive of the EU. The ECJ and the European Commission, so it is claimed, then formed an alliance to fill the gap left by the council, and from roughly the late 1960s to the 1980s, the court itself was the principal integrationist force in the EU. This story can be supported by dense case analysis showing an ECJ jurisprudence of incremental creep on many fronts toward a more complete, more penetrating body of judge-made EU law as a substitute for the bodies of law the council was not making.[14] The core of the story, however, is the great "mutual recognition" escapade.

Once the treaties themselves were enacted, the court, largely on its own and with some aid from the commission, could pursue the first stage of creating the European single market. It could and did strike down many member-state laws that acted as border barriers to free trade. It soon ran into one major problem, however, that will be familiar to those who know the U.S. jurisprudence of the "negative" commerce clause.[15]

One state may have a law, say a products labeling law, that is neither intended to, nor does in itself, serve as a barrier to trade. The product manufacturer in another state simply slaps on the label the importing state requires. The problem arises when a second state possesses a law requiring different labels than those the first state requires. This second law also neither intends to create, nor in and of itself creates, a barrier to interstate trade. The barrier arises out of the interaction of the two state laws, which results in the manufacturer incurring the inefficiency costs of having to use two sets of labels instead of one and making sure that the right label goes on each bottle, depending on what state is going to import it.

A judicial cure for this problem is extremely awkward, because it involves telling the second state it can't have its labeling law, although the first state can, for no other reason than that the first state was first. Alternatively, the court can strike down all the state labeling laws, but to do so would be a blow to legitimate concerns for consumer protection. What a court cannot do, because of its very institutional nature, is write a uniform labeling law for all the member states. So, if the central legislature, in this instance the council, is frozen, the court is stuck.

One solution to this problem that is directly available to a court is mutual recognition. The court does not strike down any state labeling law. Instead, it says that if the product satisfies the labeling law of the state in which it was manufactured, its sale must be considered lawful in all the other states. Not entirely clearly and definitively, the ECJ moved to mutual recognition in the famous *Cassis de Dijon* decision.[16] Immediately, the commission moved to interpret *Cassis* as a move to selective but wide-ranging mutual recognition as a substitute for "harmonization," that is for uniform EC-wide regulatory laws that the commission proposed but the council, under its unanimity rule, failed to enact.

It cannot be claimed realistically that *Cassis* was the sole or principal cause of the subsequent reenergizing of the movement toward completion of the single market. Nevertheless, when in the mid-1980s that reenergizing took place in the form of the Single European Act (1987), the echoes of *Cassis* were startlingly clear. The Single European Act, which is effectively an amendment to the treaties, provides that the commission shall propose a whole series of harmonizing laws and that the council shall consider them under qualified majority, not unanimous, voting. Where harmonization is not achieved , mutual recognition will come into effect. Thus a complex political incentive system is established. States favoring very low or very high regulation levels no longer can veto uniform EC-wide harmonization proposals. But high-end states must make concessions to low-end states in the harmonization process lest that process fail and mutual recognition takes over, because mutual recognition is likely to lead to a "race to the bottom," in which states with the lowest level of regulation will be economically advantaged. High-end states, notably Germany, controlled enough votes so that low-end states could not be too obdurate. In the actual event, an enormous amount of harmonization was accomplished. Thus, or so the story runs, a court-commission alliance nudges the whole system forward out of stasis to a new level of economic integration. Indeed, the court did provide the conceptual raw materials and some incremental threats.

In any event, the heroic story of the court ends on a lower note. Remember the general rule that the more efficient the legislature, the less powerful the judicial review. The core of the first story is that the ECJ stepped in to fill the void left by a council immobilized by the single-state veto. It follows that, with most of lawmaking spheres of the council shifted to qualified majority voting, the heroic period of the court should be at an end and the court's incremental policy-making steps should be shorter and fewer.[17]

An Alternative Tale of the ECJ and the EU

The second story goes beyond shorter and fewer steps forward to become one of judicial retreat. In this story, the ECJ's heroic period may or may not be an illusion, but the court certainly has now begun a retreat from any integrationist push in which it was once engaged, either because it has become frightened by member-state opposition or because its current membership is less integration minded than earlier ones, or both. This story is open to grave doubts. Even if the court were once single-mindedly in pursuit of a federal telos, it was surely a federal, not a unitary, telos in which it was in pursuit. Its case law always reflected judicial care in maintaining a "margin of appreciation" for the retained powers of the member states and respect for the "legislative discretion" of their parliamentary bodies. From the very beginning, in the crucial area of free movement of goods, the court not only gave considerable weight to the exceptions provided in Article 36 of the Treaty Establishing the European Community that allowed state derogations from free movement to protect such areas as public health but also itself invented several new exceptions and a rule of reason that permitted state derogations "proportional" to legitimate state interests.

Thus the second story, that of court retreat, must always be a nuanced one. It cannot be that any and all recent cases in which the court found for the member states and against the EU are in and of themselves conclusive evidence of retreat, because in the nature of things, there must always have been, and in fact have been, at least a few contrary cases. The centerpiece of the retreat story is a free movement of goods case called *Keck*.[18] In it and a cluster of other cases, the court has found that the member states may regulate the time, place, and manner of retail sales even when their regulations may result in a diminution in the volume of interstate flow of goods so long as the state is not using the regulation as a covert discrimination against interstate trade. *Keck* succeeds a long line of cases that heavily favor interstate trade over member-state commercial regulation. *Keck* even formally announces a partial reversal of one of the key precedents in this line. It is hard not to see retreat when the court actually goes out of its way to announce one.

Nevertheless, while the precise nature of *Keck* might not have been anticipatable, the evolution of the general free movement jurisprudence of the court could have been anticipated and can be described without invoking any special vision of retreat. Where a customs union of previously completely independent states is created by a new constitution or treaty, the dynamics of litigation will naturally impose a certain time-sequenced pattern on a constitutional court's decisions. The earliest litigation will be "easy cases" in which laws enacted by member states before ratification of the union constitution that are obviously intended to discriminate against foreign trade and with large discriminatory effect are challenged by other states or their trading companies. A stream of decisions in favor of free trade will result.

Once this brush clearing is completed, cases of covert discrimination either in new state laws or by elaborate excuses for persisting in certain old ones will reach the court in numbers. As the states learn to clothe challenged state legislation as a means of achieving legitimate state purposes, the court will respond with a balancing, and then a balancing least-means doctrine. The least-means test will be particularly convenient for judges who actually smell covert discrimination but prefer not to accuse the member state involved of lying. Instead of saying, "You claim that your law has a health or consumer protection purpose, but that is just a smokescreen to hide protectionism," the court can say "You could have pursued your quite legitimate interest by some means that would have had less negative impact on imports."

As the stream of these more-difficult covert discrimination cases continues, constitutional judges are going to be nudged from free trade to laissez-faire, particularly in the context of the least-means test. It is not always easy to keep the distinction between free trade and laissez-faire clearly in mind. Free trade is about cross-border traffic without border barriers. Thus a dozen pure socialist states in which all the means of production are publicly owned, and there is no private enterprise or laissez-faire at all, can enter into a customs union in which there is absolute free trade among them. As opposed to free trade, laissez-faire need not be about cross-border traffic at all, but instead demand only that government engage in the absolute minimum regulation of its own domestic private economic enterprises no matter what its treatment of potential imports. A protectionist laissez-faire state can exist, and, indeed, many proponents of laissez-faire at various times and places will want precisely that.

Constitutional courts at the second stage of constitutional customs unions tend to confuse free trade and laissez-faire for a number of reasons. Some of the judges may actually be ideologically committed to laissez-faire and deliberately use free trade as a means of achieving laissez-faire, as the U.S. Supreme Court is alleged to have done under the dreaded doctrine of dual federalism. Under that doctrine, so it is said, the court would strike down state business regulation on the grounds that it interfered with interstate commerce and federal regulation on the grounds that it interfered with state prerogatives of internal trade regulation.

Even in the absence of such ideological commitment, however, at stage two, faced with better and better camouflaged state trade discrimination masquerading as health, safety, and environmental and consumer protection legislation, a constitutional court simply doggedly pursuing its free trade duties will speak and appear more and more laissez-faire, or deregulatory. It will strike down a lot of purportedly legitimate regulatory legislation. And to penetrate state camouflage without openly calling the state a liar, it will more often use the simple diminution of the flow of interstate trade as a key test of unconstitutionality, because by doing so it can avoid talking about the covert discriminatory state motives it suspects. All this talk condemning the reduction of trade volume through regulation is bound to look a lot like laissez-faire talk.

It is in "burden" least-means cases that courts will be most prone to cross the line from free trade to laissez-faire. "Burden" cases are those in which no state regulation is, in and of itself, discriminatory either in intent or impact and each state regulation appears to be a legitimate, albeit regulatory rather than laissez-faire, means of achieving a legitimate state interest. It is simply the differences between the regulations of two states that creates an unintended burden on interstate trade, because a producer will have to produce slightly different products for different states.

The preferred solution to this problem may well be a single multistate regulation rather than no regulation at all, but that is precisely what a constitutional court cannot achieve on its own. Nor is it easy for a court to say, "well whichever state regulated first wins," although the ECJ came close to that in the "mutual recognition" doctrine. What it is easy for a constitutional court to do in burden cases is to use a least-means test to strike down all but minimum state regulations, driving all the states toward the least-demanding regulation, not because it is least demanding but because it is likely to be uniform state to state and thus will cause no burden.

For instance, where two or more states have slightly different substantive product regulations, say the percentage of fruit content of jam, a constitutional court is sorely tempted to say that no substantive regulation meets the least-means test. The means of protecting the consumer that would least burden interstate trade would be a requirement that the actual fruit content of the jar be indicated on its label. Notice how this holding solves the burden problem but does so by adopting a favorite laissez-faire tactic of state facilitation of consumer sovereignty in a free market rather than government-imposed consumer protection.

Clearly, the ECJ did reach a point at which it tended to confuse free trade and laissez-faire, particularly in cases in which it invalidated a state regulation that reduced the total volume of commerce within the regulating state and thus reduced the total volume of imports to the state even though there was no discrimination against foreign goods.

Is there likely to be a natural turnaround in such a growing conflation of free trade and laissez faire by a constitutional court policing a federalized economy because of the internal dynamics of constitutional litigation rather than new judicial fears of adverse state reaction? Indeed, I think two mutually reenforcing dynamics are at work.

The first of these lies in the very nature of the least-means formula. Of course, the balancing test itself, of which the least-means formula is a derivative and subsidiary part, is often criticized as too openly revealing of the element of judicial lawmaking in constitutional decision making. It might well be argued that the legislature, not the court, should balance interests. To this the court may respond that it is not naked interests the court is balancing, but two or more interests the constitution defines as equally legitimate. In such instances, judicial balancing is unavoidable.

The least-means test is even more revealing, however, of the legislative role of courts. Ultimately, under pressure of imaginative litigators, a court using the least-means test will be driven to offering a draft of the legislation that would satisfy its least-means test and flunking the actual legislation it is reviewing, because that legislation does not correspond to its model draft. When pushed to its ultimate, as it will be over time in the course of litigation, the least-means test is the judge saying, "Because I can imagine a statute that would serve your legitimate purposes at less cost to a rival constitutional value than the legislation you have enacted, your legislation is unconstitutional." Courts are not likely to feel very comfortable with their own least-means test as they are driven to say things like this more and more frequently.

The second dynamic has to do with the volume of trade test. At first a constitutional court will use this test out of politeness. Instead of saying to a member state "We've caught you covertly discriminating," it can say "We're sorry but your regulation, no matter how well meant, excessively reduces the total volume of interstate trade. Over time, however, every business that wants to escape from the "inefficiencies" imposed by the regulatory state to the blessed state of laissez-faire, will dress up its legal claims in the following form: this regulation hurts my business; some of my business involves imports or exports; therefore, this regulation reduces the total volume of foreign trade and thus violates constitutional free-trade guarantees. As these claims are stretched to reach more and more regulations, the court involved sees itself more and more pushed from free trade to deregulation and will react, unless its judges themselves are very committed to laissez faire. This is not a retreat but a refusal to be exploited any further.

The two dynamics often intersect. The deregulatory litigator claims that because the challenged regulation reduces total business volume or efficiency, it reduces foreign trade volume or efficiency and so is not the least means that the state legislature might have adopted for achieving its purposes. Some less market-restricting means could have been imagined.

Keck and company may be depicted as a judicial retreat from the ECJ's most advanced free-trade position, which disfavored diminution of trade volume. It can be seen equally well, however, as the ECJ's refusal to be pushed from free trade all the way to laissez-faire and its inevitable recognition that the least means formula, if pushed too far, completely destroys the legislative discretion or margin of appreciation the court has always been careful to preserve. Both the facts and the language of *Keck* bear this version of the story out.

Keck is a German Sunday-closing law case essentially being fought out by supermarkets. Obviously, the supermarkets care about the total volume of their local retail trade, which would be considerably improved by Sunday openings, not about the interstate wholesale volumes of their suppliers. And the supermarkets chose to litigate a case involving a supermarket near a national border so that they could argue the diminution of cross-border retail trade.

The ECJ chose to ignore this obvious ploy. What it said was: "In view of the increasing tendency of traders to invoke Article 30 of the Treaty as a means of challenging any rules whose effect is to limit their commercial freedom even where such rules are not aimed at products from other Member States, the Court considers it necessary to reexamine and clarify its case-law on this matter."[19]

Keck is far less a retreat than a midcourse correction informing litigators that the court is interested in free trade, not laissez-faire deregulation. The same thing can be said for the European Community as a whole. At the time of the Single European Act, there was much talk of deregulation. And the Single European Act was deregulatory in the sense of moving many economic endeavors from living under twelve state regulations to one EC regulation. Particularly, however, with the emphasis on the environment in the Single European Act itself and all the subsequent treaties, it is becoming clear that living under one rather than twelve regulations does relieve business of some of the inefficiencies of past regulation. But that current, harmonized EU regulation may be very far toward the high end of, or even beyond, past state regulatory demands.

A Third Tale of the ECJ

The third story is simpler and has been exhaustively told elsewhere.[20] The treaties contain an antigender discrimination clause. In dozens of cases, the ECJ has implemented the clause against unequal pay, conditions of employment, hiring, worker health and safety, retirement, and pension arrangements. As in many other jurisdictions, what was in reality a situation of role transition in which older economic gender role differentiations were rapidly but unevenly being displaced by newer ones was treated as a vast conspiracy against women's rights. Because the court's decisions flowed with the political, social, and, above all, economic trends of the times, they could hardly be condemned even by the most hostile. They have had an enormous negative financial impact on a number of the member states, particularly on state pension schemes. Indeed the potential impact was so great that the court felt compelled to mitigate it by severely limiting the retroactive effect of some of its decisions.

In reality, gender discrimination created substantial economic inefficiencies in most member states but had no particularly restrictive effect on interstate trade. This is an instance in which litigators representing a particular group with a long-term, persistent, well-defined interest and adequate financial resources forum shopped until they found the most receptive litigational arena and then worked it hard. The ECJ was dealing with a new constitution, with a general climate enthusiastic about fundamental human rights and pressing the court to declare its allegiance to such rights, and with a constitutional text in which gender equality was among the very few rights specifically mentioned. It was a court primarily concerned with economic matters, and gender discrimination intimately mixed economic and noneconomic rights concerns. Thus it proved a more welcoming arena for attacks on the gender distinctions than did many national courts, and it had far more effective enforcement powers than the European Court of Human Rights had.

As earlier noted, it is almost impossible to offer contrary evidence against the intergovernmentalist hypothesis that the member states' apparent yielding to the ECJ was illusory and resulted from the court's operating under a rule of anticipated reaction, ordering the member states to do only what they really wanted to do anyway or at least were willing to do in exchange for attendant benefits. In the gender discrimination story, the members actually did so much dislike some of the courts' decisions that they amended the treaties so as to limit the impact of some of them. And these decisions had such a large, direct negative financial impact on member states that they can hardly have been an inadvertent judicial deviation from the rule of anticipated reaction. Rather, this is at least one clear instance in which the ECJ chose to coerce the member states, albeit an instance in which the states chose to respond.

A Fourth Tale of the ECJ and the EU

The fourth story is by way of prediction.[21] The EU passed through a major legislative phase in connection with the Single European Act. Much of the new legislation consists of regulations requiring detailed and more-or-less technical subsidiary rule making or standard setting before they can be implemented. The EU depends on member-state administrative bureaucracies for most of its implementation. The main constitutional outlines of EU member-state cooperation now are fairly well settled. The treaties themselves contain few and only very general administrative procedure provisions. The commission is not anxious to move toward an administrative code. Under all these circumstances, it could be anticipated that the ECJ would develop a case law of administrative procedure to guide the implementation of EU regulatory law and to bring some uniformity to member-state administrative practices implicated in that implementation.

This prediction is rendered more certain by current developments in the politics of EU regulation. Generating the detailed rules and standards needed to implement the more general EU regulatory legislation is now done by "networks," combining government and private, EU and member-state, technically expert and nonexpert, for-profit and not-for-profit persons and organizations arrayed in an enormous web of agencies and committees whose pattern of internal and external relationships is partially structured by law and partially not; whose membership and very existence is fluctuating, sporadic, and often unknown by both outsiders and the participants themselves; and whose decisions and decision-making processes are largely opaque. There is currently a lively debate over whether this whole morass should be nonpolitical and technocratic, pluralist, deliberative, or something else. There is more-or-less general agreement that it should be more transparent and some agreement that it should be more participatory or at least that participation should be more regularized. There is an obvious and massive tension between the need for and respect for technical expertise in operating the whole system and the suspicion of rule by experts endemic to postindustrial societies.

The decisions made by the independent agencies and in the "comitology" process have multimillion-dollar consequences for regulated enterprises and touch the vital concerns of a multitude of enthusiastic interest groups. And all these decisions and decision-making processes must be lawful, although too often there are few or no concrete legal specifications for judging their lawfulness provided by the initial statutes establishing the agencies and committees. There will be a lot of litigation about these matters as well, not only by those who want tougher or less tough regulation but also by those who simply want uniform regulatory demands on their simultaneous operations in a number of member states.

Particularly because demands for increased transparency and participation in regulatory decision making are a prominent feature of the whole industrialized world and of Europe in particular, it seems probable that the ECJ is about to embark on the case-by-case creation of a whole new body of law of administrative procedure, particularly the procedure of supplementary lawmaking by those delegated such powers by the lawmaker in chief that is the European Council. This case law will be shaped by the ECJ's response to the most fundamental questions of contemporary democratic theory and particularly by the balance the judges strike between technocratic and democratic regulation. The stakes are too high and the incentives to litigation too great for the judges to avoid the fray. The administrative law traditions of the member states are diverse, and European judges, legal scholars, and practitioners are well acquainted with the "reformation" of American administrative law.[22] The ECJ has plenty of material from which to fashion an administrative law for the EU.

A Concluding Story: The ECJ and Judicial Independence

In the Maastricht Treaty, something called the second and third pillars of foreign policy and justice and home affairs respectively[23] are added to the first pillar of the European Community established by the earlier treaties. This strange pillar notion apparently has been invented because at the time of Maastricht, all of the member states were ready to add these subject matters to the EU's competencies, but only some were prepared to accept in these spheres the rather advanced stage of integration the EC had achieved in economic matters. A number of member states wanted a higher level of collaboration in these areas than had previously existed but nonetheless a collaboration that was rather far toward the intergovernmental and away from the federal. Specifically, in pillars two and three, the normal legislative processes of the EU are avoided in favor of consultative and declarative mechanisms and "conventions" that are to be negotiated bilaterally or multlilaterally among the member states essentially as international treaties.

If the pillar device is invented in general to avoid the relatively high levels of legal, political, and economic intervention of the EC or single market, one of the things the new pillars are quite specifically designed to do is avoid the Court of Justice. They both contain explicit exclusions of judicial review. Such an exclusion appears quite natural for the foreign relations pillar along the lines suggested by the U.S. political questions doctrine and the general reluctance of most constitutional courts to involve themselves in this area of broad executive discretion. To exclude the ECJ from a pillar actually named justice and home affairs, which includes the police, criminal justice, immigration, and citizenship, is quite another matter. Such an exclusion shows a very clear hostility to the court on the part of a number of the member states.

Clearly, there was a real battle over judicial review in the third pillar, because, along with the general exclusion of review, there is also a special exception under which the new interstate conventions provided for in the third pillar may each individually contain judicial review clauses should the member states entering those conventions agree to such clauses.[24] Obviously, while some states wanted to exclude review of some things, others were trying hard to keep at least the option of review open. For instance, the Europol Convention of 1995–96, after long debate, added a protocol permitting each member state to opt to allow its courts to make Article 177 references.[25]

With the Amsterdam Treaty, much, but not all of pillar three was moved into the first pillar with all the normal integrative processes the EC pillar has so far achieved.[26] Normally, that would have included full-scale ECJ review. Instead, special review provisions are attached for the pillar three to pillar one transfers. Only the highest courts in each state will be permitted to make Article 177 references as opposed to all courts as under the rest of pillar one.[27] This is particularly significant, because most of the court's most important constitutional lawmaking has occurred in Article 177 proceedings originating in quite low-level courts.

Clearly, there is a deliberate attempt not only to reduce the total volume of review but also to reduce the court's strategic resource of declaring big doctrine in small, low-visibility cases. Also, highest-state courts are those most likely to use the *acte clair* doctrine[28] to make EU law decisions on their own. Such courts are also the most likely to feel a responsibility to defend their national constitutional systems from EU incursions. The polite way to put this is that the special Amsterdam review provisions, which, it must be reemphasized against, apply only to the pillar three to one transfers, are designed to encourage high-level judicial dialogue. The other way to put it is that national high courts are set to watch the EU high court.

What is to be made of all this special attention to judicial review? If the member states historically had been directly controlling the ECJ, or it had been operating completely under a rule of anticipated reaction to do only what all the member states wanted, the member states would not have struggled so fiercely about limiting the court's review powers. Pretty clearly, the dog has bitten or the owners would not be so concerned about the length of its chain. The member states have learned to anticipate that the court will do things to them that they cannot anticipate and will not necessarily like. But many of them either like surprises or continue to prefer being bitten once in a while to losing the benefits the court provides. In the paradoxical ways of politics, the member-state attack on the court confirms its independent institutional powers in a way that a complete member-state acquiescence to the court could not.

Notes

1. In this connection, it should be noted that Alec Stone Sweet and various of his collaborators are working on very similar combinations. I can only hope to be a Braque to their Picasso, which is to excessively flatter both of us.

2. Martin Shapiro, *Courts: A Comparative and Political Analysis* (Chicago: Univ. of Chicago Press, 1981).

3. See Arthur Maass, *Area and Power* (Glencoe, Ill.: Free Press, 1959).

4. But not always—e.g., if there are regional parties or ethnic divisions on areal lines.

5. See Martin Shapiro, "Stability and Change in Judicial Decision-Making: Incrementalism or Stare Decisis," *Law in Transition Quarterly* 2 (1965): 134.

6. T. C. Hartley, *The Foundations of European Community Law* (Oxford: Clarendon, 1988), 78–79.

7. Karen Alter emphasizes this point in her forthcoming book on the ECJ. See also Karen Orrin, "The Emergence of an Authoritative International Court in the European Union," *West European Politics* 19 (1996): 458.

8. Mathew McCubbins, Roger Noll, and Barry Weingast, "Positive Canons: The Role of Legislative Bargains in Statutory Interpretation" *Georgetown Law Review* 80 (1992): 705.

9. See Alec Stone, "The New GATT: Dispute Resolution and the Judicialization of the Trade Regime," in *Supranational Courts in a Political Context,* ed. Mary Volcansek (Gainsville, Fla.: Univ. of Florida Press, 1999).

10. Article 177, European Community Treaty.

11. See Joseph Weiler, "Journey to an Unknown Destination: A Retrospective and Prospective of the European Court of Justice in the Area of Political Integration," *Journal of Common Market Studies* 31 (1993): 417.

12. See Paul Pierson, "The Path to European Integration: A Historical Institutionalist Approach, *Comparative Political Studies* 29 (1996): 123.

13. Some Article 177 proceedings arise out of litigation between two private parties in which the question of possible conflict between member state and EC norms arises, so that it is not the state but one of the private parties that persists in defending the national norm.

14. This story can be traced in any of the treatises, texts, or case books on EC and EU law. See, e.g., Paul Craig and Grainne de Burca, *EC Law,* 2d ed. (Oxford: Oxford Univ. Press, 1998).

15. See Vincent Blasi, "Constitutional Limitations on the Power of State to Regulate Goods in Interstate Commerce," in *Courts and Free Markets,* eds. Terrence Sandalow and Eric Stein (Oxford: Oxford Univ. Press, 1982).

16. *Rewe-Zentral AG v. Bundesmonopolver-Waltung fur Branntwein (Cassis de Dijon),* Case 120/78, [1979] ECR 649.

17. See Joseph Weiler, "Eurocracy and Distrust," *Washington Law Review* 61 (1986): 1131.

18. *Keck* and *Mithouard,* Cases C-267 and 268/91, [1993] ECR I-6097.

19. Ibid., paragraph 14.

20. See Craig and de Burca, *EC Law,* chap. 18.

22. Martin Shapiro, "The Giving Reasons Requirement in European Community Law," *University of Chicago Legal Forum* 1992 (1992): 179.

22. Richard Stewart, "The Reformation of American Administrative Law," *Harvard Law Review* 88 (1975): 1667.

23. "The Common Foreign and Security Policy," Treaty of European Union, Article J; "Cooperation in the Fields of Justice and Home Affairs," Treaty of European Union, Article K.

24. Ibid., Article K.3(c).

25. Protocol adopted 23 July 1996, O.J. C 2991 (9 October 1996).

26. Article B of Treaty of European Union, as amended; Article 73 of the European Community Treaty, as amended.

27. Article 73p of the European Community Treaty, as amended.

28. Under the *acte clair* doctrine, a national court may decide that an EC norm is clear enough so that the court may implement it on its own without making a preliminary reference to the ECJ. The ECJ says that the EC law must be "so obvious as to leave no scope for any reasonable doubt." See *Ciffit v. Ministry of Health (I)*, Case 283/81 (1982) ECR 3415.

15

Conclusion

Judicial Independence in
Comparative Perspective

PETER H. RUSSELL

The chapters in this book have reported on the state of judicial independence in countries in many parts of the world, drawing on a diversity of legal and political traditions and in many different states of democratization. The one thing that is clear about judicial independence in all of these countries, including those that have a long, historic commitment to the principle, is that judicial independence is never a condition that is established fully or that is enjoyed without controversy or challenge. This is the very first lesson of comparative analysis that emerges from this book. In any political community that is concerned about the independence of its judiciary—and this would seem to be the case with most countries in the world today—there is bound to be a political discourse about judicial independence, a discourse that focuses on the scope and autonomy of judicial power.

In the more well-established liberal democracies, it is indeed the growth of judicial power that has triggered contemporary concerns about judicial independence. An interesting irony is at work here. As courts, especially the highest courts, become more activist and autonomous in their decision making by upholding challenges to the activities of the other branches of government and by dealing with hotly contested issues of public law, they attract much more political attention and criticism. Thus an increase in judicial autonomy and power means that the judiciary becomes more directly connected to a democratic society's politics. This has certainly been the case in my own country, Canada. And, as the chapters in this book show, it is very much the case in the United States, the United Kingdom, Australia, Germany, and the Latin countries of Western Europe.

When the judicial power becomes more politically dominant in well-developed democracies, the pressure on judicial independence is felt not in the form of interference with individual judges in their decision making but in concerns about the judiciary as a whole—in particular, at the structural level and with the appointing system. In this context, Martin Shapiro's phrase is apt: judicial independence is secure "at retail" but not "at wholesale." This is evident in Shapiro's analysis of the European Court of Justice (ECJ), which has played such a powerful role in shaping the constitution of the European Union. There is no evidence that member states have tried to counter the ECJ's activism by pressuring individual judges. But the political leaders of the states that make up the EU's new "pillar" on justice and home affairs have shown their apprehension of the ECJ's power by being very tentative about extending judicial review to this new pillar. The ECJ, in turn, has shown its sensitivity to this political concern by drawing back from its aggressive deregulatory stance.

In Henry Abraham's account of the federal judiciary in the United States, a country in which the judicial power has historically been the strongest, again we can see that, while the individual judge's security of tenure is well protected by the impeachment process, there is constant pressure from political critics of the courts on judicial structures aimed at reining in judicial power. Never was this pressure greater than when President Franklin D. Roosevelt, in reaction to judicial vetoes of his New Deal legislation, threatened to enlarge the Supreme Court and pack it with judges sympathetic to his policies. When the court-packing bill came under vigorous political attack, this very popular president withdrew it. The episode demonstrated, in Abraham's view, that the American people would not stand for "any crass tampering with judicial independence." Conversely, we should note that this most powerful of supreme courts, without any change in its structure or membership, did adjust its jurisprudence in the direction desired by the political forces supporting the president.

Robert Stevens shows how the advent of a domestic bill of rights and the high-profile international case concerning the extradition of former Chilean dictator, Augusto Pinochet, have increased political interest in judicial restructuring in Britain. The direction of reform is interesting. Though England is the very cradle of the ideal of judicial independence at the level of the individual judge, up to now it has not treated the judiciary as a separate branch of government. Once the judiciary is cast more clearly in the role of a guarantor of rights and a check and balance on government, its close entanglement with the other branches becomes less acceptable. While Stevens assures us that Britain will not suddenly embrace a full separation of powers, he anticipates adoption of a more representative and less executive-dominated appointing system.

In Australia, reaction to a more activist and politically prominent High Court also highlights the appointing process. A right-of-center national government has used its unfettered monopoly of power over federal judicial appointments to reverse High Court decisions recognizing the rights of Australia's indigenous peoples. Though this has increased public discussion of the kind of judicial appointments commission under consideration in the United Kingdom, no Australian government has shown any serious interest in such a reform. Indeed, senior Australian judges, in a country remarkably ill prepared for the age of judicial activism, by issuing their own declaration on the principles of judicial independence, give the sense of being a judiciary virtually under a state of siege.

Israel, too, has witnessed a remarkable increase in the judiciary's involvement in hot political issues, including matters of national security. Here too, this expansion of judicial power has made the judiciary a subject of political debate. Shimon Shetreet's analysis shows how the Supreme Court has responded by fine-tuning its relationship with the political branches. In so doing, it has had to tread a fine line between not withdrawing from areas vital to the protection of citizens' rights and yet not overstepping its involvement to the point of undermining the public's respect, which is the essential buttress of judicial power.

In the chapters by Carlo Guarnieri and Donald Kommers, we can see that since World War II, the civil law countries of Western Europe have been going through a remarkable ideological change with respect to the role and status of the judiciary in governance. The essence of the change is the transformation of highly bureaucratized judiciaries into judiciaries that come closer to performing and being recognized as independent and separate branches of government. This transformation in part stems from the democratic restructuring of former fascist dictatorships. But it has also been occurring in democratic France.

This judicial mutation has had two major dimensions, both of which have important implications for judicial independence. One is the adoption of judicial constitutional review by a special constitutional court or tribunal. The other is a reduction of the executive's and senior judges' domination of the regular judiciary and an injection of political pluralism into the appointing process.

In adopting "bifurcated" justice systems, France, Germany, Italy, Spain, and Portugal have balanced off the quantum leap in judicial power that comes from constitutional judicial review, with institutional designs increasing political accountability. The specialized constitutional courts that exercise the formidable power of nullifying proposed or enacted laws found to be unconstitutional are tied closely to the political system. Elected politicians (not just from the governing party) play a direct role in selecting the members of the constitutional courts, and the pool of candidates extends well beyond the professional judiciary. Holding members of these tribunals to limited-term appointments ensures a continuing political influence on their composition.

For the judiciary of the regular courts in these countries, increased formal independence for the judges collectively as well as individually within the professional hierarchy has been accompanied by increased interaction with political life. In the Latin countries, national judicial councils have strengthened independent control of personnel and administrative matters. But as the table presented in Guarineri's chapter demonstrates, the composition of these councils have become more pluralist and to some extent politicized. Similarly, though the development of unionlike judicial associations has given the individual judge more internal independence from the judicial elite, this, together with judicial activism on the bench, has meant that judges are more closely connected to politics.

This trend appears to have gone farthest in Italy. Italian magistrates have resisted direct threats from terrorists and organized crime and have exercised enormous power in fighting corruption in the political branches. But at the same time, through these magistrates' union activity and activism, they have become highly politicized and have established close ties to opposition politicians. Also, it is interesting to learn from Kommers's chapter how in Germany, perhaps the most heavily judicialized of the Western democracies, judges are free to belong to political parties. Kommers suggests that this tolerance for judicial participation in politics offsets suspicion of judges as aloof technocrats, exercising a power that can be traced back to the German Reichstaat. But Kommers's account of the Orlet affair alerts us to the danger that campaigns of public criticism may drive judges from the bench for making fair but unpopular decisions.

Japan presents an interesting contrast with the post-fascist democracies of Western Europe. The postwar constitution provided for a strong and independent judiciary with the power of constitutional review based on the unitary American model. This was combined with a continental European-style professional judiciary. David O'Brien and Yasuo Ohkoshi's chapter reports that these arrangements, rather than leading to the judicialization of politics that has occurred in Europe, have resulted in a relatively quiescent, nonactivist judiciary in Japan. Their explanation is that the cadre of senior judges that control the judicial hierarchy has remained ideologically close to the Liberal Democratic Party, which has dominated Japanese politics since the war. In this setting, the chief threat to judicial independence comes not, as some have alleged, from politicians' attempts to manipulate the judiciary from the outside but from the conformity imposed internally on lower court judges by the judicial elite.

Post-Communist democratic regimes in Europe have kept much closer to the postwar civil law model of Western Europe, including constitutional courts with the power of judicial review. Todd Foglesong's chapter on Russia and Dick Howard's on Central and Eastern Europe show that this has produced a relatively activist judiciary fairly well purged of known Communists and capable of acting independently of the government. When this activism has led to major collisions with the government, the judiciary, especially constitutional courts, have come under serious structural threat. But as Howard's analysis of the Bulgarian case demonstrates, there may be a good deal of public support for the judiciary in these situations. A constitutional court that spends its "institutional capital" intelligently not only can survive these confrontations but also can come out of them with a stronger popular base for the judiciary's independence.

The picture is not nearly so bright when we look at the more mundane material conditions of judicial independence in these post-Communist societies. Howard relates how the ruling majority in Bulgaria responded to a Constitutional Court ruling against the Communist Party by cutting the court's budget. Foglesong and Howard both emphasize how low and unreliable levels of remuneration, combined with poor working conditions, make it difficult to attract well-qualified candidates to judicial service. In Foglesong's account of the regular judiciary in post-Communist Russia, we can see a variation on the Japanese picture. While there is a good deal of independence from forces external to the judiciary, confusion and conflict at the political level have left judicial chieftains with a great deal of power over individual judges below them. This kind of dependence has not stopped Russian judges from frequently ruling against powerful political figures. Foglesong suggests that the independence these Russian judges display in their decision making is in part a protest against the bumbling politicians who have done so little to support judicial institutions.

A strong commitment to judicial independence has been built into South Africa's new democratic constitution. The constitution provides for a judicial system that combines a European-style Constitutional Court with the English common law system of magistrates and superior courts, the latter staffed by experienced barristers. Through Hugh Corder's chapter, we are able to appreciate the tremendous challenge facing this judiciary. It must provide the stability and reassurance South Africa needs at a time of rapid social and political change. At the same time, as a powerful institution whose personnel will for some time come predominantly from the white minority, it must also show that it is responsive to the needs of the ordinary South African. The key institution for balancing judicial independence and accountability in the new South Africa is the Judicial Service Commission (JSC). The JSC plays the lead role in judicial selection and other personnel matters. Its openness and pluralistic composition provide some assurance of independence and responsiveness in judicial administration, though Corder also notes the vulnerability of the JSC to the political agenda of the governing party. The Judicial Service Commission appears to be the common law analogue of the national judicial councils in the civil law countries of Western Europe.

A Judicial Service Commission considerably weaker than South Africa's was one of the reforms introduced in Hong Kong to modify executive domination of the judiciary during the final period of British colonial rule. This institution and other features of Hong Kong's common law judicial system were carried over under the Basic Law governing Hong Kong's reunification with China. Indeed, under the Basic Law, Hong Kong's judiciary of all branches of government, in the words of Jill Cottrell and Yash Ghai "is the most independent of the central (mainland) government."

However, where the judiciary is subject to the final authority of an unreformed totalitarian dictatorship, there are clearly externally imposed limits on its power. This is evident in Cottrell and Ghai's detailed account of the recent confrontation between Hong Kong's Final Court of Appeal and the National Peoples Congress in Beijing in the case involving the right of abode of children of Hong Kong's permanent residents. The Hong Kong judiciary's survival as an independent and effective branch of government will be a unique measure of how much an independent judiciary can do to secure the independence of a political community.

Despite living under the dark cloud of an authoritarian, sovereign superpower, the people of Hong Kong enjoy the everyday benefits of independent adjudication much more than those who live in the part of the world covered in Michael Dodson and Donald Jackson's chapter. In El Salvador and Guatemala, as in much of Latin America, the most rudimentary conditions of judicial independence are lacking.

Dodson and Jackson provide a clear-headed account of the institutional changes that must be in place for the citizens of these countries to have access to credible adjudication of their ordinary civil and criminal disputes. Some progress in making these institutional changes has been made since the peace accords in these countries, particularly in El Salvador. But corruption of the individual judge and impoverished public resources remain as major barriers to an effective and independent judiciary. Yet Dodson and Jackson see grounds for optimism in the acceptance by formerly warring elites of the legal and normative framework required for a rule-of-law society. In this sense, the prospects for an independent judiciary are probably better in these settings than on the Chinese mainland.

This brief summary of the experience of judicial independence in the parts of the world covered in this volume should make us aware of how dependent a variable judicial independence is. How judicial independence is understood and institutionally provided for depends very much on the status of law in a society's political culture and on its general political circumstances.

The one point common to all the countries we have looked at is a growth in the power of the judiciary. In constitutional democracies, both new and old, judiciaries have become visible centers of power not only providing a credible adjudicative service for increasingly litigious societies but also exercising considerable leverage on controversial issues of public policy. This development has required an ironic trade-off. A judiciary cannot be powerful unless it enjoys a high level of institutional independence and its individual members are free from internal as well as external direction of their decision making. But the price to be paid for such power is close and continuous public scrutiny and contentious debate of what judges do as well as increasing demands that their selection, promotion, education, and discipline be subject to more open and representative processes. This book sends plenty of signals of the threats to judicial independence that can come from this more direct contact of the judiciary with politics. We clearly still have much to learn about how to balance the independence and accountability of powerful judiciaries in a manner that enables our political communities to be both liberal and democratic.

Contributors

Henry J. Abraham is James Hart Professor of Government and Foreign Affairs Emeritus at the University of Virginia. He holds five honorary doctorates and is a recipient of numerous grants and awards, including a Fulbright Professorship in Denmark and the American Political Science Association Law and Court Section's Lifetime Achievement Award. He has authored numerous articles and books, including *The Judicial Process: An Introductory Analysis of the Courts of the United States, England, and France,* 7th ed.; *The Judiciary: The Supreme Court in the Governmental Process,* 10th ed.; and, with Barbara Perry, *Freedom and the Court: Civil Right and Liberties in the United States,* 7th ed.

Hugh Corder is Dean and a Professor at the Law School of the University of Capetown, South Africa. A recognized expert on comparative law and judicial politics, he is author of *Crowbars and Cobwebs: Executive Autocracy and the Law in South Africa* and *Judges at Work: The Role and Attitudes of the South African Appellate Judiciary,* among other publications.

Jill Cottrell is currently a Senior Lecturer in public law at the University of Hong Kong, after having taught for more than a decade in Nigeria and at the University of Warwick, in the United Kingdom. Among her publications is *The Law of Defamation in Commonwealth Africa.*

J. Michael Dodson is a Professor of Political Science at Texas Christian University, where he is a Latin American specialist and a frequent contributor to journals and books on that subject.

Todd Foglesong is a visiting Assistant Professor in the Department of Political Science at the University of Utah. Besides contributing to journals and books, he is a coauthor of *Courts and Transition: The Challenge of Judicial Reform in Russia.*

Yash Ghai is a Kenyan who holds the Sir Y. K. Pao Professorship of Public Law at the University of Hong Kong. He has taught at the University of East Africa, Uppsala University, and the University of Warwick, as well as having held visiting appointments at several other universities. Among the many books he has authored or coauthored are *Public Law and Political Change in Kenya, The Political Economy of Law: Third World Perspectives, The Law, Politics and Administration of Decentralization in Papua New Guinea,* and *Hong Kong's New Constitutional Order: The Resumption of Chinese Sovereignty and the Basic Law.*

Carlo Guarnieri is Dean and Professor of Political Science at the University of Bologna, Italy. An author of numerous articles and books, he is an active participant in the International Political Science Association's Committee on Comparative Judicial Politics.

A. E. Dick Howard holds the White Burkett Miller Professorship at the University of Virginia School of Law. A Rhodes Scholar, he served as a law clerk to Justice Hugo L. Black, was a Visiting Fellow at the Woodrow Wilson Center, and subsequently headed the commission to draft Virginia's Constitution. Besides receiving numerous awards, he has been a consultant on constitutional reform to several countries in Eastern Europe and Africa. Among his publications are *Road from Runnymeade: Magna Carta and Constitutionalism in America* and *Commentaries on the Constitution of Virginia.* He has also edited several books, including *Constitution Making in Eastern Europe* and *The U.S. Constitution: Roots, Rights, and Responsibilities.*

Donald W. Jackson holds the Herman Brown Chair of Political Science at Texas Christian University. A former Judicial Fellow at the Supreme Court of the United States, he is actively involved with the American Civil Liberties Union. A frequent contributor to journals and books, he is author of *Even the Children of Strangers: Equality under the U.S. Constitution* and editor of *Comparative Judicial Review and Public Policy,* among other works.

Donald P. Kommers is Professor of Law and Joseph and Elizabeth Robbie Professor of Government and International Studies at the University of Notre Dame. A recipient of National Endowment for the Humanities and other awards and honorary doctorates, he is a former Fulbright Professor in Japan, former editor of the *Review of Politics,* and a frequent Visiting Professor at the Max Planck Institute of Comparative and International Public Law in Heidelberg, Germany. Among his many publications are *The Constitutional Jurisprudence of the Federal Republic of Germany,* 2d ed.; *Human Rights and American Foreign Policy;* and *Judicial Politics in Western Germany.*

David M. O'Brien is Leone Reaves and George W. Spicer Professor at the University of Virginia. He has served as a Judicial Fellow at the Supreme Court of the United States, as Visiting Fellow at the Russell Sage Foundation, and Fulbright Visiting Professor in Constitutional Studies at Nuffield College, Oxford University. He has held the Fulbright Chair for Senior Scholars at the University of Bologna and been a Fulbright Researcher in Japan. Among his publications are *Storm Center: The Supreme Court in American Politics*, 5th ed., which received the American Bar Association's Silver Gavel Award; *To Dream of Dreams: Religious Freedom and Constitutional Politics in Postwar Japan;* a two-volume casebook, *Constitutional Law and Politics*, 4th ed.; and an annual *Supreme Court Watch.*

Yasuo Ohkoshi is Professor of Political Science at Tokyo International University. An active participant in the International Political Science Association's Research Committee on Comparative Judicial Politics, he has written numerous articles and coauthored several books on comparative constitutional law and judicial politics.

Peter H. Russell is Professor of Political Science Emeritus at the University of Toronto. A Rhodes Scholar, recipient of several honorary doctorates, a Fellow of the Royal Society of Canada, and past president of both the Canadian Political Science Association and the Law and Society Association, he has held visiting professorships at Makerere University (Uganda), Osgoode Law School, the Australian National University, and the European University Institute in Italy. He is a frequent contributor to journals and has authored seven books, including *The Judiciary in Canada, Federalism and the Charter, Constitutional Odyssey: Can Canadians Become a Sovereign People?,* and *The Clash of Rights: Liberty, Equality and Legitimacy in Pluralist Democracy.*

Martin Shapiro is a political scientist and Professor of Law at Boalt Hall School of Law, University of California, Berkeley. He has taught at Harvard University, U.C.L.A., and the University of California at San Diego, as well as lectured widely, at home and abroad. He is also author or editor of numerous books, including *Who Guards the Guardians? Judicial Control of Administration, The Supreme Court and Administrative Agencies, Freedom of Speech: The Supreme Court and Judicial Review,* and *Courts: A Comparative and Political Analysis.*

Shimon Shetreet is a Professor of Law at The Hebrew University, Jerusalem, Israel. A widely recognized scholar and prolific author, he has lectured at various universities around the world and has written, among other publications, *Judicial Independence: The Contemporary Debate* and *Justice in Israel: A Study of the Israeli Judiciary*, as well as edited *The Role of Courts in Society* and *Women in the Law.*

Robert Stevens is Master of Pembroke College at the University of Oxford, and counsel to Covington & Burling in Washington, D.C., and London. Besides lecturing and consulting on courts and constitutionalism around the world, he has authored numerous articles and books, including *The Independence of The Judiciary: The View from the Lord Chancellor's Office* and *Law and Politics: The House of Lords as a Judicial Body, 1800–1976.*

John M. Williams is a Professor at the University of Adelaide School of Law, in Australia. He is a frequent contributor to journals and books on comparative constitutional law and judicial politics.

Index

abode, right of, immigration of mainland Chinese to Hong Kong, 219–21, 224–28, 306
aborigines, Australian, land rights cases, 179–80, 303
Abraham, Henry, 14, 302
abstract review: as system used in post-Communist European countries, 99; via lawsuits against encroachments by public agencies, 114, 128 nn. 12, 13
academic world, role in Japanese society, 47
Accord on the Strengthening of Civil Power and the Function of the Army in a Democratic Society (1996, Guatemala), 264
accountability, judicial, relationship to judicial independence, 5, 190, 202–3
acte clair doctrine, use by highest-state EU courts to make decisions, 298, 300 n. 28
activism, judicial: countering by ideological appointments in Australia, 183–85; of the highest courts, 301; in Latin European countries, 123–26; mandated in post-Communist European countries' constitutions, 100, 109 n. 41
Act of Settlement (England, 1701), 159, 160
Act on the Constitutional Court (Bulgaria), attempts by parliament to amend, 97
Act on the Supreme Judicial Council (Bulgaria), attempts by parliament to amend, 96
Adenauer, Konrad, 148
adjudication, Russell's definition of, 8–9
administration, judicial: as background for many justices of Japan's Supreme Court, 51–52; ECJ case laws and regulation, 295–96; effects of Russian financing, 69–74; in Guatemala, 265; proposals for Israeli system, 248; public accountability on provisions of service, 19–20
Administrative Court, Federal (Germany), on independence of judges who published letter in newspaper, 138, 152 n. 22
administrative courts, in France, Italy, and Portugal, 112
Advisory Committee for Appointing Justices (Japan), 50–51
advocates general, role in the ECJ, 281
affiliations, pre-judicial: influences on appointed judges, 10; Israel's "Rabbi Assaf Law," 243; occupations of justices of Japanese Supreme Court before appointment, 52–53, 55, 57; political appointees to Australian High Court, 183–85

age, retirement: attempts to change in Israel to keep Justice Olsham, 243; for Australian High Court justices, 175; for Japanese Supreme Court justices, 53–55; for South African judges, 199–200
Agranat, Shimon (Israel), 238
Albania, power of the chairman of the Constitutional Court, 97
amendments, Basic Law (Israel), effect on court's interpretation of legislation, 233
amendments, constitutional, use in America to overthrow judicial decisions, 34
Amsterdam Treaty (1997), on EU federalist rights and states rights, 284, 298
a posteriori review: as system used in post-Communist European countries, 99; use in Italy, Spain, and Portugal, 114
appeals, heard by Japan's Supreme Court, 41–42
appellate courts: as lower and intermediate in Germany, 140; panel decisions in Latin European countries, 123; regional courts in Russia as, 65
appointments, judicial, 257; in Australia, 174–77, 181–85, 303; in El Salvador's prereform era, 258; in England, 166–67, 170; of Germany's federal judges, 147–50; Hong Kong's current system, 212, 230 n. 17; in Israel, 243, 247–48; Japan, control of, 39, 43, 45–46; in Latin European constitutional courts, 113, 128 nn. 10, 11; limited-term affect on judicial independence, 15, 304; in post-Communist European countries, 94, 95, 107 n. 18; in Russia, 62, 68, 74–83; of South Africa's judges and magistrates, 196–99; political appointments in the United States, 17. *See also* selection; tenure
a priori review: in France, 114; in Romania, 99
Arbenz, Jacobo (Guatemala), 255
arbitration courts, as part of Russia's judiciary system, 64
Archbald, Robert (U.S.), impeachment of, 27
areal divisions of power, and higher-law judicial review courts, 275–76
Armas, Castillo (Guatemala), 263
Arzú, Alavaro (Guatemala), 264
assignments, judicial: under Germany's Judges Act of 1961, 136–37; locations as rewards or punishments, 20, 48
Atkins v. United States (1977), on reduction of federal judges' salaries through inflation, 29–30

313

Constitutionalism and Democracy

Kevin T. McGuire
The Supreme Court Bar: Legal Elites in the Washington Community

Mark Tushnet, ed.
The Warren Court in Historical and Political Perspective

David N. Mayer
The Constitutional Thought of Thomas Jefferson

F. Thornton Miller
*Juries and Judges versus the Law: Virginia's Provincial Legal
Perspective, 1783–1828*

Martin Edelman
Courts, Politics, and Culture in Israel

Tony A. Freyer
*Producers versus Capitalists: Constitutional Conflict in
Antebellum America*

Amitai Etzioni, ed.
*New Communitarian Thinking: Persons, Virtues,
Institutions, and Communities*

Gregg Ivers
To Build a Wall: American Jews and the Separation of Church and State

Eric W. Rise
The Martinsville Seven: Race, Rape, and Capital Punishment

Stephen L. Wasby
Race Relations Litigation in an Age of Complexity

Peter H. Russell and David M. O'Brien, eds.
*Judicial Independence in the Age of Democracy: Critical Perspectives
from around the World*